D0236558

Amexica

Amexica

*War Along the
Borderline*

ED VULLIAMY

THE BODLEY HEAD
LONDON

Published by The Bodley Head 2010

2 4 6 8 10 9 7 5 3 1

Copyright © Ed Vulliamy 2010

Ed Vulliamy has asserted his right under the Copyright, Designs
and Patents Act 1988 to be identified as the author of this work

This book is sold subject to the condition that it shall not,
by way of trade or otherwise, be lent, resold, hired out,
or otherwise circulated without the publisher's prior
consent in any form of binding or cover other than that
in which it is published and without a similar condition,
including this condition, being imposed
on the subsequent purchaser.

First published in Great Britain in 2010 by
The Bodley Head
Random House, 20 Vauxhall Bridge Road,
London SW1V 2SA

www.bodleyhead.co.uk
www.rbooks.co.uk

Addresses for companies within The Random House Group Limited can be found at:
www.randomhouse.co.uk/offices.htm

The Random House Group Limited Reg. No. 954009

A CIP catalogue record for this book
is available from the British Library

ISBN 9781847921284 (HBK)
ISBN 9781847921291 (TPB)

The Random House Group Limited supports The Forest Stewardship
Council (FSC), the leading international forest certification organisation. All our titles
that are printed on Greenpeace approved FSC certified paper carry the FSC logo. Our
paper procurement policy can be found at www.rbooks.co.uk/environment

Mixed Sources
Product group from well-managed
forests and other controlled sources
www.fsc.org Cert no. TT-COC-2139
© 1996 Forest Stewardship Council

Typeset in Walbaum MT by Palimpsest Book Production Limited,
Falkirk, Stirlingshire
Printed and bound in Great Britain by
Clays Ltd, St Ives PLC

This is for my Father, J.S.P.V.

1919–2007

Contents

Acknowledgements

This book would not have been considered or written without my dear friend David Rieff, whose idea of a holiday way back was to go looking for cowboy boots in El Paso and Del Rio, and stories in Ciudad Juárez and Acuña. David later introduced me to Tracy Bohan at the Wylie agency, whom many, myself included, would call a wonderful literary agent, but who I also regard as something between having one's own military wing and a sports coach with that canny enthusiasm that motivates the final extra sprint. There are three colleagues without whom the book would also not have happened: Julián Cardona, the bravest reporter I have ever met, who profoundly influenced the ensuing arguments and who remains, defying all, in Ciudad Juárez; Cecilia Ballí, whose family history is in many ways that of the border, and whose compassion for its people and their lives, and keen eye across its atrocities, likewise charge this text; and Dudley Althaus, whose generosity, commitment and expert company on the road knew no bounds.

These are times when good reporting is under siege from mediocrity, blog and twitter – but some fight on the ramparts of quality, and there remain moments in American journalism when a cluster of exceptional talent forms in one place. Mexico City is experiencing one such fortunate era, thanks to correspondents from whose work, and in many cases company, I have had the honour to benefit: above all, the great Tracy Wilkinson of the *Los Angeles Times*, who also kindly amended the draft. Also: Marc Lacey of the *New York Times*; Alfredo Corchado of the *Dallas Morning News*; the photographer David Rochkind and Ken Ellingwood of the *Los Angeles Times* – plus the inimitable Dudley, as above, of the *Houston Chronicle*, and the *Guardian* and *Observer*'s Jo Tuckman. They are the visitors. Among the Mexicans, I owe thanks to the best of those who do the difficult, right thing: in Tijuana, Jorge Fregoso of Sintesis TV; in Mexico City, to the rising star León Krauze; to Alejandro Paéz and Ignacio Alvarez Alvarado of *El Universal*; and in Hermosillo to Juan Carlos Zuniga and Marco Mendoza. Thanks to those who chronicle Juárez for *El Diario* and *El Norte*, and in terrifying Tamaulipas, you know who you are. In Nuero León, with their works of art, Francisco Benitez, Tomas Hernández and Jessica Salinas break new ground, of resistance, humour, courage and even hope.

North of the border, these folks are supplemented – and this book enhanced – by the personalities and committed work of two great heretics: Dane Schiller of the *Houston Chronicle* and Brenda Norrell of the *Censored News, Narcosphere* and other websites. Also Jesse Bogan, whose fine work *Forbes* magazine rewarded with a redundancy notice (and they're supposed to be the smart guys – no wonder the economy's down the pan), and Sacha Feinman, who writes on Sonora (and boxing) better than anyone, but has difficulty getting hired by a two-bit sports mag – God help journalism.

I am grateful for hospitality along the way: in GHQ Tucson, to Debra May, Phreddie and Olivia Bartholomaei; Trudy Duffy, Elaine Mauriole, Joan and Jen at the Ranch; Anne and Eddie; James Romero; Rene Escalante, and Bob and Peggy Feinman. In Mexico City, to León, as above; and Marco and Juan Carlos in Hermosillo. To Charles Bowden in Patagonia, Tom and Nadine Russell in El Paso, Don Henry and Leah Ford in Belmont, Raymundo Ramos in Nuevo Laredo, Mario Treviño in Reynosa, Cecilia Ballí in Brownsville and Lisa Hilton in Houston. Among these are the authors of two of four great border books to which I am indebted: C. Bowden's *Juárez: The Laboratory of Our Future*, Ford's *Contrabando*, Morgan's *The Reaper's Line* and Don Winslow's *Power of the Dog*. Thanks to Molly Molloy in Las Cruces, for hospitality but even more so for the tenacious tracking of deaths and narco violence that makes her 'Fronterizo List' the most reliable regular source of information by far, as well as an embarrassment for the amount of monitoring work we reporters could and should be doing ourselves. Other books and sources are listed in the Notes and Bibliography.

There are good and brave people in this book who will claim their acknowledgements through the narrative, but Mike Flores, Pastor José Antonio Galván, Josué Rosales, Paula González, Marisela Ortiz, Norma Andrade, Rosario Acosta and Julia Quiñonez need special thanks for their company and the influence they had on things. I owe perennial thanks to John Mulholland, editor of the *Observer*, for commissioning some of the articles that gave rise to all this, and to Paul Webster, my main editor for two and a half decades at the *Observer* and *Guardian*. Also thanks at the *Guardian* to Holly Bentley for her assiduous research across the archives, Arnel Hecimovic for the picture research and Finbarr Sheehy for drawing the map. There are debts and thanks due to the main editor of the English edition of this volume, Will Sulkin, and his American counterpart, Eric Chinski, for terrifying faith at the outset and subsequent guidance on the text. Also to Kay Peddle, Eugenie Cha, Laura Mell and Laurel Cook for their kind efficiency and patience. Thanks to Alison Tulett and Cynthia Merman for their copyedits. Thanks also to Elena Cosentino of the BBC, Rob Yager and Philip Breeden at the US embassy in London.

Some precious friends propelled this book and its background: John Cale with a steady stream of information and his own caustic but always velvet observation; Paul Gilroy and Vron Ware, without whose wisdom, company and friendship over four decades I would have been locked away; Marco '*El Sexto Sol*' Roth, with his irrepressible faith in uprising and complicated love for his native Mexico; Mark Dowie and Wendy Schwarz, in the most beautiful place on earth, and Tom Rhodes, whom I met in the storm of another war. Deep thanks to Josh Lord at East Side Ink, grand master of the chisel, for our mutual design, and his execution with painless finesse of the Guadalupe/Coatlicue/'Amexica' protective tattoo.

There are deepest personal thanks, too, for this has not always been easy: to lovely Elsa and Claudia for being who they are and putting up with me (if they do); to Victoria for the desert and for bearing with it all so kindly (if she did); and to Mum, Tom, Clara and Louisa. In New York, thanks to Roger Cohen and Frida Baranek, Arabella Greene, Stacy and Leslie the propeller girls, Nebojsa Shoba Serić and Iris Kapetanović. There was a lot of tiring and miserable hobbling on crutches getting ready, during which many thanks to

Hawkwind, Fairport and the LSO for music of delight and encouragement; to Angela, Kate and Thomas Turley-Mooneyham in Chicago, to the Uxbridge Arms and Tomano pub, to the Frontline Club, to the Tavola Calda '*da Maria*' for *vera cucina casalinga*, even in Notting Hill Gate and to the Kop on the lock at The Constitution for never having to walk alone, even on crutches. For repairing the damage and getting me mobile, thanks initially to Tamara Cilliers, then Kerry Dowson and everyone that morning at Royal Liverpool Infirmary – but no thanks at all to the Paterson wing at St bloody Mary's hospital in Paddington, which did its best to stop the whole thing happening.

Crucially, thanks to Echols the Arizona alley cat.

Credits

The author and publishers would like to acknowledge and thank the following artists and photographers for their kind contribution to *Amexica*. Every effort has been made to trace and contact the relevant primary copyright holders in each instance. The publishers would be pleased to correct any omissions or errors in any future editions.

Lyrics

When Sinatra Played Juárez
Words and Music by Tom Russell © 2001 Frontera Music (ASCAP)/Administered by Bug Music. All Rights Reserved Used by Permission.

Where The Dream Begins
Words and Music by Tom Russell © 2001 Frontera Music (ASCAP)/Administered by Bug Music. All Rights Reserved Used by Permission.

The Road It Gives, The Road It Takes Away
Words and Music by Tom Russell and Andrew Hardin © 2001 Frontera Music (ASCAP) and Alligator Farm Music (BMI)/Administered by Bug Music. All Rights Reserved Used by Permission.

Illustrations

1. Amexica: the corpse of an executed man hangs, decapitated and handcuffed, from the Puente Rotario in Cuidad Juárez © Alex Tellez / *Periodico PM*
2. Joaquín Guzmán Loera: picture sourced from a Mexican police handout
3. Osiel Cardenás Guillén © Getty images
4. The devil's highway © David Rochkind
5. Urban Frankenstein: children foraging in the aftermath of a massacre © 2010 by Julián Cardona. Reprinted by permission of Anderson Literary Management, LLC. All rights reserved
6. Here begins the homeland © Shaul Schwarz/Getty images
7. Urban Frankenstein: a body chained to a fence © Alejandro Bringas/Reuters
8. The human junkyard © 2010 by Julián Cardona. Reprinted by permission of Anderson Literary Management, LLC. All rights reserved
9. Wind of knives © Guillermo Arias/AP
10. The road it gives, and the road it takes away © Robert Yager
11. Eat off the floor ©Antonio Olmos Zazueta
12. Gateway to the Americas: migrants prepare to jump and ride a train © Photo by Gary Coronado/Palm Beach Post/ZUMA Press
13. Amexica © Robert King/Polaris/eyevine
14. Gateway to the Americas: the daily line to cross the border on foot © *New York Times*/Redux/eyevine
15. Iron river © Getty images
16. Santísima Muerte © Redux/eyevine
17. The Virgin of Guadalupe: tattoo © Josh Lord, East Side Ink, New York; photo © Arnel Hecimovic

Map

Amexica: The US–Mexican borderland © Finbarr Sheehy

Amexica: the US-Mexican borderland
Principle locations and cartel influence

Cartel influence: contested
Sinaloa cartel
Arellano Felix Organisation

Cartel influence: contested
Sinaloa cartel
Beltrán-Leyva cartel
Juárez cartel

Cartel influence: contested
Sinaloa cartel
Beltrán-Leyva cartel

Los Angeles

CALIFORNIA

ARIZONA

Phoenix

Tohono
O'Odham
Indian Nation

NEW

Calexico
San Diego
Yuma
Tijuana   Mexicali   San Luis
Lukeville
Tucson

Columbus

Sonoyta
El Sasabe
Nogales Douglas
Paloma

Nogales Agua Prieta

Caborca   Altar

BAJA
CALIFORNIA
NORTH

SONORA

CH

Hermosillo

PACIFIC
OCEAN

BAJA
CALIFORNIA
SOUTH

Ciudad Obregón

Los Mochis

Culiacán

La Paz   SIN

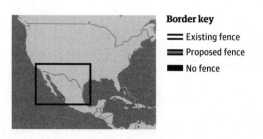

Border key
━━━ Existing fence
━━━ Proposed fence
━━━ No fence

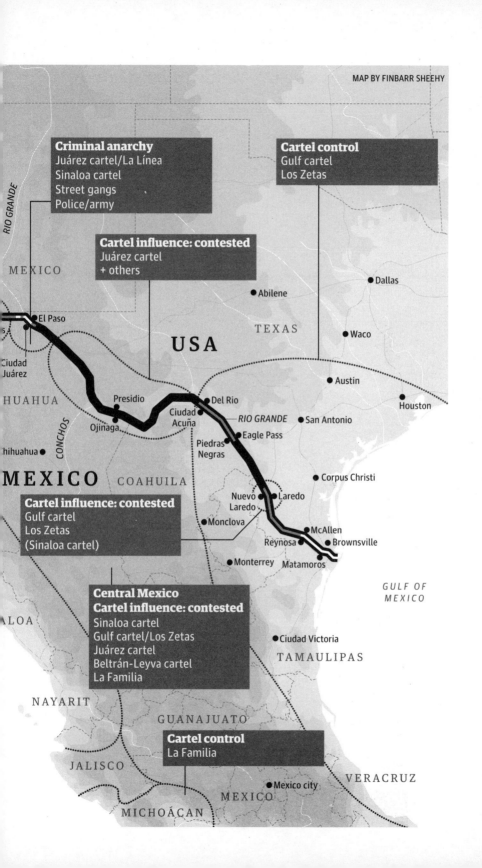

MAP BY FINBARR SHEEHY

Criminal anarchy
Juárez cartel/La Línea
Sinaloa cartel
Street gangs
Police/army

Cartel control
Gulf cartel
Los Zetas

Cartel influence: contested
Juárez cartel
+ others

Cartel influence: contested
Gulf cartel
Los Zetas
(Sinaloa cartel)

Central Mexico
Cartel influence: contested
Sinaloa cartel
Gulf cartel/Los Zetas
Juárez cartel
Beltrán-Leyva cartel
La Familia

Cartel control
La Familia

RIO GRANDE

MEXICO

USA

TEXAS

Dallas

Abilene

Waco

El Paso

Ciudad
Juárez

Austin

HUAHUA

Presidio

Del Rio

Houston

Ojinaga

Ciudad
Acuña

RIO GRANDE

San Antonio

hihuahua

CONCHOS

Piedras
Negras

Eagle Pass

MEXICO

COAHUILA

Corpus Christi

Nuevo
Laredo

Laredo

Monclova

McAllen

Reynosa

Brownsville

Monterrey

Matamoros

GULF OF
MEXICO

ALOA

Ciudad Victoria

TAMAULIPAS

NAYARIT

GUANAJUATO

JALISCO

VERACRUZ

Mexico city

MICHOÁCAN

MEXICO

Amexica

As dawn breaks over the vast desert, the body is hanging from a concrete overpass known as the Bridge of Dreams. It has been there for two hours – decapitated and dangling by a rope tied around the armpits. The sun begins to throw its rays across the busy intersection, with its rush-hour traffic and former American school buses carrying workers to sweatshops. It is still there an hour later, this grotesque, headless thing – swaying, hands cuffed behind its back – in the cold early-morning wind that kicks up dust and cuts through the Mexican border town of Ciudad Juárez, the most dangerous city in the world.

Next to their prey this morning – left hanging just as the factory shifts were about to change – the executioners, or *sicarios* as they are called, have hung a sheet, on which they have painted a message: '*Yo Lázaro Flores, apoyo a mi patron, el monte perros*' – 'I, Lázaro Flores, served my boss, the dog-fucker'. '*Atte. (Atencion), La Línea*' – 'Look out, The Line' – it concluded. A crowd assembles to watch in unsurprised silence. The straps underneath the corpse's armpits creak, and its feet flap in the wind, but the crowd remains gawping at this hideous, buckled thing, perhaps fearing, if they leave, they might take with them the curse of that which was done. So that before they could go, it must be dealt with, erased from view and from the morning. Finally, after three hours, firemen arrive and erect ladders in order to take the carcass down, wrap it in canvas, put it in a red van, and drive it away to the morgue, to be examined and 'read' for any message contained in the mutilations. And so Juárez could get on with a day that would see another four narco murders before it was out. Which was an unusually low count:

with the year 2009 but a month old, 227 people have already been killed in this city on Mexico's border with the United States.

La Línea is a recent mutation of what was once the Juárez narco-trafficking cartel run by Amado Carrillo Fuentes, known by the *nom de narco* 'Lord of the Skies', so called because of the fleet of Boeing planes that was at his disposal for smuggling cocaine from Colombia. But *La Línea* is now just one of the miasma of factions and interests – cartels, street gangs, corrupt police units, military detachments – fighting with ever more inventive twists of violence for the 'Plaza', the river of drugs running north through Juárez into El Paso and from there across the US. Fighting, too, for the resultant plazas of Juárez and northern Mexico themselves: for where the river runs through, people will drink, and as a direct consequence of the Mexican cartels' near-monopoly of the supply of narcotics to the United States, northern Mexico is ravaged by crack and methamphetamine addiction, and by the bloody battles for terrain on which to sell them. The sheet, known as a *narcomanta*, and its message, known as a *narcomensaje*, are common features of the executions, designed to charge the slaying with menace or even opacity: Lázaro Flores was not the dead man's name, but that of a prominent local businessman – something for the city, and indeed Mr Flores, to ponder.

This macabre, barbaric execution, in November 2008, took the number of murders in the anarchic city of two million people to about 1,300 that year. The toll would cap 1,700 before the end of December. The national figure of those killed across Mexico reached over 5,400 in 2008. In 2009, despite successive waves of military re-enforcements and a promise by Mayor José Reyes Ferriz on 1 January that Juárez 'cannot have another year like that' the toll was even higher: 2,657 people murdered, making Ciudad Juárez the world's most murderous city, with 192 homicides per 100,000 citizens. The total of those murdered across Mexico in 2009 reached 7,724.[1] This means that by the end of that year, more than 16,000 people had been killed since Mexican president Felipe Calderón launched a military offensive against the cartels in December 2006, with many of the victims mutilated, like this man, horribly and carefully, then exhibited to convey some message or threat. By summer 2010, the total killed since December 2006 had exceeded 24,000. The killing is everywhere across Mexico, but concentrated along the border with the USA – 2,100 miles long, the busiest border in the world and a place that belongs to both countries, and yet to neither.

Ciudad Juárez lives cheek by jowl with the United States and its 'twin city' El Paso, on the other side of the frontier. Sometimes the proximity is surreal: from the campus of the University of Texas in El Paso, one sees, in the foreground, the diligent enjoyment of life – students strolling to and fro. Across mid-distance, less than half a mile away, runs the border in two forms: an articulately harsh wall decorated with barbed wire and the trickle of the Rio Grande. And beyond the boundary, one of the poorest barrios – or *colonias* as they are called here – in Mexico: a bleached, ramshackle shanty town called Anapra, thrown up out of wood and corrugated iron on the edge of a burgeoning city. The desert dirt and dust on which Anapra is built is criss-crossed by outlaw electricity supply cables to the barrio huts. El Paso and Juárez form the heart of, and midway point along, this singular strip of land conjoining two countries. The borderland is a place of paradox: of opportunity and poverty, promise and despair, love and violence, beauty and fear, sex and church, sweat and family. Even the frontier itself is a dichotomy, simultaneously porous and harsh. The US border patrol recognises the contradiction in its recruiting billboard on Interstate 19 north of Nogales, Arizona, advertising 'A Career in Borders, But No Boundaries'.

The frontier itself can be brutal. In 1994, the United States initiated 'Operation Gatekeeper' in San Diego, 'Operation Hold the Line' in El Paso and another similar operation in the Rio Grande Valley. Since then, under five administrations (Bill Clinton's twice, George W. Bush's twice and now Barack Obama), the border has become a military front line, along which runs more than 600 miles of fence enhanced by guard posts, search-lights and heavily armed patrols. In places where there is no fence, there are infrared cameras, sensors, national guard soldiers and SWAT teams from other, specialist law-enforcement columns, like the Drug Enforcement Adminstration and Bureau of Alcohol, Tobacco, Firearms and Explosives, plus the newly empowered border patrols and their own special forces, called BORTAC and BORSTAR. From the other side, apart from the tidal wave of drugs and migrants smuggled across the border, there are the killings:

of Border Patrol agent Robert Rosas in Southern California in August 2009, shot when he tried to interdict an armed incursion; and of the respected rancher Rob Krentz near Douglas, Arizona, when he chanced upon what were believed to be smugglers moving across his land.

There is a striking contrast between the asphalt of the United States and the instantaneous jumble and tumble of Mexico. When you fly over the border, you see streets arranged in a grid on the US side give way suddenly to those, if arranged at all, like a crazy-quilt. And the discrepancy is even greater between poverty on the US side and poverty on the Mexican side. One is struck by a stark, brazen inequality of wealth and power as one crosses the line, be it through the busy, click-clunk-click-clunk of turnstiles between sprawling Mexicali and tiny Calexico, or along the remote desert road between Lukeville, Arizona, and Sonoyta, Sonara; or over the trickle of the Rio Grande from El Paso into the cauldron of Juárez; the lustier flow between Eagle Pass and Piedras Negras or the last remaining cross-border ferry, between Los Ebanos, Texas, and Díaz Ordaz, Tamaulipas.

But the border is, as I say, porous. The more the United States builds its fence, enhances its technological stockade and empowers its patrols and customs officers, the more people cross the border *legally* – currently about a million of them every day. Families live astride the frontier; workers, shoppers, relatives and schoolchildren commute across the line; it takes twenty minutes to walk from downtown El Paso to main-street Juárez, from what is supposed to be the First World into what looks like the Third, yet is not. More commercial traffic crosses the US–Mexico border than any other in the world, currently worth some $367.4 billion a year.[2] Five million trucks cross the border annually, and thousands of freight train wagons each day, carrying goods from across the Americas into the USA, and from China via the Mexican port of Lázaro Cárdenas – as well as southwards, bringing exports from the United States. A necklace of thousands of sweatshop assembly plants, called *maquiladoras*, has been established all along the border to provide the US with cheap labour just across its own frontier. American and Mexican fire services answer each other's calls and, during 2008, more than fifty victims of the drug violence in Ciudad Juárez were treated for multiple gunshot wounds at Thomason Hospital in El

Paso. The border country has its own music, '*norteño*', and its own Spanglish slang spoken on both sides of the frontier, a lexicon that sometimes just jumbles the two languages together, as on the door of a bar in El Paso: '*Minores and Personas Armadas Strictly No Entrada*'. Friends may address each other as 'Mano!' mixing 'hey, man' with the Spanish '*hermano*' – brother. Across Mexico, a bicycle is a '*bicicleta*', but on the border it can be a '*baica*'. Someone's wife can be his '*waifa*' rather than '*esposa*'. In the US, a Chicano gang-banger is a '*vato*', but on the border he's a '*cholo*'.[3] Then there's the word for diarrhoea: '*turista*' – tourist, for obvious reasons. Perhaps the most useful border term of all is *rasquache* or *rasquachismo*, defined by the writer Tomás Ybarra-Frausto as being 'to posit a bawdy, spunky consciousness, to seek to subvert and turn ruling paradigms upside down. It is a witty, irreverent and impertinent posture', and if it doesn't define the borderline, there is certainly no shortage of it.[4]

The borderland is a territory in its own right, astride the line, estranged from both Washington and Mexico City, the centres of power whence decrees about its daily life are issued often without much understanding of how the borderland works or fails to work. There is as much seamlessness across the border as there is contrast. There is as much that bonds the two sides of the frontier as there is that divides them, though these adhesives and points of common-ality are being tested and strained by the narco war. Gloria Anzaldúa, who revolutionised the Chicana writing of her generation, called the border '*una herida abierta* – an open wound – where the Third World grates against the First and bleeds. And before a scab forms, it haemorrhages again, the lifeblood of two countries merging to form a third country – a border culture.' [5] The borderland has an identity and flavour of daily life that spans the frontier, and I call this land – 2,100 miles long and about 50 miles wide, from the Pacific to the Gulf – *Amexica*. Now, because of the flood tide of narcotics running through and along it, Amexica is a battlefield, but a battlefield wrapped in everyday life. And for all its inquietude, the border is every bit as charismatic, complex and irresistible as it is fearful and terrifying.

'Amexica' is not just a play on words. The original and proper term for the Nuahatl-speaking Aztec people who migrated south to build their great city at Tenochtitlán – later Mexico City – and found their empire is 'Mexica' (pronounced 'Meshica'), and they came from just north of the border, around the so-called 'Four Corners' where New Mexico, Colorado, Arizona and Utah meet. The Chicano consciousness movement of US Latinos during the 1960s resurrected the notion of a cradle land of the Mexica people – in the northern (or southwestern, to the Americans) deserts – called 'Aztatlán', or just 'Aztlán'. This land was important to Mexica creation mythology, based, like the border today, upon a concept of duality and complementary opposition. The creator God Ometeotl incorporates both male and female, and his/her children, Quetzalcoatl and Tezcatlipoca, are both allies and adversaries, representing harmony and conflict, balance and change.[6] According to some accounts, it was from Aztatlan that the primary God, Huitzilopochtli, led the Mexica south to what would become their imperial capital.[7] It was in what Mexicans now think of as the northern desert borderland that Huitzilopochtli was born to his mother, Coatlicue, primal mother and principal goddess of fertility and destruction, womb and tomb, who wore a skirt of serpents and a necklace of human hands and hearts.

The Spanish word for a border is *La Frontera*, with all the intended connotations of the word 'frontier' – as in the American 'Last Frontier'. While the south-western USA is 'the frontier' in American parlance and nineteenth century folklore, so *El Norte* – the same terrain, through Mexican eyes – struck a similar chord of mystique in the lore of both Spanish conquistadores and Mexicans after them. *'El Norte'* is even symbolically charged in ancient Mexica legend: according to the Aztecs' coloured system of the flat world's four directions, north was white: its stone was white flint, and the white Ceiba tree, the tree of abundance, was said to grow there. But north was also associated with death and winter, and was the way to the underworld. Before it actually became a border, what is now the borderland was a territory charged with the myth of exploration, risk, opportunity, outlaw glamour and danger. More recently, while the Americans had Billy the Kid, Mexicans had El Zorro; to Americans, the cowboy is in the south-west; to Mexicans, *el vaquero* is in the north – they are the same personage in the same place, on *La Frontera*. Miguel Olmos Aguilera, a quietly spoken musicologist who directs the Cultural Studies Department at the *Colegio De La Frontera del Norte* in

Tijuana, posits, in conversation, that 'the *"Frontera"* has always had an imaginative and emotional meaning, as well as a geographical one. Since pre-Hispanic days, it has been a place in the imagination of death and fame, suffering and heroism, as well as a reality which kills people.'[8]

To citizens of the United States the word 'America' usually refers only to that country. To the rest of the continent, though, it refers to the entire continent – as well as to Mexico City's most famous football team, Club América. Mexico's powerful and ubiquitous symbol and icon, the Virgin of Guadalupe, is the Mother of God and Queen of Mexico – but she is also Empress of the Americas, all of them. There is, furthermore, academic debate about how and whence the masculine word 'Mexico' emerged – 'Mexica', like 'America', having been initially feminine.[9]

The border was created by the Treaty of Guadalupe Hidalgo in 1848, which ended the US–Mexican wars, after which the Gadsden Purchase of 1853, known in Mexico as the Sale of La Mesilla, pushed what is now Arizona and New Mexico south of the Gila river to the present frontier.[10] Ever since, people have kept arriving on the border, not just to cross it, but to remain by it. The more the populations grow, the more each pair of twin cities is bound together, the closer the two countries have become – an adhesion now challenged by the narco war. The demographics of migration across the border are, meanwhile, astounding: one in five Mexicans either visits or works in the United States at one time or another in their lives.[11] But *Amexica* is not about (to use that dreaded shorthand expression) 'the Hispanicisation of the USA', or that moment in 1996 when salsa overtook ketchup as the United States' favourite condiment. True, the Hispanic population of the United States now takes Amexica to and beyond the Canadian border, and especially to such places as Los Angeles of course, and thence Chicago, New York and the Carolinas. But this book is not about the estimated twelve million Mexicans and twenty-eight million Mexican Americans living legally in the United States nor (probably) another 28 million illegal Mexican residents. It is about the quintessence of 'Amexica', the borderland itself.

Amexica found me as much as I found it. For years, I have worked along the borderline: narratives about international trucking and sweatshop factories, abducted women and the breathtaking desert,

all set against a backdrop of adventure and hard grind, love and
lust, achievement and tribulation, scintillescent light and occult
shadows. This is a place of impenitent heat by day and bitter winds
cutting through the darkness of night. I have been a war reporter
on many battlegrounds, yet nowhere has violence been so strange
and commanded such revulsion and compulsion as it does along the
borderline. War deepens the dichotomies, intensifying Amexica's
magnetic field. It darkens the already opaque shade, making the
colours even more lambent. The edge gets edgier but the ready smile
more winning; the danger deepens but the welcome becomes warmer.
The perversion of values makes the everyday more valuable; the
feral physical cruelty of the slaughter accentuates the borderland's
spirituality and its sensuality and libido. The narco war has a suffocating claustrophobia about it, in counterpoint to the unique beauty
and infinite *scale* of the landscape – the eternity of desert and sky
that form its backdrop. The distances are all the more liberating but
they are deceptive, and savage also: something is always about to
happen in Amexica, hence the dread and expectation, apprehension
and tenterhooks of every moment.

This is not a story with a beginning, middle and end, it is a slice
of very recent, unfinished history. Or to take from Brian Delay's
introduction to his greatest of all books written about the border,
War of a Thousand Deserts: 'This is a shared story. This is American
history, Mexican history and Indian history.' This book is not so
much about a war as it is a view of a singular place in time of war.
It is about the ways in which war impacts Amexica, but it also shows
how the war is a consequence of other – mainly economic – degrad-
ations and exploitations, quite apart from drugs, from which the
border's people have suffered. A suffering due not least to the fact
that narco cartels are corporations like any other, applying the
commercial logic and following the same globalised 'business models'
as the multiplicity of legal enterprises that have wreaked a different
kind of havoc along the borderline. Indeed, the drug violence is in
many ways a direct result of the deprivation and misery caused by
the legal globalised economy. The cartels are not pastiches of multinational capital – they are pioneers of it, integral to it, and apply
its rules and logic (or, rather, lack of rules and logic) to their marketplace just as would any other commercial enterprise.

The book is also a journey from west to east, Pacific to Gulf. It begins in Tijuana, opposite San Diego, where two cartels are locked in battle. Thence into the deserts of Sonora and Arizona, and the deadly trails followed by half of all illegal migrants into the US across the border – a business being commandeered by the narco cartels. The kernel of the voyage is Ciudad Juárez, where the idea of a war between cartels implodes into criminal anarchy and terrible suffering from violence, addiction and deprivation. The road then winds through breathtaking country, on the US side in Texas and on the Rio Grande's right bank side into cities like Ciudad Acuña and Piedras Negras, utterly transformed by the arrival not so much of drug cartels as *maquiladora* factories. Next is the border's main trade corridor and temple of its commercial porosity, from Nuevo Laredo into Laredo, Texas. This is the truck route between Mexico and the USA: it is also where the latest drug war began, for the trade is contaminated by a river of smuggled drugs. The journey ends in the border's richest and most complex territory in terms of history and identity: Tamaulipas on the Mexican side and the Rio Grande Valley in Texas, between which the cartels' drugs flow north – and the guns run south across the borderline to the terrifying 'Zetas', a paramilitary cartel.

The voyage will not only be a geographical one. It will afford a glimpse behind the insistently glamorous associations which the drug business enjoys. When the narco trafficker looks in the mirror, he sees not a criminal, but a romantic bandit. As Roberto Saviano, author of the remarkable book *Gomorrah*, about the Neapolitan Camorra syndicates, put it in conversation: 'They love to think of themselves as Scarface; it's their favourite movie.'[12] But because of the singular product in which the narco *traficante* deals, the mass media and society also see in the narco more than a little bit of Scarface, thanks to the packaging of drug culture by our media and mass culture. We have become vogueishly obsessed with 'fair trade' consumerism to the point that supermarket chains compete with each other's rhetoric about where and how the mange-tout peas are grown by happy African villagers. Multinational coffee-shop chains strive to make consumers feel good about the 'sustainable' Andean or Indonesian plantations their particular brand of latte comes from. But this pop-moral advertising lexicon does not apply to the origins of drugs: public fascination with celebrity drug-addiction has exempted drugs from the touchy-feely vocabulary of 'ethical' consumerism. For all the concern, however laudable, with the lives ruined to make cheap clothes or an unethical cappuccino, few ever stop to ask how many lives just went up a supermodel's nose – the opposite, indeed: the same media that pontificates about ethical consumerism treats celebrity drug-taking as fodder for tittle-tattle gossip, laced with a giggly – only slightly disapproving – waggle of the forefinger. Or even excessive sympathy for the stars in rehabilitation, or admiration for gutsy appearances on reality TV. *Amexica* offers a backstage pass, access all areas, behind the celebrity gossip and those glittering cocaine nights in Los Angeles, New York, London and Madrid.

There is another way in which the narco war fits into our contemporary modus vivendi that make it very much a war of its time. It is the first real twenty-first-century war, because it is about, in the end, nothing. Mexico's war is a conflict of the post-political era. It is being fought in an age of belligerent hyper-materialism as an ideology in itself, the leading exponents of which run their corporations or banks with personal greed as their sole credo, and their brands as icons of this post-modern religion. Until this hyper-materialist era, the human race has populated a world where, unfortunately, Muslims and Jews fight each other, communists and fascists, Serbs and Croats, Tutsis and Hutus, Americans or British soldiers and Islamic insurgents, and so on. We may all have different readings of why they do this, but they do so – at least nominally – for a cause, faith or tribal identity, however crazy. But Mexico's war (some do not like calling it a war) has not even the pretence of a propelling cause. Mexicans are mutilating, decapitating, torturing and killing each other ostensibly over money and the drug-smuggling routes that provide it. Some would argue that all wars are fought indirectly over money and resources, be they wars of empire fought in the nineteenth century until 1918, or wars of ideology or religion in the twentieth century. But most of the savage violence in Mexico is for the smaller profits of the domestic market and local street corner, meted out for its own sake. There is no financial stake in killing a street addict. There are regional and clan identities, to the states of Tamaulipas, Michoacán or Sinaloa, but they are fluid and subject to too many whimsical alliances and betrayals for the war to be defined as tribal as it is in, say, Rwanda. Mexico's war has no ideological pretentions or window dressing – its only cover is that it was originally fought, like other, lesser, Mafia wars, over the now diversified product lines that get America (and Europe) high. But the *casus belli* is now even more vacuous than that. The narco war is fought for the accoutrements of a new post-modern social kudos, social performance, the ability to show off the right labels, brands and products in accordance with advertising; to wear the right clothes, to be accompanied by the appropriately desirable girl, chatter on the latest mobile phone with the latest 'applications', own the right gadget and drive the right SUV. For these definitions of status, thousands die. The narco war is fought on YouTube and mobile phones as well as in the streets and back-room torture chambers: cartels use YouTube to threaten rivals and public officials, boast of their killing and set up rogue 'hot spot' digital sites to broadcast their savagery and invite comments. One such site hosted from El Paso received more than 320,000 hits and posted more than 1,000 comments.[13] Murders, mutilations and executions are posted on the Internet, themselves a blend of cyber-sado-pornography. Unlike the cyber-strutting of al-Qaeda, from whom it is sometimes argued they got the idea, the narcos use digital communication not as a weapon of insane Holy War, but with something approaching a sense of humour with which to goad and boast across cyberspace – gift-wrapping their real-life bloodlust in the electronic ether of titillation and non-meaning.

One striking feature of the post-political war is that neither the political left nor right has managed to muster the slightest resistance. There is no significant trade union, nor any revolutionary or overtly workers' movement against the narco cartels (though civil society organisations doing their level best tend to be of the left). Similarly, there is no sign of a rightist, fascistic or vigilante movement for law and order (at least not on the Mexican side of the border); the army's role is a mercurial one, and no Mussolini figure to the right of President Calderón has come to the fore. Instead, a war that is quintessentially materialist and largely male meets resistance from two quarters that do not belong to conventional politics. The post-political, materialist war meets resistance from the 'pre-political' clergy and church groups more than any other constituency of society – both Catholic (though not entirely from the organised Church) and reformed. And the male war meets resistance from strong women, as individuals, organisations – and in the home. That these social quarters provide the only measureable, let alone cogent, counterweight to narco violence at street level is something with which a secular mass media, forever seeking policy options and conventional political or military 'solutions', is deeply and visibly uncomfortable, not least because they all, serially, fail.

This was the kind of war being fought by the cartels during the two weeks over Christmas in 2008:

- A man masquerading as a fisherman, calling himself Enrique Portocarrero, is arrested in Colombia for designing and building twenty fibre-glass submarines to bring cocaine ashore in Mexico. He was known as 'Captain Nemo'[14]
- A sudden escalation of declamatory *narcomantas* in public places, usually naming and warning local police officials, reached a zenith in every sense, hung from Monterrey cathedral and ominously denouncing President Calderón himself for favouring the Sinaloa cartel over its principal rival, the Gulf cartel[15]
- A member of President Calderón's personal and permanent bodyguard was arrested and charged for being in the employ of – and feeding secrets about the president's policies and movements to – the Beltrán Leyva brothers cartel
- After five men were arrested and charged in El Paso alone for procuring firearms in Texas and smuggling them into Mexico, US Secretary of State Condoleezza Rice insisted that the lifting of a ban on semi-automatic weapons had nothing to do with the vast quantities of such weapons seized in Mexico[16]
- The decapitated bodies of twelve federal army soldiers are found in the southern state of Guerrero, the most audacious single execution of serving military personnel since the Mexican revolution of 1910. They are gagged by the arms and feet when executed, with a message reading: 'For Every One of Mine You Kill, We Kill Ten'[17]
- The US National Drug Assessment Threat report for 2009 declares that 'The Mexican drug-trafficking organisations represent the greatest organised crime threat to the United States'

During the first two weeks of the New Year, 2009:

- Twenty-one people are killed within forty-eight hours in and around Ciudad Juárez
- Twenty-seven people are killed within one week in Baja California
- A television station in Monterrey is attacked with grenades after reporting on narco murders[18]
- General Mauro Enrique Tello Quiñones, who left the army to work as a security consultant for the mayor of Cancun in his efforts against the narcos, is abducted, tortured and executed along with two adjutants. Among those arrested in connection with the murder are Cancun's police chief and several of his senior officers[19]
- In Tijuana, Santiago Meza López is arrested, charged with disintegrating 300 bodies in acid
- Four decapitated seventeen-year-olds are among twenty-one people killed in Tijuana during the first week of the year[20]
- Twenty-one senior law-enforcement officers in Tijuana are arrested for protecting the Arellano Félix cartel. There is speculation as to whether this is a genuine offensive by authorities trying to clean up corruption, or said authorities working for the rival Sinaloa cartel

The transition from Christmas 2009 into the New Year, 2010, went thus:

- During the first four days of December, twenty-five are killed in Ciudad Juárez, as the city is blanketed by a rare snowfall, bringing the anuual total of dead to 2,390 for a single city[21]
- It emerges that only 2 per cent of the much-vaunted $1.4 billion 'Merida Initiative' of aid from the United States to Mexico to help fight the cartels has arrived in the recipient country due to bureaucratic problems, contracting rules and difficulties getting helicopters to Mexico[22]
- Thirteen Zeta gangsters are killed as Mexican marines burst through the gates of a narco compound outside Monterrey. Several passers-by, including a twelve-year-old girl, are injured by intense fire. The Zetas call for help, which arrives in the form of a dozen armed vehicles that then engage an army patrol it meets on the way[23]

- An American teacher and school district councillor from Southern California, Bobby Salcedo, is abducted and killed in Durango while visiting his wife's home town of Gómez Palacio during a twinning celebration between his town and hers. Four others were also kidnapped and killed
- The Inter-American Court of Human Rights rules that Mexico failed to investigate the deaths of young women abducted, tortured, violated and murdered in Ciudad Juárez. The ruling applied to three test cases
- Antonio Mendoza Ledezma, a member of the Azteca street gang that acts as an enforcer for the Juárez cartel, is charged with involvement in the murders of 200 people[24]
- Journalist Bladimir Antuna of Durango, who bragged to his colleagues after serial death threats that he wouldn't mind being killed but was terrified of torture, is found strangled and tortured to death. A note beside his mangled body reads: 'This happened to me for giving information to soldiers and writing too much'[25]
- Six decomposing bodies are found at the seaside resort of Puerto Peñasco in Sonora, two hours' drive from Tucson, Arizona, beloved by and known to American tourists as 'Rocky Point'[26]
- Naval special forces mount the most successful raid ever against a leading cartel drug lord: Arturo Beltrán Leyva, head of the rebel cartel pitched against *Chapo* Guzmán's Sinaloa cartel and the Mexican government, is killed at his home in the smart Mexico City suburb of Cuernevaca
- A special forces naval ensign, Melquisedet Angulo Córdova, was killed during the shoot-out that eliminated Beltrán Leyva. Two days after his official funeral, gunmen burst into the home of Angulo Córdova's family, killing four of his immediate family, including his mother[27]
- The body of thirty-six-year-old Hugo Hernández, abducted in Sonora on 2 January, turns up in Los Mochis, Sinaloa, though not in one piece. His torso is in one location, his severed arms and legs boxed in another place, and his skull found in another. But his face had been flayed, left near the city hall of Los Mochis, sewn to a soccer ball[28]
- The death toll in Ciudad Juárez for only the first week of the New Year, 2010, reaches the abominable figure of fifty-nine[29]

The last day the body of this book was being written, 30 January 2010, began with the receipt of the following email from Molly Molloy who – at the New Mexico State University campus in Las Cruces – keeps the most reliable tally of drug violence in Ciudad Juárez. Ms Molloy's introduction to today's bulletin reads as assiduously as it does most other days:

> Diario reports 12 people were killed in shooting incidents yesterday
> . . . Or it could be more. I checked stories in Diario before I went to
> bed at about 10:00 and several women and a baby were also injured
> in these incidents. Below is a post from Lapolaka [a Juárez website]
> posted at 23:10 last night that says 10. Then, another at 1:03 that
> describes another massacre after midnight in the Oasis neighbor-
> hood that left 3 more people dead. The tally yesterday [for the year
> so far, one month old] was at about 183, so with these the toll is now
> at least 195 or 196. It would seem that an apparent lull came to a
> very violent end on Friday night. Molly[30]

The following night, sixteen teenagers were shot dead as a unit of gunmen stormed a party of young people.

On New Year's Eve, a week before Mr Hernández' face was discovered tied to a football in Los Mochis, the bound, beaten and tortured bodies of two men had also been found nearby, with their hands tied behind their backs. A message beside them read: 'This Territory Already Has An Owner'. But the twist was this: these last deaths of 2009 were bodies hanging from an overpass, just like the headless man from the Bridge of Dreams in Juárez.[31]

CHAPTER ONE

La Plaza

My friend Jorge Fregoso and I were drinking a beer at a bar in a labyrinth of quiet alleyways away from central Tijuana one Saturday afternoon in September 2008 when the shooting started. It targeted an art-deco mansion in the upscale Misión del Pedregal suburb. Federal army trucks arrived to its left, state police shock troops to the right. Few shots were fired from inside the building, it seemed, but a deafening fusillade of fire was aimed at the villa. Only next day was it revealed to have procured, for the authorities, Eduardo Arellano Felix – 'The Doctor' – chief of the clan trying to defend the plaza of drug traffic between Tijuana and California for his Arellano brothers syndicate from the raiding Sinaloa cartel. Misión de Pedregal is clearly marked as being, says the sign adjacent to Arellano's house, a '*Vecinos Vigilando*', Neighbourhood Watch, zone – yet, says a woman cleaning her porch opposite Arellano's next day, 'I didn't think there was anyone living in that house.' What followed the announcement were seventy-two hours of carnage even by Tijuana standards, which took the death toll for the city to 462 in the year 2008, and caused even the local *El Sol de Tijuana* newspaper, accustomed to such things, to run the headline '*Bano de Sangre*', bloodbath.

Fregoso, a reporter for the local Síntesis TV news channel, and I receive our first alert shortly after 3 p.m. on the Monday when we are called to a *colonia* called Libertad, where a corpse lies slumped in the dirt beneath a rung of steps made of tyres. A crowd of young people arrives to observe the busy forensic aftermath in a disconcertingly knowing silence, punctuated by the odd giggly joke or mobile phone call, while some 30 metres away the iron wall that

marks the border with the USA also looks on, the old fence made
of metal landing sheets used by the US air force from Vietnam to
Iraq in 1991.

Three young women from the forensic team (wearing identical
grey shirts, black jeans and pony tails) take careful photographs and
notes, then, like the accompanying trucks full of balaclava-covered
federal police, speed off to a different location, Mariano Matamoros,
and a major artery on the city's outskirts where another corpse lies,
visible by the green light of a Pemex gas station. The windscreen
of the victim's Ford Explorer (with California plates) is pitted with
three bullet holes, and he seems to have made a run into the street,
followed by twenty-five further shots, each shell casing marked by
a blue number on a yellow card. Before the forensic women have
even finished here, we are immediately summoned across dirt tracks
– tearing, zigzagging, between cement buildings – to a crossing of
back streets in the Casablanca district, and a lifeless body beside the
doorway of a corner shop painted with yellow flowers. When
the ninja-clad cops pull back the sheet, we see a teenager shot at
point-blank range in the face, blood oozing onto the flagstones, and
a watching girl turns away to weep into her mobile phone. But now
the night really begins.

Fregoso, with his access to police communications, receives
the news so fast that we barrel our orange Volkswagen between the
fourth and fifth jeeps of a machine-gun-toting police convoy (to the
hooting fury of jeep number five) heading for the next slaughter.
The cordon of plastic tape reading '*Precuacion*' is not even in place
yet outside the 9/4 minimart in Villa Foresta, in theory selling '*Vinos
Y Liqores*', where a blanket covers the remains of the security guard,
with two more dead inside. There is wild wailing from the womenfolk as this body outside was revealed: his flesh has been grated into
something like raw kebab meat by fire at point-blank range from a
Kalashnikov, or *cuerno de chivo* – goat's horn – as an AK-47 is known
around here. Yet more screams follow the sight of those killed inside
the store, brought out on stretchers and loaded into the white 'DIF'
Forensic Department truck now carrying five former people. The
shop, says the *susurro* – the rustling whisper through the crowd –
was a stash for drugs being loaded for export aboard two cars,
presumably intended to join the 65,000 that cross from Tijuana into

San Diego every day, but which the police now tow away. Meanwhile, heavy-set men in sharp suits arrive to look from a slight distance, embracing each other in a way that suggested burdensome comradeship and solace, but little sadness. Any attempt to speak to them is rebuffed with menacing silence and a glare. One of them goes over to console a young woman clutching a baby, in paroxysms of grief, beneath a mural advertising Viper auto alarms.

Yonkes − repair yards for fixing up cars with second-hand parts − are a hallmark of Tijuana's byways, and next morning another group of *sicarios* − or maybe the same squad − return to Villa Foresta in brazen, broad noonday light, past the mural of a girl in a bikini sprawled over an SUV and into gate number one of *Yonke Cristal*, killing one man whose body, wearing a red shirt, is visible through the bars of a red gate. Two other corpses are hidden behind a white van, the skeletal metal frames of the vehicles all around, detached wheel hubs like prying eyes, and the words '*Jesucristo Excelsior*' carved into the hillside above. This is now Tuesday, and on Wednesday morning Tijuana awakes to the news that while the city slept, three more bodies were found in an abandoned van and another in a car. The van has been dumped in a quarter called Los Alamos, at a meeting point between ramshackle hillside *colonias*, a smart gated community and an electronics factory, and the dead men have been tortured, mutilated and strangled − one of them handcuffed. People killed and dumped in vehicles are known in this war as '*encajuelados*', literally 'entrunked'. The body in the car is that of a police officer called Mauricio Antonio Hernándo Flores. It is his personal car, and the officer had parked beneath a great statue of an open-armed figure of Christ, presiding over Tijuana in imitation of Rio de Janeiro, with its engine running, just past 1 a.m. apparently awaiting someone. Whoever shot him, leaving his body to be discovered slumped in the blood-soaked driver's seat, knew him, and was expected at the scene.

There are two kinds of cop-killings in the narco war. One was illustrated in January 2008 when the narcos crossed some line in the etiquette of drug warfare. The *sicarios*' car pulled off a main road onto the dirt track into the wretched *colonia* of Loma Bonita. They would have parked next to the Swap Meet jumble-sale hangar and walked to what is now a vacant lot for sale, marked by a white wooden cross, where officer Margarito Zaldano lived. They entered the house and executed not only Zaldano but also his wife Sandra and twelve-year-old daughter Valeria. Zaldano's crime? Being a cop and doing his job trying to arrest criminals who were protected by his own police force. The other kind of slaying of police officers – or *la chota*, as they are known on the border, the fuzz – involves those who become embroiled with the narcos, work for them or add to the income of their day job by moonlighting for the cartels, often with the same uniforms and weapons. These officers get caught out if they renege on a deal, charge too much for their services, over-sights or information, or if their work for one cartel becomes irksome to another. Mexicans joke that a police officer is offered a simple career choice: *plata o plomo* – silver or lead – and many, while they can get it, inevitably opt for the former. After the killing of Officer Flores, the authorities, in contrast to their outpouring of tribute to Zaldano back in January, refused to fuss much over this latest execu-tion of one of their colleagues by a single *tiro de gracia* – a 'mercy' shot to the head. In Tijuana, as elsewhere, the municipal police can be working for one cartel, the state police with another, and the *Federales* with yet another. None of this happens in a vacuum.

Like every war, this carnage has a history, and we need to under-stand the background to the narco cartels' business, lest the war appear to be the senseless bloodletting it is not. Or, at least, was not at first. Indeed, one needs to know one's Mafia history as much as that of any major player in the global economy and polity, because the syndicates are more powerful, more astute, and handle higher turnovers than most multinational corporations, as well as fuel our society with their products. The drug cartels were prototypes and pioneers of globalisation; the Neapolitan 'Camorra' was the first multinational into post-communist Eastern Europe, harvesting Kalashnikovs produced under Soviet licence. The Camorra was also among the first capitalist enterprises to penetrate communist China, dealing in textiles and drugs coming into the port of Naples. Now that the 'legal' global economy is in crisis, narco cartels respond to their own crisis within that economy in their own – but by no means separate – way.

Unlike their Italian counterparts, the Mexican cartels cannot trace their origins to the eighteenth century, but they were drug-dealing before the Italians. The smuggling syndicate based in Ciudad Juárez was not only the first narco syndicate run by a woman, 'La Nacha', Ignacia Jasso, but among the first to trade in heroin to the USA, after the market for supplying America with alcohol, during Prohibition, came to an end in 1933. The Mexican heroin-growing and opium market in Sinaloa gained impetus during the Second World War, when the United States signed an agreement to buy opium to meet its wartime medical needs.[1] The Mexican narco smugglers did start dealing in drugs on a major scale at the same time as the Italians, towards the end of the 1960s, when it became clear that demand from the United States and Europe was insatiable. 'The narco economy,' wrote Guilermo Ibarra, an economist at Sinaloa State University, 'and family remittances from the United States actually keep our state on its feet.'[2]

At first, Mexico's role was that of producer, of 'Mexican Mud' heroin, poppies for which were ideally suited to the climate of the Pacific coast state of Sinaloa, home of the 'classic' narco cartels – then and now. Two initiatives by the US government during the 1970s and '80s changed things, and in part laid the foundations for the modern cartels. First, during the 1970s, the United States steered the Mexican government through 'Operation Condor', which succeeded in all but destroying indigenous Mexican heroin production, incinerating and defoliating the Sinaloan poppy crops, in dichotomous partnership with the same Mexican political apparatus that had ruled in close co-existence with – protected by and protecting – the *gomeros*, or heroin barons, so called because of the gummy texture of their merchandise.

Second, Washington embarked on its covert backing of right-wing Contra rebels against the Sandinista government in Nicaragua.[3] The Contras would be armed with weapons secretly transported from the US, with the criminal underworld acting as supplier and mediator. But the arms had to be paid for in 'currency' that would not call attention to itself, and they were: in cocaine from Colombia. Luckily for all involved, narcotic science and narcotic fashion both coincided with Washington's interests, as well as those of the cartels in Colombia and Mexico. Just as the US needed Colombia's natural currency to procure and pay for arms to the Contras, cocaine was

becoming the drug of choice: in powdered form for American entertainment and other smart circles, and in its chemical derivative form,
crack, on the street and in the ghetto. According to a fictionalised
account in *The Power of the Dog* by Don Winslow, the Mexicans
became the courier service for arms in one direction and cocaine in
the other – a service that became known as the 'Mexican Trampoline'.
Mexico's cartels combined three things to act as a conduit in flooding
America with crack and cocaine: their knowledge of smuggling
routes as old as the border itself, the unofficial acquiescence of the
Reagan administration, and their conviviality with Mexico's
Institutional Revolutionary Party, which had ruled since 1917. In so
doing, they realised, as Winslow put it: 'that their real product isn't
drugs, it's the two-thousand-mile border they share with the United
States. Land can be burned, crops can be poisoned, people can be
displaced, but that border isn't going anywhere.'[4]

As masters of the border, Mexican narcos were in a position to
assume control of the hemisphere. Cocaine supply routes through
the Caribbean and Miami were strangled by US authorities still
earnest about fighting a 'war on drugs', which only increased the
flow through Mexico, which it was impossible to throttle. The
Mexican traffickers demanded that their Colombian suppliers pay
not in cash for the necessary transportation, but in kind; and the
percentage of cocaine payable as commission for the delivery service
increased, and increased. Colombians trying to penetrate Mexico
themselves were promptly killed. So that now, according to the US
Drug Enforcement Administration, 90 per cent of all drugs entering
the United States do so as part of Mexican cartel business. The major
imports are still cocaine and marijuana, though recent Mexican
mass-production of methamphetamine accounts for most US consumption of the drug, as it does across Latin America. The bust of
a methamphetamine factory in Argentina in September 2008
involved predominantly Mexican nationals. Drug-enforcement agencies also blame Mexican cartels for the sudden spike in heroin
availability, and the precipitous fall in street prices, from $5,000 per
ounce in 2004 to $1,000 per ounce in 2008.

But when we talk about 'The Mexicans' we talk not about a
homogenous organisation; quite the reverse. We talk about cartels
operating, during this period, under licence from the authorities.

Franchised by municipal, state and federal government officials and police forces, the system was based, through an organised network of corruption until the fall of the PRI in 2000, on what is called the '*Plaza*' – a word used in Spanish to mean a place of gathering, be it a square in the centre of a town, or the *Plaza de Toros* – a bullring – or the jurisdiction of a police or military force. Apart, crucially, from its eastern stretch towards the Gulf, the border was strategically carved into drug-smuggling 'Plazas', each considered the territory of a sub-division of the original Sinaloan mafia, which would pay the authorities for protection and cooperation – with percentages shaved off at every level, to the top – on its turf. In return, the mafia would finger freelance or rival operators so that the authorities could give the impression of an authentic enforcement operation.[5]

Even if it sometimes feels a bit like train-spotting, we need to be familiar with the names and heritage of the major trafficking organisations that operate the trade worth an estimated $323 billion a year[6] – pushing drugs into the veins of the wretched, up the noses of the rich, and frying the brains of the young. People refer to 'the Mafia' as though it were some amorphous alien force or – worse – a romantic brotherhood operating to some code of honour laid down by 'Godfather' Corleone, a Marlon Brando don. 'Mafia' is a useful generic term, but applies properly only to Cosa Nostra of Sicily, the syndicate with which the world is most familiar because of its history and mythic presence in mass culture. But in Mexico, as in Italy, the dramatis personae of narco traffic is more complicated than 'the Mafia', and we need to know the cast.

The pioneer of Mexico's narco trafficking mafia was Pedro Aviles Pérez, from Sinaloa, who escalated the smuggling of marijuana and heroin into the United States during the late 1960s. But the original Mexican Godfather was Miguel Ángel Félix Gallardo, a protégé of Aviles' who took over his operation after Aviles was killed in a shoot-out with the police in 1978. Félix Gallardo founded the Guadalajara cartel and became perhaps the biggest narco trafficker in the world during his zenith. In 1985, however, a calamity changed the cartel, the Mexican government's conviviality with it, and US complicity with that relationship. An undercover agent for the US Drugs Enforcement Administration, Enrique 'Kiki' Camarena, was fingered, kidnapped and tortured to death in Guadalajara (there is evidence that the CIA knew and may even have trained the people who did it, to a point that relations between the two agencies have never since fully recovered).

The truth behind Camarena's death has eluded all attempts at excavation, but whatever that truth, Washington demanded that Mexico do something – and that something was to arrest Félix Gallardo. In 1989, Gallardo was convicted for ordering Camarena's abduction and murder, but from jail he sought to keep his organisation together, allocating its various component Plazas in which to operate. There was even a council, held in an expensive Acapulco hotel, to which the jailed Gallardo sent messengers to clarify the Plazas, exhort the cartels to cooperate against their common enemy, US law enforcement, and offer advice on how to negotiate with the Mexican authorities and impose discipline.[7]

Gallardo's vision was one which in Italy is called a *Pax Mafiosa* – the Mafia's peace – whereby criminal syndicates know their place with reference to each other, law enforcement knows its place in the same scheme of things, the product keeps flowing, and politicians understand that this kind of quiet comes at a price – protection. A *Pax Mafiosa* can guarantee the politician votes, and a power base, in return for nothing more than the tranquillity of a blind eye at least, or cover for, even adherence to, a particular cartel at best. But this is not how the criminal mind works. If the cartels are greedy, why should they not become even greedier? If their modus operandi is to break laws, why would their modus vivendi be keep to them? When things become bloody in the world of narco trafficking, and the peace is blown apart, this means power is shifting, disintegrating or resisting disintegration and being claimed across the ordained Plazas. When Cosa Nostra famously blew up the anti-Mafia judges Giovanni Falcone and Paolo Borsellino in 1992, it was taken wrongly to be a sign of the Mafia's strength. Cosa Nostra was reeling from what the judges had achieved against them, and – crucially – the tables were turning across the Plazas of Italy. Cosa Nostra was being overtaken by new – leaner and meaner – operators: the Camorra of Naples and 'Ndrangheta of Calabria. The old guard was in trouble, the Plaza unquiet. Nor, in Mexico, could such a momentous event as Gallardo's arrest occur without leaving a vacuum, any more than any of his lieutenants could resist trying to fill it. The Guadalajara cartel split, different branches claiming its mantle: one, led by Gallardo's nephews and nieces, established the Tijuana cartel: another, led by Avilés' nephew, Joaquín Guzmán – *El Chapo* or Shorty – founded the Sinaloa cartel and a third formed the Juárez cartel. But the shattering of *Pax Mafiosa* did not result in a reduction in the flow of drugs, it means only that control of the flow, of the Plazas, is up for grabs. It has also come to mean, in Mexico, that unfettered greed and a terrible surplus has created a new Plaza on home turf, contaminating Mexico itself. And so a draft map of the present war came to be drawn.

The most famous Plaza, that between Tijuana and California, was featured in Steven Soderbergh's film *Traffic*. It was run by the Tijuana cartel, or Arellano Félix Organisation, the AFO, but is now contested. The Tijuana cartel is the only one to claim a direct (but disputed) family connection to Gallardo: Gallardo had five nephews, the Arellano Félix brothers – Eduardo, arrested that Saturday in Misión Pedregal, was the last to remain at large. Joaquín '*El Chapo*' Guzmán's first round of offensives on the border followed the borderline itself, west to east, starting in the early 1990s in Tijuana, soon after Gallardo's arrest, when Guzmán claimed the *Padrino*'s mantle, and the heritage of his own uncle, Pedro Avilés Pérez. In those days, the AFO kept Guzmán at bay: the early 1990s were the days of the 'Narco Juniors' in Tijuana, who flaunted a style that the recent violence has only just forced out of date. The brothers and their entourage would cruise the city and its nightlife, dressing outrageously, on their motorcycles or in SUV *trocas*. In many ways, they invented a narco style of yuppie razzmatazz. The AFO most infamously perpetrated the highest hit against the Catholic Church by any crime syndicate, when its hit men killed Cardinal Juan Jesús Posadas Ocampo, on 24 May 1993 at Guadalajara airport.

The AFO can be said to be prime movers in changing the rules of engagement to include women and children as well as clerics – something the 'old guard' narcos prided themselves in avoiding. In August 2008, Jesús Rubén Moncada – aka '*El Güero Loco*' the Crazy Blond – was arrested in Los Angeles for a famous massacre in 1998 of nineteen people, including a baby clutched in its mother's arms, on a villa veranda near Ensenada, down the coast south of Tijuana. He had been living illegally in LA for ten years.[8] In 2002, the cartel's leader, Ramón Arellano Félix, was shot and killed by federal police. And in the latest round of violence since 2006, the AFO has been subjected to a battering by Guzmán's cartel, which abated only recently when his man in Tijuana, Eduardo García Simental, known as '*El Teo*', was arrested in January 2010. The arrest of Eduardo Arellano Félix that Saturday afternoon in 2008 leaves his sister Enelda as commander of the Tijuana clan (a first for a woman since Ignacia Jasso in Juárez during Prohibition), while Eduardo's nephew, Fernando Sánchez Arellano, 'The Engineer', runs the street operation. Enelda is an important figure, because narco trafficking had become a male domain — until now, when more and more women have become engaged in the business. Drug trafficking is seen as a more dignified profession than prostitution, as women elect to serve as smugglers, with a better chance of passing border controls and checkpoints than men. There have been some major arrests of women, and the body of María José González, singer and winner of the Sun Festival beauty pageant, was found by a road in Culiacán in spring 2009 near that of her drug-trafficking husband and a sign reading 'Don't Throw Trash'. The authorities believe she had become involved with the Sinaloa cartel, one of many beauty queens to become cartel mascots, then victims of their rivals.[9]

A stretch of land between Tijuana and Ciudad Juárez is variously controlled by an organisation that switches allegiance to bigger cartels in order to operate. It was once run by two brothers called Arturo and Alfredo Beltrán Leyva, who come from the same range of mountains as *Chapo* Guzmán, near the town of Guamúchil, in Sinaloa. For years, the Beltrán Leyva brothers operated their stretch of frontier on behalf of the Sinaloa cartel, to which they were allied. They acted also as a security wing for Guzmán, overseeing squads of *sicarios* and protecting *El Chapo*'s lieutenants and their families. But two things happened in rapid succession: in December 2007, while Guzmán's cartel was fighting the Gulf cartel and its military wing, the Zetas, leaders from the Beltrán Leyva cartel held a treacherous meeting with the Zetas in Veracruz, purportedly to discuss opening a space for the brothers in Central Mexico, independently of Guzmán. The meeting fitted into a series the Zetas were said to be holding, offering their services as hit men for a 'super-cartel' comprising anyone prepared to challenge Guzmán.[10] In January 2008, a month after the meeting, Alfredo Beltrán Leyva was arrested, and in this moment lay a turning point in the war. Guzmán is said to have commented that Beltrán Leyva's meeting with the Zetas necessitated his having to 'cut off that arm of the organisation'. The Beltrán Leyva clan deserted Guzmán, convinced that he had delivered Alfredo to the authorities in order to court, or even secure, their favour. The younger brother, Arturo Beltrán Leyva, '*El Alfa*', exacted revenge on senior public officials, including the Federal Police Commissioner, and on Guzmán's son, Edgar Guzmán López, whom his *sicarios* gunned down in a shopping mall in May 2008. As head of security for Guzmán, Arturo had the home addresses of the families of his senior affiliates, and the violence unleashed by Beltrán Leyva against his former protector's entourage accounts for some of the worst recent killing in Sinaloa.

Over Christmas and New Year 2009–10, a government offensive against the Beltrán Leyva cartel reached high drama. On 16 December, a unit of naval special forces, backed by helicopter cover, stormed Arturo's dwelling complex in Cuernevaca, shot and killed him – the highest narco drug lord to be assassinated by the military since President Calderón's offensive, and the first since Ramón Arellano Félix in 2002. Beltrán Leyva's bloodied corpse was subject by his military assassins to an official rite associated with the narcos themselves. Photographs showed his jeans pulled down to his knees and his torso adorned with rows of bloodied $100 bills, and in another shot with spiritual accoutrements. Such a display angered commentators such as Jorge Chabat in *El Universal*, who called the rite 'the typical modus operandi of narco traffickers',[11] but that newspaper, like others, eagerly published the images.[12]

During the raid of 16 December, an ensign from the commando unit, Melquisedet Angulo Córdova, aged thirty, had been killed as Beltrán Leyva's bodyguards exchanged fire. He was buried with full military honours, and the response of Beltrán Leyva's supporters was immediate. The day after the commando's home-town funeral in the state of Tabasco, gunmen burst into his grieving family's home, killing his mother, sister, brother and an aunt.[13] By targeting the immediate family of military personnel serving in the war against them, the narcos had escalated the stakes in Mexico's war by yet another notch, but the authorities' response was equally swift. With both senior Beltrán Leyva brothers removed, leadership of the cartel fell to the younger Héctor Beltrán Leyva. He remains at large, but on 2 January 2010, another brother, Carlos, was taken by a bloodless swoop in the Sinaloan capital of Culiacán. The government could not have made itself clearer: the war was being cranked up still further. But who stood to gain? The President, of course; but also, said the whisper on the street – which on the border is called a *susurro*, a rustle of leaves – the Sinaloa cartel, who had everything to win from the government's war against its rivals, as the government well knows.

Ciudad Juárez was always the core of Amexica, formerly '*El Paso Del Norte* – portal to the North – a trading route long before the border and a smuggling route as old as the line itself. *La Nacha Jasso* was the unchallenged heroin and then marijuana queen of Juárez from the legalisation of alcohol until the 1970s. But the modern Juárez cartel was forged by Amado Carrillo Fuentes, who emerged as a force after he attached himself to the most powerful drug lord of the central border area, Pablo Acosta Villarreal, during the 1980s. Acosta operated out of the isolated town of Ojinaga, opposite Presidio in Texas, and in an unparalleled series of interviews with the writer Terrence Popper, detailed how his syndicate enjoyed the protection of the state and federal police, politicians and army.[14] But, spotting his chance, Carrillo arranged for his mentor to be killed by federal officers during a raid on his home village of Santa Elena in 1987, which involved cooperation with forces from the US side. In his excellent account of Carrillo's building of the Juárez cartel, *Down by the River*, Charles Bowden relates how Carrillo paid a federal commander a million dollars to mount the raid and ensure Acosta's death.[15] Carrillo Fuentes then shifted the cartel's power base to Juárez itself and strengthened it: in the mid-1990s, according to the DEA, the Juárez cartel was the biggest drug trafficker in the world, shifting more than 50 per cent of all narcotics consumed in the USA. In 1996, Carrillo died during facial surgery – if he did die: mystery still surrounds his passing, with all four surgeons engaged for the operation subsequently murdered. Violence in Juárez followed his death, as Carrillo Fuentes' heir and brother, Vicente, tried to secure the terrain, but even that bloodbath was moderate compared to the present savagery in the city, which is supposed to have begun when Joaquín Guzmán's Sinaloa cartel laid siege in 2007. Whether the Juárez cartel remains a force in the labyrinth of competing interests that are killing across the city today has yet to be ascertained; but one can only presume that its present incarnation, *La Línea*, retains potency in the maelstrom, alongside some 500 street gangs, the Sinaloa cartel, different strata of corrupt police forces and the armed forces. How fitting, and gruesome, that '*La Línea*' is also a common term in everyday parlance for the border itself.

As a man who perceives himself as heir to the Avilés/Gallardo empire, and as Avilés' nephew, Joaquín *El Chapo* Guzmán saw the Plaza of his Sinaloa cartel as a national one, almost of birthright. The moment Gallardo was arrested, Guzmán, who had built solid alliances with cocaine exporters in Colombia, declared war first on those whom he disdained as pretenders in Tijuana and, with time, every other criminal organisation in Mexico. Guzmán was captured, however, early into his leadership of the cartel, in 1993. It was from jail, in luxury confinement at El Puente Grande maximum-security prison near Guadalajara, that – US intelligence sources believe – Guzmán adapted his tactics to build alliances in public office and high politics. Perhaps because of those contacts, Guzmán escaped spectacularly in 2001, just before he was due to be extradited to the United States, thus becoming poster boy for the latest wave of cult narco folk heroism. 'Breakout Of The Millenium' was the title of one *narcocorrido* ballad commemorating the escape. Another, by Los Buitres (The Vultures) and broadcast across radio airwaves, juke boxes, the Internet and YouTube goes: 'He sleeps at times in houses / At times in tents / Radio and rifle at the foot of the bed / And sometimes his roof is a cave / Guzmán is everywhere.' Guzmán is semi-literate, but issues communiques boasting that he pays out five million dollars a month to corrupt officials, and makes sudden, brazen appearances like that in May 2005 at a restaurant in Nuevo Laredo (on Gulf cartel terrain he was contesting at the time), when some forty diners found the doors suddenly locked by his gunmen. The clientele was asked not to use cell phones while Guzmán and his entourage enjoyed their own meal and drinks, after which *El Chapo* himself pulled out thousands of dollars in cash and paid for everyone in the room.[16]

From jail, Guzmán had directed successive assaults on the border

Plazas, which chronologically followed the frontier from west to east. After Tijuana came Juárez, following Carrillo's death. But it was after Guzmán had escaped that he launched the offensive which detonated this latest phase of the war by unleashing his forces, unsuccessfully, against the Gulf cartel in 2005, and in pursuit of the prize: Nuevo Laredo, the busiest commercial border crossing in the world. The offensive in Nuevo Laredo was both an end and a beginning: it was the last of Guzmán's first round of attacks but also the onset of the current war, taking the violence to another level altogether. Some expert observers believe that Guzmán has become something of a figurehead, a symbolic narco monarch who wields less power than notoriety, and that the cartel is now run by others with lower profiles but greater ruthlessness, Ismael '*El Mayo*' Zambada – who in 2010 gave a unique interivew to *El Universal*, boasting about the cartel's prowess – and Ignacio Coronel until he was killed by Mexican troops in July 2010. It is often speculated, on the *susurro*, that if it was part of the Mexican government's strategy to restore a *Pax Mafiosa* by backing one cartel in its bid for a monopoly, then that cartel would be the Sinaloa. But it is now too late to pursue such a goal, because of the ferocious power wielded by Guzmán's main rival, the Gulf cartel.

Until 2005, the drama was mainly among and between Sinaloans moving up to the border, which initially excluded the only syndicate to whom Gallardo had conceded its own indigenous terrain, the Gulf cartel, based in the north-eastern state of Tamaulipas, opposite deep south Texas. At the time of writing, it is too early to discern any specific outcome to the offensive launched by President Calderón in December 2006, but one partial result is clear: the Gulf cartel and what was formed as its military wing, Los Zetas, have held their terrain against both their rivals and the army. While *Chapo* Guzmán remains Mexico's most powerful drug lord, and his cartel appears to remain that closest to political power, the Zetas' insurgency and resilience makes them the Mexican government's gravest problem, along with the very different nightmare of the anarchy in Ciudad Juárez. For this reason, the Gulf cartel and Zetas warrant special attention.

Unlike the other syndicates with leaderships from Sinaloa, the Gulf cartel grew out of – and is fiercely proud of – its territory and home state, which runs along the border from Nuevo Laredo to the river's mouth. The cartel was founded by a whiskey bootlegger from the 1930s, Juan Nepomuceno Guerra, when he moved into the mari-juana and heroin business during the 1970s. He is said to have had the only rival on his terrain, Casimiro Espinosa, killed. That murder, in 1984, was reportedly organised by Guerra's nephew, Juan García Abrego, and marks the birth of the modern Gulf cartel. By moving the cartel into cocaine, García Abrego became the first drug traf-ficker to make the FBI's Ten Most Wanted list, and was duly arrested and extradited to the USA in 1996, leaving the leadership contested but easily won by Osiel Cárdenas Guillén. Cárdenas, who hailed from a poor ranch on the outskirts of Matamoros, consolidated his power within the cartel by killing his rival, Chava Gómez — earning himself the nickname '*El Mata Amigos*', the friend-killer — and led it from his home city until being arrested during a gun battle in 2003. He was subsequently extradited to the US in 2007, and sentenced in Houston to twenty-five years in jail in February 2010, after a trial held in secret. Cárdenas, in his way, defines the present narco war: from a very humble background in the police force, he sought not to manipulate high politics, but secured his position within the cartel and against its competitors by recruiting an enforcement wing trained by former members of special service military units, which Cárdenas named *Los Zetas*, after their leader Arturo Guzmán's call sign in the police, Z1. The Zetas emerged to take over the cartel as a syndicate in their own right (a position facing a challenge from within the cartel at the time of writing). They are now one of the most terrifying and formidable drug-trafficking organisations in the world with a paramilitary army estimated by the DEA to number 4,000 highly trained soldiers. Arturo Guzmán and his deputies Rogelio González, 'Z2', and Heriberto Lazcano, known as 'Z3', enticed former members of Mexico's special airborne anti-drug military unit, the GAFE, to defect and train up others. Some of the Zetas' troops were reportedly trained by the US at Fort Benning in Georgia, but this has not conclusively been proved. After 'Z1' Guzmán was killed in 2002 and 'Z2' Rogelio captured in 2004, Lazcano, a former commando in the Mexican GAFE special forces, took on the lead-ership. The recruiting continues: the Zetas, calling themselves a '*Grupo Operativo*', hung a 'narcomanta' banner from a bridge in Nuevo Laredo in 2008 calling for men with 'Military Experience' to call a displayed number. 'We offer a good salary, food and medical care for your families,' it taunted. The Gulf/Zetas claim as part of their territory the most lucrative smuggling point on the border and prize coveted by any cartel: the freight road and rail bridges that cross the Rio Grande between Nuevo Laredo and Laredo, Texas – the busiest commercial border-crossing point in the world. In 2005, the Sinaloa cartel attacked, in pursuit of a share of the contaminated traffic that crosses the frontier every day. The assault was the beginning of the current war, the latest and most vicious phase not just in the long history of narco violence, but in Mexico's history since the revolution of 1910.

Meanwhile, the Zetas have all but secured their goal of a route down the Gulf Coast and into Central America, affording direct access to the traditional cocaine-producing country of Colombia, and new export markets of the drug in Peru and Venezuela. The advantages of coastal supremacy were illustrated by a novel haul on 16 June 2009: dozens of mysteriously dead sharks in two containers brought ashore by the marine authorities at the Gulf port of Progreso turned out to have had their bellies stuffed with bags containing a total of 1,965 lbs of cocaine.[17] In order to secure a clear route to the cocaine producing countries, the Zetas are combating the Sinaloa cartel in guerrilla warfare in Guatemala. The Zetas are the cartel with the best international connections to markets in Britain and Europe, aligned with their opposite numbers: the 'Ndrangheta of Calabria. When in September 2008 some 175 operatives for the Gulf cartel were arrested by US authorities – to whose intelligence services the cartel is known as 'The Company' – ten were in Calabria.[18] The alliance is important in the light of remarks made by the then Mexican attorney general, Eduardo Medina Mora, in March 2009, saying that the crack-down against cross-border traffic was forcing Mexican cartels to shift their attentions and potentially their operations, and 'focus more closely on Europe'.[19] The alliance is equally cogent in the wake of recent briefings by the Mexican diplomatic service indicating that a slight decline in cocaine consumption in the USA entails a surplus needing to be shipped somewhere – which may explain why Britain, Spain and other European countries serviced by the 'Ndrangheta have now overtaken the US in the consumption per capita of cocaine and its 'cooked' derivatives. There have been recent reports of direct contact with drug gangs on Merseyside in Britain.[20]

An alliance between the Zetas and 'Ndrangheta is also logical in terms of narco social style. Although the parallels are not exact, some similar progression can be traced in the decline of the 'classical' Sicilian Cosa Nostra as matching that of the Félix Gallardo federation during the 1980s, as both were overtaken by more ferocious syndicates emerging from poorer backgrounds and without pretensions to become 'Godfather' figures – epitomised by the Zetas from Tamaulipas (challenging Sinaloa) and 'Ndrangheta from Calabria (challenging Sicily). In Mexico as in Italy, there is a ubiquitous nostalgia, however misplaced, for 'old time' gangsters with almost aristocratic pretensions for their codes of 'honour', debonair style and political connections. But they have been superceded, both generationally and in terms of savagery: in the Italian instance by the Camorra and 'Ndrangheta, and in Mexico by the leaner and meaner Zetas, who came from a background of rural slums, urban street gangs and the police or military academies. In both cases, the old Fedora or Western Stetson has been replaced by a shaven buzz-cut and tattoos; the appointment with a politician by that with a personal martial arts trainer. Osiel Cárdenas was an auto-mechanic before joining the police, and as a modest dresser is seen as the style guru of this transition to what one could call 'Generation Z' in the genealogy, without end, of drug dealing.

The Zetas are, moreover, leaving an ever-heavier footprint within the United States. Apart from their deep penetration of the most important border hub city of Houston, they have been linked to appalling violence in the deep south. In August 2008, five men were found with their throats slit in Columbiana, Alabama; they had been tortured with electric shocks. The FBI claims the victims owed a debt of $400,000 to the Gulf cartel. During the big raid against the Gulf cartel in September 2008, twelve of its operatives were arrested in Atlanta, where authorities reported an increasing level of cartel-related violence. In July that year, Atlanta police had shot and killed a Gulf cartel operative arriving to pick up a $2 million kidnap ransom, while in summer 2007, police had found a citizen of the Dominican Republic bound, gagged and chained to a wall in the Atlanta suburb of Lilburn; he owed $300,000 to the Gulf cartel. In 2001, a haul of $41 million in Gulf cartel cash was uncovered in

Atlanta, and another $2.3 million in Houston. In the United States, the battle for distribution is now essentially between Guzmán and the Gulf. After the swoop against the Gulf cartel in September 2008, 750 affiliates to the Sinaloa cartel were arrested by another famous round-up across the USA, Operation Xcellerator, in February 2009. The swoop had started in the Imperial Valley of California, but many of those arrested were in Washington DC and the capital's suburban hinterland. Some $460 million in cash was seized, along with 24,000 lbs of cocaine and 1,200 lbs of methamphetamine.

In its essence, then, Mexico's cartel war is becoming a three-way battle between the army, Guzmán and the Zetas – but there is a final and more recent addition to the list: *La Familia*. *La Familia* emerged during the 1990s as a syndicate entirely indigenous to the state of Sinaloa's coastal southern neighbour, Michoacán. It was devoted to claiming drug-trafficking from and across the state for its own against a subsidiary of Guzmán's, the Milenio cartel, run by a family called Valencia. According to some reports, the rift was due to rivalry over a woman between a member of the Valencias and the man who founded *La Familia*, Nazario Moreno González, known as '*El Mas Loco*' – The Craziest One. *La Familia* 'came out' with a famous incident on 6 September 2006, when twenty masked men burst into a low-rent discotheque, the *Sol Y Sombra* in Morelia, the state capital, and bowled five decapitated heads across the floor, accompanied by a message that was bizarre even by the wayward standards of narco communication: '*La Familia* does not kill for money. It does not kill for women. It does not kill the innocent. Only those who deserve to die. Know that this is divine justice. '*El Mas Loco* prosletyses from a book mixing quotations from the Scriptures with his own excruciating mantras, such as: 'Don't View Your Obstacles As Problems But Accept Them and Discover In Them The Opportunity To Improve Yourself'.

To fight off its Sinaloan neighbours, the emergent *Familia* had elected to be trained by the Zetas. In 2007, however, *La Familia* decided to carve an identity for itself, throwing off the Zetas, who were coming to dominate the *Familia*, as had been their intention all along. The response to the rebuff from Tamaulipas was a brazen act of terrorism against civilians: a bomb was thrown at crowds of families celebrating the Mexican tradition of '*El Grito*' – the Cry of Independence – on the night of 15 September the eve of Mexico's Independence Day. It killed eight people and injured more than 100 in the president's home city of Morelia. *La Familia* sent a flurry of messages to local media disavowing the attack, and hung *narcomensajes* accusing the Zetas of responsibility. After the swoops against first the Gulf cartel and then Guzmán, the US authorities next targeted operatives working for *La Familia*, with 305 arrested during mid-October 2009 by a sting known as Project Coronado. The concentration of arrests was around Dallas, where seventy-seven were arrested for operating a distribution network feeding Illinois, Minnesota and Mississippi.

As the year 2006 drew to a close, some 2,000 people had been killed in violence between the cartels, mostly in Nuevo Laredo and Michoacán. Against this mayhem, on 11 December 2006, only ten days after he had been sworn in, the newly elected President of Mexico, Felipe de Jesús Calderón Hinjosa mobilised 40,000 troops. Calderón, a Harvard-trained lawyer and devout conservative Catholic from Morelia, was the second president to be elected as a leader of the National Action Party (PAN), of which he had been a co-founder, succeeding PAN's first president, Vicente Fox, a former executive for the Coca Cola company in Mexico. For the previous seventy-two years, Mexico had been ruled without interruption by the Institutional Revolutionary Party, which had become more institutional than revolutionary by building and managing a byzantine system of government by corrupt patronage, thereby exercising political party power or influence in every pore of the social fabric to a degree unknown elsewhere in the West. Fox's victory in 2000 was seen at the time to have broken with a stifling epoch, liberating Mexico into the Elysian fields of free-market capitalist meritocracy. His victory was an overwhelmingly urban one and especially resounding along the border. Fox won every border state and sixteen of the nineteen electoral districts adjacent to the United States.[21] It is seen by commentators in the USA and Mexico as unfortunate that the narco violence coincides with the transition to a genuinely capitalist free market in Mexico; but it is essential to the argument of this book that the violence is not, however, a counterforce against what the title of one learned account of this mutation in the country's history calls 'opening Mexico'.[22] The violence occurs not despite but, in large part, *because* of these changes; it is at best an inevitable side-effect of 'opening Mexico', and at worst an integral to it. La Plaza is a marketplace like any other, and narco cartels are not criminal pastiches of contemporary, multinational 'late' capitalism – they are part of it, and operate according to its ruthless values – or, rather, lack of values.

It would have been almost impossible for the narco cartels to operate without the help of the PRI; they mirrored and were part of the party's pyramidal, monopolistic system. But a newly competitive economic environment and the defeat of the PRI obliged the cartels to look again at their own operations, tighten international alliances and diversify their merchandise beyond the cocaine line that had been the main product of its boom years, the 1970s and '80s, during which cohabitation with the PRI had been sustained. A new generation of cartel leaders, typified by Osiel Cárdenas, expanded their catalogue range and strengthened their production and supply of synthetic drugs like methamphetamine or crystal meth. And with cocaine consumption declining in the United States, they also returned to the best-seller of yore, heroin, researching new permutations suitable to the latest taste – such as the craze for 'cheese heroin' in Texas, mixing heroin with over-the-counter drugs to make it cheaper, more impactful and longer-lasting. These are products of Mexico's Fox–Calderón era.

President Calderón's foursquare young spokeswoman, Alejandra De Sota Mirafuentes, meets me at the Brasserie Lipp (the one in Mexico City, not Paris, and part of an international luxury hotel complex) to insist, over mineral water: 'We cannot turn a blind eye to criminality. The power of the cartels has become a very real threat to the security of the Mexican state – the ability to buy off local and state authority, even federal government. For years,' she says of the PRI epoch, 'the authorities just gave in.' But, 'this is very important: Mexico has changed, politically. If in the past, the government was greedy and wanted to take advantage of the cartels, that is no longer the case.' The initial intervention in Michoacán, she says, 'opened the body, and once the body was opened, we could see that it had contracted severe cancer: Juárez, Sinaloa, Tamaulipas, whole regions were controlled by the cartels'. It seems odd that this bright young woman – let alone Calderón's government – had not known that all along. President Calderón has, after all, needed to purge his own apparatus of corruption in an initiative he called 'Clean House'. His former acting police chief, Gerardo Garay, was arrested for protecting the Beltrán Leyva brothers, and his 'drug czar', Noe Ramírez, for taking a $450,000 bribe from the Sinaloa cartel. Both are awaiting trial, both have denied wrong-doing. Operation Clean House had failed, however, to net another of Mexico's apparently trustworthy drug czars, José Luis Santiago Vasconsuelos, who was warmly embraced by Washington, and the man who extradited Osiel Cárdenas. Vasconsuelos was killed in a mysterious plane crash over Mexico City in November 2008 and six months later, in May 2009, a DEA report named him as being on the payroll of the Beltrán Leyva cartel.[23]

The thrust of the offensive, says De Sota, is to challenge the cartels militarily while 'aggressively' reforming the legal system and institutions, starting with the federal structure. The task, she says, 'begins with the military, but by the end of the presidential term, we aim to have established an honest and well-structured federal police. We start with the military because we cannot count on the municipal and state police. In a number of places, the traffickers control the police'. So that is official, at least. As is this: 'The military is going to stay in there for as long as it takes.' As long as what takes? 'So long as it takes for the state to fulfil its basic obligations: public security and the collection of taxes, which are currently threatened by and even subverted and imitated by levies imposed by the cartels.' Strangely, and with estimable honesty, De Sota adds: 'The president is clear: the fight is not against drugs, it is against the violence and the ability of criminal organisations to subvert the state. The president knows that drugs will not disappear.'

That is the map at the outset, the template of the cartel war, to bear in mind as one explores the border, though there is no predicting how the lines on the map will blur or demarcate the narcotopology. However, a journey along the map as it stands entails, loosely, three stages: first, the road from Tijuana to Ciudad Juárez, across terrain of warfare between the Sinaloa, Tijuana and Beltrán Leyva cartels. Then a meltdown in Juárez, as the cartel pyramids collapse into a murderous anarchy. Finally, from Ciudad Acuña and Nuevo Laredo eastwards, the road leads into a land where there was, between 2005 and 2010, relatively less fighting, but which is the most terrifying stretch along the border. Until early 2010, this was terrain subject to an iron reign consolidated by the Zetas and Gulf cartel. Only now they are no longer synonymous with one another, the 'classical' and military wings at internecine war with each other.

With the election of Barack Obama, the map has also changed at the level of US government. After decades of the United States seeing the narco-trafficking problem as essentially an all-Mexican one, there is now a sense of officially acknowledged 'co-responsibility' over crucial areas of policy. During visits to Mexico City by Secretary of State Hillary Clinton and the president himself, the matter of arms trafficking from the USA to Mexico, previously taboo, has been addressed. There has been acknowledgement of the fundamental fact that the root cause of the crisis is addiction to drugs in American society. In March 2009, President Obama announced a Janus-faced package with two themes: man the border defences, while also attacking the root causes of addiction. He increased the allocations of all federal agencies along the border, with $700 million that year towards personnel and technology, and more to come. President Obama said he would upgrade intelligence-gathering, and improve cross-border interdiction, but also that he would 'redouble' efforts to diminish demand for drugs in the US and staunch the flow of weapons from the US to Mexico. 'It's really a two-way situation here,' said the president, speaking a language never before heard from the White House. 'The drugs are coming north, we're sending funds and guns south.'[24]

The reality on the ground is mercurial and in places much worse than the map suggests, because if the map shows a war caused by fighting between cartels for smuggling routes and a consequent government crackdown, it does not show another, monstrous reason for the war: that the Mexican side of the borderline has become a place accursed by addiction to hard drugs. This seems of little conse-quence to the United States, and is virtually taboo in Mexico, but is cause of most of the killing and most wretched of circumstances in the drug war. All warfare creates resultant 'sideshow' horrors. The consequential sideshow of America's addiction to hard drugs supplied from Mexico, and both countries' war against the traffic, are two-fold: first, the ravages of hard drugs along the border, and subse-quently, the feral war for control of this domestic 'Plaza', which is just as savage as that for narcotic exports, if not more so. Fundamental to Mexican government strategy and to the thinking of the DEA is that to fragment the cartels is to weaken them, thereby damaging drug traffic and reducing violence. 'We want it to be disorganised,' says Eileen Zeidler, spokeswoman for the DEA in San Diego, of the cartels' fragmentation since President Calderón's offensive. 'If they're not organised, they don't function. We want it to fall apart.'[25] Ms Zeidler's boss, the DEA's chief of intelligence, Anthony Placido, went so far as to call the violence a 'sign of success', and to speak of 'wounded, vulnerable' cartels.[26] But fragmentation does not mean a weakening of narco traffic, it simply nuances the market: the domestic Plaza is fought over by the plethora of gangs that serve the big cartels when drugs cross the frontier, but fight one another when dealing on home turf, bringing death and misery to the *colonias*. Like any other corporation, the cartels nowadays 'outsource' – as corporate jargon has it – much of their business to subcontractors such as street gangs or corrupt police forces who tender for a slice of the profits. Narco outsourcing even has a name: *el derecho de piso* – the right of tender, of passage.

Our journey begins where the desert sun sets into the Pacific at Amexica's western edge, the frontier between Tijuana and San Diego. The latter is not really a border town – it is too big, too Californian. But one can already feel the frontier at the 12th Street and Imperial transit centre, which during the early morning stages a two-way rush hour through the mumbling homeless pushing their belongings in supermarket carts: of people arriving for work from Tijuana, and people leaving for work in Tijuana.

The blue line trundles towards the railway yards and dockland base of the US Pacific Fleet, frigates and masts thick with radar, and painted murals illustrate the 'History of Our Community' at Barrio Logan (a Hispanic settlement named after an Irish pioneer), featuring a Mesoamerican Indian blowing into a conch shell, fishermen hauling their catch and dolphins at the Sea World theme park. Through factories and the lights and smoke of dawn, Rosebud Law Enforcement services and Tactical Assault Gear is right next door to Rosa's Mexican Diner, just as it would be anywhere else in America. But anywhere else is not the suburb of Chula Vista, two miles north of Tijuana, nor San Ysidro, end of the line – and of the United States. Thirty minutes south of downtown San Diego, on the platform teeming by 7.30 in the morning, the two-way rush hour is in full swing, as is a McDonald's, which is a border hub of its own: customs agents, girls laden with huge packs of diapers, Mexican businessmen who have fled to Chula Vista but return each day to work in Tijuana and Mexican ladies on their way to clean American toilets are all eating breakfast . . . and there it is: the concrete barrier, the footbridge, and beyond it, Mexico. *Aqui Empieza la Patria* – Here Begins the Homeland – is Tijuana's municipal motto, and a Mexican flag, defiantly and desperately giant, with its eagle clutching a snake on a cactus, which legend has it predicted the birth of the nation, flies in America's face, at the border.

CHAPTER TWO

Aqui Empieza la Patria –
Here Begins the Homeland

Tijuana's image north of the border was always that of a festive party town. And for the Americans who poured into 'TJ' by the thousand every day, and by the tens of thousands every weekend, it was. 'You are in the Most Visited City in the World' claims the sign above Avenida Revolucion, and whether statistically true or not, people thronged here to savour Mexican exotica, buy souvenirs, drink Margarita by the jug (at an age younger than the USA permits), get teeth fixed cheaply, invest in a spare pair of spectacles and, latterly, buy Viagra or Prozac and other medications for a fraction of the price back home. Tijuana grew during the nineteenth century, after the loss of 'Alta California' to the USA in 1848. The downtown area acquired its reputation for selling an ersatz 'Mexico' to North Americans in 1915, when Tijuana decided to echo that year's great Panama–California Exposition in San Diego with a fair of its own called the *Feria Tipica Mexicana*, to lure visitors across the border. Since which the city has specialised in sombrero hats, reproduction Aztec bric-a-brac, ponchos and other trinkets that actually have nothing to do with the country's sixth largest city of 1.5 million people. Every Mexican border city and town divides itself between indigenous northern '*Norteños*', '*Sureños*' from the south and '*Chilangos*' from the capital. There is even a constituency which calls itself '*Fronterizos*', from the border itself – and these are crucial points of identity.' Over half of the population of Tijuana does come from 'traditional' southern Mexico, not to live according to some folklore kitsch, but to work in sweatshop *maquiladora* factories or eek out some other living in desperately poor *colonias* on the city's outskirts. For the southerners, or those from El Salvador, Honduras and Guatemala, Tijuana can be harsh, unwelcoming, dangerous and violent. Attacks on Mixtecs, Mayas or Zapotecs are routine. Until recently, when vast estates of uniform housing were built around the city, whole communities from South and Central America lived on the *dompes*, or landfills, of domestic and industrial rubbish.[2]

Tijuana's reputation for naughtiness grew during Prohibition, soon after the *Feria*, when the city became a magnet for those seeking not only off-the-peg Mexico but also alcohol, gambling and the go-go good-time vices that accompanied them. The existence of the biggest naval base on the Pacific edge at San Diego guaranteed steady off-duty customers in addition to civilian tourists. But the narco war has changed all this, so that now, says Enrico Rodriguez in his empty shop full of unbrowsed jewellery, trinkets and Western wear, 'I cross myself every time I make a sale, and have not crossed myself for two days.' No one wants a polaroid picture taken of themselves wearing a sombrero next to an old donkey painted black and white like a zebra, and the strippers pole-dance pretty much to one another. Apart, perhaps, from the odd scurvy vagabond from California, too stoned to care about any potential danger, and, of course, the local backsliders, equipped with a limited supply of greenbacks. The famous district around the cross streets of Avenida Revolucion and Constitucion is now more about sleaze than aphrodisia. On its uppers, Mermaid's Club and Hotel, with its Western saloon-style swing doors, is forced to offer 'Two Massages for the Price of One'. The Adelita Bar (est. 1962), with the Hotel Coahuila situated conveniently next door, has seen better days, now hoping to attract guests with neon signs of girls wearing *bandolero* bullet belts and brandishing Kalashnikov machine guns. A passing *gringo*, I am ushered inside with desperate insistence and quickly introduced by a heavily tattooed doorman to comely Gabriela in a glittering, fluorescent turquoise bikini and train of plastic feathers like a peacock's. She asks if I would like to buy her a drink while the doorman, whose height reaches as far as Gabriela's articulate bust, runs down a list of offers – including stiff alcohol, sex and a card game – very easily refused. The cavernous depths are not quite empty: a group of Mexican men share a bottle of tequila while their female company sip sodas and a lone, palid American with a goatee and skin that has not seen daylight for a good while watches the writhing pole-dancer. But that's about it for the night, concedes the doorman. The Narco Juniors, as they became known, once cocks-of-the-walk, have disappeared too. Since war broke out, the modern *narcotraficante*, out of prudence and self-preservation keeps a low profile, partying at the villa and entertaining ladies through home delivery rather than brazenly in public – as they did not long ago.

How well she remembers those days. How could she ever forget – when the Narco Juniors were in their prime: flashing their wealth around Tijuana, dripping gold with a scantily dressed beauty hanging from each arm? Cruising in their SUVs, taking over nightclubs in which they would only drink champagne. Cristina Palacios Hodoyán, lighting ultra-thin cigarettes with a gold lighter held in her ultra-thin fingers, remembers them with a sorrow in her eyes that even her polished demeanour cannot hide. How could she forget the Juniors, when two of her three sons were among them? The eldest, Alejandro, was kidnapped twice – once in 1996, and again the following year, since when he has never been seen again. The youngest, Alfredo, became known as '*El Lobo*', the Wolf, and is serving 176 years in a Mexican jail, convicted of multiple murder and criminal association. 'I had wanted them to become lawyers, or go into their father's business as civil engineers,' their mother reflects. After finishing her cigarette, she picks at a smoked salmon sandwich, at a table in the Merlot Restaurant, near Tijuana Country Club, where the better class of people go. Mrs Palacios turns sixty-nine the day after we have dinner, and says she plans a quiet meal with close friends, nothing extravagant.

Her boys had had the city at their feet. As heirs to the Palacios Hodoyán family, they enjoyed automatic membership of and access to the 'Club Campestre' and so-called '*Instituo Set*', alumnae of the elite Tijuana Institute. There was an auspicious future in their father Ramírez's legitimate businesses if they wanted it. Alfredo was confirmed into the Church by the then Bishop of Tijuana, a family friend who would become Cardinal Posada Ocampo, assassinated by the very cartel Alejandro and Alfredo later joined. 'Ocampo was very dear to us,' recalls Cristina, 'known and loved by Tijuana'. Born in the USA, the boys could cross the border any time, and set up in business there if they preferred, with their father's rolodex of clients at their disposal. And the Hodoyán brothers were heading that way, until Ramón Arellano Félix arrived in town from Sinaloa.

'I remember Ramón,' says Cristina with a shudder. 'He always wore a mink coat, even on a hot day, and shorts – with a big golden cross against his bare chest. There was a place by a tree where children had always played with tricycles and bicycles, and later they might meet up there in the evening, chatting up the girls or boys. Alex was in college studying law, aged about twenty-five, Alfredo was eighteen or nineteen. And Ramón Arellano Félix and the boys from Sinaloa used to come up to the tree, presenting themselves as interesting and exciting, flashing their money, and the girls wanted to be seen with them.'[3]

'So that the people who would start bringing drugs into my house – only I didn't know that at the time – were children I had known since kindergarden,' says Cristina Palacios. 'Ramón would take them to the clubs. He would walk in and commandeer a table, even if it was taken, just send the people away. He would buy champagne for his company all night; but if you talked to anyone else, you were considered a traitor. Any time, they could take someone out and kill them, and they did. Once you were in, you were in, and there was no way out. My sons had become part of it all, they were among people who would laugh while cutting someone's fingers off, or chop someone into pieces for fun. All this I learned later, when Alex had been captured and Alfredo was in prison.'

On 11 September 1996, 'Alejandro disappeared in Guadalajara. And from September to February he was in custody, held by General Jesús Gutiérrez Rebollo of the Mexican army.' During this time, in December 1996, General Gutiérrez Rebollo was appointed to the top post as Mexico's 'drug czar', leading the government's effort against the cartels, not least because of his success in procuring Alejandro Hodoyán. Alejandro was 'singing', telling the general all he knew about his AFO cartel.

It emerged when Alejandro talked to his family, says Cristina, that the confessions were ill-gotten, and that the general had played a vile game with his quarry. 'The soldiers,' recalls Mrs Palacios, 'used electric shocks on his eyes and feet, and burned him with cigarettes and lighters to get him to talk. Gutiérrez Rebollo,' she goes on, 'had arrived later, after others had tortured him, so that Alex felt beholden to him and would tell him everything.' In late November, once he had softened his prisoner, Rebollo called in prosecutors from Mexico City, who recorded a videotaped confession in which Alejandro, between gulps of water, recalls how his partners in the cartel would 'laugh after a murder, and go off and have a lobster dinner.' Killing, he told his captors, 'is a party for them, it's a kick'. Alejandro told the prosecutors that he had started running errands for the cartel, progressed to running drugs across the border and then joined a unit of *sicarios*. After they had the information they needed, the Mexican Public Defence Department handed Alejandro over to the Americans, who were preparing an indictment against the AFO. 'We also now know,' Mrs Palacios adds with a shiver, 'that the Americans were aware this was how he was forced to talk.'[4]

'On February 10 1997,' she continues, 'Alejandro was flown to San Diego, he told me, and put in custody by the FBI and DEA. At that point, both my sons were in San Diego, in different prisons, because Alfredo had been arrested too. But Alejandro was not arrested, it was worse than that: he was to become a protected witness. "I know a lot of things," he told me, "and I need protection." But he had no protection: what they did not tell Alex was that everything he had said in Mexico City had been leaked by the Ministry of Public Security to the Tijuana cartel, and that General Gutiérrez Rebollo was working all along for the Juárez cartel. Only two months after taking office in his new job at the apex of Mexico's supposed anti-cartel offensive, Gen. Gutiérrez Rebollo was convicted of collaboration with Amado Carrillo Fuentes – the general even lived in a villa owned by the 'Lord of the Skies'.

After ten days in DEA custody in San Diego, 'Alejandro was asked to testify against his brother,' says Cristina. Alfredo Hodoyán, her younger son, had been charged with murder and was about to be extradited for trial in Mexico. He was in an impossible position between the rock of family loyalty and the hard place of his own survival. Mrs Palacios says: 'Alejandro ran back to Tijuana. By then, he was a condemned man: by the AFO for having squealed to Gutiérrez Rebollo, and by the Juárez cartel for belonging to a rival.' Alejandro hid at home. Two weeks later, Cristina was driving her son in the family's SUV: 'We were in a parking lot, when a truck blocked our way. Men surrounded us, with guns, and told us to get out of the car. I said no. They didn't have masks or anything. Then they pulled Alex out and drove away. I never saw him again.' She lights another ultra-thin cigarette, draws in the smoke with a deep breath and says, 'It all made sense. They're all working for one cartel or another. When I went through a police album of intelligence officers, I found the face of the man I saw in the van, who kidnapped my Alejandro. But I still have Alfredo. He is in jail in Matamoros, and we are trying to get the sentence reduced.' Alfredo Hodoyán had been extradited to Mexico shortly after his brother's disappearance, held in Mexico City and convicted on several counts of murder.

All this is in the past, she insists. Cristina has updated her expectations of herself, working with parents or families of people kidnapped and probably killed by narco traffickers — trying to pressurise the authorities into tracking their lost loved ones, and doing something that only very rarely happens: go after the kidnappers and killers. 'The problem is, though,' Cristina continues in a matter-of-fact way, 'most of these people, once kidnapped, were dissolved in acid.' We are joined by Fernando Ocegueda Flores, whose son, also called Fernando, was taken from the family home, he says, on 10 February 2007. 'The police were so uncooperative, even obstructive, that at first I thought they themselves had taken my son,' he says. 'Then the whisper from neighbours told me that it had been the Arellano Félix Organisation. From the authorities, all this time, I have had nothing, zero, no investigation, not even a reply. I went crazy, and decided to conduct my own investigation. For two years, I searched — I went to everyone I knew in the cartel and asked them point blank to tell me. I went to their houses, I knocked on their doors in rage'. 'We were worried,' says Cristina, 'that he would not survive this line of investigation.' 'Someone did this, and I had to find out who,' retorts Fernando. Finally, he says, 'I went to a very dangerous place, and they put me in a car and I talked to this man. My request had gone high up the chain, and they told me my son had been killed and the body dissolved in acid.'

On 24 January 2009, Federal police raided a *narcotraficantes*' party at an upscale seaside resort on the coastal highway from Tijuana to Ensenada, and arrested one Santiago Meza López, universally known and wanted in Tijuana as '*El Pozolero*', the stew-maker. *Pozole* is a

popular ragout made of pork, vegetables and seasonings, but this is
not what Meza was brewing. He confessed to having disposed of
some 300 corpses by dissolving them in vats of lye or hydrochloric
acid, initially at the service of the AFO but defecting to the Sinaloa
cartel, for which he was paid $600 a week.[5] Meza's confession was
a straightforward one: he would fill a vat with water and two bags
of lye, don a pair of protective gloves and goggles, boil the pinkish
brew and dispose of the bodies delivered at his lair by truck, one
by one.

Accordingly, Fernando Ocegueda came to know that the answer
to his and hundreds of other distraught families' questions lay along
the road south-eastwards from Tijuana to the satellite *colonia* of
Florido, a place of shrivelled orchards, ramshackle houses, home to
the Silza propane gas terminal. Up a dirt track into the desert lies
the hamlet of Ojo de Agua, the Eye of Water, above which are two
small graveyards nestled into the hillside. The *Pozolero*'s lair is
surrounded by a blue tarpaulin and guarded by an encampment of
bored *federales*. It is a square of ground, about 30 by 30 yards,
enclosed by walls of grey breeze-blocks, open to the sky, with a little
hut in the corner. For a tip of 400 pesos ($32), the *federales* open
the padlock and slide the heavy white gate, for a guided tour. Across
the compound, earth is piled in mounds, and blue plastic barrels are
scattered across the dirt. Two steel containers stand beside a cistern
at the top of the slight incline on which the lair is built. 'This is
where he put them into the acid,' says the federal police captain, in
a plain-speaking, unadorned way, but with something between a
grimace and a smile.

The unofficial tour is economically informative: 'They would have
been brought by truck, and unloaded over here,' says the captain,
striding around, 'then taken here, probably on wheelbarrows, put into
the vats, and there you go, no more bodies!' But a potent smell rises
through the afternoon heat: the inimitable, sickly sweet, putrid smell
of death and decomposition, of human remains. 'It's always stronger
when it gets hot, around this time of day,' observes the captain, as
though by way of apology. So the *Pozolero* was not as thorough in
executing his task as the public were led to believe – nor, clearly,
were the police investigators whose duty it is, in theory, to collect
any remaining DNA on the site, seal it, endeavour to identify the

dead and seek out their relatives. In fact, here we are, stomping around a crime scene that is abandoned but littered with evidence. 'We haven't noticed any sign of the detectives for three months – no one, nothing, we're just told to stay here and . . . well, watch for anyone who arrives,' complains the bored captain. This was August 2009, seven months after the arrest and confession. The captain points into the cistern, from which an especially pungent stench ascends into the afternoon. 'There's still plenty down there,' he informs, kindly but unnecessarily. And not only 'down there' – we take a look inside one of the blue plastic barrels, and there is a lower gum, with teeth still attached, which somehow escaped dissolution. At the bottom of one of the steel tanks, there is raw flesh, and jelly-like human tissue.

There are also quite a few remnants from the recreational life led by the stew-maker and whatever apprentices he needed to prac-tise his craft: a barbecue, several dozen empty Tecate beer cans strewn here and there, bits of seafood in the dust and a thriving marijuana plant. The arrest was made in January and in the little hut in the corner of the settlement, the *Pozolero*'s Christmas tree remains, complete with decorations made of festive red velvet ribbon and sparkly tinsel.

During the recent war, the killing has become qualitatively, as well as quantitatively, more grotesque – savage mutilations, decapitations, tortures to a point of perverse cruelty. The carnage has come to require a deviant sense of innovation, a twisted creativity: 'bone-tickling' involves scraping the bone with an ice-pick sunk through the flesh. Doctors are employed to ensure that those being ques-tioned or tortured do not lose consciousness. Methods of execution are almost inventive in their calculated atrocity: one of the Arellano brothers' victims was left tied to a chair and his hands chopped off, so that he bled slowly to death, alone. The killing has been extended to include families and children among the victims. This is not entirely new: at one point during the 1980s, Félix Gallardo needed to deal with an encroachment into his Guadalajara business by an interloper called Hector Palma. Gallardo tasked one of his operatives to seduce Palma's wife and run off with the lady and her children – which he did. One day, the cuckolded Palma received a package by courier. It contained his wife's severed head. He learned later that Gallardo's man, Clavel Moreno, had proceeded to push his children to their deaths off a bridge. Palma built a special little chapel in their memory.

The children of some lesser narcos attend Valentina Farias Gómez primary school in Tijuana. The school is kept beautifully clean and the children, wearing red uniforms, chirp around the playground before settling in for lessons with orderly discipline. One morning in March 2008, however, the children arrived to find a message for them to bear in mind as they prepared their futures in the community: twelve festering corpses piled across the road from the school gates, naked, tortured and with tongues cut – people who talked too much. It was a lesson to the pupils not to do the same, says the principal, Miguel Ángel González Tovar, simultaneously courteous and exhausted as he understates what he tries to do in running a school where 'the children of narcos, children of police officers and children of ordinary workers attend. The situation is very delicate. There are evil people in our area, but they still send their children to school.

'It was terrifying,' he says of that morning in March. 'The children were terrified, the staff were terrified and I had to pretend not to be terrified, but everyone knew what was happening. It was a warning, and it means what it means. We try to teach here, to teach against that message, like an island of education and peace and security for the children, but we are fighting a form of barbarism here, and cannot be isolated from what is going on outside. That is not easy, however. They gave me a CCTV video camera, but it doesn't work. They gave me an alarm button, but that's broken. It's terribly sad, a situation we despise, are scared of but fight against.'

Dr Hiram Muñoz, a forensic pathologist assigned to the Baja California state prosecutor's department in Tijuana, talks about how 'each different mutilation leaves a clear message. They have become a kind of folk tradition. If the tongue is cut out, it means they talked too much – a snitch, or *chupro*. A man who squealed on the clan has his finger cut off and maybe put in his mouth.' This is logical, a traitor is known as a '*dedo*' – a finger. Sometimes fingers are stuck up the rectum. 'If you are castrated,' continues Dr Muñoz, 'you may have slept with or looked at the woman of another man in the business. Severed arms could mean that you stole from your consignment, severed legs that you tried to walk away from the cartel. Decapitation is another thing altogether: it is simply a statement of power, a warning to all, like public executions of old. The difference is that in normal times, the dead were "disappeared" or dumped in the desert. Now, they are executed and displayed for all to see, so that it becomes a war against the people.'

At another school, in the deserted resort of Rosarito Beach down the coast from Tijuana, an official visit is being put together on the tarmac basketball pitch. Victor Hugo, a fifteen-year-old pupil at the Abraham Lincoln Secondary School No. 32, was gunned down in a narco shoot-out earlier this year, for reasons that are still unclear. And today, the recently appointed state prosecutor of Baja California, Rommel Moreno Manjarrez, has chosen the school to make a speech reassuring teenagers that there is a force out there trying to hold the *traficantes* to account. 'The police are now with us, and there is new hope against violence,' says the prosecutor. And the pupils applaud; '*Viva México!*' shouts one.

Prosecutor Moreno stepped into a difficult job when he became state attorney general in 2007. His predecessor, Antonio Martínez Luna, stepped down after a video released in May that year by a known drug dealer accused Martinez of protecting the Sinaloa cartel; he even had a nickname: '*El Blindado*' – the bullet-proof. The trafficker in the video was found dead soon after it was released so the veracity cannot be tested. Mr Martinez, now reported to be living in the United States, has denied all connections with the Sinaloa cartel, but he stepped down and Moreno was appointed nonetheless to clean up the image of a pivotal office during a drug war.

It had seemed worth giving Moreno the benefit of the doubt. When we first met in 2008, he seemed immediately engaging, not least because he had studied law at Sapienza University in Rome, and taken many trips to Sicily to learn from his mentor, the great anti-Mafia judge Giovanni Falcone. He has an affable if somewhat vague manner, and we enjoyed sharing recollections of the inimitable Falcone, and speaking Italian in Tijuana. He remembered, too, the campaign by another mutual acquaintance, brave Leoluca Orlando, who mobilised a mass popular movement against Cosa Nostra called '*La Rete*', the network. 'This is what I want to see here in Mexico,' said Moreno. 'A culture in the magistrature similar to that in Italy, committed to going after the Mafia, supported by movements in the civil society like that organised by Orlando.' It all sounded good, and I was hoping to talk on, towards an elusive point in the discourse, the bit about efficacy, arrests and convictions. But Moreno did not make himself available for a follow-up conversation for weeks afterwards.

Most mornings, I hovered about like a courtier at various official engagements that featured Moreno and a rolling dramatis personae, like an acting troupe in repertoire, also featuring City Mayor Jorge Ramos and José Osuna Millán, Governor of Baja California. The format was always the same: the panel sat in the shade of a large open-sided marquee and applauded one another's speeches about combating the cartels, after which its members were served cool drinks by waitresses in high heels and mini-skirts. On one occasion, launching a fleet of high-tech vehicles for use by the state police, that morning's edition of the Tijuana newspaper *El Méxicano* carried a front-page story about the murder of lovely Adriana Alejandra Ruíz Muñiz, a model and cheerleader for the local soccer team, *Xoloitzcuintles de Caliente*.[6] The horrific scene of her death had been found filmed on the mobile phone of one José Carlos Meza, known also as '*El Charlie*' in narco circles, who had been detained and put under investigation by Moreno's department. Meza protested his innocence, claiming that Adriana Alejandra was an informant for the police, furnishing the authorities with information on Guzmán's man in Tijuana, Eduardo García Simental, *El Teo*. Meza implied that Adriana Alejandra had been *El Teo*'s lover, and provided what he claimed to be the name of the man who duly kidnapped and killed her. Adriana Alejandra had her fingernails pulled out and the bones in her fingers broken during the interrogation, after which she was decapitated.

While the paper told the story and Rommel Moreno made speeches, Dr Muñoz, in the forensic autopsy department of Moreno's prosecution service, is inspecting Adriana Alejandra's corpse on his slab. He is anxious to oblige my request to join him while he conducts his analysis of the corpse, in order to develop and illustrate his decoding of mutilations with a visual aid. But Prosecutor Moreno's assistant says this is impossible, beyond the prosecutor's authority, a matter for the courts. Dr Muñoz is annoyed, for he is considering this case carefully, weighing up the various hypotheses: 'that it could be the big narcos, as they say, or that this is a crime specifically against a woman, a so-called "crime of passion" by a common criminal, for what passion is more wrathful and violent than that of a man towards a woman he is obsessed with and cannot have? And this is, actually, my inclination in this case. I've looked very carefully at how the fingers have been broken, and it has not been done very well – you could almost call it careless, or reckless, and when the narcos are torturing an informant, the tracks they leave are never careless. They would have sliced the fingers off at the joints, not merely crushed them, maybe so as to send them to someone. But my job is not to pass judgement of this kind, I'm not a police officer and the police do not ask me who I think did it, or why. My job is to make a report, and the rest is up to the prosecutors and investigators, and – how can I say this? – that's where the farce begins. The authorities don't look at any of this socially or forensically.' Dr Muñoz produces a bullet from a plastic bag and brandishes it between his thumb and forefinger. 'If I find bullets from the same weapon in different bodies that are brought to me, and put this in my report, but no one takes any notice. The narcos give us signs, they leave unique marks, like fingerprints, only the authorities do not heed them. They have the files, they have the register of weapons, but they will not make an inventory, bullet by bullet.'

Dr Muñoz gets out a pen and draws four boxes, labelled: 'Me', 'Prosecutor's Office', 'Judge' and 'Jail'. 'For every hundred bodies sent to me, twenty go to the prosecutor's office, ten go before the judge and one ends up in jail – no, fewer; in less than one per cent of cases do they ever get the real killer. And that one per cent is probably not a criminal boss, it'll be the little guy. Meanwhile, they convict people for things they couldn't possibly have done.' There are not many people in Mexico, or anywhere, brave enough to speak so freely and boldly from inside the system about their own employer, but there is no stopping Dr Muñoz. 'There is a woman called Jacinta, from the south, a Mixtec lady who is supposed to have kidnapped six armed federal agents all by herself. The strategy of the authorities is show business. They need to make a spectacle out of these cases – you can see, whenever they do catch a narco, they parade them, with all the drugs and guns. It is pure theatre, to impress the president like I as a child tried to impress my father. To the press, they feed this phrase '*presunto responsabile*' – presumed responsible – what on earth does that mean? Is that conviction by a court? It's a lot of rubbish. And all the while, I have these victims of torture and mutilation brought before me, knowing that they will never catch the people who did this. But I love my profession, I love my job. It combines medicine and law in practice: the corpse is my patient, and my job is to interrogate the corpse, to ask it questions. Because the dead cannot speak, I have to find ways of getting them to tell me what happened.'

Tijuana is a strong city, and, after all, the local Mexicans are still here even if the tourists are not. A 'Fab Four' Beatles tribute is sold out. Taking your lady for a skinny-vanilla-frappuccino at a branch of the D'Volada chain – a Mexican Starbucks – is a cool date, especially if it has wi-fi so that no one need actually talk. 'Sanborn's' is a landmark institution which characterises any Mexican city, combining a restaurant and rendezvous with a small department store, and Tijuana's is no exception, brimful every Sunday lunchtime, its waitresses in their hallmark 'traditional' costumes with wings on their shoulders. The *Cinepolis* is packed for the latest movie glorifying violence – fantasy violence – made up the coast in Hollywood.

After reading all that Hemingway and D. H. Lawrence, I decided I really must sample a *corrida* at the bullring near the border fence by the sea, only to be reminded how little I admired either writer, failing utterly to feel any macho-libido rush as yet another knackered bull is slashed according to plan and his carcass hauled off with ropes. But couples cheer, the band plays and ladies wave handkerchiefs at the matinée idol matador clad in the regalia of Old Spain.

Far more authentic is the *Sótano Suizo* pub, which was heaving on the Sunday that Eduardo Félix Arellano was being flown to the capital, but not because of him. There was another, different arrival in Mexico City that day: by the Chivas soccer team from Guadalajara, for the match Mexicans call *El Clasico*, against Club America. On screen in Tijuana, both teams unleash attack after attack in a tremendous game-to-the-death, Chivas winning 2–1. A joyful Guadalajara fan in the bar, Adán, likens snatching victory in the capital and seat of power to 'robbing your boss's house, and fucking his wife on the way out'. But the temperature of *El Clásico* was nothing compared to that eight months later for Mexico's make-or-break World Cup qualifying match against none other than its neighbour, the USA: the transborder Amexica derby. Quite apart from its complex piquancy on the border, there is history to this fixture. Mexicans find it hard to admit that Americans play very good football nowadays, and it is a deeply-held belief that while the *gringo* subjugates Mexico, there is one thing that the boys in green do better than their northern neighbours: play soccer. Or so they thought, until a terrible night during the 2002 World Cup in Japan, when the USA dismissed Mexico 2–0 in a knock-out round. The wound cut deep, and right to the top. Before the game, then President Vicente Fox proposed to George W. Bush that the two might watch the game together at a venue on the border, as a gesture of friendship between the two nations. But the dismissive answer came back from an aide: since the game was being played in Asia, the president would be asleep at that time of night. America slept through its historic victory while Mexico was wide-eyed with anguish.

Now, with Mexico trailing the US in the 2010 World Cup qualifying table, defeat today in Mexico City would entail a serious risk of shameful elimination from the finals in South Africa while the *gringo* sailed through. The Americans score first: Mexico 0, USA 1, in Mexico City. Adán from last time cracks the inevitable sullen joke about the boss robbing YOUR house this time, and fucking YOUR wife. But then Israel Castro equalises with a glorious shot from 27 yards and with minutes to go, Miguel Sabah controls a perfect cross to score the winner for Mexico. Then one of those things happens, as they do, by word of mouth from bar to bar, *colonia* to *colonia*: head for the border. Which they do, by the thousand, on foot and in hooting, flag-waving motorcades. They paint their faces, stick fingers through the fencing, and sing their songs. Finally, the whooping crowd blocks the frontier traffic crossing and six are arrested. 'Look,' says my friend Delgado, trying to explain, 'we clean their toilets, we pick their fruit and water their lawns. But we can beat them in football.'

The gaiety in Tijuana even has a certain surreality: at the height of the killing in winter 2008, couples and excited parties of schoolchildren in pressed uniforms lined up to see a museum exhibition

of mummies with preserved skin like parchment that stare haunt-
ingly across the centuries from pre-Aztec Guanajato. The crowds
make no connection between these cadavers and other events in
town, somehow affirming that Mexican cult of death.

The Sunday crowds fill Tijuana Cathedral, outside which market
stalls sell unmistakably Mexican devotional accoutrements: it may
trouble the Vatican, but it is of deep meaning to many devout
Mexicans that the Virgin of Guadalupe, national symbol and
'Empress of the Americas', can also represent Coatlicue, mother of
the Aztec primary god. Such dichotomy – ubiquitous in the 'folk
Catholicism' practised in Mexico – is incomprehensible to dogmatic
Christians, just as the ambivalence of the Mexica gods themselves
were incomprehensible to the conquistadores, whose religion the
Mexica incorporated into their own. During the Credo, in which the
congregation proclaims its faith in 'One God', a text message arrives
to say that Eduardo Félix Arellano was arrested during that shoot-
out at the villa. After administering the Host, Archbishop Rafael
Romo gives an interview, despite having only just been briefed on
the arrest himself by a whispering aide, on his way to the sanctuary.
'It is a time of challenge for us, as Christians and as citizens whose
quality of life and lives themselves are in real and immediate danger,'
he says. 'The violence is now strategic, against all society, and this
is the difference. Not to mention the problems that the drugs cause
in our diocese. What we can do is offer resistance, and an affirma-
tion of hope.' Most of the narco aristocracy, and more than a few
of the *sicarios*, though, are devout Catholics, or at least they go
through the motions of devotion – baptism, church marriage, cash
donations and confession. There is even an unofficial narco 'saint'.
Santo Jesús Malverde, a bandit with a Robin Hood legacy to whose
shrine in Sinaloa devout traffickers pay homage with devotional
pledges – *mandas* – in return for the Holy outlaw's blessing. During
the 1980s, the narcos actively aligned themselves with the Church's
conservative wing against priests advocating Liberation Theology.

Archbishop Romo is direct for a man of his austere authority.
'They expect to come to us and talk about what they do. Our word
to them is clear: we will talk about these things, these dangers. If
they think they are religious, we will debate them, urge them to

leave behind this evil and these activities against God. They are like those "Ultra" football fans that come to the stadium – they support your team but the club doesn't want them there to behave like that, but it is still your team and you are not supposed to turn them away. Moreover, it is not easy in the barrios for priests dealing with them face to face.'

This was October 2008. Perhaps the bishop would have replied more severely had we spoken some months later – after a terrible narco execution in July of 2009. Father Habacuc Hernández and two seminarians training for the priesthood were ordered out of their pick-up truck on the road into Ciudad Altamirano, 180 miles south of Mexico City and repeatedly shot. Hernández had travelled by horseback and truck for hundreds of miles across mountainous terrain to serve his scattered community. He was one of ten children from a poor family who had worked for a while, illegally, in Texas. Villagers believed he must have fallen foul of instructions by the narcos not to meddle in their affairs.[7]

On the Day of the Dead, 1 November 2008, the daily *El Sol de Tijuana* carried a front page which looked like a heavy-metal album cover, with a hooded skeleton brandishing a scythe and a headline quoting a carefully timed pronouncement by the bishop: R O M O : LA SANTA MUERTE NO EXISTE – Holy Death does not exist. The archbishop was taking a public swipe in a popular paper at the cult in which the borderline is steeped, on both sides. *La Santísima Muerte* – Most Holy Death – adorns car windshields, T-shirts, mobile phone holders and hangs as a silver pendant on chests all along the borderline. To the uninitiated, they look like trinkets from a Goth shop at Camden Market in London or the Lower East Side of New York, but they are not. Most cogently, wayside shrines to *La Santísima Muerte*, also called *La Señora de las Sombres* – Lady of the Shadows – have been erected on the outskirts of most cities skirting the border on the Mexican side. In these shrines, built as little temples, she stands, the hooded skeleton holding the orb of the world in one hand and her scythe in the other. She usually wears a crown or mitre, and her cloak is often white, but sometimes painted in the colours of the rainbow. In some shrines, the skeleton is a real one, draped in fabrics. And around her, offerings are made: cigarettes, fruit, photographs of the deceased.

Candles are lit to her, which bear her image on glass around the wax. Messages and petitions are written, asking for protection. Sometimes she is adorned with flowers.

This cult has its origins in the syncretism between Catholicism and pre-Columbian faiths and the cult of death, and has been dated to the eighteenth century. In the 1960s, the first public sanctuary to *Santísima Muerte* was built in the poor Tepito neighbourhood of Mexico City. In 2005, the cult was removed from the Mexican government's list of religious rites licensed to practise, and only since then has it captured the imagination of the criminal young, winning a rapidly expanding number of devotees among narco traffickers and the street gangs affiliated with them. *Santísima Muerte* has become an icon to which drug dealers and killers plead for protection against their own death, a talisman and mass cult accompanying the war. Though *Santísima Muerte* is regarded outside the country as yet another exotic piece of Mexican mumbo-jumbo, the cult can make one's flesh crawl as one watches others pull over their cars and whisper their devotions to her at these shrines. *La Santísima Muerte* has a calculated didactic iconography. In mystical Catholicism, the figure of the Antichrist – the notion of Satan in the guise of the Messiah – is more terrifying than the devil himself, because of the deceit. Perhaps that is why the Antichrist is so rarely portrayed in Christian art (among the few portrayals is Luca Signorelli's very unsettling depiction in the Orvieto cathedral of Satan preaching to the prayerful masses, wearing a mask of Jesus). The point is this: all the accoutrements of *La Santísima Muerte* echo exactly the iconography of devotion to Mary Mother of Christ in general, and the Virgin of Guadalupe in particular – the shrines, offerings, prayers, flowers and candles decorated with her image. *La Santísima Muerte* is not, like Satanism, an inversion of the faith. Rather, she wears the garb of faith – like the Anti-christ, she is not an inversion but a masquerader.

Priests are afraid to fathom the cult and its potency, while authorities are afraid enough to attack it both legally and physically. In Tijuana, almost all the roadside chapels which stood in 2008 had by the summer of 2009 been demolished – by the army, said Mayor Jorge Ramos, though the military will not accept official responsibility. Demolished, but not gone. One especially prominent one had been erected above the concrete sweep of the Abelardo Rodríguez

Dam. High above the reservoir, I remember the shrine: painted white, with low front walls through which one could enter into a space for offerings and pleadings for intercession; the 'saint' looking out from behind a real human skull, adorned with a headshawl of rainbow colours and wearing a mitre over which necklaces of beads were strewn. The hideous figure usually clutched a bunch of fresh flowers, regularly laid. The shrine is now demolished: jagged masonry and broken bricks, but there remains a defiant shrine within the rubble, crammed with candles bearing the image of *La Santa Muerte*, a few of them still burning. The butts of cigarettes given in offering are lined up in neat rows, wedged in the broken masonry. Cigars have been left, and personal trinkets. To the side is a mound of hundreds of empty glass candle-holders, most of them decorated with the familiar figure – hundreds of people have been this way since the destruction, and there is more: messages painted on the shrine's toppled walls, now scattered across the terrain. 'Though they destroy you, I still believe in you,' reads one. The next one says: 'They have taken my child, my parent, my penance, my condolence.' Watching us all this while, guarding the rubble of the shrine, is a black Ford F-150 truck with darkened windows and a CD hanging from the mirror. Next day, I return to find a different vehicle, a Toyota truck this time. I wander over, cheerily, dumb *gringo* complimenting the shrine. The truck's passenger window is open, and there are two men sitting in it; the younger looks straight ahead, out of the window, at the shrine. The older man turns towards me, stares, nods twice and stares again. '*Vete a la chingada*' – go fuck yourself – he says nonchalently, and without further word flicks the electronic switch to close his window.

The Day of the Dead in Mexico is syncretism in action, a profoundly charged entwinement of ancient faiths with imported Christianity, of Aztec communion with the underworld with the Catholic days of All Saints (1 November) and All Souls (2 November). Elaborate meals are cooked, and special breads baked to share with the departed. Musicians are hired to sing them ballads and laments, toys brought for dead children, special prayers whispered and rites observed. Most feasts across the country are held in cemeteries, but in Tijuana this can be the occasion for a family reunion astride the border itself – by the beach where California and Mexico meet.

This may sound more idyllic than it is. The turquoise ocean looks distantly seductive, but this is a scrappy piece of land divided by a mesh fence, which is the border – across and through which families sit down for picnic lunch, one half on the American side, the other in Mexico. This is the last stretch of fence along the whole border as flimsy as this, and during earlier visits to Tijuana, it was an evening pastime to come down to the *playa* and watch people climb over and run for it. Sometimes boys used to pose atop the fence, balancing, while family members or tourists took pictures, before darting into the United States of America, knowing that the border patrol, the *migra*, would catch some, but could not catch all. Another favourite crossing point was a dry cement canal running between Tijuana and the USA, along which so-called 'roadrunners' would hurtle at dusk, timing their sprint across the *territorio de nadie* – no man's land – between passes by the *migra* patrols and helicopters above.[8] These days, fence-hopping as a spectator sport at sundown is over; it ended after the Clinton administration mounted 'Operation Gatekeeper' in 1994, overseen and enforced by the then United States Attorney in San Diego, Alan Bersin, now 'border czar' for President Barack Obama. But the crossings continue and so do the picnics as a matter of weekend ritual, especially on the first day of November.

The Giovanni family assembles: Salvador Giovanni on the Mexican side with his daughter, Jessica, holding her baby, Jorge, so that the child's father, her husband Ricardo, can play with his son – a game of finger-tickling through the mesh, the international border – and catch up on his wife's weekly news from the southern side of the border. Salvador's other daughter Chantelle, a student of criminal justice at San Diego University, has also come to the US side 'for the first time, when I heard that my brother could meet his wife and baby at the fence', along with her boyfriend Luis – so it becomes quite a Sunday reunion, only with an international frontier running through it. 'It sure is a picnic with a difference,' says Salvador in perfect English, cutting his son a slice of water melon to a size that will fit through the fence. Dollar bills as well as tamales get passed to and fro through the wire. 'Some of us can't get across at all, and others who did cannot go back again if they return to this side – like my son-in-law. He made it over, got a job, earns money and sends most of it back — what father of a girl and grandfather of a little baby in this town is going to have a problem with that?' Salvador 'spent a while over there myself, working in Los Angeles. But they were different times. We used to come and go as we pleased. For ten years, I worked in an auto shop and came home every two weeks.' Not any longer: Jessica and her husband kiss through the wire, she lingers a moment, sadness flickers in her eyes, Dad tickles his baby, and it's time to go. 'I gotta work,' says Ricardo, and slouches back across the parking lot. However, says Salvador Giovanni, the US will soon end these traditional Sunday picnics and replace the mesh fence with the reinforced version that already runs for over 700 of the 2,100 miles of border. It is concentrated at and around urban centres, so that these family assemblies become a vulnerable point in America's defences. 'But the thing is,' says Salvador, 'there's always a chance', and he gestures towards a no man's land at the fence's edge, near the ocean. 'Every six or seven days, a big group just makes a run for it and the Americans know as well as the Mexicans that they can't catch everyone — there's always a few who'll dodge the cameras and infrared lights, and God bless 'em.'

Some make it, others are caught and deported — after hours, days, sometimes years in the United States. An afternoon at the border dump for deportees shows most of the deported to be like Natalia González, aged thirty-eight, who lived twenty-two years making batteries in Los Angeles before a check on documentation by the immigration authorities. 'There's work here in the *maquilas*,' she says, 'but my son's in LA, so I don't know what to do next.' But there is another small constituency among the deportees, says Victor Clark Alfaro, for years a campaigner for human rights in Tijuana, a minority extremely useful to the cartels: 'they speak English, they have contacts across the USA, many have been in gangs like the Latin Kings and Mexican Mafia, one third have been in prisons, they know about drugs and how to use weapons. They cover up their gang tattoos when they cross, are dumped without work, but quickly find it.' A man with teardrop tattoos arrives in the pound, the kind of tattoos you get as a gang member, or in prison. Julio César is a confident and friendly, if intimidating, alumnus of Huntsville jail in Texas, America's capital of capital punishment, where he served time for dealing in amphetamine. 'You're looking at my tattoos, ain'tcha?'

He speaks the obvious with a blend of menace and amusement. 'Yeah, I got 'em, and you know what for, don't you?' Though César is not going to elaborate, I recall having it explained to me in a scary quarter of east Los Angeles by gang members with teardrop tattoos that for each person you killed a teardrop was filled in. They were a form of initiation into and protection by the Mexican Mafia or some other gang inside and outside jail. César sheds many tears of ink, two of them filled in. He says that in the three jails in which he served time in America, 'I got looked after by the *Raza* ['the race', as Mexicans call themselves by way of assertion in the USA], 'by the brotherhood.' By which brotherhood? Mexican Mafia? Latin Eagles? Latin Kings? I ask. 'Now that'd be telling,' César says, but concedes: 'One of those.' It is a conversation I probably could not have had were César not in the compound and overseen by the police – and that he cannot continue for the same reason. César was due to be deported in 1993, but the jail lost his records, he says, so he remained inside until 2001, got deported, slipped back into California for five years and was caught yet again: 'just because I like to smoke'. Now back, 'I'm going to get whatever work I can find here in TJ that'll get me the money to get back there', he says. 'I have some contacts. TJ's cool, only there's no way for an honest man to make a living, if you understand what I'm sayin'.'

Others who cross the border are never seen again: they are never greeted by the relatives to whom they were headed, nor are they received back home, unless it is aboard a plane, in a coffin paid for by the Mexican government. For some in Tijuana, *Dia de los Muertos* 2008 has a special purpose, which is to pay homage to those who died in the deserts of America on their way to what they had intended to be a better life – the theme which dominates and defines the next stage of this book's journey along the border. The procession of homage in Tijuana is by those who survived the journey but were deported, and now assembled at the Salabrini hostel, which receives deposited, homeless deportees from the United States. Each marcher carries a white cross bearing the name of a compatriot who died attempting to make it to the USA – of exposure in the desert, heat or cold, thirst or hunger, attack by bandits or venomous snakes. The deportee marchers walk as far as the Mexican side of the fence, onto which, after saying prayers beside a little shrine of flowers and candles, they affix the crosses. 'Lord, hear our prayer,' chants Revd Luis Kendzerski, 'for the migrants and the poor, the abandoned and the dead, of the border.' Of every ten who die, he says, two are women or children.

East of Tijuana, through Tecate, along Mexican Highway 2, there is the first of many heart-stopping moments along this journey: the heat of early afternoon rises from the land below the road and across the desert, stretching into Southern California and on, it seems, for eternity. Hues of red, pink and burnt sienna wrap the distance, ascending into the smoky-blue haze of sky as it meets the horizon. There is complete stillness in the apparently boundless landscape. On the Mexican side, the road winds through Tecate onto a high mountain ridge and a parallel border road on the Californian side through leafy glades to a lonely but hospitable little town called Jacumba, with a spa motel, and into the cauldron of Imperial Valley. Here, the crossing into Mexico connects two towns with names that place both of them didactially in 'Amexica'. They are called Calexico and Mexicali, California and Mexico spliced and shared. Much of the Imperial and Mexicali Valleys lies below sea level, and both cities cohabit in a geological bowl in which air is trapped, so that neither the pungent stench of livestock, feed-lots and fertilizer on the US side nor the waft of chemicals drifting on the breeze from Mexicali can escape. Though this is a desert, Imperial Valley boasts some of the most productively fertile farmland in the western United States, thanks to the All-American canal, running from the Colorado river and benefitting farmers on both sides of the border, due not only to intended irrigation but also to an unforeseen life-source in the Mexicali valley: seepage. Water seeping from the canal created wetlands in the desert and has been pumped from the ensuing aquifer by farmers on the Mexican side, and used to grow crops. Until, that is, April 2009, when the rebuilding of the canal along 23 miles of watertight concrete was completed, saving an estimated 3.1 million acre-feet of water per year.[9] The canal lining was seen in California as a popular environmental and economical recovery of lost water for use by farmers in the Imperial Valley Irrigation District and domestic taps in the Metropolitan Water District of San Diego. Except on the border, in Calexico, which sided with the outraged Mexican farmers. A former mayor, Alex Perrone, argued that 'economically, if Mexicali loses, we will watch Calexico die. We're near totally dependent on the development and spending power of more than a million people on the other side. If the water goes, the farms suffer and the industries suffer. And if they suffer, Calexico suffers.' And so, concludes Perrone, who was born in Mexicali, 'We opposed the lining of the canal. Water is scarce, and our joint community has been developed around what has been available. Now the farmers are losing land over there, because the water is limited. This'll stop creating jobs, which means you contract the economy. It impacts on the agro-businesses, the people who sell the seed and fertilizer, or supply and maintain the machinery, and then it will impact us.'

But in this sweltering valley, and across the land to the east, water – *agua* – has a significance way beyond matters of irrigation and farmland. Along Highway 98, the road from Interstate 8 down into Calexico, the temperature rises with every mile – well over 100 degrees – and blue plastic tanks have been placed along it at regular intervals. Above them fly blue flags, and each is marked with the word *AGUA*, stencilled in white paint. There is a connection between these water posts and a plot in the cemetery at nearby Holtville, where those who died in the desert without a name are buried. This road takes us out of California now, into the state of Arizona and on to the narrative that lies behind both the water stations and the cemetery – that of the desert as graveyard. For something else is happening here, which has nothing to do with the canal, and whereby even a few drops of *agua* can make the difference between life and death.

CHAPTER THREE

El Camino del Diablo –
The Devil's Highway

There was a northern road, cut wood-blackened and
flower-sided; wing feather bowstring, down feather bowstring-sided
/ On that side, North, bad were my thoughts. And I uprooted it,
broke it, threw it down, stamped on it/ Thus you may wish and
plan, various kinsmen.
Opening speech in preparation for war, Tohono O'odham tribal
ceremony.[1]

The hinges of hell would cool this land; it is a pyrexia, and breath-
lessly still. Not a zephyr to disturb the simmering air. Beneath the
mesquite trees, creosote bush and agave cacti with blades like
drawn swords, are thousands of holes in the dust, some burrowed
by kangaroo rats to escape the sun. These animals have kidneys
that can reabsorb water and concentrate urine so as not to lose
fluid; their nasal passages are designed in order to recycle any
moisture from breath they exhale. Also invisible until the impenitent heat has abated are kit foxes, whose dens are so ubiquitous
that it seems there must be hundreds of them in just two square
miles. Not so: this animal changes dens frequently, and changes
vixens with every season, but never leaves its terrain and always
rests underground during the day.[2] The spindly branches of the
ocotillo appear like a fan of parched, dead sticks – only they are
alive, hibernating, feigning dry death. They would spring to verdant
life with the slightest fall of rain or during a desert storm, for
weeks if not months, storing the water, then return into their
disguise of mummified kindling. And when its leaves do grow, and
flowers that look like flames blossom from its stems, there is a
spike behind each tiny leaf, to punish and warn off any thirsty
animal tempted by sapless thirst to steal its moisture with a
refreshing bite. The 'Teddy Bear' cholla cactus, back lit, looks as

cuddly as a furry toy, but its spines are barbed and stick to anyone who brushes against them. Its big cousin, *cylindropuntia fulgida*, aka the Jumping Cholla, has treacherously weak joints that can dislodge themselves and, it appears, fly into the skin, implanting their spikes. Then there is the Arizona barrel, with fish-hooked spines that can bury themselves into your flesh, and cannot be removed. At dawn and dusk, rattlesnakes appear along the pathways, flicking their forked tongues, and the wilderness echoes with the haunting range of howls, yaps, cries and growls of the coyotes – songs of the trickster in Native American lore, one of the most resilient, cunning and adaptable of all animals on earth, even in this barren land. In the legend of the Navajo, north of here, the First Coyote flipped a blanketful of stars into the heavens, creating the Milky Way.[3]

In this xerosis of the land, any organism that has been shed to desiccate in the dust cracks underfoot like old parchment. Discarded snakeskin lies by the wayside, dry as burned paper. The stillness itself is immense: only broken by the occasional dart of a lizard across the rock, or the flight of a black-and-white backed woodpecker through the cavity it has excavated into the wall of a mighty saguaro within which it nests and whose fluids it extracts. The only persistent movement is on high, circling eagles on the fly, ready to dive at any chipmunk or jackrabbit with the audacity to move across country at this time of the afternoon. Or else vultures, seeking out those who could not make it. In the distance lies a boundless world and a constant drama of colour and light; of predator, prey and survival. The immensity stretches into the Cabeza Prieta, or 'Dark Head', mountain range of western Arizona – black volcanic peaks laid bare by millennia of erosion, and coloured a smoky indigo as evening considers its options. There are other dark colours, from granite and mica, which beneath the unrelenting sun create a haze of navy blue across the wild: the Diabolo Mountains, Growler Valley, Scarface Mountain, Black Mountain, Gunsight Hills, Alamo Wash, John the Baptist Mountains . . . As the writer Luis Alberto Urrea said: 'the poems on the map read like a dirge'.[4]

The esteemed Mexican naturalist Exequiel Ezcurra wrote that his 'work in the Gran Desierto changed my stereotype image of a competitive nature, where killing and conquering was the rule for he survival of selfish genes, into a different and somewhat opposing view: Life is driven not by contest, but by symbiosis and a drive for reproduction. It is not so much about supremacy as it is about co-operation of organisms and passion of the senses.'[5] And that is all very well, but for an animal or plant to evolve and endure this terrain takes millennia of natural selectivity and mutation. To be a frail human in this land is quite another matter, for over all this presides the sun. There are some scattered signs of Homo sapiens. Off a hiking trail running through the Buenos Aires Wildlife Refuge in southern Arizona, abandoned: empty plastic five-litre water canisters, grimy shoes, soiled fake Nike track-suit ziptops, school backpacks with pictures of Hannah Montana, a shaving set, exercise books, used batteries – all collecting sand and fading in the heat. Most poignantly of all, a pocket photograph album, the images bleached, just discernible, show a group of people smiling at what appears to be a celebratory meal of mostly seafood. There are three men with moustaches, three big ladies in best dresses; another man plays a guitar. These things are discarded slices from a journey being undertaken out there, in the baked distance.

This trail of dust – which winds south from Wellton, Arizona, over the Mohawk Canal and out across the US Air Force Barry Goldwater bombing range and Cabeza Prieta National Wildlife Refuge – was named by Spanish explorers who used it as an exploratory route north from their mission at Caborca, now in Sonora, in the mid sixteenth century. The name, marked in square Y 23 on the map of Yuma County you buy at the gas station, is *El Camino del Diablo*, the Devil's Highway.

The *Camino del Diablo* was an ancient trail first laid by Pima tribes native to the Sonoran Desert, but the route was pioneered for the historical record by order of Francisco Vásquez de Coronado, governor of Nueva Galicia, initially in pursuit of a mythical cluster of seven cities of gold called Cibola. A missionary and explorer, Melchior Díaz, is said to have set out from Coronado's encampment near Caborca, to seek Cibola and establish a route to the Sea of Cortez, into which the Colorado flows. The hardships encountered by Díaz's expedition earned the road its name. It was mapped more than a century later by the man whose memory remains ubiquitous across northern Mexico and southern Arizona, Father Eusebio

Francisco Kino. Father Kino – a seventeenth-century missionary, philosopher and astronomer – converted, but also defended the rights of, the Pima and was the first to chart not only the Devil's Highway, but also the water springs along it, called *tiñajas*. Knowledge of the *tiñajas* had been a means of survival and of wisdom among the Pima, and the instinct for locating them separates real desert people from transient inhabitants and boarders even today. In 1775, a band of 200 colonists under Juan Bautista de Anza endured the highway's hardships on their way from what is now Tubac, Arizona, to found the city of San Francisco.

The Devil's Highway won back its name in May 2001, when fourteen migrants recruited by criminal '*coyotes*' in the Mexican state of Veracruz, were found dead from dehydration and exposure. Their smugglers, heading from a border crossing west of the Mexican town of Sonoyta for the Arizona town of Ajo, became hopelessly lost on a doomed meander across some of the most unforgiving terrain.[6] The last stragglers were rescued in an operation no agent at Wellton's little border patrol station will ever forget, just south of a lovely palm-lined oasis and aquifer of water from the Colorado, and a service station on the freeway called 'Dateland', which sells date milkshakes. They were just fourteen among the many who die; but in Mexico, they were, absurdly, turned into folk martyrs by the country that exports people – through desperate poverty – across the border into America.

There are names for the players in this business of people-smuggling: the migrants are known as *pollos*, chickens, and those that recruit them therefore *polleros*, chicken-runners, working for *coyotes*, who control the networks. Bottom of the criminal ladder are the *guías*, the guides, who actually do the walk. To the border patrol, the migrants are 'wetbacks', even if all they have crossed is sand, otherwise 'bodies', 'wets' or 'tonkies'. Mexicans use the word *mojades* themselves: literally, wetted. The border patrol, of immigration police, is, of course, *la migra*.

The causes of migration from Mexico into the United States – about which much has been written – are deep and many, but are all variations on the theme of extreme poverty in criminally unequal Mexico, the lure of the economic superpower along its northern border and that country's demand for cheap labour. The first

Mexicans came in flight from the revolution of 1910, and to fill jobs created by the First World War — leading to the establishment of the border patrol in 1924. During the Great Depression, as now, opportunities for work shrank and migrants were made less welcome, only to return dramatically with the Second World War. Such was the demand for cheap labour after 1941 that the US government devised the Bracero Program to regulate it (the name comes from the Spanish word *brazo*, an arm), whereby employers could register immigrant workers and pay them specified wages for specific work over specific periods. The demographics and economics of the modern border began as many employers preferred to use the programme as cover to pay lower wages to illegal immigrants, while the migrants themselves would settle on the Mexican side of the border when their time was up, rather than return to the interior, in order to sign up again for further work in the United States. With the war over, migrants continued to flow north, so that the US felt obliged to mount 'Operation Wetback' in 1954, a round-up of illegal 'aliens'. The abolition of the Bracero Program in 1964 led directly to a second and even more momentous step in forging the border's population and economy: an agreement between Washington and Mexico City the following year to allow the building of the *maquiladora* assembly plants on the Mexican side of the line, 'bonded' for duty-free export across the frontier. The scheme, a precursor to the North American Free Trade Agreement, was devised primarily so that American corporations could pay Third World wages just across the southern border, and in Mexican terms to find employment for *braceros* returning home en masse, but remaining on the frontier.[7]

The direct cause of the deaths along the Devil's Highway in 2001 was a sudden exodus of migrants from the time-honoured border crossings into San Diego, El Paso, and cities along the Rio Grande Valley, into the deadly wilderness, in response to the boldest offensive against illegal immigration the US government had hitherto mounted. In 1994, Bill Clinton's administration escalated Washington's perennial battle with three 'Operations': 'Gatekeeper' in San Diego, 'Hold the Line' in El Paso and 'Operation Rio Grande' in the valley — three fronts which constituted a genesis of the process intensified by President George W. Bush after the al-Qaeda attacks of 11 September 2001. President Clinton's Operations proceeded chronologically from west to east, with 'Gatekeeper' over-seen by the then US Attorney for San Diego and Imperial Counties, Alan Bersin, defying his own favourite description of the trans-border community as 'San Tijuana'. 'Gatekeeper' brought the first stretches of the present-day border fence, night-vision cameras, infrared spy cameras, a reinforced border patrol and high-tech sensors that could detect movement. And it worked: by the end of the decade, figures for arrested migrants had plummeted – in the cities. But from the point of view of those smuggling migrants, let alone those being smuggled, 'Gatekeeper' entailed not a suspension of operations but a by-passing of the concentrations of fencing, technology and border patrol – and a redirection along the *Camino del Diablo*. The fourteen *pollos* who died near Wellton were only fourteen of what Enrique Morones – founder of a humanitarian organisation called Border Angels, which placed those blue water stations along the road to Calexico – believes to be 10,000 people who have died in the desert since the inception of Operation Gatekeeper. But numbers are of as little use on the border as they are in the desert. There is simply no way of knowing how many have crossed and died, or how many have crossed and survived; how many corpses will never be found for each one that is. Or how many Mexicans or Central Americans are still illegally but busily working away in America for each one who is dead or deported. All we can know is what a friar called Francisco Salazar already knew in 1650 when he wrote that the *Camino del Diablo* was 'a vast graveyard of the unknown dead . . . the scattered bones of human beings slowly turning to dust'.[8] There is no sign of the exodus along this widened *Camino del Diablo* abating – only of it becoming better organised, and exposed to different dangers and cruelties, now that narco cartels are taking over the business end of things.

The Reverend Robin Hoover of the First Christian Church on Speedway in Tucson leans back in his chair, feet on the desk, soles in my face, and describes his many good works. He dismisses descriptions of the work of others, like Morones and his Border Angels, as 'exaggerated'. He points out that I 'must be the thousandth journalist' to interview him. 'CNN were here only last week.' But there is a reason for his attitude. He has saved lives and gathered valuable information that no one else in America has compiled about deaths in the desert.

During the 1980s, the decade of President Ronald Reagan's support for military regimes and fascist militias in South and Central America, an ecumenical cadre of clerics together with some 500 congregations based on the border and in a network across America organised the Sanctuary Movement to protect political refugees from death squads in El Salvador and Guatemala, and the murderous US-backed regimes in Chile, Argentina and elsewhere. From his time with the Sanctuary Movement, Revd Hoover went on to establish and run another organisation, Humane Borders, which agitates on behalf of migrants and organises the placement of lines of water stations throughout Southern Arizona, and especially along what Revd Hoover's data shows to be the new corridors of death. One is across the land of the Tohono O'odham – 'Desert People' – Native American tribe, their 'reservation', across which the border now cuts like a gash, cutting off its people on the US side from the Mexico and vice versa. The other is a corridor running either side of Interstate 19 between Nogales on the border and Tucson, 70 miles north. These two corridors account for 42 per cent of recorded deaths in Arizona, says Revd Hoover, which in turn account for half the total deaths along the entire border. The clusters of corpses on Revd Hoover's screen show, he says, 'that although we had an overall reduction year over year until 2007, the numbers of migrants dying is now on the rise again. If the border patrol and new security measures were effective, the numbers dying would be dropping. But they are not: in the mid 2000s, we were seeing one hundred deaths a year. Over the last three years [to 2009], that figure has increased to two hundred, and the reason is that, as we can see from this diagram [and he flicks to another chart] the more the roads are patrolled, the more the migrants cross more remote and dangerous terrain. The deaths occur further from the roads, where you may be less likely to get caught, but less likely to make it.' The collation and analysis is estimably thorough: maps from 2005 show the majority of deaths between 5,000 and 6,000 metres from paved roads. The latest figures show them at least 9,000 metres away. 'The distance from the roads where people are perishing has nearly doubled,' says

Revd Hoover. 'We are the authority for mapping this shit out – the government doesn't do it.'

Revd Hoover calculates that 'up to twenty-five per cent cross using contacts they know – relatives or cousins – people concerned with the well-being of everyone in the group, should anything go wrong. Then there is a group of people who strike out on their own. That leaves a huge majority, about seventy per cent, in the hands of the *coyotes* whose only interest in getting you there will be a bit of extra pay, but who will not wait if something goes wrong, walking across country where a twisted ankle is a death sentence.'

The fourteen dead on the Devil's Highway in May 2001 had used as their point of departure in Mexico the border town of Sonoyta, opposite the outpost of Lukeville, Arizona, gateway westward to the *Camino del Diablo* on the US side. At that time, Sonoyta was abuzz with human traffic: the main square bustling with movement. Coaches from the interior disgorged load after load of people from the south, ready for the journey. The town was full of flophouses where itinerants would stay cheaply, and be picked up by prowling *polleros* and *coyotes*. Now, Sonoyta is quiet – uncannily quiet. The town seems to have shut. '*Chapo*' Guzmán chose Sonoyta as the location right on the border to deliver an order, according to US intelligence, that operatives for his cartel 'use their weapons to defend their loads at all costs' while crossing into Arizona.[9] So, informs a dentist in Sonoyta who asks not to be named in making this observation: 'the *polleros* have gone. This is now a place for another kind of crossing. You will see them only at night, and it is a good thing not to see them. From here, the bad guys now transport drugs, not other people.' The *Ajo Copper News* on the US side gives a weekly update on shootings in Sonoyta, while the sheriff's log is a litany of drug seizures. For the *pollos*, says the dentist, 'you need to go to Altar'.

Altar, some 30 miles south-east of Sonoyta and 60 miles back from the frontier, is by no means the most dangerous town in the borderland, but it is one of the eeriest. There is no way of arriving in Altar without being thoroughly checked out, heart-in-mouth, for there is no reason why a *gringo* like me would be in this place, other than to pry into its main trade. Altar is the new hub, in the western half of the borderland, for the arrival of migrants in transit from ıthern Mexico and Central America. In the heat of late morning, ,alls along the sides of the square, and up the back streets, are selling the equipment needed for the crossing and ordeal ahead: black backpacks, black T-shirts, camouflaged combat pants, flashlights – and, of course, the necessary spiritual protections: key rings, prayer cards and purses for change bearing the image of the Virgin of Guadalupe and San Judas Taddeo, cousin of Jesus Christ and the patron saint of lost causes, to whom one turns in time of difficulty.

Throughout the town are flophouses of the kind a while back found in Sonoyta – shelters where migrants pay between $3 and $5 for a bunk-bed made of wood, used blankets and the possibility of a mattress stained with dried semen and sweat. There are dormitories like those on Panteon Street, into which we are not admitted by an administrator apparently nervous about the other men lounging around the reception area – *polleros* plying their trade, preparing to bake chicken in the desert. There is one shelter, however, which is free, and where there is a welcome, the *Centro Comunitario de Atención al Migrante y Necesitado* (CCAMYN – the Community Centre for Assistance to the Migrant and Needy), supported by the diocese of Hermosillo, the state capital. The centre, clean and wholesome, is run by Marcos Burruel, who was once a quality control supervisor at the brewery in Tecate, using his sense of smell to pick out a substandard brew, but who now uses similar instincts to prevent anyone who has been drinking alcohol to sleep here, or a *pollero* disguised as a migrant but looking for custom from conniving his way into the dormitory. At CCAMYN, there are clean mattresses and linen for the deserving. Outside is a carved plaque and dedication: '*A Los Caídos En Los Desiertos de la Muerte*' – To the fallen in the deserts of death. '*En memoria de aquello que por buscar una major vida / Lo único que encontraron fue la muerte*' – In memory of those who searched for a better life / But the only thing they met was death.

We sit and talk while the shelter is closed during the day. 'How different it was when I was a boy here,' recalls Burruel. 'There were no fences, and people would cross and come back, cross and come back. Which they still do – there's much more coming and going than one hears about. Most get taken straight off the bus, the *coyote* is waiting there. They're cunning – the migrant may say, "I'm looking for Roberto, or *El Tigre*", and the *coyote* will say, "I'm *El Tigre*'s friend" and make a fake phone call: 'Hey, *Tigre*, your people from Chiapas have arrived.' And if they don't want to go, they're sometimes taken with violence and held until they pay. The authorities don't give a shit, and do nothing – besides, there's always a deal between the police and the *coyotes*: the police can get one hundred pesos for each migrant, which is more than they earn working for the police.'

Burruel estimates that 'about eighty per cent of the people who cross know of the dangers, but many don't have a clue. From here to Tucson or Phoenix can take them four to five days, but the *coyotes* tell them it'll take three to four hours. It's become a dirty business. Not just the heat, but kidnapping. Every day there's kidnapping, here in Altar and the desert. They kidnap the wetbacks and ask for ransom [Burruel uses the term *mojado*, 'wetback' migrant, although he is Mexican and though there is no river here]. They hold them for days, weeks, I have no way of knowing how many just disappear. They kidnapped and held a crowd of them in that house just across the street there', and he gestures behind him, through the window.

Burruel, a slight man wearing a beige shirt, talks about his work and his charge with a certain detachment, for all his commitment, as though such an attitude may protect him from the many people in Altar who disapprove of him, and of whom he is clearly afraid. 'The migrants are here because they're eager to cross, but know nothing apart from what they heard back in the villages, where they see the *coyote* as someone important. In some ways, I'm here to help them in this madness: I feed people, give a bed to a few – but I must also make them aware of what's about to happen. I warn them about kidnapping, show them videos about the dangers. And some do change their mind. They see the films and decide to go back. One time a man kept asking to change the video, and that's how I knew he was a *coyote* infiltrating the shelter. That's how my trouble begins.

'What I do here,' Burruel continues, 'angers the *coyotes*. If I talk about the dangers, this upsets them.' But, as he has implied, it is more serious than that. 'Here in Altar, other people have come who are part of organised rackets, to kidnap people; criminals who are not *coyotes* but related to the drug-trafficking cartels. The drug smugglers use Altar too, to stash and transport drugs and to tax the *polleros*. And this is very dangerous for me. They insult me, threaten me, tell me they're going to kill me.' Burruel is suddenly haunted, loses his detachment, and confides: 'Since I got my job here, I've been terrified of the night.'

Most of the narcos and *coyotes* working Altar are from Sinaloa, says Burruel, 'as are the *bajadores* – bandits – who come with guns and rob people before they cross. What his conversation drives towards is a recent development: that the traffic in migrants between here and the border crossing town of El Sasabe is being taken over by the cartels. 'The narcos control the frontier. From here to Sasabe, the *coyotes* have to pay a tax to the mafia, which they collect from the poor *pollos*, between 700 and 1,200 pesos [$50-$80] for each. If they don't pay, the narcos stop the truck and beat hell out of the driver, maybe beat the migrants and burn the bus.

'So why do I do this job? I must be crazy, I know. It's not because I think it matters, because it doesn't. Actually, what I try to do is pointless, against their business. It's because I believe in God, and because the priest is a friend of mine. But I'm only human, and of course I'm afraid. I'm also, by the way, a postman, and must do my rounds now.' These duties delivering mail, he says, afford a break, a breath of air beyond the stifling claustrophobia of this deceptively sleepy town, apparently calm but saturated with the movement and violence of which Burruel speaks.

But there is more to learn. In the thicket of back streets behind the square is a shop selling clothing, aimed like every other at the migrants' needs, but a little less like a military surplus store than the stalls: there are children's clothes and sunhats that are neither black nor camouflage. The shop is run by Amanda Ortiz Reina, wife of a man I had met briefly when he was mayor of Altar a decade ago, Francisco García Aten, a schoolmaster who had warned then that drug dealers would move in on the sumggling of migrants. In 2009, Ms Ortiz herself campaigned to win the office her husband occupied until 2003, on a ticket challenging the power of organised crime in town, but was beaten by her rival, Rafael Rivera Vidrio, who refuses to see us.

Ms Ortiz, by contrast, admits two unannounced strangers rolling up on her doorstep – after a brief but visible sizing up – and makes sweet tea, to drink with cakes served on a tray with a paper doily. She came to Altar aged twenty, to marry, in a city 'where everyone knew each other and supported one another'. Most of the population 'worked in the fields, like my father, and no one got rich from the collective farms, but they fed us. It was companionable, and we lived in symbiosis with the desert.' But now, 'incomers from Sinaloa have taken over the town and subjugated the local authorities and police. This has escalated even over the past two or three years; things have changed even since the government began the offensive.' So far as the cartels are concerned, Ms Ortiz posits tentatively, the terrain is contested between Guzmán and those loyal to the Beltrán Leyva clan, now allied to the Gulf cartel. 'While they fight each other for the Plaza, they both extort from the migrants, up to one hundred dollars per head smuggled, I understand.' But there is a twist to the cartels' involvement. As they swing their organisational muscle behind migration, so 'it becomes more efficient. And safer, in some ways though not in others. Our indications are that there is less rape by the *coyotes*, less robbery by bandits, less harassment on the way to the drop houses, less of anything that will attract the authorities' attention to the drugs, or get in the way of the money. But there is a terrible price to pay for this. Once they reach safety, the migrants are at their mercy.'

Then Ms Ortiz reverts from this distant menace to what is before her. 'My greatest worry for our town,' she concludes, 'is that children along the border are growing up with this as their world. My sons used to play in the streets; now that is simply too dangerous. We're terrified of the kids from Sinaloa, but the criminals become role models for the young people. When I ran for mayor, the old people wanted me, but the young people voted against me – when we used to go into town campaigning, there would be kids of twelve or thirteen years old, with walkie-talkies, reporting on our movements – to whoever. The truth no one wants to admit is that the young don't want to take a stand against what is happening. They're happy with this new culture, these new opportunities; they're growing up with it. Many parents have left, leaving us who remain scared, alone and frustrated. We're afraid to talk to our neighbours, because we're unsure who we are talking to.' As we look around her shop, minibuses heave by, up the little street and out across the land where the Buckhorn cactus changes colour in response to stress, turning a purple colour in times of severe drought or cold, then blooms in the many colours of fire during spring – the desert's mixed messages to those about to cross it.

They sit in what shade they can find around the main square, and wait, plan, figure out the next move. They are people in flight from what they have left behind, and in fear of what lies ahead. Some are on their way, others on their way back. The latter have less to lose now and are readier to talk. 'We knew the risks, and we took them,' reflects Ramón from Tabasco, who has now crossed twice, and been deported twice, 'and that's enough'. Ramón has paid *coyotes* $1,200 since he left home near Villahermosa four months ago, 'and there's nothing left. I have nothing for it but to go home, where there is nothing'. There are a lot of 'nothings' in that sentence, *mucho nada*. Ramón has a tooth missing, wears a pale blue shirt and a smile incongruous to his lot. He worked the land back home, 'where it's very beautiful, but I couldn't feed my family, I could hardly feed myself'. The second crossing was the worst, says Ramon's friend Victor from Chiapas, with whom he teamed up on the bus from Villahermosa. 'The first time we crossed and were picked up by the *migra* as soon as we found the main road. We were back in El Sasabe within three days. But the second time, it was hotter, we walked longer. The first guides knew their way, it was just bad luck the *migra* spotted us. But the second pair were useless, a couple of *pendejos* [idiots]. They thought they were the real thing, but in the end they were *cobardes* [cowards, weaklings] who argued between themselves. After two days, we were still on the Indian reservation, they said, when we should have been near the freeway services where the bus would take us to Phoenix. We were spotted by helicopter, and this time all the *migra* were Mexican, real *sabelotodos* – smart-asses – kids like I would walk past in the street back home, but they called us all kinds of shit.'

There are much edgier people in Altar embarking on their first journey across, on which they have staked their life. Some do not want to talk at all, and groups of boys with tattoos and cropped hair switch their conversation to an indigenous language as soon as we approach. But one man, Rodolfo, manages a joke. He is travelling with two cousins to join his eldest son in Minnesota, where, he says, 'I've heard about the cold in winter and how it'll kill me, but now I'm more worried about the heat.' The bridge home to Jalisco is burned: 'All I own I have put into this journey,' he says. 'I sold my house and my animals to pay the *coyote* and to buy clothes and things we need for the trip. Yes, I know the risks, but we have to take them; I cannot sell even the little I grow any more, the prices for produce are so low I'm paying to grow it, so we'll pray all day, and leave before dark.'

The road from Altar to El Sasabe, across a spectacular landscape called the *sierrita*, is a route to take during daylight. A sporadic flow of rickety white minibuses crammed with migrants, or open-backed cattle trucks with wooden slats to contain the human load, account for the only traffic to speak of. The beauty is breathtaking – grassland and low trees against a horizon of lilac-coloured rock and buttes against a deep blue sky – but hard to enjoy, as the minibuses kick up dust and the Arizona plates get us waved down and pulled over by men in bomber jackets and jeans. There is no demand for money, no sign of weapons, but there are plenty of questions, nods of disapproval and partial belief at the answer that we are researching migration patterns – one does not mention the words 'drug' or 'trafficking' around here. And there are stories told, whether true or false, with menace: about a hamlet called Los Molinos where a carload full of people was 'shot off the road, with everybody killed'. Ten miles on, however, approaching El Sasabe, the incinerated skeleton of a minibus adorns the roadside.

The town of El Sasabe itself is set slightly back from the border, giving the migrants a diagonal line to walk before they cross, hoping to avoid the concentrations of agents around the town of the same name in Arizona. It is low-slung, a main drag of buildings made of bricks on hastily applied cement, including the Super Coyote Café selling fresh water. The migrants line up at a makeshift hut to register with a branch of the Mexican public safety ministry called Grupo Beta. These men and women wearing orange T-shirts and driving orange jeeps, have a peculiar role: a kind of migrant social services branch of the government's social welfare administration, the '*Desarrollo Integral de la Familia*'. Grupo Beta agents take the names of those crossing, lest they be needed or never heard of again.

They fill the migrants' water cannisters and even provide maps of the US side, where there is disquiet among the authorities as to whether Grupo Beta is helping to save lives or facilitating, if not encouraging, illegal immigration into Arizona. One agent, called Aleman, remarks that 'we are doing the best we can to make what is happening anyway less dangerous for the migrants crossing. We're not encouraging them, we just try to stop them from dying.' He says that 'the flow of migration has slowed down, because it's getting much harder. We all know now that just over there, not only are the border patrol waiting for them, but even the National Guard.' And waiting in numbers recently increased by Homeland Security Secretary Janet Napolitano who was, until summoned by President Obama, governor of Arizona, the promised but parched land, receding from view up the Devil's Highway. A group of migrants camp down in the dust, wearing black hoodies and carrying their backpacks, and joke that it is in the interest of Grupo Beta to help them, because if they make it, the government benefits from the money they send home. But if they die, the government has to pay for the coffin and the plane to carry it. 'That would be the first time the government did anything for me,' cracks Jorge, a young man from Chilpancingo. 'If only they had given me that kind of money when I was back home!'

Only one trafficker is prepared to mumble a few words. Introducing himself reluctantly as Mario, he is a lean youth with spiky hair and a T-shirt reading 'Metal Rock On'. He says between cigarettes that he has been doing this for two years, after losing his job in Ciudad Obregón in the south of the state. 'I'm good,' he assures us, but adds nervously, 'You can write that all these people will make it to Phoenix' – as if he could know. One's mind runs back to the famous guide, Antonio López Ramos, who accompanied those who died on the Devil's Highway in 2001. He was identified by all the survivors as having a fleck of died red hair, for which he was nicknamed 'Red Rooster', and was apparenlty as cocky as this young man in El Sasabe now, who even echoes López's reported dress sense. Eleven miles of wall are under construction here: steel poles that mark the frontier as it disappears through scrub and creosote, being filled with concrete and standing four inches apart, a service dust-road along the American side – nothing but desert grass to the south. Suddenly, about four miles west of the hamlet, it stops, and the border continues as a line of squat metal bollards, around and over which the migrants will go, into the furnace.

The journey had been easier than Vicente Sánchez Morin feared.[10] A bus arrived as promised to take him and a cousin from Cintalpa in the west of Chiapas to the airport at Tuxtla Gutiérrez, from where a charter plane flew them to Hermosillo. 'I had never flown,' says Vicente, 'that was the only time I was scared, before we crossed the border.' From Hermosillo, another bus drove them to Altar, though there had been a breakdown and short delay at a place called San Agustín – Vicente remembered the name because it is the same as his brother's, whom he was to join in Denver. Agustín had a good job, or jobs, in Colorado: working fields and orchards during summer, fixing cars and casual shifts packing meat in winter. The crossing at El Sasabe had been 'easy', said Vicente, 'we went at night, the guide knew where he was going'. By now, they were in a party of ten, including a man from Azipaco, in Tlaxcala, who said nothing and who Vicente did not trust. 'He wore a black T-shirt and camou-flage pants, he was always watching people, he never talked or seemed worried.' A minibus duly appeared, Vicente could not remember where, but we worked out it would have waited for them at Arivaca, 20 miles from Sasabe, with a connection to Interstate 19. Vicente saw the lights of Tucson at dusk, 'and I thought it was Phoenix already. They told us in Altar that's where we were headed and I'd told Agustín to pick me up there.' The van arrived in Phoenix during the heat of afternoon in May 2009 – Vicente does not know where, although: 'I know where it is now,' he says, safely in the care of a church group. 'I've been back to look at it a couple of times.'

When the van arrived the group of men were corralled into the back of a building in the outskirts of town. 'There was a group of four people waiting for us, and they were scary to us. By now, I had been separated from my cousin, at the place where the bus picked us up in the dark. The mood had changed. It wasn't like they were trying to get us to our relatives, it was like we were going to jail.' Weirdly, 'the man from Azipaco, who we had thought was one of us, knew them, like he suddenly switched sides'. The windows of the house were blackened, the door locked, the men left alone.

'Everything had gone wrong. I had no idea what was happening. Some hours later, more men came, with guns. These were completely different people. They were wearing masks, while the other people we had dealt with until now showed their faces, though they never told us their names. They'd had nicknames, the one who took us through the desert was called *La Flecha*, the arrow. Now I was really scared. Then they took all our papers, our money. Two days past, maybe one night and a day. I tried to keep count with a man from Campeche. It was only when I finally found Agustín by telephone that I realised what was happening. It was almost more terrifying for him.' Agustín had been contacted by telephone and asked for $3,000 to buy his brother's freedom. 'He panicked completely. He hadn't expected anything like it. He'd sent me $1,000 for my trip, and hadn't anything like that kind of money. He was running around, asking anyone he knew. They told him that if he didn't find it within a week, they'd kill me. I knew nothing about all this.'

Vicente is a rugged man who looks older than his age of thirty-two, though he is physically fit. He tells his story in the office of a church as though it were happening to someone else. He wears a clean shirt, pressed slacks, smart shoes with buckles on them. Vicente is one of more than 1,000 people from Mexico and Central America whom Phoenix police have freed from captivity – in the city becoming known as the 'kidnap capital of America'.[11] Out of 368 kidnapping cases handled by the Phoenix Police Department in 2008, says spokesman Tommy Thompson, seventy-eight were calls to migrant drop houses. During the first six months of 2009, another sixty-eight had been identified or raided after emergency calls. In a raid on another drop house in a suburb called El Mirage, conditions had been even more frightening, some thirty men kept half-naked and pistol-whipped, their relatives shaken down for $5,000 before the property was raided in June 2009.[12] This is the delivery end of the narcos' taking over of the migrant business, using their contacts in the drug distribution network, based on street gangs and family associations, to recruit those prepared to hold migrants to ransom. Phoenix, now America's fifth city, has long been a destination for Mexican migrants, and especially from Sinaloa. According to the police department, Sinaloan gang members cruise the bars in Phoenix frequented by people from their towns back home, Culiacán and Los Mochis, recruiting for migrant kidnap operations, offering to pay cash advances with the balance payable upon receipt of the relatives' ransom money. As the mortgage market crashes, so the work is made easier by the number of properties to rent, which has increased by 75 per cent since 2000.

'We waited, and after a day they brought us some food,' says Vicente. 'They provided water, but no food until now. A woman came to help the men give it out – she told us she was 'cooking for them', but I think I know what that means. This time a man showed his face. We were told to sit and wait. They needed more money, he said, and they asked us for the names of the relatives who were waiting for us. A man said he wouldn't give it, and they hit him, and told him: 'If you want to live, give us the name and number.' He gave them a number in Chicago. I gave them Agustín's number in Denver, which I had learned by heart. They were all young, kids, nothing, but frightening.'

After four days, police stormed the property, without major incident. 'It happened quickly and suddenly. It must have been before daylight, because when they took us out into the front area, it was dawn. They took our names, and arranged for our relatives to be contacted. I didn't know how the police found us; I know now, but I'm unable to say.' Vicente, which I do not think is his real name, avoided deportation by agreeing to testify against the man from Tlaxcala. For the moment, Vicente is safe in Salt Lake City, protected by his church and US law enforcement. 'But I worry about my brother. For him, all this has been much more alarming and he has had to leave Colorado – although they were arrested they have his number, they knew where he was.' Vicente will probably get deported in the end, says the pastor looking after him at the evangelical sect to which Vicente belonged back in Mexico. And if so? 'I'll try again,' says Vicente.

The agricultural centre of Caborca, 60 kilometres west of Altar, is regarded as the Spaniards' point of departure along the *Camino del Diablo*. At least, the histories have it that the expedition set out from an Indian village near Caborca, leaving the possibility that this may have been Pitiquito, where the loveliest church in the area nestles between the back streets of town and fields beyond. The cool and the damp, musky scent of plaster and stone inside the chapel of the Misión San Diego de Pitiqui, give relief on a baking hot afternoon, especially when the walls speak as they do. Built in 1687, the aisles were decorated in 1719 with monochrome frescos depicting Death and Glory, a magnificent eagle's head representing St John the Evangelist, a bull's head for St Luke, a majestic Virgin of the Apocalypse and skeletal figure of all-conquering death, pointing the way towards the Resurrection by prophesying the exact month and year of Christ's crucifixion, as in the Book of Daniel.[13] 'All the bikers want their photo taken underneath it,' says the priest, Father Claudio Murrieta. He is in his mid-forties, handsome, energetic, forever at work around the fields or at his computer writing a history of this corner of Sonora. Pitiquito was an Indian village, populated by people the Spanish called *Pima* because it approximated their word for 'No', says Father Murrieta — the natives' initial reaction to the arrival of his Catholic faith. Altar became a city of commerce, legal and illegal, while Pitiquito remained agricultural, a place of orchards and crops: cotton, wheat — and eventually asparagus. But this last was emblematic of what has happened here since the government of President Carlos Salinas de Gortari ended the system of village landholding, privatising communally owned lots of farmland known as *ejidos* during the 1980s and allowing agribusinesses to take over the peasants' plots. 'Asparagus was new here: it was the big business crop which takes the nutrients and leaves the land barren,' says Father Murrieta, 'it is typical of the system now, exploiting the land and the people, bad production for quick profit, and low wages.'

We set off in the priest's truck to survey the scourge of poverty that followed President Salinas' privatisation of the *ejidos* — and the arrival of narco ranches on the land. The initial buyers were big landowners who turned the self-sufficient peasants (who were also small traders in their produce) into serfs, or else the rural unemployed. It is about this process, and its devastation of Mexican agriculture, along with the NAFTA free trade agreement, that Father Murrieta is writing his book. 'This is a route I do every day,' he says, 'to keep an eye on what's happening.' Which is, he says, 'that the average Mexican salary in the fields is fifteen pesos [about 8 pence or 12 cents] a day' — in a country where prices are not far below those in the

United States. We pull up at a hamlet called La Stacion, beside a disused railway line in the shadow of the spectrally beautiful Cerros mountains. Another of President Salinas' rackety ideas was to privatise Mexico's railways, selling thousands of miles of track to American freight rail companies and ultimately closing the entire passenger network. Behind us is the old station – once a bustle of meeting and greeting, arrivals to and departures from this now still and subjugated community, the building in ruins.

Father Murrieta greets a woman putting her washing through a mangle, chickens clucking around her ankles on the scrap of land surrounding the shack that is her home. 'She once farmed this land herself, when it was communal,' says Father Murrieta. 'But the privatisation was a pre-condition imposed by the Americans for entry into the free trade zone. The peso collapsed around the same time, and none of the peasants could afford even a slice of land. So first came the big ranchers with political connections,' he continues, 'then American agribusiness, buying up vineyards like that one, owned by a winery in California' – and he points to rows of vines, climbing the hillsides. Dogs lie in the shade of the mesquite trees; in a yard, a girl gets ready for a date, washing and applying make-up beside a tub of water with a cracked mirror balanced against a rusty pump. Along the dirt road adjacent to the railway line, posters have been erected by the rival political parties, PRI and PAN, for an upcoming election. The candidates' faces beam out at the hamlet. 'They're just messing with the people,' scoffs Father Murrieta, 'there's no difference between them, so they agree to fight it out with each other for the right to steal from the village' – and we agree that this is hardly a phenomenon unique to Mexico. In the yard of a bigger house with acacia trees in front of it, is parked an incongruously brand-new SUV with tinted windows. 'It's not hard to spot the ones who are working for the narcos,' Father Murrieta says with a shrug, 'but these are just the footsoldiers. After the landowners and the Americans, the narcos came, needing to clean money and stash drugs. They may keep horses, but obviously they don't farm.'

In late October 2009, an agricultural union leader called Margarito Montes Parra, who had tried to defend the rights of peasants, was ambushed by gunmen and killed while visiting Sonora. The Worker, Peasant and Popular General Union of which he was president is based in Oaxaca, but Montes Parra was trying to organise fishermen off the Sonoran coast, and arbitrate disputes involving the Yaqui Indian tribe. He had repeatedly criticised the authorities for protecting narco traffickers, and his son Adrián had also been shot here in Sonora in 2007, a murder the authorities said was linked to narcos buying land. On 30 October, Mr Montes was leaving a ranch with a party of families when a convoy of three trucks sped by, firing AK-47s at the small crowd. In all, fourteen people were killed, including four children.[14]

This war has butchery for its badge, or cachet, and it was also not far from here that a massacre of unimaginable brutality took place. A white SUV was found abandoned, and inside it a stew of mutilated bodies – hacked, chopped, castrated, decapitated; literally, cutlets of severed head, arm, leg and torso crammed into the vehicle with no relation one to the other until they were matched by the forensic police. Unpublishably gruesome pictures of the discovery and its aftermath were taken by the authorities, showing the deeply disturbing sight of human pieces laid out on a tarpaulin across the floor of a hangar. It is a scene from Hell from which even Hieronymus Bosch in his most vividly imaginative moments of pious terror would have flinched.

We drive through this terrain with Father Murrieta, the Cerros mountains cloud-capped in mid-distance, and pass a compound by the old railway, fenced off by chainlink topped with barbed wire, with a gas cylinder and trucks and trailers parked up on the gravel within. 'That's them,' Father Murrieta says, 'transferring, and loading up drugs; they don't even bother to hide it.' He accelerates, for this is not a place to be caught snooping. Soon, there's a fine-looking ranch with a wide gateway, and horses visible behind a fence along the driveway lined with cypress trees. 'That's another,' Father Murrieta says almost nonchalantly. 'You're now driving past quite a big operation. They have some fine stables there, but that is not their line of business.' He confirms Amanda Ortiz's diagnosis: the warring factions here are the Sinaloa and Beltrán Leyva cartels, the latter representing the Zetas' western front. We tell the priest that we slept a second night in Caborca, wary of Altar, to which Father Murrieta retorts, with laughter: 'You fell for the appearance of things, did you? For sure, you're more likely to get kidnapped in Altar, or your car hijacked. But there's a much greater chance of getting killed in Caborca, even if it looks quiet. It's far more dangerous, because that's where the infrastructure the narcos need is located: distribution centres, support industries – packaging, transport, that kind of thing.' He points past a burned-out former cotton mill, American-owned now, but deserted: 'There's an important archaeological site over there, which no one can visit after a narco bought the land.'

Father Murrieta is now livid and needs some refreshment. The advantage of being a parish priest in Mexico is that the old ladies of the village are delighted to cook lunch for he who nourishes them with communion each Sunday. Father Murrieta registers no objection, as we are welcomed into María Bonilla's little house for a hearty meal of pasta, seafood and beans, with a bottle of Tecate for the priest, over which he tells a funny story. The Father had always wanted, he relates, to go for a beer-drinking holiday during the Munich Oktoberfest, and recently he made it. There had been a convention in the Veneto, after which most of the faithful wanted to go to Rome, 'apart from the priests!' he jokes. So Father Murrieta and a friend headed for Bavaria, 'and we lived on beer and potatoes for a few days. They had glasses THIS BIG!' and he raises a hand above the lace tablecloth to illustrate the height of a stein. 'But oh dear, the hotels were so expensive. We used to go up to the airport and sleep there, on the seats, then back to the *bierkeller* in the morning. Which was fine, but if I go again, I'll save up for a bed.'

Of the two 'corridors' along which Revd Hoover's charts showed people dying in the largest numbers, the more deadly was the land of the Tohono O'odham Native American tribe, for whom smuggling, and the US government's war against smuggling, constitute just the latest chapter in a history of striving against – and living with – subjugation and persecution ever since the white man, first Spanish, then American, stepped on its ancient land. The O'odham were a people from what the Spanish called the 'Pimería Alta' region, unified by traditions and the O'odham language, but for centuries the tribe lived and were bound in groups without tribal government or centralised secular leadership. The O'odham had no formal laws; individuals and families were expected to maintain 'order and proper decorum, and people who went against customs were asked to leave', writes the historian of the tribe, Winston P. Erickson.[15] They farmed with no idea of private land ownership, but were constantly raided for goods, food and women by people they described with the O'odham word for 'enemy' – *Apache*. Their land was crossed by the Coronado expeditions, missions established by the Spanish, and colonisation accelerated after the discovery of mines in Sonora. The O'odham were quick to show an interest in the growth of wheat as a crop, and European tools with which to grow it, which led the Spanish to think they might be potential converts to Catholicism. In the last years of the seventeenth century, the tribe was caught between the Spanish military's abuse and the favour of Father Kino, whose shrine at Magdalena in Mexico remains a pilgrimage route for many O'odham Catholics. When the Spanish moved permanently on to their land in the early 1700s, in search of gold and silver, the O'odham came to distrust them, hiding their sources of precious metals – and the Spanish responded ruthlessly and violently towards the O'odham and their neighbours, the Yaqui. In 1821 both tribes exchanged Spanish for brief Mexican rule, and in 1848 the border between the US and Mexico was drawn across O'odham land. 'The splitting of O'odham land between two countries inconvenienced the O'odham somewhat, but it would be many years before strong enforcement of border policies would occur,' writes Erickson, with understatement.[16] Under US law, he continues, 'the O'odham had few or no rights as intruding Anglos took what they wanted and ignored the rights of the native peoples'. By the turn of the century, the killing and destruction of the O'odham and their ways had begun in earnest: the reservation was designated across 4,800 square miles, as cut off as it was expansive, and the cash economy ravaged the O'odham and Yaqui ways of living, as many native people migrated to Tucson in search of employment as construction workers, railroad labourers or domestic servants, or to the copper mines of Ajo. During the 1930s, the first border fence was erected, although the O'odham remained – and remains – the only tribe in the United States which enrols Mexican citizens and allows them to vote in tribal elections. The tribe is one of the poorest in the south-western USA, with an average annual income of $8,000 per family and about one third of its citizens unemployed.

When the world's press descended on southern Arizona after the

deaths of the 'Yuma 14' in 2001, the Tohono O'odham tribal authorities greeted visitors with pride and courtesy. The chairman, officials
and employees of the tribe would discuss education and the dilemma
between retaining the native Uto-Aztecan language and culture
while giving young O'odham a chance in modern America. Now,
attempts to contact the tribe officially disappear down a black hole
– messages to its gatekeeper Pete Delgado hit a brick wall. Even
America's most respected and tenacious reporter on Native American
affairs, the indefatigable Brenda Norrell, is forever, through an
estimable website called 'Censored News' and others, hammering at
the door in search of answers to questions about abuse of land,
heritage and people by construction of the border fence, and about
where profits go from casinos operated by the tribe, most of whose
members live in extreme poverty. The generous inference is that
tribal affairs are private, and privacy must be respected. The less
charitable interpretation of the stonewalling is that things are
happening of which the tribe is aware but which are unfit for prying
eyes. 'I'll say it on the record,' Revd Robin Hoover had volunteered
back in Tucson, 'because I can and I have, and few others would:
there's a degree of complicity in the smuggling of drugs and people.'
In the eyes of some tribal members, their authorities have, ironically, done something even more serious: having vowed to oppose
yet another invasion by the white man in his attempt to reinforce
the border with fences and hundreds of agents, they have instead
cooperated with the militarisation of their own land. The tribe is
again exploited, caught again between a rock and a hard place:
between smugglers of drugs and migrants exploiting the poverty of
its people, and US authorities trying to stop them.

People cannot be silenced, however, and where there is grievance
the courageous talk, whether out of rage, pride, despair or all three.
Mike Flores is one such person. 'Who are you?' he asks by way of
introduction, in the inimitable way in which Native Americans ask
the question, with an implied enquiry after one's ancestry. Flores is
a Native 'Amexican' in the deepest sense. He lives in a caravan on
a patch of land behind the roadside café on the main highway
through Sells, but his father comes from Quitovac, across the border
carved through his ancient land, and migrated north to Ajo in the
United States – just west of the reservation – to work in a copper

mine. Flores' mother was born beside a natural spring, a *tiñaja*, in what has since become the Organ Pipe Cactus National Monument park, adjacent to the border on the US side.

Flores is a true son of this land we are calling borderland, but with an identity that precedes any borders and transcends Spanish colonisation, Mexico, the arrival of the white man and the United States. Spiritually, he feels close to the Mexica, calling himself a 'traditional', according to the ancient beliefs of his ancestors, rather than what are called 'progressives' who converted to and still accept the Catholic faith. 'My grandfather told me: This is our way, the four directions, the four winds and what we call *him'dag*, the way, the journey. When I went [to Teotihuacán] to see the pyramids, I felt part of *that*,' he insists; 'those people were looking at things the way I do, they saw it the way we see it, and that's not surprising, they came from here.' I foolishly mention the journey of the Mexica to Tenochtitlan from around here, but Flores scoffs: 'Oh yeah, people have all these anthropologies and sociologies and all kinds of "ologies", but I'm an O'odham, not an 'ologist – all I know is what I was told by my father and grandfather, which was what they had been told by their fathers and grandfathers: that I can rub the dirt on my face anywhere between Alaska and Mexico City, and call it me, because that's where I come from.' The uniquely complex and beautiful emblem of the Tohono O'odham tribe portrays the human journey within the scheme of *him'dag*: a small figure, representing birth, stands atop a circular maze which winds, via a penultimate point in the far corner of the pattern, to a 'dark centre' of eternal life, in which one is cleansed and reflects back on knowledge gained during the journey. Just now, reports the O'odham paper *The Runner*, *him'dag* is a subject taught in school on the reservation, and a popular one. Pupils are reported to look forward to the special day of the week when traditional food replaces the usual junk served at lunchtime.

Flores would have learned how the Creator God I'itoi led his ancestors from the underworld, up into this land; he would call months *masads* or moons, the first being the *eda wa'ugad masad*, backbone month, beginning with the winter solstice to commence an annual cycle divided into halves, with its mid-point as the summer cactus-wine feast on the longest day.[17] During the 1970s, Flores became involved in the militant American Indian Movement, and 'I still feel the war, like it never ended'. Flores wears an AIM hat when we meet for breakfast in Sells. 'Right behind my caravan is where the US army set up its first base on our land. And sometimes at night, it's like I can hear our warriors preparing for battle. The past is very close by around here, you know – it's with us all the time. And the ancestors are watching to see how we deal with this latest situation. The land has fallen sick from being raped over and over. First, the white man, then the border, now this: ninja guys prowling around, helicopters flyin' over making the people and the horses scared.' Flores spits words of fire but with an expression of deep calm that is disarming and compelling, his vocabulary ablaze, but his eyes wide, voice soft.

The border patrol has Flores's unmitigated contempt: 'They come from Texas, South Carolina, upstate New York, and they don't know jack shit about this land. They act the tough guy, but if you put any of 'em out on the land under the sun without their toys, they'd be dead in two days. I can walk for weeks across this land, light and dark, 'cause I know it, I know where the springs are and what to eat. We've been close to the land for all time, we understand these things – how the birds hatch, how the water flows, how lizards stay cool in 110 degrees, so we can imitate them. But these guys: they think they're big boys but they ain't nothing on this land.' Which makes it even more offensive to Flores that 'they're interfering with *him'dag*, the way itself. We can't get the elders to perform the sacred rites from the Mexican side because they don't have the papers. Last year, we held our traditional ceremony, and it's the custom for our warriors to hunt a Pronghorn deer; it has to be caught, cooked and eaten in the correct way. But last year, the border patrol drove up on the warriors, handcuffed and detained them for eight hours, for having a weapon on their homeland.' Such audacity is 'overstepping the line', fumes Flores. 'It's part of the same shit that gets these kids in gangs who are twenty-one, twenty-two years old, using drugs and alcohol, and I get on my soap box and tell 'em that's not the way, that's the way the white man sent us. He taught us that to get anyone's attention you gotta show 'em a thousand dollars and that's what it's come to on the rez. Whoever offers the money gets their way.' This affects the tribal authorities too, says Flores. 'There's a switch

in tactics,' he continues. 'At first, the tribal leadership opposed the
border fence. But they feel more confident now, against us of the
old way, 'cause they've seen a little money in it. Now they're happier
about co-operating with anyone who wants to trample on this land,
whatever they're messing in.'

We drive south, off the main highway running parallel to the
border and down the road towards the frontier, marked with an arrow-
head as 'Indian 19', leaving behind the shacks and trailers, the land
rising so that we are surrounded by agave, chollas, mesquite and
creosote. To the east, a conic mountaintop rises above the other desert
peaks along the ridge and pierces the horizon like the tip of an arrow.
Flores says: 'That's Baroquivari, which our ancestors considered the
centre of the universe'; and one feels a strong sensation from the passive
but passionate way in which he says this, and from the mountain
itself. 'It's the land which keeps us going,' he says again. 'We and the
land are the same.' We pass a compound of buildings and a holding
pen for people, signed 'Law Enforcement Area', out of which a bus
bearing the name and insignia of the Wackenhut security company
tears towards and past us. This is one of the vehicles that commutes
between the law-enforcement area and the border, taking illegal immigrants apprehended in – or rescued from, depending on how you
look at it – the expanse, corralled and now shipped to the border and
dumped on the other side to make their way back to Altar whence
they came. 'One time,' says Flores, 'the tribal police stopped one of
those buses and found the guards had stolen a tortoise from the desert.
You know, to keep as a pet – a beautiful desert tortoise. That's how
they see our land.' After 19 miles of Indian Highway 19, the paved
road veers left towards an outpost community of trailers called San
Miguel, clinging to the border, while we take a dirt track to the right,
at the end of which is a clearing in the desert scrub, a border patrol
van, electronic surveillance tower, fence made of steel poles of
alternating height, and a heavy electronic gate. This is a pedestrian
thoroughfare, which is not an official 'Port of Entry' but a passageway
for members of the tribe only, upon production of ID. Behind it is
an old fence made of sticks linked by two strands of rusty wire,
intended – with little success, usually – to stop cattle wandering
between the United States and Mexico. This latter was the border
until recently. And beyond both these frontiers, across earth identical

to that on which we stand, lies a place with two names: Flores calls it the continuation of ancient Tohono O'odham tribal land. The world beyond the tribe calls it Mexico. 'On the weekend,' says Flores, 'there used to be a market here. People would bring stalls and line them up along the border and sell tacos and clothes and stuff over the fence. That doesn't happen any more.' The markets, recalling those Day of the Dead picnics at Tijuana beach – themselves soon to be a thing of the past – are hard to imagine in the empty silence under the gaze of the border patrol and, no doubt, its quarry of smugglers on the other side.

On the edge of Sells is Poltergeist Lane. No one seems to know its real name: it was baptised by the gangs that patrol it, and tag the empty houses: 'Poltergeist Northside,' reads one graffito. This is the newer housing on the reservation, considered better than the trailers or shacks in which many O'odham live. One of the local gangs, explains a boy putting up a flier for a tribal rock poetry event in the café, is called the 'Dream Walkers', because 'they can kill you in your sleep, by spiking your dreams with curses and stuff'.

'There's a lot going on out there at night,' says Angelita Ramon, who lives at number 18 Poltergeist Lane, pointing past the creosote bushes. 'A lot of people coming through the wash right there, a lot of drugs coming through. I hear them, and it keeps me awake.' But Mrs Ramon's sleeplessness and struggle arise from the impact of all this movement on her own family. In the living room of her house, two daughters busy themselves with housework, cooking and television; but her three sons are present only as portraits on the wall. One 'committed suicide after the police took him into the desert one time and gave him a hard time. He was so mad at them, he killed himself; he was sixteen,' says Angelita. A second, Joseph: 'he's in jail, in New Mexico . . . they say he shot . . . you know . . . oh, I don't know . . . He's very protective of me now – always calling to see if I'm okay.' And there's the third: Bennett, who died a death so strange and unexplained 'it's driving me over the edge'.

At four thirty in the morning of Friday 9 April 2002, Bennett Palacio, aged eighteen and known as 'BJ', was walking home to Sells from a party following a baseball game. He turned from a dirt track onto the main road near a village called Cowlic, where he was struck by a border patrol vehicle and killed. Ever since, his mother and stepfather Ervin Ramon have avowed that Bennett had stumbled upon a drug transfer involving members of the border patrol on the dirt track, and was killed after making a getaway run onto the asphalt. It would not be so far-fetched: the FBI's Operation Lively Green in Arizona and the associated Operation Tarnished Star in Oklahoma resulted in ninety cases being brought against serving soldiers and government agents for drug smuggling in this region; among them were 13 guilty pleas entered during a single trial in Tucson in 2005, including a National Guard Sergeant Robert Bakerx, jailed for smuggling cocaine and getting other soldiers to do so.[18] Between 2001 and 2004, sixty-nine members of the military, border patrol, prison guards, law enforcement and other public employees had been convicted of accepting bribes to help smuggle cocaine.[19]

After years of tribulations through the courts – the Ramón family constantly spurned by tribal and federal authorities alike – and the emergence of court papers naming two drivers behind the collision who were never called as witnesses, the Ninth Circuit Court of Appeals in February 2006 and May 2007 rejected the family's action for unlawful death. The driver concerned was ruled not criminally responsible for killing Bennett Palacio. Applications to talk to the border patrol about the case for this book, as well as the wider issues of migration and rescue, were informally accepted during approaches made locally, but declined in Washington.

'Year after year, the pressures have eroded who we are as an original people,' says Ofelia Rivas, organiser of O'odham Voice Against the Wall, a campaign against the means of fortification of the border. 'Now, it's not just a border,' she says, 'it's a wall across our land. It stops people crossing, including our elders, and has already disturbed our burial sites. Some of our ceremonies are in Mexico, and I can't go. We've had tribal members on the American side arrested and deported while visiting relatives on their own tribal land, because they came from Mexico and didn't have the right papers. It's even disrupted the pathways of mountain lions which have to find new areas of habitation because they can't migrate. This is our ancestry, not a Kokopelli on someone's coffee mug! I'm fifty-three years old, and fifty-three is just fifty-three – but even I can remember when we got water out of water holes, and had to understand the land in order to eat and organise the year. I saw it all change during the

80s and 90s – the young people became lost, television took over our lives, then the militarisation. Twenty years from now', Ms Rivas predicts, 'our children will look back and say: "That is when it happened, the second destruction of our people." And it's all happening at such speed, after so many thousands of years. For all time, we just went to what's now Mexico and visited families, and people would come here. The authorities don't seem to realise that we have the spirits walking before us when we have to do these things. You must understand that we feel the eyes of our ancestors upon us, and have to explain to them that our history's being eradicated at this pace.' On the road off the reservation, into Tucson, a sign with a picture of smiling young O'odham reads: 'We lived and survived the desert for more than 500 years. Will we survive the next 500?'

Some 28,000 O'odham live on the US side of the border, and only an estimated 2,000 on the Mexican side, most of whom prefer to be called by the name the Spanish gave them, *Papagos*. Towards their villages, through the Sonora Desert, is some of the most majestic land in the Americas, over which tower the Saguaro cacti, monarchs of the desert, and the organ pipes, with rounded ribs and fruit from which the O'odham make jelly, wine and seed meal. As do the people of Quitovac, which lies up a track from the main road between Altar and Sonoyta. Quitovac is a village of fifty people, the largest single *Papago* settlement on the Mexican side, with a kindergarden that prepares children for 'Mexican school' in Sonoyta. A lady called Leticia keeps the little village *bodega* selling tortillas and household basics. She says that 'teachers come from Sells to run special programmes in O'odham traditions and culture, but the children tend to lose it when they grow older – and hardly ever go over to the American side because they get arrested if they don't have papers. They'll grow up as Mexicans, and only go to Sells if they need to see a doctor at the hospital ... Most of our families are on the American side, but it's hard to visit them, and almost all traditional activities happen on the American side, apart from religious pilgrimages,' says Leticia. 'Most of us here are Catholic, and make pilgrimages to Magdalena more than the traditional rites; most of us still like to be called *Papagos*, like our parents called us, not O'odham.' This is more significant than it seems: for while Flores and Rivas feel quintessentially of the borderland in its most ancient sense, and an identity endangered by the white man, and now by the materialism of the cartels and the fight against them, the O' odham on the Mexican side seem less discontented, even though their culture has been thoroughly more eroded by Hispanic culture and religion.

Sitting on a chair outside his home is Eugenio Ortega Velasco, aged seventy-eight and the last man to speak the O'odham language in Mexico. 'At least I think so,' he says. 'When I was young, I moved around the whole territory, both sides of the border. There was work on the US side, and we used to go all the time, to and fro, and to visit family. Then, one by one, all my brothers and sisters went to work in the US, and never came back. Nothing much has changed since then, apart from the fact that it's very hard for most people to cross the border. I could if I wanted to' – he produces a pass with his photograph on it, valid for a year – 'but I don't feel the inclination. It's so much trouble – all those guards.' He folds his dog-eared letter from the Department of Homeland Security with a dismissive air, puts it back in his pocket and adjusts the brim of his hat downward, as the sun sinks low over the earth. Then he shifts his chair for no reason, and continues staring out in silence across the desert, from the porch of the house in which he was born.

The Tohono O'odham's cash-cow casino, on an annex of the reservation called San Javier, south of Tucson, is packed this summer Saturday night. The song belting out beneath a full moon after a thunderstorm is called '*Contrabando y Traición*' – 'Contraband And Treason' – and it is the one the audience has been waiting for. The young people on the lawn behind the amphitheatre whoop and sing along; the elderly folk and families in the more expensive seats 'rattle their jewellery'. The number, with its swaying accordion and rollicking bass line, is about a couple, Emilio and 'Camelia the Texan', smuggling drugs from Tijuana into San Ysidro, 'their car tyres replete with naughty grass'. They cruise through a questionnaire at customs, make it to Los Angeles and collect the cash, which they split, Emilio telling his partner that he is now proceeding north to meet the love of his life. Upon receipt of this news, 'Seven shots sound; Camelia kills Emilio', but when the police arrive, they find only a *pistola tirade*, a fired pistol – 'of Camelia and the money, nothing ever more was known'. The song was an early hit for the band on stage, Los

Tigres del Norte, recorded in 1972, when the now middle-aged men were teenagers. Though not the first *narcocorrido*, it was the first to become a hit on every jukebox and across every dance floor in Mexico.[20] It was so popular that the band recorded two sequels: the first in which Camelia is tracked and gunned down by rival *traficantes* in Guadalajara, and a second, 'The Son Of Camelia', about her offspring killing five members of the Tijuana cartel and hunting down others to avenge his mother's murder. Los Tigres – three brothers and a cousin – are the kings of the genre they created, the undergrowth of which now provides a soundtrack to the narco war. They are the originals who have gone glitzy and international while the seeds, or some would say weeds, they planted grow thick and healthy, for the glorification of criminals.

Tonight, Los Tigres are dressed in flagrant red silk emblazoned with shameless gold; their pants skin-tight to show their bulging efforts to best advantage, their heels are high and their posturing lusty, for these are the pin-up boys of *narcocorrido*, from the state of Sinaloa, of course, but playing to a home crowd in the Arizona desert. Tucson – a name derived from the O'odham phrase '*Cuk Son*', at the foot of a black hill – is 70 miles from Mexico and not strictly a border town, so much as a border hub. It is a heart-warming place: scrappy but funky, sun-dried, vibrant and eclectic. It comprises a university, thriving bohemian arts and music scene, gated suburbs in the northern foothills, horse heaven towards Saguaro National Park and a downtown through which railroad trains hoot and rattle on their way from Yuma to El Paso and beyond, past the Congress Hotel where John Dillinger stayed before he was arrested. The south side of the city, including a separate entity called South Tucson, lies on what is regarded as the wrong side of those tracks: a burgeoning and mettlesome Mexican-American community, umbilically connected across the border. During 2008 and 2009, the city saw a sudden rise in drug-related crime and home invasions, resulting in most cases, said the police, from unpaid debts due to cartels smuggling people and narcotics.[21] But tonight it's all bandanas with the Mexican flag and 'Los Tigres del Norte – Gira USA 2009' emblazoned upon them. For all the Tigres' bravura as the godfathers of *narcocorrido*, this is a family outing. The entire Mexican-American spectrum is here: elderly couples with their children and grandchildren, boys in baggy shorts and tattoos on their shins; a scary-looking man with a long black coat and a fedora hat and gaggles of girls pressed up against the fence at the front of the standing area. Jorge Hernández, the bandleader, raises his stetson with a debonair bow to the crowds and presents the musicians: '*mi hermano Raúl, mi hermano Hernán, mi primo Oscar*', my brother, my brother, my cousin.

Next up is a blustering number called '*El Avion de la Muerte*' – The Airplane Of Death.' It is a true story, supposedly, compiled from news reports, featuring the narco Manuel Atilano, captured and tortured by the Mexican army into flying them to his cartel's hideaway landing strip in Sinaloa. Atilano, however, seizes control of the plane and broadcasts details of his treatment over the radio: '*Con pinzas machacaron Partes nobles de su cuerpo*' – with pincers they crushed the noble parts of his body. The song ends with an act of heroism, as Atilano changes his plan to crash the aircraft into a police compound when he sees a schoolyard full of children next door, and instead plunges himself and his captors to their deaths against a hillside, bidding fond farewell to his friends in the landing strip's control tower – '*adíos a sus amigos camaradas de aviación*.'

Los Tigres have no connection to any cartel, but one is left uncertain whether the brazen inclusion (on a tape, of course) of rasping, rapid automatic machine-gun fire which carries along Los Tigres' next song called *Pacto de Sangre*, 'Pact Of Blood' is being faithful to their roots or offensively tasteless. There is no uncertainty, however, about how much the audience relishes all this gaudery: the gunfire, which sweeps in stereo from stage left to stage right, gets 'em dancing with even more splash and splurge.

Jorge Hernández puts it this way: 'Poor people idolise the narcos: they admire their bravery, and they want to be like them. When you sing the songs, the audience feel that they're living through the characters, as if they were watching a film. That's why people love the *corrido*. It lets them dream.'[22] Within weeks of tonight's concert, Los Tigres would become involved in their share of controversy. The band pulled out of an appearance at the prestigious Las Lunas music awards show because its organisers refused to allow them to play their latest song: '*La Granja*', 'The Farm', a critique of President Calderón's offensive against the narco cartels, accompanied by a video showing pigs representing politicians getting rich on the back of the poor.[23] This peacockery is the razzmatazz side of this genre. However, more recently emerged *narcocorrido* bands are sometimes recruited to sing the glories of one particular cartel over another, a hero against a villain or, more usually, against the army. This, of course, makes them fair game for a rival cartel.

In a separate but chilling incident, the most famous murder of a musician occured in Matamoros, the easternmost city on the Mexican side of the border, on 1 December 2007: that of twenty-eight-year-old Zayda Peña, the raven-haired singer for Los Culpables – the Guilty Ones – a best-selling band. Peña, who sung a famous hit entitled '*Tiro de Gracia*' – a single 'mercy-shot' to the head – was staying at a motel in Matamoros after a concert the previous evening when gunmen came to the door and opened fire, killing a male companion and the hotel manager. Peña was taken to hospital and given emergency surgery, but as she emerged from the operating theatre a squad of *sicarios* was waiting in the corridor to deliver a '*Tiro de Gracia*' through the recovering star patient's head. 'Nothing, nothing, nothing,' was the response of the Tamaulipas state prosecutor's office when asked for possible trails in search of Peña's killers.[24] Ms Peña's mother has been working for the prosecutor's office since 2007, the year of her daughter's murder.

The Spanish word for 'walnuts' is '*nogales*', and there are two towns of that name, facing each other across the border south of Tucson, so called because of the walnut trees that grew wild and in orchards across the verdant slopes that rise into Mexico from the thirsting desert of Arizona. On the southern edges of Nogales, Sonora, is a new building, opened to great fanfare, called '*Camino a Casa*' – the highway home – another border project of the government's *Desarrollo Integral de la Familia*, or DIF. The brief is simple: to gather children who have been smuggled north across the border, caught and deported, and to get them home. But the process is complicated: in the clinically clean reception area, a couple, Cesar and Yvet, waits. He wears a white T-shirt and tattoos, she wears lines of exhaustion and her cheeks are tear-stained. They are in their thirties, from Acapulco where, says César, 'there is nothing for a family', and had crossed just east of Nogales, into the desert. They were caught near the town of Patagonia, having paid one *coyote* $1,000 in Acapulco and a further $400 in supplements in Altar and along the way. They had been deported separately, their daughter Francesca brought to *Camino a Casa*. Cesar signs a last piece of paper, and the security guard retreats through a magnetically locked door. Some time later it opens, emitting a chorus of high-pitched, young farewells – '*Adíos*, Francisca!' – and the couple's daughter, aged twelve, runs into her weeping mother's arms. 'There's nothing more to say really, thank you,' says Cesar, sweeping his womenfolk towards the door. 'We're going to find the bus home.' Across the road, other children chirrup and run around an urban schoolyard; Francesca shoots them a glance of envy, takes her mother's hand, and disappears back to Acapulco.

At first, the imposing María Mayela Alessi Cuevas appears as a set of long, painted fingernails with a woman and shoulder-padded jacket attached. She is the impeccably dressed director of this branch of *Camino a Casa* and runs the place with a mixture of no-nonsense authority and a degree of compassion, no doubt. She took the job when her husband moved his business to Nogales. Ms Alessi explains the situation with straightforward clarity. 'We get about five hundred a month,' she says, 'of whom twenty per cent are fetched by their families and eighty per cent are sent home.' When they cross into the United States, most have both parents living there, and are forwarded by relatives who put them in the care of *coyotes*. 'Some cross the desert, some through the official Ports of Entry (PoEs) with false visas or fake documents, with other families. They get asked what their name is, questions about things on the papers, get confused and get caught. A child's instinct is to tell the truth, and if the customs ask "is that your mom?" they give the game away. Often they're drugged to sleep when they cross but the customs wake them up, and when they're drowsy they make even more mistakes; we sometimes get girls who have had their hair cut to look like boys in the fake papers.' They, however, are the lucky ones. 'For the ones who cross the desert, things are harder,' says Ms Alessi. 'We get girls who have been raped, as young as twelve, and some are pregnant after having been raped on the way north. Others sustain physical injuries: we had a group deported after they had been in a car crash, a chase by the border patrol – one boy was in a wheelchair, his bones broken from his feet to his hip. Often we'll get one left behind by their brothers or sisters – two who made it and one who didn't, with everyone traumatised, and parents trying to get in touch from the USA. They sometimes think when they come here they're being arrested and going to jail. When the child is introduced to their parents or, more often, grandparents, they usually burst into tears. A few have so little to go back to that one or two older ones want to stay and work here; but most, by the time they get here, all they want to do is go home. So much that they often try to escape, break the windows at night to try and run for it.'

Most of the children, Ms Alessi explans, come from the south; then the bombshell: 'most of the kids from Sonora, from around here, are being used by the cartels as *burros* – donkeys – to carry drugs, some as young as thirteen. They cross over, know the territory and deliver the drugs, then try to hitchhike their way home and get caught. The Americans don't arrest them because they're minors, and the cartels know that. And some of them are doing and selling the drugs they run – it's a way of paying them.' Ms Alessi leaves us, with permission to talk without supervision to the children.

Two large recreation rooms off the courtyard house boys and girls respectively. In each, about a hundred faces traverse the spectrum of youthful emotion. Some are puckish, full of mischief; some are melancholy, even lachrymose. Some of the boys wear their courage – or their fear – behind an appearance of steadfastness, even aggression. Some of the girls wear theirs behind a mask of exuberance, while others wear their distrust out loud. The boys speak first, with César Magaña cursing the *pocho* – Mexican American – *migra* agent who 'kicked me in the back' when he was apprehended after two days walking. His father in North Carolina had paid the *coyote* who had taken him from Tabasco and 'things had been going well, until we were chased by the *migra*, first in a truck and then, when we dived into the trees on the mountainside, they were on foot. They caught us, kicked and punched us and said "that's for making us run, *mojades!*" They were all *pochos*, apart from one, and the *gringo* wasn't kicking!' Next to César is Marcos – aged sixteen from Campeche, with a heavier air, speaking more softly. 'After three days, we were desperate,' he says, his gaze far off. 'By then, we were looking for the *migra* to get caught, looking for them to save us. My father had paid the *coyote*, and I had to pay no more; I was told to follow everything the man called Zepeda said; I had to meet him off the bus in Altar. But Zepeda was a liar; he didn't know the way and got lost. They got us on a night it rained so hard you couldn't see in front of you. One day, nothing to drink; another day, wet through. When the border patrol caught us, they were kind – they knew we were pleased to see them. The older men ran, but we walked towards the border patrol, because all we wanted was go home.'

Two boys sit silently, more shy than taciturn it turns out, not because of us but of the others. Xochitl, sixteen, and Itzel, a year younger, are not the usual Mexican mixed *Mestizo*: they are pure Aztec, from Veracruz. Everything is '*más o meno*', they say, more or less. Do they want to go home? More or less. Was it frightening in the desert? More or less. Then Xochitl adds: 'It was okay, until our friend was gone. Then the guide was gone. There were eight of us left, and we didn't know where we were, in the dark, in the night. After they found us, they brought three of us here, but I have no idea what happened to the others.' 'I don't care about Texas any more,' says another boy, Adan, aged fourteen, from San Luis Potosí. 'I don't want a rich blonde *gringa* from Dallas. I thought I did – it's what I imagined, that and my mama and papi, but I was wrong. I don't care about anything else now – I don't even want to see my parents in Texas – I just want to go home.'

A show of hands is hardly a scientific way to gauge opinion, but sometimes it suffices, and when asked whether they wanted to go home or try again, only one hand out of about eighty is raised in favour of the latter. This is Gabriel, aged seventeen, from Cacahoatán in Guatemala, with no return ticket. It is strange he is here; the DIF in theory only administers to Mexican citizens, those from further south being regarded with greater contempt than Mexicans in the USA. 'I came on the train,' he says. 'All the way, with my uncle. In the south of Mexico, they robbed us, and again in Nogales; the first time was Mexicans, the second time was Salvadoreans. This town was our last chance, my uncle said. And after a day, the helicopter came over us – we scattered. I lost my uncle, and ended up here. The lady who processed me said not to tell anyone where I am from, and that I could leave with some others, and try again. I have to try again.' He is seventeen, but seems either twelve or thirty-five he is so strong-willed, but so poignantly and utterly alone and a child.

'This place is the middle of nowhere,' says Arturo from Hidalgo. 'I hate it. They give you two tortillas a day and some water. That's it. They don't let us play football in case we try to escape; and we wait – wait for them to find our relatives and for our relatives to raise the money to get us home.' I had naively assumed that because the poetically named *Camino a Casa* was a government agency, the government might pay a bus fare to see these children home. 'Of course the government doesn't pay,' scolds a girl called Magdalena from Chiapas, and with a wisdom and humour she really should not possess at fifteen: 'The government only pays if you're in a coffin.' And at last, everyone laughs, a hollow but badly needed laugh, and we talk about football and the inevitable rivalry of *El Clásico* – felt as keenly by the girls as the boys – between Chivas and Club América.

'America' is a beautiful word, especially when it is the name of a child. And the group marooned in the purgatorial care of *Camino a Casa* in Nogales is sustained by its collective fascination with, and care for, the shelter's most heart-searing resident: America, aged four. In any other life she would be headed for the stage; as it is, heaven knows what awaits her. The little girl's parents are living in Florida, and she was sent across the border by relatives in her native Acapulco, ostensibly to join them. However, Ms Alessi had explained, 'the *coyotes* took her to the border with two others, aged five and six, in the middle of the night, sent them through the fence and pointed to a house, saying: "If you follow the lights and go into that house, your parents will come and pick you up." They did, the children walked up to the door, and the Americans called the border patrol. They were dumped at 4 a.m. in the deportation pound on the Mexican side, alone, with no explanation or adult present. They're not supposed to deport minors after 6 p.m., but in practice they don't care. So we went to get them, and America is still here while we try to locate her family.' This has taken two weeks so far, without success.

There is a teenaged boy called Francisco and a girl called Lizabeth who are very proud of their special role in minding America. 'Things can happen to a little girl that she cannot understand,' says Francisco, horribly perceptive. 'And we cannot let you talk to her without our presence,' affirms Lizabeth, thirteen, with authority. 'I want to go back to Acapulco,' cheeps little America, 'because there is a fairground there, and my mother [that would be her grandmother] has my lovely pair of boots there, in the *Calle de Chile*.' The child starts blowing kisses down the corridor. 'Then I got trapped,' she says suddenly. 'I went through the gate to play, and the men came. But now I'm going and after the fair my mother and me will sit and watch Amy on television.'

There is a sudden frisson along the corridor, the sun glinting through the frosted glass ceiling and firing a ricocheted shaft of light across the tiled floor. Amy is a character in a TV soap the children know from home, and they want America to sing, as she does. One of her favourite songs is by Danna Paola, who plays the title role of Amy in the hit Telenovela *Amy La Niña de la Mochila Azul*. America walks towards the shaft of sunlight and stands for a moment, gathering the words in her head, eyes closed. Then she opens them, takes a deep breath and sings: *Fiesta, Fiesta/La vida es fiesta/Escucha tu Corazón/Fiesta, fiesta/Que poco cuesta/Dar un poquito de amor.*

How little is that, to give a little love. Then America stops; everyone claps; she smiles a big, sunny grin, claps herself too, and bursts into tears.

The Business End of a .12-Gauge — Barrett and Morgan's War

The Gadsden Hotel in Douglas, Arizona, is grander than it probably needs to be nowadays. But that doesn't stop one catching one's breath walking into the lobby, to behold those marble columns, that imperious winding stairway, and walls echoing with the sounds of Wild West war along the borderline. Built in 1907, the hotel bears the name of Lieutenant James Gadsden, president of the South Carolina Canal and Rail Road Company, rabid Southern nationalist, advocate of States' Rights and slavery. Later, he became US ambassador to Mexico, and secured the purchase in 1853 of all land, including southern Arizona, south of the Gila River, for the United States from Mexico. The purchase was a territorial postscript to the Treaty of Guadalupe Hidalgo of 1848 which ended the Mexican–American war, though some around would say that the war was still being fought, for the borderline here is fraught with tension. In late March 2010, a respected rancher called Rob Krentz was shot dead by Mexicans coming through his land, fuelling rage as well as grief, and strengthening the hand of a growing anti-smuggling, counter-migration vigilante movement. A month later, the Arizona state governor Jan Brewer signed into law a measure enabling police to stop and demand that immigrants produce documents proving their status as legal residents, on pain of arrest and deportation if there were none. The measure was eyed by other border states with a view to similar legislation, and polarised Arizona. Thousands of protesters took to the streets of Phoenix and Tucson and sheriffs for two counties, Pima and Yuma, said they would not enforce the new law.

But the border road has now led us east of Tucson and Pima Counties, into hard-line Cochise County, via the gun stores and bike repair shops of Sierra Vista, a vigilante stronghold, in the wild south-east corner of Arizona, where rancher Krentz was shot dead. Here lie two neighbouring towns, both of them former copper-mining centres: Bisbee, a hip, liberal outpost and arts centre, and gritty Douglas with its Gadsden Hotel, built before Arizona became a state on St Valentine's Day 1912, and while Geronimo was still leading troops of the Apache against both Americans and Mexicans. For all the quick-draw legends and pomp of the hotel's surroundings, Butch Barrett dresses casually in the searing heat; he wears shorts and a star-spangled baseball cap for our appointment in the lobby. Barrett was for decades a customs special agent in this corner of Arizona, riding horseback and fighting regular hand-to-hand shoot-outs with narco traffickers from Agua Prieta over the border. During his time patrolling this land, the territory between Nogales and Arizona's eastern border with New Mexico had become known as 'Cocaine Alley', such was the volume of white powder coming through from Agua Prieta.[1] To Barrett and a partner of his called Lee Morgan, this country was both home and castle.

Not many stories like those of Barrett and Morgan's war get to be told first-hand any more, in the days of high-tech border policing, with sensors and virtual fencing. But Lee Morgan set it out in a memoir called *The Reaper's Line*, which tells it like this: 'The outlaw took aim with his Blazer and went for Miller's plump, round silhouette. The agent dropped the spikes and took aim at the driver with a .12-gauge pump shotgun. Looking down the business end of the .12-gauge convinced the smuggler he was about to commit a grave mistake.'[2]

Morgan's book is the best action movie never made about the border: a latter-day high-noon Western set largely at midnight, because Morgan was in the thick of the nascent years of the narco war, which he saw coming a decade away. After graduating from Border Patrol Academy in 1975, Morgan was initially stationed in Douglas, but worked across America and the Caribbean in the immigration service's anti-drug task force before returning as a customs special agent in 1987. After which he and Barrett fight perpetual, total war on two fronts: against their quarry, the smugglers, and against what they call 'REMFs' – rear echelon mother fuckers – who get paid by the taxpayer to push pens in Washington and throughout the bureaucracy. 'What did I learn from my first gunfight as a federal agent?' Morgan writes rhetorically.

'Well, I learned that as usual the REMFs are wrong and the grunts know what they need in the field to get the job done.'

For this book, access to the current border patrol was, sadly, declined by Washington – so what better than to hear it like it was? As a special agent out of uniform, Morgan teamed up with Barrett and another agent called Allan Sperling on horse patrol. Both Morgan and Barrett were Vietnam veterans, though, says Morgan, while 'I've seen my share of hell when the shit hit the fan in the jungle, Butch saw some really BAD shit. Try to imagine floating in a body of water so thick with bloated bodies that you actually had to lance the corpses with a bayonet so they would sink.' Back from fighting the Vietcong, Morgan's and Barrett's enemies were the Agua Prieta cartel, allied to Ciudad Juárez, and Morgan's favourite horse was called Cougar. Through the turn of the decade, Morgan and Barrett ride against the bareback narcos, fight shoot-outs against them and apprehend them in unarmed combat; it is late twentieth-century Wild West desert war, as thrilling as it is ominous of what is to come in the twenty-first: 'I yelled to the asshole that I would blow his face off if he brought the barrel of his rifle up. I hate to cap a guy if I don't absolutely have to. God-fearingly correct in his decision, the outlaw dropped his assault weapon to the floorboard and raised his hands above his head.' During an incursion by Mexican soldiers protecting the cartel: 'let me be perfectly clear about this: these armed black uniforms were not patrolling Mexico. They had invaded our country and were conducting military combat manoeuvres on US soil.' As for the narcos themselves: Morgan respects the mules carrying *la merca* – the dope. 'You know how those mountain-climbing pro dudes use the picks and pitons to ascend a rocky mountain bluff that goes straight up? Mickey Mouse crap! We've seen mules go up the same incline using only their bare fingers and tennis-shoe-covered toes.' On the narcos themselves, however: 'Being the chickenshits these behind-the-border backshooters are, any show of superior force causes them to run like scared jack rabbits being chased by coyotes.' And: 'But the Mexican outlaw wasn't quite done yet. The son of a bitch fought Butch tooth and nail while he kept hitting the accelerator with the tip of his cowboy boot. The truck kept surging and spinning in a tight circle like a wounded duck with one wing shot off.'

Not only did Butch Barrett's son get married on the magnificent staircase at the Gadsden Hotel, he also joined the Border Patrol recently, 'and I'm mighty proud of that', says his father, for all Barrett's misgivings about the service these days. His were 'days when you had to provide your own horses and saddles', he recalls, 'until the REMFs were persuaded by a couple of successes we had that we deserved us a team of four. But it worked – tracking 'em down on horseback proved very successful. We knew the terrain, we knew how to get 'em and we got 'em. It was another world back then: pre 9/11, pre-technology, pre Generation X and Generation Me before it – but more heroes, I'm tellin' ya. Yes, they'll laugh at you now, but we did it for God and country. Some did it for the highs and the adrenalin, but they likely pulled out from the sheer terror of having someone carrying a load and trying to kill you to get it through.' We sit in armchairs at an old, low wooden table. There is no tea, coffee or beer, just talk and a big empty lobby around us. 'The kids now, they do it mostly for the money, and because it's a job. I don't blame them, but it's just an existence nowadays – in our time, you had to prove yourself, produce bodies, getcha hands dirty and take 'em on. The dope smugglers project this image of being the macho man, but they cry like babies when you got 'em in handcuffs.'

But, says Barrett, 'I still talk to some of the young agents. They're no fools, and they get into situations when they need a little old-school advice, particularly when it comes to dealing with the people with their feet under desks. That was the only mistake I made, to get promoted behind a desk! The problem is what it always was: the REMFs in Washington DC. They'd come down in my day, look around for fifteen minutes with the press secretary, and we'd offer them a tour out with us, good to go. But they never even sat in a car with us.'

Butch is proud of Douglas, but unsure about what that frontier has done to Douglas of late. 'If you go to City Hall and look at the portraits of the mayors, you'll find that the white guys suddenly stop and after a certain time, around 1980 when Phelps Dodge [the copper mining company] up and went, they're all Mexican. Well, I don't say I have a problem with that, except if the town is Mexican, then there's going to be a lot of them in the smuggling trade, you know, part of the picture. There's going to be a situation where you have a guy in law enforcement and his cousins are across the border. And he's going to get a call saying "hey, we'd like you to join the customs service and do as you're told", let this car through or turn a blind eye there. And that's gonna be said by your cousin on the other side, and it's going to be an offer you can't refuse. And that has happened, because I know it has.' There was a customs officer, says another agent, who was passed by the same pretty girl every day: '*¡Hola!*' she would say, smiling and waving, until, to script, he asked for her number. After a little rendezvous and one or two drinks, a car load of men arrived at the supposedly discreet bar with a briefcase containing $250,000 in cash, put it on the table and made a suggestion: take the money, or we call your wife – now. All he had to do is what he'd always done: wave back, and wave her through, only now he was in – and once in, there's no way out.[3]

Long before the Obama administration finally found a buzzword to admit the United States' 'co-responsibility' for Mexico's drug war, Lee Morgan wrote: 'Maybe we, as the decadent, arrogant *Norteamericanos*, should start questioning our own insatiable appetite for drugs.' He was also on top of the smuggling of guns to the south, when the matter was taboo: after one terrifying 'surreptitious excursion' to Agua Prieta, a man whom Morgan was trailing was arrested with 'enough ammo to start a small war', which indicated, along with Morgan's progressive seizures of weaponry from China, that the business ends of .12-gauge shotguns would soon be superceded by those of AK-47, AR-15 and TEC-9 machine guns. No one saw the narco war coming, writes Morgan, because: 'We have an entertainment and media industry that thrives on keeping our vegetating minds stuffed with compost . . . so there's no real need to think for yourself in America.' And his conclusion: 'The border is a line of barbwire and spiked pillars that seems only to serve as a symbol of one man's futile lifetime endeavours, his attempts to define Mother Nature's boundaries, as well as man's national claims to a piece of what no human can ever call his own possession. Men will always be willing to fight and die in follies of nationalism, but they will never be able to continually control their own borders.'

Morgan and I meet further along the road, in San Antonio on the river walk opposite the Alamo which, we note with amusement, has become Texas' leading tourist attraction and icon of the Texan revolution against Mexico, despite having fallen to the Mexican army during the famous battle of 1836, with all but two of its defenders killed. In smart casuals, he looks younger, and certainly trimmer than the rugged desert rat on the inside cover of his book, clutching binoculars.

'We were wild,' says Morgan. 'We were outta control, socially unacceptable. But we were effective. Now, it's all just policy, policy, policy and orders from the top. The good people are getting thrown out, pushed aside − "do it our way or get out of our way" − and it's been like that ever since we told 'em this was coming, that the drug lords were getting serious, like these people in Washington don't want to be told the truth. They don't understand the drug lords, they don't get it that you can't deal with them. Look at the things they do to people! You can't offer 'em a better job because they don't want to be in any other business unless it's another form of crime.'

And there is a surprise by the Alamo. Morgan and Barrett had a mentor in the customs service, a man called James Rayburn − the team leader, a slightly older man who knew every grain of sand in the desert and taught Morgan a few of the tricks in the book. Rayburn has joined us, for a chat by the river. They are two of the best special agents their service ever had, but have trouble figuring out the silly computerised machine that distributes timed tickets in the parking lot, for display on the dashboard of the truck they have driven into town from hill country. These men don't like to be controlled, and good for them. Both men smoke, and enjoy their cigarettes. Morgan and I order Mexican Dos Equis beer; Rayburn wants a Bud Lite. Rayburn's expertise, among many things, was to run informants in Mexico − people regarded, says Morgan, by defence attorneys as 'Judases' and by prosecutors as 'a painful but necessary black plague'.

On 2 July 1988, the Clinton administration signed an accord with the Mexican presidency of Ernesto Zedillo that became known as the 'Brownsville Agreement'. The agreement obliged US law-enforcement agencies − principally customs, the DEA and FBI − to notify, through the embassy in Mexico City, the Mexican attorney general's office of their undercover investigations and informants. Intelligence agencies, markedly the CIA, were exempt. 'For us border narcs, it was like being the only blind son of a bitch at a poker table,' objects Morgan. 'Everyone is reading your cards but you!' In practice, the accord meant that a Mexican government deeply infiltrated by narco cartels was being informed who the snitches were, to disastrous effect in Douglas alone, and on informers run by Morgan. One of whom was infiltrating a syndicate manufacturing and smuggling methamphetamine. But after being informed by their government who the informer was, the smugglers avoided a sting Morgan had prepared for them at the local Motel 6 in Douglas. Instead, the informer became one of three out of the four undercover spies working for Morgan across the border in Agua Prieta to be gunned down soon after the Brownsville Agreement.

The events recalled the cornerstone murder of DEA agent Kiki Camarena in 1985, to which James Rayburn, sipping on his Bud, has a connection. Rayburn had controlled an informer, Benito Suárez, who was commandeered by US customs to look for Camarena, kidnapped on instructions of the Godfather himself, Miguel Félix Gallardo. But when Suárez arrived in Sinaloa, the Gallardo clan appeared suspicious of his timely return from Arizona. He and a fellow Mexican informer based in Phoenix were taken to a private house in Jalisco where Suárez was tortured and beaten, and believed he heard Camarena's voice in an adjoining room. Afterwards, the two men were driven to a cliff edge, and Suárez put in the driver's seat while his friend's face was crushed by the butt of an AK-47, and Suárez was whiplashed at the base of his skull. But as the car was pushed over the cliff to the bottom of the canyon, Suárez was miraculously thrown from it, and survived. Rayburn did all he could to have his man rescued out of Mexico and carried across the Bridge of the Americans from Ciudad Juárez into El Paso. 'The last time I saw him when he went hunting for Camarena,' says Morgan, who took turns with Rayburn driving Suárez to physiotherapy, he had been a 'healthy young man with fire in his eyes and a zest in his heart for life. But what met me at his apartment door on my first visit was the pitiful remains of a man I didn't recognise.' Suárez died of AIDS in 1998, a secret he preferred to keep rather than be treated, after being repeatedly sodomised during torture.

'It was the beginning of the end,' reflects Rayburn. 'After the Brownsville Agreement, it became almost impossible to do an effective undercover operation; it became harder to deal with Washington than to fight the criminals. When you go undercover, the REMFs hate it while you're doing it, then go on TV and claim all the credit when you pull the outlaws in. Nothing substitutes human intelligence and infiltration, and that's something we're losing, just as the drug lords are gaining it. While it gets harder for us to infiltrate them, they'll use relatives and friends to infiltrate us, they'll call a cousin on the US side and tell 'em: "Hey, we need you to work in border law enforcement – for US", and there ain't no saying no to them. We've seen it happen; we arrested one of our own customs people smuggling cocaine for a drug boss called Yolanda Molina. They told us to our faces, years ago: "if we can't beat you with weapons, we'll infiltrate you" – I had that told to my face by a man I arrested. We reported this, but no one listened. And sure enough, next we knew, the assistant special agent in charge of Nogales had been working for them all along.' They were refering to Richard Padilla Cramer, another decorated Vietnam veteran who served three decades in law enforcement, locking up corrupt officials, busting drugs and promoted to become attache for immigration and customs enforcement at the US embassy in Mexico City. By which time, according to the prosecution case at the time of writing, as Cramer waits to stand trial, Cramer was selling his knowledge to the cartels, a treachery dating back to his days as head of ICE in Nogales, Arizona. 'This,' said Rene Andreu, former assistant head of the ICE customs division in Tucson, 'is impossible to grasp.'[4] 'We didn't believe it,' hoots Morgan, 'must've talked with him a thousand times – all that time, he was one of them.' Cramer has yet to stand trial and has denied all wrongdoing.

'When they called us cowboys,' Morgan ponders, 'it was intended as an insult. I was told I had a John Wayne attitude – well, what in hell's wrong with that? Dammit, the smugglers sure have a John Wayne attitude: they live like smugglers and expect to die like smugglers, and we were the same. You gotta know your enemy, you gotta know his terrain better 'n he does. The way we did the job was to get inside the smuggling organisation and hit it head-on. We were working with the inside view of how they work, who they are, what they do – get to know the basics, and the pressures they're under. That's what I try to tell the young guys now: get to know 'em, don't look down on them – but we could never do it now; I just wouldn't be allowed to work the way we did. We were in the right place at the right time.'

Since it is a beautiful afternoon by the river, another round of beers seems in order, and we turn the conversation to a favourite subject: reading tracks, or 'cutting for sign', as it is known in the trade, a skill that precedes even mankind's presence in the desert, where covering and detecting tracks are everything. The Red Fox walks the desert in such a way that its hind paws fall near or directly onto its fore prints – known in zoology as a 'direct register' – obliterating the forepaw tracks; it changes coat with the seasons for both insulation and camouflage, taking on what is called a 'dark morph' when necessary.[5] The art of covering and 'cutting' sign was perfected by Native Americans for hunting animals, and latterly by law enforcement for hunting humans. There is a special unit of the border patrol on the Tohono O'odham reservation called the 'Tracking Wolves', cutting for sign. And of course, sign-cutting was perfected by men like Morgan, Rayburn and Barrett. You need to know, says Morgan, the difference between a chevron and a starburst imprint, when a mat of some kind had been attached to the shoes, when footprints have been swept away by the last person in a convoy, walking backwards and brushing the terrain, as tribal raiders have done ever since this arid land was inhabited. And to read the sign that tells you exactly when these movements occurred, for your quarry may be near, or too far; the kind of thing you learn from whether the track of a bug runs over or beneath a footprint.

Back in the lobby of the Gadsden Hotel, Butch Barrett had recalled the romance of sign-cutting. 'It was something handed down to us country boys,' he says. 'My father used to take me hunting animals when I was twelve years old, and the first thing I learned was how to read their tracks. So I took that knowledge, and applied it to hunting people. The real hunt starts when you get off the roads: working out when a footprint isn't a real footprint, when they've made a mistake trying to lay a false trail – that's something the best of the young 'uns who are interested in getting results love to ask us about. "Back in your day," they say, "when you used to cut for sign . . ." and they ask us how it was done.'

By the river, Morgan confesses: 'I'm still always looking for tracks. Habitually, every time I go for a walk. Fact is: it worked. All these sensors and gadgets, they break, they malfunction. [He imitates a dumb voice on the end of the phone:] "I'm sorry, the system's down."

And they can lie. But the ground can't lie. A piece of fibre caught by a cactus can't lie. The smallest shift in the sand on terrain you know can't lie. Just like a border fence can hold you up for twenty minutes, but it can't arrest you – it don't have no John Wayne attitude. Unlike the drug lords, watching all this and laughing.' They might also be laughing at a report by the General Accounting Office filed in August 2009 finding the Secure Border Initiative launched by President George Bush in 2005 to be running seven years behind the schedule it set for putting the latest gizmos in place, and running millions of dollars over budget because of maintenance bills. The 'virtual fence' system designed by Boeing had 'fallen prey to weather and mechanical problems', said the report by the GAO's Richard M. Stana. The total bill will come to $6.5 billion over twenty years, he estimated. During the same week as the report's publication, the government extended Boeing's contract for another year.[6]

The cartels will also, says Morgan, 'be wondering how all this'll enhance their ability to infiltrate us deeper, corrupt the system and keep the money flowing around'. He pauses. 'Kinda strange, ain't it, how Washington got all this technology, but never goes after the money – billions of dollars of it? Billions of dollars moving around the US banks, and going back into Mexico. They never go after it. That ever strike you as strange?'

The heresy has been spoken: Morgan, who saw the war coming, now wonders about the money-go-round that circles between Mexico and the United States, just as the late sun aims its last, deep rays against the Alamo. Further along the border road from Morgan, Barrett and Rayburn's terrain of eastern Arizona, an anthropologist at the University of Texas, El Paso, Howard Campbell, suggests that we should try re-labelling the narco cartels, because of the money-go-round, calling them the Sinaloa-Phoenix-Denver cartel, the Juárez-El Paso-Chicago cartel or the Gulf-Houston-Atlanta cartel, so as to more accurately reflect their sphere of influence. It is out across the desert towards Campbell's seat of El Paso and its twin city of Ciudad Juárez that the road now beckons. But first, one last round with the horsemen of the John Wayne attitude, a toast to the reaper and his line in the sand.

CHAPTER FOUR

Urban Frankenstein

'If Juárez is a city of God, that is because the Devil is scared to come here' – *street* dicho, *or saying.*

'Ciudad Juárez: right now I'd say it's the safest city in Mexico' – *Lt. Col. Jorge Alberto Berecochea, upon taking over the 6th police district, March 2009*[1]

Of all the enthralling landscapes in America, none is more complicated in its awful beguilement than that southward from the balcony outside room 262 on the upper floor of the La Quinta Motel on Geronimo Avenue in El Paso, Texas – with a sixpack, a lime, hot salsa and bag of tortilla chips for company. In mid-distance runs the border. And beyond the boundary lies the factory smoke, the sea of lights, the lure and menace of this most charismatic and daunting of cities: Ciudad Juárez. While El Paso is the United States' third safest city of its size, with only sixteen homicides in 2008, Juárez is currently the most dangerous city in the Americas and, by some counts, the world. The scene is especially cogent at dusk, when fleets of cast-off American school buses have done their rounds taking home the day shift in the *maquiladora* sweatshop factories, so that a layer of grey, dust stirs around and settles on the lanes and the labyrinth of outlaw electrical wires supplying the *colonia* shacks.

To get here, the road from eastern Arizona has crossed the border state of New Mexico on the US side, and western Chihuahua, on what many Americans living on the frontier still call 'Old Mexico' when wishing to convey a rugged affection. The small town of Columbus, New Mexico, faces Palomas, Chihuahua, across an expanse of otherwise wild and empty land populated by ghosts from the Mexican revolution – the Pancho Villa park is nearby. Alima McMillan lives in remote Columbus but enjoyed her work across the border at a medical centre in Palomas, where mayor Estanislao

García was kidnapped and shot dead the week after Ms McMillan and I met in September 2009. Ms McMillan had already decided that the eruption of violence in the town a short walk from where we had lunch in a café should prevent her from carrying on her regular surgeries there. Quite often, victims of the violence would appear at the border crossing in need of help, like a teenaged boy the previous week, who had been beaten, shot, doused with diesel fuel and set on fire. Palomas had been a place to which visitors from New Mexico went regularly to get teeth fixed and buy cheap medicines until new arrivals in town, says McMillan, 'put the fear of God into everyone and started clearing the territory'. Palomas was turned quite suddenly into a three-way battlefield between the army, the Juárez and Sinaloa cartels, now a place in which one family remains dominant, among the silence, the emptied houses, new narco villas, and the army Blackhawk helicopters overhead, 'flying their noses right up to the line', says Ms McMillan, 'to blow a bit of Mexican dust into Columbus'. From Columbus, the road clings to the border through a village called Malpais – bad country – a suburb of El Paso called Sunland Park, which is nonetheless still in New Mexico, then across the Texas state line, but cheek by jowl with the rusting iron fence, the barbed wire and the colonia of Anapra, which tumbles down into Ciudad Juárez, just yards away from the highway into downtown El Paso.

The scene from El Paso across the border is all the more surreal on the night of the *Grito* – the cry – commemorating Mexico's independence from Spain in 1810. This is the United States, but on a stage at the northern end of San Jacinto Square, a full mariachi band launches a night of festivity to precede the day commemorating that on which the Mexican nation was born 199 years before. '*Viva La Independencia!*' shouts the singer, in a long, very tight cocktail dress from which she bursts. '*Viva!*' answers back the crowd of several thousand families, cuddling teenagers, and old ladies with Indian faces from Mexico's deep south, wrinkled with hard work, smiling beneath the round brims of their hats. '*Viva México!*' shouts the singer, the *Grito* – the cry – itself. '*Viva!*' replies the crowd as the band strikes up the national anthem, whereupon the crowd stands still, hands across the chest, clutching the heart, here in Old El Paso. Long lines wait for food served from stalls – sweet fried churros, tacos and shredded beef, though the longest queue approaches the sign promising 'Turkey Breast, Bratwurst, Hamburgers'. Other stalls have games: pop the balloon and win a 3-foot-high plaster cherub for the garden, or a big cuddly gorilla.

Down a side street, a lone van with flashing lights advertises 'Sodas, Aguas, Gatorades', and plays a tune more disturbing than jolly. As well he might, given what is happening over the border in Ciudad Juárez. The crowd of some 10,000 in El Paso can hear its counterpart across the river four times the size, the whooping and music that happens only rarely in a city that lives under effective, self-imposed, curfew. At 11.00, fireworks fill the skies both sides of the border, bursting with a sound like gunfire – thereby concealing the fusillades of murderous, real gunfire across Juárez at exactly that moment. In fact, some of the witnesses to the killing of ten people in a drug rehabilitation centre thought the rasp of AK-47s was a part of the celebrations.

The killers burst in though the gateway of the *Anexo de Vida* – annexe of life – rehabilitation centre in the heart of Barrio Azul, a poor *colonia* of little streets, and threw a grenade into the first room on their right, occupied by a sixteen-year-old guard. Inside the room next morning, a mattress is splattered with blood, the floor next to it saturated, but the teenager seems to have made it through the door before falling to the ground where his workout weights still lie. The killers have soaked his blood into the soles of their heavy boots and stamped it around in horribly clear footprints – that anyone who cared to solve the crime might examine, only no one ever seems to solve the crimes.

The cement and whitewashed walls of Barrio Azul are staked out with the blue graffiti tag of the local *pandilla*, or gang, the BAZUL, to claim the *colonia* and remember: '*In Memoriam, Zaiko y Nordiano*', presumably two street-fighting 'brothers' who died 'defending' it. A dog rests in the stinking trash strewn along Via Juan Escutia. A burned-out building is likewise tagged by the BAZUL, next door to which a neat pink house with flower pots on the window sills flies the flag for Independence Day. Turning into Via Jaime Nuño, there is the entrance to the *Anexo de Vida*. The words '*Para Enfermos De Drogadiccion y Alcoholismo*' are written in careful letters on the white paint – for the sick from drug addiction and alcoholism. Only there is no '*vida*' in this place now, chains on its padlocked gates, and a black tarpaulin hiding the aftermath of the horror unleashed just as the mayor of Juárez, José Reyes Ferriz, rang the bell and shouted the *Grito* last night. The previous week, seventy-five people had been killed in Juárez, including one man beheaded and another hung to die by handcuffs from a chain-link fence. And this was only a few days since 3 September, when seventeen people were killed at another rehab clinic, the *Aliviane*, a few blocks from city hall and the downtown bridge to El Paso. Black-clad gunmen had burst into the *Aliviane* and lined up the young male inmates against a wall before summarily executing them. The father of one of the dead said that his son had completed his rehabilitation, but went back to *El Aliviane* for prayer meetings.

We clamber onto the roof and down into the courtyard of the *Anexo de Vida*, still a mess thirteen hours after the killing, the hiding and flight. Sneakers are discarded in piles, crates are upturned and furniture scattered across the ground – following the painted signs to the '*Ruta de Evacuación*'. Off the courtyard are the rooms that were death chambers overnight, and still stink of the sickly-sweet stench of sticky blood which congeals in pools around us – wrapped in the other scents of what was until last night a rehabilitation centre run by poor people for people below poverty: stale sweat, rotting broccoli piled up in boxes, and the ashes of a fire on which dinner was being cooked. It does not take a policeman to work out what happened, only there is little sign of any police work, and no question of guarding the crime scene, or preventing us from contaminating it, nor the young boys who follow us inside, scavenging for souvenirs and things left behind to sell: medical drugs, tools, pairs of shoes, packets of cookies.

After the killing of the teenaged guard, the carnage then divides into two directions, along each side of the courtyard. To their left, the death squad headed towards the room of the centre's director, who seems to have made it outside, where a pond of his blood putrifies on the cement. Next were the quarters of the vice-director, a woman whose room is a pitiless sight: blood splattered across her floral bed spread, and rushing to the floor beside it where she seems to have been raked with bullets, then horrible smears where she appears to have collapsed onto her sofa beneath the window. Now, two boys play and cast their eyes over the ransacked drawers, taking two baseball caps. The dead woman's handbag lies on an armchair – it contains Christian magazines and a paperback guide to sacred sites in the Holy Land. Her CD collection is scattered on the floor – *Metal En Rosas*, a compilation of Guns 'n' Roses, and Radiohead. Curiously, only a single bullet casing lies on the floor; perhaps the children have taken the rest. Or maybe even the police.

The assassins moved past the main dormitory, in which mattresses still lie, and posters line the wall warning that '*La Adicción Es Una Enfermedad*'. And in this room a man now appears, wearing a Dallas Cowboys cap, returning to pick up the set of tools and shoes he left behind in the flight last night. 'I used to sleep over there, at the end. It happened about eleven o'clock,' he testifies. 'We were watching the boxing on TV. We heard the explosion, then the shooting, and hid under the mattresses at the end there. The whole thing took about two minutes.' How were they dressed? He doesn't remember. Why did they do this? 'I have no idea. The people who ran this centre did it just by themselves, and we came by ourselves, after they had taken us off the streets. We never received any threats, and we never threatened anyone. We hid nothing from the *narcotraficantes*, and we had nothing to hide from the *narcotraficantes*.' He breaks open a packet of biscuits, and eats. No, he will not give his name – '*Anónimo*', he insists – and no, no photograph. The death squad proceeded to the room at the far left-hand corner, where two beds are now empty, in between which is a pool of blood so thick that it is still sticky underfoot, thirteen hours later, its darker coating over the still congealing red glistening in the shaft of sunlight that penetrates the door.

Meanwhile, another squad of executioners continued on from the entrance up the courtyard's right flank, past a storage area, the '*Area de Fumar*' and cooking yard, where blackened pots hang in which soup would have been cooked, and a metal tub for washing clothes. The grate of the fire that warmed, well, the last supper, is still full of ash. The scene in the next small room suggests that the killers were looking for something – a mattress overturned and shot to shreds, but no sign of murder. In the far right corner, however, there is a brutal scene, in and outside the *Enfermeria* – the medical centre. In the courtyard is another pool of blood, and the wall is pitted with bullet holes. Whoever came to investigate the scene has scrawled '*CUERPO* I' – Corpse I – on a piece of paper placed on the ground. Inside the infirmary is a fearsome sight: a cupboard of medicines has been ransacked, with much of its contents left, and a closed door shot through with a bullet. There is a pool of blood by the door, but someone seems to have forced a desperate way out, like a trapped beast, for his blood is splattered all over the bullet-riddled wall outside and the metal door – ajar – is gnarled at the base, as he staggered and fell outside to become '*CUERPO* F'.

This room must have been a sanctuary of sorts: there are sports trophies and a bookcase with several editions of the same paperback Bible. This collection belonged to a man called José Ángel Torres, who obviously read, maybe even taught, English, for he had several copies of a volume called *Famous Christians*. He had potted cactus plants, a CD/cassette player and had just sipped at a plastic bottle of Diet Coke when his murderers arrived: it is about 7/8 full. To the rear of this hospital reception area is a bunk-bed, more copious blood, and a label reading '*CUERPO* H', next to a cabinet behind which is the doctor's stethoscope, on the floor. As we rummage around trying to recreate the crime, an SUV with blackened windows pulls up in the otherwise empty street outside the gate. Having climbed in, there is no quick way out – we're trapped. While it remains there, motionless, the flesh creeps with goose pimples for all the 35-degree heat, and one's vision blurs with fear. Then it purrs away.

Oddly, there are *CUERPO* F, H and I, but no *CUERPO* A, B, C, D, E or G. Either too much trouble or the kids had taken the labels as souvenirs. It doesn't matter – no one is going to look for the men wearing the boots that left further bloodied marks here in this corner. Although that is not what they are saying at the press conference in the Chihuahua state offices. 'We continue in our unrelenting work against the criminals,' affirms Patricia González, state prosecutor, with as little menace as hapless Rommel Moreno in Tijuana. 'We have shown the world that the struggle against organised crime is resolved and determined.' The new police chief is 'confident in our continuing investigations' into this latest carnage in yet another rehabilitation centre. Being the police chief of Juárez is work on a high wire. In February 2009, the narco traffickers decided that Chief Roberto Orduña, a retired army major who had been in office since May 2008, should go. After the purging of 300 police officers accused of working for the cartels, the narcos vowed to kill a police officer every forty-eight hours until Orduña resigned, starting with his operations director Sacramento Pérez Serrano and three of his staff. On 20 February, Orduña – who had lived in the police station for several months – quit his post and fled the city. He had replaced another chief who had also fled to live in El Paso. The mayor of Juárez, José Reyes Ferriz, has also received death threats, one in spring 2010 written on a severed pig's head, and keeps houses on both sides of the border. Interviewed in El Paso, he vows: 'I am not going to give in.' After inviting me to attend a summer cultural festival in Juárez, the mayor lists the things he needs, including an encrypted radio network so that he and the police do not have to constantly listen to the knocking sound followed by a *narcocorrido* with which the cartels hack in to announce that another officer has been or will be shot. Reyes Ferriz has been menaced by communiqués threatening to kill and decapitate him, even in El Paso, if he 'continues to help you know who', as one message put it. [2] The mayor and authorities decline to speculate on what the message – implying favour towards one cartel over another – could have meant. The governor of Chihuahua, José Reyes Baeza, was also the target of an assassination attempt: a car in his convoy was hit by machine-gun fire in February 2009. This time, one of the five gunmen, an ex-soldier, was arrested. These people preside over a city that was in January 2010 confirmed as having the world's highest homicide rate, by a group based in Mexico City called the Citizens Council for Public Security and Social Justice. The organisation calculated Juárez as killing 191 citizens per 100,000, way ahead of second-placed San Pedro Sula in Honduras with 119, New Orleans with 69, Medellin in Colombia with 62 and Cape Town with 60. [3] What characterises the killing in Juárez – or what fails to characterise it – is that no one knows who the killers are, or what they seek to gain from the killing. There is no reason why a 'drug lord', as newspapers call the cartel leaders, would want to liquidate ten wretched addicts in a rehab centre.

A week after the mayor shouted the *Grito* of independence, the black plastic sheet covering the gate of the *Anexo de Vida* in Barrio Azul has been removed. Inside, the blood has been whitewashed away with limestone; all that is left are bullet holes, mattresses, a Toronto Blue Jays cap and a newspaper from the day of the massacre (which would itself become the next day's front page). Its cover carries vividly illustrated coverage of the previous day's atrocity, but the paper is open at the pin-up spread showing a girl wearing a studded leather bikini, gagged at the mouth and bound in chains.

I had first crossed the Rio Grande into Juárez in 1981 for the same two reasons as anyone: the opening line of Bob Dylan's 'Just Like Tom Thumb's Blues' ('When you're lost in the rain in Juárez, and it's Eastertime too'), and to gawp at the salacity and audacity with which anything and everything was for sale, most of it carnal. And although the fleshpot, the dope-den and the Kentucky Bar in which Marilyn Monroe celebrated her divorce from Arthur Miller are certainly not the 'real' Juárez, they are not entirely deceptions either. Not because Juárez was superficially a playground of danger and vice for visitors but because it was and remains, above all, a market-place of the purest, unfettered kind. Juárez is a pioneer of, and monument to, economic deregulation. When I returned two decades later in 2001, Ciudad Juárez was ready to implode, and has now imploded. The implosion was not sudden, and its roots are deep. Juárez is at once a very singular city and one that encapsulates many things common to most other cities, though in extremis.

Juárez lies, so they say, *entre algo y la nada* – between something and nothing. It is a city of transit: a military, then road, then railway junction. A pivot of Spanish colonisation, it is the oldest settlement along what is now the border, established as *Misión de la Nuestra Señora de Guadalupe de los Mansos del Paso del Norte* in 1659, as Spanish explorers and then traders and missionaries prepared to cross what they called the *Rio del Norte* – what Mexicans now call the Rio Bravo and Americans the Rio Grande. ('*Mansós*' was a loaded and thoroughly unpleasant Spanish colonial word applied to those indigenous to the area, equivalent to 'the tamed', or 'meek' – the subjugated.) [4] Paso del Norte was a commercial junction and entrepôt for trade between New Spain and its province of New Mexico, then between independent Mexico and its northern reaches.

Until the international border was drawn across Juárez' face in 1848, along a line following the river as it takes a sharp eastward

turn, there was little on its northern left bank; only after the frontier was etched, was the city of El Paso established on the US side.
The metropolis on the Mexican right bank expanded as a market
centre for the surrounding cotton fields, but towards the end of the
nineteenth century had become urbanised by the arrival of
the Mexican Central northbound railway from Mexico City, which
connected Paso del Norte to the railroad network that had woven
an industrial infrastructure across the United States. The railway
brought hundreds of thousands of Mexicans to the doorstep of the
USA and the siding yards of the new American sister city and transport hub, so that a flow of goods and human traffic now connected
the border city to the industrialising United States. Letters sent from
El Paso by a German immigrant, Ernst Kohlberg, describe the border
city on the US side as 'nearly the end of the world, and the last of
creation', while in El Paso del Norte on the Mexican side, after a
reinforcement of cavalrymen, he had 'never seen so many cut-throats
together at one time'. The businessmen of the city, he noted, were
each extorted for $160 for the military's stay. 'The money will not
be lost if no other party gets control,' he wrote, but, 'if another
crowd gets the upper hand, they will declare the levying of the tax
as illegal and make us pay again.'[5] Whether Kohlberg's remark was
a more apposite prediction of the arrival of the PRI and PAN or
of the drug cartels is a matter of subjective judgement in hindsight.

In 1888, El Paso del Norte changed its name to Ciudad Juárez, in
honour of Benito Juárez, president of Mexico during the 1860s, who
had used the city as his headquarters. For a short while, the city even
acted as Mexico's provisional national capital, while Juárez's republican forces fought French intervention in Mexico. Juárez became a
capital city of a different kind during the Mexican revolution of
1910, of which it was the cradle. In the reconstruction that followed,
Juárez grew into a manufacturing base in its own right, making
copper wire. But the city's economic recovery from the revolutionary
violence was also due to a thriving trade in smuggling during the
prohibition of alcohol in the USA between 1919 and 1933. Juárez
meanwhile opened its doors to anyone wishing to come and consume
banned firewater rather than have it illegally delivered. And so the
city's reputation for opportunism in illicit markets was born, enhanced
by the shift, orchestrated by Ignacia '*La Nacha*' Jasso González, from

alcohol to heroin once the former was legalised over the river. *La Nacha* was dope queen of Juárez until the 1970s, by which time another wave of commerce was about to engulf the city with far greater impact: the *maquiladoras*. Hundreds of thousands of Mexicans would arrive in Juárez from the interior and desperately poor south, not to cross the border, but to work on it, in the proliferation of assembly plants that suddenly spread across the borderland like an invasion of bland low-rise Lego bricks. Initially, and for complex reasons of exploitation and demographics, the majority of those employed in these soul-destroying factories were young women. Juárez attracted more *maquiladoras* than any other city along the border, and therefore more workers, but did not create an infrastructure to house or shelter them, let alone keep them warm, light their shacks, or school their children. Let alone protect them from the nightmarish kind of metropolis that resulted from this smash 'n' grab of cheap labour. For the big landowners, markedly the Bermúdez family, after whom Juárez' biggest *maquiladora* park is named, and by whom it is owned, the industrial explosion was a boon beyond their wildest dreams. As the photographer who has captured this city's descent, Julián Cardona, puts it: 'The rich of the city had paid the politicians to raise taxes from the poor, in order to turn the place where they lived into an urban Frankenstein.'

I met Cardona long after first seeing his work: he had curated shocking, striking pictures for a book called *Juárez, The Laboratory of Our Future*, with a text by Charles Bowden, which I had bought in 1998. The volume proved even more pessimistically prescient than it dared presume when published. Juárez has indeed become, since then, the laboratory of our futures: a prototype for the post-political global economy and now also the arena for post-political war that that economy has produced in the city. A decade after *The Laboratory of Our Future*, Bowden would reflect, in another book about the city: 'Juárez is not behind the times. It is the sharp edge slashing into a time called the future . . . This is not some break-down of the social order. This is the new order'.[6]

Off a road leading south-east from the city – past road bridges built by the big landowners to connect their properties to the indus-trial parks – a dirt track turns into the scrub, towards the main cemetery. The concrete gateway and breeze-block walls are tagged by gangs when they come to bury their casualties: 'RIP Hulk' and 'RIP Oxxy'. 'RIP Onza' refers to someone named after the Spanish word for an ounce. In one corner is a section marked with white paint on a yellow wall: the *Fosa Común*, the common grave, stretching into the desert — mound after mound of earth beneath which lie those unidentified who died in Juárez without a name, though some have blank wooden name-boards, and others even have crosses and name plates, only those are bare too. Some, oddly, have flowers placed in memory — perhaps by a fellow patient at a rehab clinic, a fellow addict, or a family member who dare not give their murdered loved one a name. Traffic from over the horizon sends a distant hum of life from the road running through the army checkpoint and out into the desert, and a northerly wind scatters stray garbage and rustles the petals left in memory of the anonymous dead.

Hugo de León, proprietor of *Marmoleria Hugo*, one of the head-stone salesmen at the entrance of the cemetery, watches the funeral cortèges come and go, and reckons that 'about eighty per cent are to do with fighting over drugs — and too many of the dead are young. But some of the funerals still bring the mariachis and have a party.' Some are without names, he suggests, 'because the family couldn't afford to get the body from the morgue', and some 'because no one dared come forward to claim the body in case they got killed as well'. Of course, many of those buried in other parts of the cemetery do have names: 'We've had eighty bodies in the last five days, most from the violence, and most of them went over there, to the regular cemetery,' says de León. The walls to the 'regular cemetery' are tagged like the entrance: 'RIP Flozo 2008', and 'Sad Dog'. There are photographs on some of the headstones, like that of Miguel Ángel Juan Pavilla, who turns his firm, almost belligerent gaze out across the cemetery, having been killed the night of the *Grito* in 2009 — possibly one of the victims in the Barrio Azul rehab centre — just before his nineteenth birthday. He had a strong jaw, close-cropped hair and a blue zip jacket with 'Rocket' emblazoned across it. Someone has put a pink teddy bear on the grave of Luis Ramos Vega, killed on 20 June 2009, aged twenty, and picked out the letters TQM in pebbles — *Ti Quiero Mucho*, I miss you so. They have also left a bottle of Coca-Cola in which yellow and white flowers are placed, struggling to drink the soda into their stalks. Beyond the latest headstones, the gravediggers have done their hefty workload well: deep, fresh holes dug already, mounds of earth beside them, ready to welcome tomorrow's harvest.

If Juárez is a city of God, that is because the Devil is scared to come here, goes the old *dicho*, or saying. But Julián Cardona, braver than the Devil, remains in Juárez and is building himself a new home here, to which his Alsatian guard dog Caesar is only just acclimatising. In November 2008, Cardona and I had embarked on a forensic tour of the scene around the decapitated body suspended from the Bridge of Dreams on the day of the killing. The *narcomensaje* was itself a puzzle. 'I, Lázaro Flores, served my boss, the dog-fucker' – but that was not the dead man's name. Lázaro Flores is a prominent businessman – with no connection to this killing – who owns an event palace and narrowly escaped kidnapping allegedly by police officers working for *La Línea*. There was also written a menace to a named senior police officer, whose son was rumoured to have defected from *La Línea* to another trafficking cadre. Around the time of the execution, *La Línea* took to publishing lists of police officers it was about to execute on public *narcomensajes*. A list of twenty-six officers was posted at a dog-racing track just before Christmas 2008, above the bodies of four civilians, one of them wearing a Santa Claus hat.

The Bridge of Dreams overpass is officially called *Puente Rotario*, after the Rotary Club whose cogwheel emblem it bears, right next to where the body was hung. It is one of the city's busiest junctions, so there would have been no shortage of witnesses, especially at 4.30 a.m., with the morning tide of shift workers just then heading for the *maquiladoras*. Hundreds of people must have seen it done. How quickly and surreptitiously can a vehicle or possibly a small convoy of vehicles pull up on an overpass, unload a bloody victim, suspend him between the hoardings advertising Frutti Sauce and Comida Express fast food, tie and fasten the ropes, and hang the sheet bearing the message? The killers would have driven their getaway vehicle passing a late sports bar called Hooligans, the GMC car concession and a *maquiladora* belonging to Honeywell, which would have changed shifts while the headless body was being hung there.

The severed head of the victim, from Sinaloa, was found days later in the *Plaza des Periodistas* – Journalists' Square – at the foot of a statue of a boy hawking newspapers, a celebration of old Juárez's pride in itself as the cradle of a free press during the Mexican revolution. The message to journalists could not have been more articulate. A few days later, on 14 November 2008, one of the leading reporters on crime in Juárez, Armando Rodriguez of the local paper *El Diario* – who had reported on both the execution at the Bridge of Dreams and the discovery of the head beneath the statue – was shot dead while warming up his car. His eight-year-old daughter, whom he was taking to school, was in the passenger seat.[7]

'There's a lot of world-class business here,' says Cardona, as we pass the *maquiladoras* along the executioners' getaway route. 'And these worlds entwine, they're inseparable,' he explains. 'Young families come north, the girl gets a job in the *maquila* and the man is sexually potent but economically impotent. But he can earn money working for the narcos, part of a waiting labour force, and if he has a habit himself, which he probably has, he turns to crime and drug dealing to maintain it. So his addiction becomes an economic activity in the marketplace. If you keep things separate,' counsels Cardona, 'you will not understand what is happening in this city. Narco – *Maquiladoras* – Migration, that's the triangle, they're all related. And of course, there's narco money in the construction you see everywhere.' We pass the iron girder skeleton of a building that never seems to get finished; it was under construction when I was here seven years previously, and it still is. 'Narco installation art,' says Cardona. And later, a car with its windscreen shot out: 'the new Juárez window design'. In the waggish parlance of Juárez, recent architecture is categorised as being of the 'Early Narco', 'Mid Narco' or 'High Narco' periods. A series of arches proclaim the entrance to the upscale *Rincón San Marcos*, or St Mark's Corner, a gated community of villas inevitably re-christened *Rinconces de San Narcos* on the street. Around a pleasant green is arranged a quiet retreat of mansions, each more garish than the next, and advertisements for facial and cosmetic surgery. Here is a metaphor for the economy of power in Juárez. Outside some villas are vehicles marked with *maquila* corporate logos, and in the forecourt of others belonging to well-known drug barons, are powerful four-wheel drives with blackened windows – which are now illegal in Juárez, but what the hell.

* * *

In Juárez, the map of the cartel war frays. Any preconceptions about combat between narco-trafficking structures dissipate into a delta of violence. The chains of narco command have, apparently, collapsed. Something else is happening, something differently terrifying and more murderous. Before proceeding, there is a cautionary word from one of the more renowned Mexican journalists to call Juárez his home, Alejandro Paéz Varela, Editor of *El Universal*. Paéz is back home from Mexico City to greet a group of friends at a Cultural Centre called *Cafébreria* – coffeebookshop – and launch his novel, *Corazón de Kalashnikov*, about two women who become involved with narcos. The *Cafébreria* is an agreeable space, an oasis in Juárez, frequented by a slice of life in the city whose existence is scarcely acknowledged outside it: a beleaguered intelligensia with tortoiseshell spectacles and pony tails gathers together to talk on white sofas beneath an ironwork staircase. But even this is considered worthy of the cartels' attention. The *Cafébreria* is run by José Pérez Espino and his wife Claudia. José is a former reporter with *El Universal* and runs the Juárez alternative news website Almargen. In January 2010, he posted this message on his Facebook page: 'I am afraid for my life. I've been a journalist for 20 years and I've overcome many threats. A person has threatened me with death. I know that he could be an extortionist as there are very many of them. I just wanted to post this information here.'

Red wine is served after Paéz's reading from his book. Then Paéz tell me: 'Juárez has been ruled by the Juárez cartel, it is true. But forget what you have read and heard about who controls what. Whoever the controllers are, they leave those who remain in the city to fight a battle to the finish, which involves the extermination of rivals and others. This has become crazy warfare, not even necessarily between the Sinaloa and the Juárez cartels, it is anarchy. Yes, they are all there, Juárez, Sinaloa and Zetas trying to get in. But the pyramids have collapsed, and not one of the big bosses in the battle for Juárez has been touched, not one – they are far away. This is a fight between the groups and gangs on the ground that used to work for them, and it has become a massacre.'

Julián Cardona cautions that 'it simply doesn't make sense, as the media and government think, to draw lines between cartels in Juárez. Along the smuggling corridors into the US, maybe, but not on the streets. The cartels cannot even see those lines themseleves here any more. Of course the drug cartels exist, they are players, but they are no longer the main reason for the violence here. Look at this as a factory. You have a product and a production line. There are bosses, managers, middle management, line workers, accountants, bankers, shippers – they are all part of the process, but they never meet each other and most of them are not directly employed by the corporation. We'll have counted 1,700 dead in this city by the end of the year [he said, rightly, in September 2008] and in most cases, the executioners don't even know which cartel, if any, they're working for. If they change sides, from someone far from here who is part of the Juárez cartel to someone far from here in the Sinaloa cartel, they won't know it. All they have is their assigned task, their piece of turf, and maybe an order to do this, do that, or kill someone. Not why, or who for. They have no idea about the big money, or who their bosses are.'

This comes as a partial surprise (if anything surprises in Juárez), subverting the official 'map' of the cartel war. But it is utterly convincing. The notion that the cartel war has imploded and no longer explains the bloodshed in Juárez is a heresy against the versions of what is happening as expounded by the US and Mexican governments and many of the media in both countries. It funda-mentally challenges the notion of carefully staged cartel war on a narco Monopoly board, as well as that of a government 'offensive' against drug dealing in the city. The heresy was formulated by two reporters, Cardona and his friend Ignacio Alvarado Álvarez, who ran the investigative Almargen media service now run by Pérez Espino from *Cafébreria*, but who has since been persuaded by his co-citizen Paéz to work at *El Universal* in the capital. 'I have a family,' Alvarado says, explaining his decision to leave Juárez.

But we had first met when Ignacio was still living in Juárez, with Cardona, later in the morning after the decapitated corpse was hung from the overpass, in the inimitable and inevitable Sanborn's coffee house, for what was for me an unforgettable briefing. The cartels, explained Ignacio, have 'substituted the old pyramidal chain of command for the same concession or franchising system as any other corporation marketing any product or service in the globalised economy'. It takes a moment to realise how sarcastically funny Alvarado is being about the legal economy around us. 'You know how a corporation will not do its own detailed work any more – no! – that's not cost effective, that's monopolistic. So like a good capitalist, the cartel outsources, puts contracts out to tender, gives other people a chance to compete in order to reduce its own costs. Why should drug traffickers be any different? They're a business like any other. The cartels have got much more democratic in the capitalist sense: out-sourced, meritocratic and opportunistic,' he says, half-laughing, his eyes widening in mischief, disgust and fear. 'There really are far more opportunities for the small investor nowadays, with of course a higher risk, and more people getting killed. But think of the freedom to operate! The small guy pays a commission for the cartel's control over corrupt officials and the border, and occasionally they'll tell you who to kill, though not necessarily. The cartels don't need to control the streets, because they cannot, so they franchise them, they get other people to kill and die. The problem is: what happens if they have outsourced so much that they lose control completely? Do you see outsourcing making modern capitalism any more efficient? Of course not, it's a complete mess! So the cartels find that it's not so much that they need not control the streets, but they *cannot*.' 'What wealthy drug lord,' adds Cardona, 'would want to try and control *this*?

'I used to call my town a city of two economies,' Cardona continues, ordering *huevos rancheros*, 'one legal, the other illegal. But now that both are globalised, the dividing line has gone. Both the *maquilas* and the drug Plaza are based on the notion that the market will find its proper balance, and the market alone will dictate how Juárez will do business. And that is exactly what has happened. The "legal" economy brought hundreds of thousands of people to Juárez, me included, to work in *maquilas*, as I did, and offers to pay them three dollars a shift. The illegal market needs people, and offers better opportunities, to double that money for street dealing, multiply it by ten for a carrier, and by a hundred for killing. The *maquila* jobs market can't support what it created, so it sends you to get sucked into the other market, the parallel drug market, where you get paid in kind, you become an addict, you cut the drugs to sell, so that your addiction becomes an activity in the market, and you become an economic agent. When the recession comes, the *maquilas* find cheaper labour in Asia, so more people lose their jobs and turn in even greater numbers to buying, taking and selling drugs. And killing.'

Long before Juárez became the economic model for an inflation of killing, it was often in its history a place of tussling between smugglers of goods into the USA. But now, this late-capitalist, post-modern battlefield is for a Plaza that did not show up on the 'map' in Chapter One. A Plaza which is more fiendish in its violence than any war over trafficking into the USA: the battle for the internal drug market of Juárez – indeed of Mexico itself. In the aftermath of the cartel war and the throes of this new conflict, Juárez is blighted by drug addiction, markedly to crack and methamphetamine. Indeed, one reason Ignacio Alvarado gave for the erosion of cartel structures and boundaries, especially in Juárez, is 'that Mexico has become a country with a vast internal consumer market for drugs that is deliberately underestimated by government lies, and too anarchic for the cartels to control, even if they wanted to'. 'If we divide the drug market into eras,' says Cardona, 'we can see the smuggling era as that of the cartels – the monopoly capitalist era, if you like – and the explosion of domestic drug-taking as that of the free market, of criminal anarchy. Before, in the monopoly era, everyone knew their place: drug lords, the politicians, state police, local police, mid-narcos and gangs. Now, Juárez has become a formless, horizontal hierarchy, responding to the free market – some become very rich, most go into the trash.' Juárez is a city of 500 *colonias* with no municipal facilities to keep up with what were (until the recent recession) its 8,000 weekly arrivals. In each *colonia*, wasteland is drug-dealing territory for one of the 500 *colonia* gangs, apart from big spaces in the outlaying barrios like Anapra. There, says Cardona, 'the waste spaces are controlled by a gang called the police'.

Each *colonia* also has what in Tijuana were called *tienditas* – little shops – outlets for cocaine, marijuana, synthetic drugs and heroin. In Juárez they are called *picaderos*, usually marked by a shoe tied to a nearby telegraph wire. As the cartel pyramids collapse, so they lose control of the burgeoning domestic market for drugs, each *picadero* claiming and operating its own Plaza, protected by the local gang. The more the domestic Plaza expands, the looser the grip of the cartels, and the need for them to operate not so much a chain of command, but an affiliation system of 'outsourced' gangs. As a result, Juárez is now being fought over by a labyrinthine Pandora's Box of warring interests. Some of them are street gangs collated into a federation called *Los Aztecas*, which in turn serves *La Línea*, a street-level resurgence of the old Juárez cartel thought wrongly to have been shattered by Guzmán. Another federation of gangs is the *Artistas Asesinos*, affiliated to the Sinaloa cartel's siege of Juárez, as are *Los Mexicles*, also at the pleasure of Guzmán, who will kill anyone they can find who had any business with *La Línea*. An especially vicious animosity exists between *La Línea*'s *Aztecas* and *Los Mexicles*, since the latter defected from the *Aztecas* to join Guzmán. This betrayal led to a riot in Juárez prison in March 2009 in which twenty-one *Mexicles* were killed by *Aztecas*, reportedly with official sanction. Then there are the various police forces. In January 2009, the police chief tasked with gang-busting, Francisco Ledesma, turned out to have himself been a coordinator for *La Línea*, and was murdered. Partly as a result, the rogue element in Chihuahua state police, formerly a wing of the Juárez cartel, is now believed to be an independent force of its own. The municipal police has meanwhile been liberated by the domestic market from its attachment to politicans and cartels, and can operate as it wishes. The army and federal police, supposedly in town to quell this murderous farrago, we shall consider later.

There is some idea abroad that the killings are contained within one sector of society, or in the shanty barrios, but not in town or the exclusive quarters. Not at all: we drive to a smart villa currently 'under administration', where nine bodies were found recently, just opposite a fancy hall called *La Cité*, let out for weddings and functions. Then along the Avenida Rivera Lara, past Desperado's disco and rodeo, into the Calle Sierra del Pedregal, to arrive at a white, gated property where up to thirty-six bodies (depending on which account one heeds) were found buried beneath the patio in March 2007. At another house at 3363 Parsioneros, known as the House of Death, twelve bodies were found buried. These were killings over which controversy raged, with reports that an informant for the US government was part of the cell that carried them out, and that those who 'ran' him in the customs service were warned in advance of most murders and knew that the massacre – in which state police officers on the Juárez cartel payroll took part – was ongoing.[8] In the yard behind the House of Death, the picture of a mysterious and beautiful woman has been attached to the wall and 'shot' in the mouth, as though she were used for target practice. 'The general pattern was,' says Cardona, 'that if you exhibit the bodies, you are not killing for the police. If you hide them, either you are killing for the police or you are the police.' On the roadside round the corner from the House of Death, a police recruitment poster features a ninja-cop in a balaclava, and the words: '*Juárez te necesita!*' – Juárez needs you.

Only guesswork could explain why the satellite town of Riberas del Bravo is where it is: about an hour's drive from Ciudad Juárez, clinging to the borderline on the city's eastern edge. According to the *susurro*, these communities of relentlessly identical little houses – built to install *maquila* workers previously living in cardboard shacks – were erected where they were to suit landowners acquainted with politicians making the decisions, with both set to gain financially from an agreed deal over some far-flung location. Or maybe it is just that the city authorities somehow thought it a good idea to hurriedly throw up this maze of streets on a swamp by the river, on what were previously paddy fields of rice and cotton plantations, cut off from the city, with no attempt at transport connections apart from a single bus route downtown. There has apparently been some idea for a park in which children could play: the remains of a rusting round-about are still there, half-submerged in the swamp water seeping from the Rio Bravo. And anyway, to build all these houses during the *maquiladora* boom appears now to have been optimistic: since the emergence of cheaper labour in Asia and the onset of recession, row upon row of them have been abandoned and ransacked after their owners were laid off and returned home to the south. The PFK gang – whoever they are – seems to have made crack dens in most of them, tagging the walls or else incinerating them. On one street, four houses in a row are burned out, whether as a result of gang warfare or just pyromaniac recreation. Another posse in town is, apparently, the MK 18, which has taken over a row of empty houses leading down to an open sewer, so that the stink of excretia wafts on the breeze through its territory. At the end of Rivera de Zempoala, two lookout guards stand watch with a walkie-talkie. Ten years ago, this was a city of cardboard boxes growing out of the mire; now it is a showcase for the urban Frankenstein. As so often, the only respite or sign of resistance emanates from the church, surrounded by a high fence with a locked gate ever since the priest's computers were stolen. Here, children abandoned all day while both parents work at the *maquilas* can find a meal and company, lining up in shifts − girls, then boys − chatting over polystyrene plates divided into three sections of beans, pasta and a tortilla, before adjourning to the common room to watch Michael Jackson videos. When the priest is out doing his rounds, the centre is run by Alfredo Aguilar, once a gang fighter on these streets, now a recent father and guardian of the next generation. 'Here, they are left alone,' he says, by way of opening our conversation. Left alone by whom? 'By their parents, older youths, their families. We deal with trauma from sexual harassment by fathers and elders; the most common form is violation of girls by their stepfathers, and in some cases a man will kill the children of the woman he takes on, if she has them from a previous marriage.' Next to his desk, Aguilar's computer has a screensaver showing a paradisal tropical scene − waterfalls, birds and lush vegetation.

'The little ones are abandoned when their parents go to work,' says Aguilar, 'and fall prey to everything imaginable. We try to give them shelter, some glimpse of other values. It's not easy − we have ten-year-old boys trying to hit on girls who are even younger, because it's what they see at home. There's so much violence in their lives, so many drugs and that too starts in the home: five to ten people living in a tiny house, on top of one another, with abuse, violence against the children, no privacy and no one able to sleep. So most of the gangbangers are fifteen to sixteen years old, some as young as thirteen. I was one of them, not serious, but I grew up among these people, girls raped, boys joining gangs and getting killed; I lived with them.' Aguilar, twenty-eight years old, wants to make a point rather than deliver a confessional. 'The main point,' he argues, 'is that these are people spat out by the *maquiladora* factory system, and out of that come the gangs and the drugs. These people arrived from Veracruz, Tabasco, Oaxaca to work in the *maquilas* and when the *maquila* spits you out, drug dealing becomes a way of staying, a way of living. You stay and survive the best you can, or you leave and your house becomes a crack den. But not only the *maquilas*: the city has spat these people out, too. No wonder truancy is a problem if you have six small primary schools for seven thousand families and no secondary school.' To get to secondary school in Ciudad Juárez can be a two- to three-hour cross-town journey each way because the bus routes are arranged like a fan from outlying places like this. Every retired American school bus converges from the *colonias* on the city centre as its destination; there is no transport between one satellite and another, so pupils must travel via what is considered by most to be a no-go downtown zone before daylight in the morning and after dark at night.

Father Roberto returns a few days later, and tells me: 'When I first came here, I was doing many children's funerals, children who had died after accidents at home – well, I say accidents, I mean they were killed by their stepfathers – raping them and killing them. I found that in order to have a lover, a woman had to agree to this choice: kill the child or lose the man. I had six of those funerals in my first two years.' Then Father 'Beto' as he is universally known, relates a few statistics. 'There are twenty thousand houses in this colonia, of which eight thousand are now abandoned,' leaving more than 60,000 people living in 12,000 tiny houses. The proportion of empty houses is high, even for Juárez, though the figures for the city itself make terrifying reading. A report by the *Colegio de la Frontera del Norte*, published in January 2010, found that there are 116,000 vacant houses across the city, out of a total housing stock of 416,000 units. The empty dwellings, says the report, 'result from the economic downturn that began in 2001, and the depopulation has increased greatly in the past two years because of the violence and insecurity. Many migrants who came from southern Mexico to work in the *maquiladora* industry have decided to return to their places of origin. Others have migrated to the United States. Various neighborhoods contain mostly deserted and vandalized houses. In addition, statistics from the tax administration offices show that since 2008, more than 10,670 businesses have closed, the majority according to the business leaders, due to the economic crisis and the insecurity. There are many factory buildings vacant and these cannot be sold for any price to manufacturers due to the current conditions. The vacancy rate in industrial real estate is now at 14 per cent. Many of these businesses have abandoned Juárez.' The author of the report, COLEF researcher César Fuentes, told the *Diario* newspaper. 'The economic, public security and social crises in the city have important

repercussions in terms of economic and social viability. It is difficult for someone to invest in the city if they know that they will
become victims of extortion, robbery and kidnapping.'

With Father Beto, we take a walk. In the cool of the open sewer,
on a hot afternoon, two dogs roll in the excrement in a kind of embrace,
occasionally snapping playfully at each other's throat. According to
the tagging on the walls, we arrive in territory contested between
'West Side' and 'Siglo XIX', where some attempt at another little park
was once made. There is a three-way see-saw, rusted and inoperative,
stranded in a puddle of sewage. The benches, their paint peeled, have
not been sat on for a while, and have weeds growing through them.
We walk on, over another putrid and motionless waterway, past what
was once a paddy field lined with trees shimmering in the wind, to
a trickle of water winding its way through banks of arid grass. It is
the Rio Grande, and the other side, 20 yards away, is Texas.

'The border is all about trash,' says Cardona. 'Think of Juárez as
perpetual motion by different kinds of trash: someone else's trashed
fridge or car recycled; turning human beings into trash in the *maquilas*,
dead human trash in the rehab centres – though you can't re-fit the
dead people in a '*yonke*' and put them up for sale like you can the
trashed cars.' We hold this conversation on a ridge of precarious
housing above the sprawling *colonia* of Poniente, to which Cardona
originally came himself, from the state of Zacatecas, to work in a
maquila. Brought up by his grandparents in the country, he has stayed
ever since, apart from a spell back home, during which he tried to
organise resistance to the break-up of communally held and farmed
land, after privatisation. But neither the campaign against big
landowners grabbing the little holdings nor a love affair worked out.
So he headed back north, settling into the miasma of little dwellings
spread beneath us, where we have just been visiting a man called
Antonio, once a fighter in a gang called *Callejon*, who now runs a
centre for gang members to try more creative ways of expressing
what he calls 'our territoriality'. Cardona surveys the panorama, with
its views of downtown El Paso in one direction, and to the south,
burgeoning breeze-block and cement housing crawling down into the
valley and up the other side, dogs and children scattered across the
maze of streets and radio masts piercing the sky. 'More than half a

million people,' says Cardona, 'and only a single high school. Anyone who can't make it, throw them on the trash heap.'

Trash can bring work back in Riberas del Bravo, where a man called Marco wheels an old pram heaving with scrap up the street towards his house, one of the few that has not been abandoned and burned out. Marco is surrounded by four of his six children, who also carry pieces of rubbish, all of it with value in Ciudad Juárez: tin cans, steel piping, bath taps – the discarded appliances of other people's former lives. Finally, they wheel their swag up the little driveway of the fifth house from the end of the row. The family came from Durango sixteen years ago, explains Marco, but both he and his wife lost their jobs in the BRK *maquila* two years before. The pay in the factory was 600 pesos ($50) a week. Collecting trash – 'anything metal, anything iron, anything we can sell' – pays 'one hundred pesos on a good day, sixty on a bad day'. Marco's six children all help, on a timetable he has laid down: 'we work Monday to Wednesday, take Thursday off, and work again Friday to Sunday'. There is no question of them going to school, since 'school demands a fee of twenty-five dollars per family, plus money for the heating, lighting and books. And that's before the bus fares, six tickets costing six pesos, twice a day – that's seventy-two pesos a day – where am I supposed to get that from?' One of his sons wears a T-shirt with a heavy-metal band called *Angeles del Infierno* – Angels of Hell – on it, and the family's pet dog is called *Satanas*.

The main problem, says Marco, is that when he returned from the USA and started collecting scrap, 'I was only the third person doing it. Now, there are too many, and there's only so much trash to go round, even in a place like this!' However, this is a better state of affairs, Marco insists, than Durango, 'where there is nothing'. Another *nada*. Better here, despite permanent harassment by drug addicts: 'One day, I came home and they were taking the door off my house! I chased them off. Now, they come and go through those houses [he points towards the end of the street]. All four between here and the end are empty, and after that is the border so we're the closest family to the United States!'

A spaghetti junction of slip roads connects US Interstate 10, as it skirts within yards of the border fence and roars through El Paso, with the Patriot Freeway that runs north from the frontier. Today, the cars are arrayed in all their glistening glory. No, not those above on the freeway, but in Lincoln Park below, where they are attended to with loving care by people from the tough barrios on the edge of town. A 1968 Impala Caprice convertible from the fourth generation of Chevrolet's iconic line is flanked by two Mexican flags and has the slogan '*Viva La Raza*' emblazoned across the bonnet in palace script. Its interior consists of puffy cream-coloured cushioning. A 1961 Impala, in burgundy, has the famous 'bubbleback' roofline and bears the motto 'Low Riding Girl'. Indeed, in front of the car is a child's doll dressed in a micro-skirt in the colours of the Mexican flag – next to which is a real live girl to match, subject of quite a few photos as she poses against the vehicle on the highest of heels, showing off the hair she combs, her legs, tattoos and, supposedly, the 1961 Impala. The car seats are upholstered in – what else? – green, white and red with 'Chicano Power' embroidered into them. The occasion is a heart-warming one: the Chicano Arts festival – part car show, part family cook-out, part girlie catwalk, part gang convention, part arts fair, part afternoon disco, part Mesoamerican costume parade for children. On the concrete stilts supporting the freeway are graffiti paintings of the pyramids at Teotihuacán and the assertion: 'Lincoln Park: *El Corazón de El Paso*', the heart of El Paso. The pillars cast shadows in long straight lines along which rows of people, mostly extended families, align their deckchairs in order to eat barbecued picnics, their lines rotating like the shadow cast by a sundial, in order to stay in the shade. But the real matter in hand is the battle of the car clubs, which loosely reflect neighbourhoods and even gangs – or clans – and in which mutual respect and rivalry co-exist in roughly equal measure: the Oldies Car Club of New Mexico pitched against the Imperials of El Paso, the Latin Pride Car Club against the Natural High Car Club, the Our Story Car Club against the Ekztazy Car Club. 'It's about cars, it's about Chicano pride and it's about your own pride in your own club, which is your brother's,' says Alejandro Dávila from eastern El Paso – an imposing man with the Aztec calendar tattooed on his shoulder and a two-headed serpent on his shin below the cargo pants. 'It all started here, man – hot rods, Zoot Suits, that's our heritage here in El Paso and we're conscious of that. The *chicas* are part of that

scene, they go with the cars. You got the car, you get the *chica*; if
you don't have the car, you gotta find some other way, see what I
mean?' And he laughs, begging the obvious awkward question about
gangland and drug dealing. 'Yes', he says carefully, 'there is a role
for some *chucos*' (someone from El Paso) and what Alejandro
calls '*Segundo Juárez* which I guess means Juárez USA, you know
– overspill of what's going on over there. There's a kind of connection between Juárez and a gang this side by the name of *Barrio
Aztecas.*'

'But,' Alejandro continues, 'most folks aren't involved in the other
side. That's gone way heavy now. We stay this side, just *chuco* clubs,
car clubs. The crazy stuff don't come over here too much, and not
at all on the car scene. The car scene is family, brothers, maybe
people who've been in jail, but come out again and cleaned out. We
do heritage now, Chicano heritage. And I mean they're beautiful
things, man, very beautiful objects and a lot of work and money to
get to that condition. It's all connected in the cars, you know –
brotherhood, neighbourhood, all kinds of connections, and sure it's
a pussy connection too.' A woman arrives and ends the conversation.
'This is my mother,' Alejandro says, introducing a cleaner for the
school district, and they wander off together to admire cars and join
the extended family for empanadas.

Alejandro has a point: the much-vaunted 'spillover' of violence
across the Rio Grande has not occurred (yet) other than as a series
of episodes. Drug traffickers and their support systems in gangland
– never mind the 'legitimate' financial sector – seem reluctant, so
far, to draw the authorities' attention on the border itself. Of course,
there are exceptions that go beyond the daily routine of trans-border
carjacking and mugging. An edition of the Juárez morning paper
El Diario[9] in September 2009 carried a grisly picture of a pair of
severed arms folded and resting on the chest of their former owner,
Sergio Saucedo, aged thirty, kidnapped in the El Paso suburb of
Horizon City one fine afternoon in May. Three men wearing black
baseball caps and black gloves burst into his home and took him
away in a maroon Ford Expedition, as recounted by his wife and a
bus load of schoolchildren who bore witness to the abduction. Saucedo
had convictions in the USA for money-laundering and cocaine possession with intent to distribute, and had been taken by his captors

across the border to Juárez where his mutilated body was found four months later, dumped in a busy street. Soon after the kidnap, on 15 May 2009, José Daniel González Galeana was gunned down outside his hacienda-style villa in El Paso: he had been a lieutenant for the Juárez cartel, turned informant for the customs service – apparently rumbled and tracked down by his erstwhile *compadres* to become what the FBI in El Paso considers to be the highest-ranking member of a Mexican cartel to be assassinated in the US.[10] One in eight El Pasoans is employed by the military and, in August 2009, the FBI arrested an eighteen-year-old soldier based at nearby Fort Bliss for being contracted by the Juárez cartel to carry out the execution.

The fate of informants, and those in flight to the USA from direct personal threat, is among the preoccupations of a tireless man who helped organise the car club corral and works from a little office on the low-slung Yandell Drive in El Paso: Eduardo Beckett, of Mexican-Irish descent, managing attorney at the Las Americas Immigrant Advocacy law centre. Most of Beckett's clients are families facing deportation, or those with citizenship issues or the other problems of any large migrant or immigrant community – appointments with families: mum and the boys in Beckett's office, daughter staying behind in reception to take a nap. 'Most people we see here,' says Beckett, 'have spent their whole lives in the United States, commit a crime and get deported. They're not educated, and they end up taking odd jobs back in Mexico. A few get a break, others end up in whorehouses or committing another crime. Then you have the others, who have worked sometimes ten years for US government agencies in Mexico – DEA, FBI, customs, police departments – on the understanding that if they give up information, they'll get a visa in return one day. It's called an 'S-Visa', better known as 'Snitch Visa'. But in my experience, once they're found out, or after they've testified, they're just clipped off, they're garbage. The agencies I deal with won't even admit they were informants, and they're sent back to the wolves waiting for them.' These special cases that demand Beckett's energy and motivation are of people who face almost certain torture or death if they return to Mexico, having fallen foul of the narco cartels for one reason or another.

Beckett surveys the paperwork, his caseload that looks like a truck-load, with the air of an exhausted gladiator. This is a man who spent his student days knocking door to door for the United Mineworkers of America in Gillette, Wyoming, where 'all these folks wondered: What's this *brown* person doing up here?' He judges that 'most of my clients are looked upon as trash by the system, and that's the starting point. With the informers, it's even worse – that they were doing it for the money, and they're snitches. They know that if they cross back over, they're going to get tortured and killed. They have nowhere else to go, they're banged away before they get to court, and they're stuck. And still the feds just say: "No, I never saw this man." We argue that they're in danger and a hell of a situation, and they just wash their hands of them or say these things can't be decided in open court because it constitutes a danger to their operations and the way they do things. They argue for internal relocation within Mexico, but there's nowhere to hide in Mexico. And if you're an honest cop, put in an impossible position and in fear of your life, they argue that if you're a cop of course the criminals will be out to get you. They say that's not persecution. We're accused of imputing some kind of politics into what the narcos are.' So the law on asylum, persecution and torture is not ready for post-political war, unable to recognise persecution unless it has a political colour. The law of the United States is not ready for, and cannot cope with, the post-political nightmare of which the narco war is herald – organised terror by branches of the state whose only political colour is white powder.'[11]

Among Beckett's cases is the extraordinary story of Martín Espino Ledezma. Ledezma was a mounted police officer in Juárez but left the force due to the personal strain of his division's duty digging up the bodies of young women who had been kidnapped and murdered. He left Juárez in 1993 for his wife's native town of La Junta, to work as a singing teacher. La Junta lies at a strategic hub for the transportation of drugs into Juárez from the south and there Ledezma was approached by the leadership of the local PAN party, and asked to help in establishing order in 'a lawless town'. Then Ledezma found out, he claims in an affidavit filed in a federal asylum case in El Paso, that his sponsor in the PAN 'was a puppet for [the narcos] in La Junta'. One day, 'two individuals came to my office and said they came on behalf of Pepe Estrada [the local municipality president] to put me at his disposition, for me to work for organised crime, and for this they offered me a substantial amount of money . . . My job would consist of distracting the federal police officers at the checkpoints near La Junta. I would also have to put the officers under my authority at their disposition. When I denied this they went from being kind people as they had presented themselves at the beginning to being very overbearing and threatening.' After Ledezma refused to cooperate, 'on 3 March 2008, Mr Estrada sent some men to kill me. This occurred that day, which was my birthday,' says Ledezma. His wife answered the door, outside which two SUVs had parked and 'at least six individuals with high-calibre weapons who had surrounded the house and pointed their guns toward it. They told her I should watch out, and wherever they found me, they would kill me, that it didn't matter where I went, that they could find me anywhere because they had connections all over Mexico.' It was later 'confirmed', claims Ledezma in the same affidavit, that Estrada was working for *La Línea*, the Juárez cartel."[12]

I wish life was still like that, my Uncle Tommy says/
But everything's gone straight to Hell since Sinatra played Juárez/
You could get a cheap divorce, get your Pontiac tuck and rolled/
You could take your dolly to the dog track in her fake chinchilla stole.

The Fiesta Club, The Chinese Palace, The Old Kentucky bar/
The matadors and baseball heroes and great big movie stars/
Those were truly golden years, my Uncle Tommy says/
Cause everything's gone straight to Hell since Sinatra played Juárez

Now Uncle Tommy Gabriel he still plays Fats Domino/
He speaks that border Spanglish well, He owns a carpet store/
He lives out on his pecan farm, 'I don't cross the bridge,' he says
Cause everything's gone straight to Hell since Sinatra played Juárez[13]

It's a song by Tom Russell, who arrived in El Paso in 1997, from Brooklyn, in a U-Haul truck. Before that, he had taught criminology in Nigeria, worked in Canadian lumber camps, took time out in Norway and elsewhere besides. But now Russell is the deep-voiced bard of the border, 'one of the people who still thinks songs should tell stories' as he says himself. And of El Paso: 'Hell, the town has been semi-dead for pretty much half a century. If you turn off towards downtown, you'll hit the central Plaza with its fountain of fibreglass sculptures of leaping alligators. Up until the 1960s, there were real gators in there, but the drunks fell in and lost their arms and legs.' Russell likes to recall Johnny Cash's song 'Mean As Hell', in which the Devil is looking for Hades on earth, and God gave him 'a plot of land near the Rio Grande which sounds like El Paso'. Notwithstanding which, Russell bought an adobe on three acres 'not to find my identity so much as to lose it', he says. Up the hillside was Cormac McCarthy, who 'lived in a rattle trap, trying to do the same thing. To be left alone to write. Unfortunately, fame and fans hunted Cormac down and chased him to Santa Fe. I'm still here.' El Paso, he says, 'is an abandoned midway of cultural impoverishment. When big corporations and big business came calling, decades ago, the city council and powers that be delivered an ultimatum, which went something like this: We'll allow you to move in here, but what are you going to do for us? Big Money squirmed with distaste and walked away.' As a result, Russell adds, 'the city fathers left in charge bought up water rights by paying off the city council and turned El Paso into one big freeway, the agricultural land both east and west chewed up to build strip mall sprawl and substandard housing'. For all that, however, 'El Paso is my own Patagonia. Outside and over the edge. Lyrical in its essence, tragic in its fate, comic in its existence. But it's a peaceful place. You find that amusing? The war has not spilled across the Rio Bravo. Life is cheap and simple. I like the people.'

We are sitting over dinner at a restaurant squeezed between the suburb of Sunland Park, just over the New Mexico state line, and the border, the other side of which is Anapra, the poorest *colonia* in Juárez. Another train rumbles by, the railway line backlit by the glow of the city Russell sings about in another song called 'The Hills Of Old Juárez' – a smuggling ballad. It is the city his fictional 'Uncle Tommy' loved until everything went 'straight to hell', and which Russell used to love to visit for bullfights and the Kentucky Club, the city where Steve McQueen died. But Russell, like Uncle Tommy, thinks twice about crossing the bridge since everything went to hell; moreover, he says: 'I wouldn't sing some of those songs now, like "The Hills Of Old Juárez"; any idea that drug smuggling was in some way dare-devil or romantic – bandits under the mesquite trees

– just ain't admissible any more. But that ain't to say I don't miss Old Juárez, and the way it was.' Russell has a new song now, about drugs coming north, guns going south, and the ghost of Benito Juárez watching on, and shedding a tear.

Like Tom Russell's, my memories of Juárez are of a city that explodes at night. On a Saturday, the *Esfinge* – Sphynx – disco, shaped like an Egyptian pyramid behind what was the Holiday Inn, was pullulating with a multitude of drinkers and dancers, mostly girls spending their *maquiladora* wages like there was no tomorrow. For this is a strange economy: wages are pitiful by US standards, but not by those of the Mexican interior and if you want to go out dancing with your friends on a weekend, there might be the change with which to do so. Life on the border is all about inspection: you are forever clocking in and clocking out at the *maquila*, your productivity is overseen, your lunch break and even your toilet break are monitored, papers are scrutinised by the police, the army and at US border checkpoints if you are able to cross the bridge. You even get checked by the doorman and security guards here. But once inside, *Esfinge* is a different kind of inspection: that of a factory girl's body by every male in this ruffian ballroom tripping the light fantastic. And it is an inspection she passes with flying colours, whether she is here to court the boys in earnest, flirt a little or just shake her bones with the other girls with whom she makes harnesses for car distributors by day, and then head home. I remember them along the podia and catwalks, dancing and strutting, all flutter and flicker; simultaneously humiliating and bedazzling their drop-jawed, wide-eyed audience, nine times out of ten refusing the offers of drink or whatever. Factory girl by day in cap and apron, *danseuse* by night, dressed to die for. But not all the men in their spiffed-up shirts and tight slacks will be content to admire from a distance, nor will their attentions be necessarily amorous. The horror of extreme violence against women came to curse (but also to define) this city, and predict the present way of violence in narco warfare.

In here, though, aphrodysia and the music were all that mattered. Like the concupiscence of Nero's Rome, that of Ciudad Juárez was connected in some perverse way to the impending collapse out there: the superabundance, the flowing drinks, the mellifluous arc of a perfect arm and a toss of the hair were a devil-may-care defiance of death in the streets and of hard factory grind. Kisses blown and conjoined, acceptance and rejection; tease and tussle; the chessboard diplomacy of the dance floor as it is anywhere else in the world, only in Ciudad Juárez it was lascivious like nowhere else – both in spite of what was happening outside and because of it. The girls who saved up to go to these glitzier places were called *fresas* – strawbarries – back in the day – the 90s and early 'noughties'. Those who preferred to economise or could not afford the $8 entry fee could go instead to a less lavish bawdyhouse like *El Patio* and listen to a band singing *narcocorridos* rather than the thumping techno at *Esfinge*. But *El Patio* was voluptuous enough, the debauchees in skin-tight jeans and boots of blue, red and green crocodile clinging onto the girls' fingertips as they spun them round with elastic arms but a firm grip, watching the skirts flying and breathing smoke rings in the thick, damp air. On the border, by the way, a *corrido* (masculine) becomes a *corrida* (feminine) when it is being danced to.[14] In *El Patio*, a visiting foreigner was a space alien, unworthy even of a threat – in fact, so absurd that the *bravos* would buy me a drink – just one. At *Esfinge*, though, an outsider who is not American got drawn in. It was all 'welcome to Juárez!' and clinking glasses of '*Paloma*', which normally means a dove, but in this dive is tequila and grapefruit. It was written in the fake luminous stars on the ceiling: one was irrevocably part of the strawberries' game in a place where no one really belongs, apart from those counting the laundered money.

Back in Juárez seven years later, in 2008, the *Esfinge* was subdued. Amexica's great city of the night, over decades of naughty-but-nice, was ill at ease after sundown. Back again in 2009, the *Esfinge* has shut. The nine-storey hotel into which I check is empty apart from a boxing team from Chihuahua City on its way to fight in Finland. In 2008, Cardona and I went for a beer at another dive, Bar Amsterdam. There, one of the barmaids wearing the uniform red micro-dress, Giselle by name, had joined us for a drink. She told the quintessential Amexican life story about making it across the border when she was fourteen, getting as far as Denver and a decent job, only to be stopped ten years later because of a faulty rear light on her car, caught without papers, and deported. Back home, Giselle took the job in Amsterdam where she could be leered at for a living. She seethed with palpable frustration at it all. She wished the men who came to do whatever they thought they were doing here to cream their jeans would please just play Creedence Clearwater Revival on the juke box instead of that endless fucking *norteño*. Some time afterwards, in July 2009, Cardona sent a story from *El Diario* which read: 'Five men were assassinated in a spray of gunfire last night, while meeting in a bar called "Amsterdam". First reports said that two of the victims were beside the bar, and three were in the toilets . . . Word reached the first agents on the crime scene that one of the victims had been terminated with a so-called *Tiro de Gracia*.'[5] Giselle, according to the *susurro*, had apparently found herself a narco she liked and gone to work in another place, Dallas, which had been closed after its owner was kidnapped and shot dead. Cardona and I return to Amsterdam in October 2009, after the killing. As we walk in, all six barmaids come and sit in a row opposite us, like a chorus line. We are the only customers there. We drink a quick beer and leave through the dark, deserted and menacing streets. 'The narcos,' says Cardona, 'decided to take over the night life, and in doing so, they killed it.'

Anyway, all this hanky-panky caper in no country for old men is all very well until you get close to the other old men. On my last night in the empty hotel, the boxing team and I were joined by an American whom it was my dubious privilege to meet in the lift. He was sweating profusely through layers of fat and the polyfibres of his San Antonio Spurs sportswear, at the prospect of an evening with the teen lovely accompanying him to the floor beneath mine. The kind of sleazebag who needs to forget that she is the same age as his daughter, he slapped together two packs of lingerie like a baseball into a glove. '*Duerme Bien!*' I offered cheerfully – sleep well – to which he replied: 'You too', with a look that said he wanted to punch my teeth down my throat, while the young belle smiled with a mixture of defiance and humiliation. I retired instead to watch Telemundo's unrivalled broadcast of global highlights from every major football match that day across the Americas, Britain and Europe, which the Mexican channel does with a cosmopolitan panache and excitable love of the game, wherever it is played, that puts the parochial myopia of American and British sports coverage to shame.

Even in changed Juárez, there are still attempts at public life. In the parking lot of the *Plaza Renacimiento* there's an impromptu night rally of customised cars – not vintage classics like El Paso's, but roaring, grinding, screeching Toyota Camrys and Volkswagen Golfs, genetically modified with overdeveloped hubcaps and souped-up engines, and low-slung to make sparks against the tarmac. The young drivers race a little, but mainly just take turns to wheel around the lot making as much noise, smoke and smell of burning rubber as possible, for the benefit of onlookers. It's edgily hysterical, certainly, but 'the best fun in Juárez', says Antonio González González, proud owner of a white Ford Focus with what look like wings over the rear wheels, and a chassis millimetres from the road. 'During the day, in the maquila, it feels like everyone is driving the machines apart from me, but when I'm in my car, I'm driving,' he says. At the other end of the spectrum, 2 October 2009 was a big night when – as if Juárez hadn't suffered enough – Sarah Brightman came to sing, and close the fifth Chihuahua international festival of culture. There she was, onstage in the Benito Juárez stadium in the most dangerous city in the world, wearing a dress that seemed to come from the costume-drama wardrobe, flanked by crooning tenors and a bevy of dapper musicians. La Brightman's saccharine voice wafted across the air, heavy with sulphur fumes from the chemical works and this evening's news of seven more murders. The lyrics were inescapably bizarre in such a place: 'And I think to myself / What a wonderful world'. The finale, 'Deliver Me', rose to a crescendo of fake, packaged hope for Juárez, making way for the second elaborate and extended fireworks display in a fortnight (the *Grito* of independence was just two weeks beforehand). 'Deliver me, loving and caring / Deliver me, giving and sharing / Deliver me, the cross that I'm bearing,' she sang sweetly, into the murderous night.

And credit to Ms Brightman; many, influenced by the headlines, would have shied away from the appearance; she was right to keep it. For Juárez surprises those who come here on business or to take a peep. Journalists who arrive expecting to find a besieged Sarajevo or Grozny are disappointed (or relieved); BBC news presenters talking to cameras in bulletproof vests look downright silly. By day, not much has visibly changed in the little streets behind the cathedral and the plenteous Cerrajeros marketplace, especially on Saturday, when the shroud of work is lifted and Juárez's face is hearty and sanguine. This landscape of flotsam and jetsam for sale could only exist in a border town, and only on a border with America. Everything that is not quite *à la mode* north of the frontier lines the streets in overload quantities: sixties' furniture, soda fountains, hair curlers, Kelvinator fridges and Osterizer blenders, as though the sets of hundreds of post-war movies had been ransacked and put up for sale along Mexican sidewalks. There's a *Venta de Boilers Electricos y de Gas Termostatos*, a block of sixties' sofas and armchairs, another block of sixties' fridges and another lined with pre-digital electronics: reel-to-reel tape recorders and mono record players, even some early stereo. What a bloated modern city nowadays calls 'retro', Ciudad Juárez calls the Saturday market. The centrepiece, though − the masterpiece − is the car mart.

Here is Amexican border economics at its most eccentrically creative, supplying Mexico with refurbished, formerly discarded or crashed (and written-off) American cars between twenty and five years old. While the periphery of Juárez is an infinity of *yonke* auto-repair yards, the arteries running from the marketplace are lined with miles and miles of refurbished models. The man selling one stretch of them, Enrique, explains the system: 'We go all together in the back of a van, to the auctions, all over the US, then drive or tow back the cars that have been discarded. Some have been in car crashes and we rescue them from wrecking yards because we know we can do things with them the Americans won't. Others are just old, or damaged in some way, and the *gringos* offer such low prices that it's worth our while fitting them up. Sometimes, they're in a really bad state, and we need to do some work on the other side − in our relatives' workshops. That's why we usually go to the sales in North Carolina, Texas or Chicago.' One by one, the cars are fixed up to the point of being able to get them back, via a bribe to Mexican customs. In Juárez, they are made roadworthy again, driven back to the US, re-licensed, returned to Mexico and either registered with a Mexican plate or driven as a coveted American car. The export 'duty' paid to Mexican customs for this second, more delicate, crossing is usually an informal settlement with a specific officer or shift, explains Enrique. The system works: People come from all over Mexico to buy these cars.

This matey discourse carefully skirts any connection between this trade and that in drugs. As everyone knows, part of the *yonkes'* work

is to fit up the ingeniously secret compartments within a private
vehicle for hiding drug shipments across the border. Fitting out the
cars is an expert business, with container spaces hidden in batteries,
tyres, door panels and elsewhere, often treated with mustard, engine
grease, hot chilli pepper or perfume in order to foil the dogs. But
even without the more lucrative kitting up of vehicles for smuggling, the economy of the resale market is all the more baffling
when we learn how cheap these cars retail for. I asked Enrique's
understudy Emilio how much a beautifully done-up Chevrolet
Impala costs. 'About a kilo,' he says, by way of a telling Freudian
slip, with a completely straight face, meaning a thousand dollars.
Most of this business is probably semi-legal, with customs officers
working out private import duties, says Emilio, and creates badly
needed jobs in a city busy training mechanics. But, given Emilio's
ambiguous word for a grand, the term the Mexicans use for a car
loaded with drugs for smuggling is a *clavo*, literally, a nail. And there
is a bar just up the road – the local, indeed, to which the mechanics
and salesmen retire for a beer and snack – with a great nail rising
from its roof, called, of course, *El Clavo*.

To say that little has changed in the marketplace is not strictly
true. There are army Humvee jeeps patrolling the crowds and
fridges, soldiers in pale desert camouflage, weapons at the ready,
safety catches off. And similar trucks driven by the federal police,
in dark blue ninja uniforms, eyes peering from behind their ski
masks. And nobody is quite sure what exactly the Mexican army –
an enigmatic but highly potent power throughout the country's
history – is up to.

One of the striking things about the spiralling violence in Juárez
is that it escalated dramatically during 2009 despite wave upon wave
of military reinforcements. The Mexican government's insistence that
an increased military presence is the only way to confront the drug
violence makes Juárez the litmus-test city of its policy. It is a test
spectacularly failed. In January 2009, there were some 5,000 soldiers
in Ciudad Juárez. On the first day of March, an additional 3,200
troops were deployed in the city with a massive show of force alongside 700 federal police officers, all under the banner of what the
military now called Joint Operation Chihuahua. The new troops had
new uniforms which could not be duplicated, said the operation's

spokesman, Enrique Torres, after accusing narco death squads of dressing up as soldiers to carry out their executions[16]. There was a brief respite in the slaughter, but only a brief one, and as soon as 26 April, Mexico City sent 5,000 more soldiers to Ciudad Juárez, bringing the total to over 13,000. His efforts at police reform in ruins, Mayor Reyes Ferriz announced that the military would take over police functions and other arms of civilian authority, would man checkpoints, conduct house searches, challenge extortion rackets and guard crime scenes[17]. By 21 April, a former air force lieutenant, Jorge Alberto Berecochea, who had taken over the 6th police district, took journalists from the *Washington Post* on a tour of the Casas Grandes *colonia*, to demonstrate what the paper reported to be the 'sudden, surprising calm' in Juárez.[18] 'The cartels are basically wiped out here now,' Berecochea said, making a point barbed with half-truth. 'They're not operating, at least not in Juárez.' He explained the 'cockroach effect' the army had, scattering drug traffickers, and proclaimed: 'Ciudad Juárez: right now I'd say it's the safest city in Mexico.'[19]

It was an extraordinary claim, and a bizarre report. Two months later, the plot thickened: the army said it had captured twenty-five cartel gunmen who went about their murderous business dressed as soldiers. They were never named, and if they were ever charged, the case disappeared like almost all the others. By early June, the escalation and pattern of killing continued − often targeting teenagers. Three adolescents were among five people executed on 13 June, according to the magazine *Proceso*. Three more the following day, next day, another five.[20] By midsummer, Howard Campbell, an expert and author on the Juárez drug war at El Paso University, estimated that 90 per cent of those killed were street-level drug dealers, not smugglers of drugs into the United States.[21] And so it continued through 2009, by the end of which 2,657 deaths had been recorded in Ciudad Juárez alone.[22] From these statistics, and the nature of the executions, a second heresy arises among the attempts to explain the inexplicable in Juárez: that the violence has intensified not despite the army's increased presence, but because of it.

One especially savage massacre was metered out in August 2008, off the Avenida de los Aztecas, at a drug rehabilitation centre outside which a car pulled up on the dirt track, the *sicarios* alighting and shooting to death nine recovering addicts while they were at prayer.

The executions lasted fifteen minutes, and accounts from eyewitnesses reported in the local press (in a rare public indictment of the army) suggested that military jeeps had blocked off any impediment to the executioners' progress, guarding their way, while others said the killers were dressed in military uniforms (something, claims the army, that cartel killers do). Certainly, the rehabilitation centre is only a few blocks from the impressive Camp Militar 5-C, on the main road. Gangland graffiti painted on the stricken building and in the alleyways give some clue as to why, perhaps, the authorities had a stake in this carnage: '*Locos* 23. *El Signo*', and '*Signo* RIP' read the paint-sprayed tributes. *El Signo* was a member of a street gang, apparently now pentient or at least 'clean', whom rivals wanted rubbed out, possibly with army approval. Or maybe the army wanted him and his fellow patients killed – no one knows, for the systematic massacre of the city's most wretched outcasts is Juárez' cruellest mystery. 'The army,' says Ignacio Alvarado, one of the original heretics in the Juárez media, with Cardona, 'is like Spiderman. It has a double. There is the real Spiderman, and there is his dark *doppelgänger*.' No emergency services arrived to help the wounded from the rehabilitation centre massacre – they were taken to hospital by trucks driven by staff and neighbours. Hours passed before the police arrived. No one has been arrested. It was after this attack that the Red Cross in Juárez said it would stop treating gunshot wounds in rehab centres and would not respond to emergency calls after 10 p.m. after death threats made over their internal radio network.[23]

There are three interpretations of the why, who and wherefore of mass killing in rehab centres. One is that of Pastor José Antonio Galván, who runs a rehab clinic and asylum on the outskirts of town called *Visión En Acción*: that the cartels – Guzmán's Sinaloa and the *Línea* heirs to the Juárez cartel – are picking out former *sicarios* and other operatives who once worked for their rivals. A twist to this is added by a former patient and now an assistant at another rehab clinic who wishes to remain anonymous: that the cartels have an interest in eliminating their own: the logic being that if former cartel foot soldiers are trying to clean out, rehabilitate and fix themselves a new life, they would become dangerous – no longer bounded to the organisation and knowing too much. And there is a third possibility, the heresy, advanced by Cardona and Alvarado: that the

Mexican army is using the crisis to either facilitate, by default, or even engage in a campaign of what they call '*limpia social*', literally 'social cleansing' of society's unwanted outcasts, the undesirables, drug addicts, street urchins and petty or more-than-petty criminals. The army hardly dispelled this notion when the general in charge of the 11th military district of which Juárez forms part described each death on his watch as that of '*un delinquente menos*' – one criminal less. The occasion was a press conference on 1 April 2008, at the State Palace in Chihuahua City, when General Jorge Juárez Loera told the assembled journalists and cameras: 'The media are very important to us. Tell the truth, say what you have to say, but say it with courage. And I know that the media are sometimes afraid of us, but they should not be afraid. I hope they will trust us, and I would like to see the reporters change their articles and where they say "one more murdered person", instead say, "one less criminal".'[24] Neither is the idea that the poorest of the poor are in some way targets in this war dispelled by such killings as that of a waif cleaning car windscreens at traffic lights, for a peso a time, as happened in October 2009, one of seven murders that day. Requests were made for access to the army for this book, to ride with its patrols, discuss general strategy as well as these allegations in Juárez – including a request at the highest level with President Calderón's adviser, Ms De Sota, in Mexico City – but were not granted.

The most compelling public figure to emerge from Juárez' war believes that all the above explanations of the killing in rehab clinics and of the poorest on the streets can be concurrently true, including the heresy of *limpia social* by the army. Gustavo de la Rosa Hickerson is a fascinating man. Born to a middle-class family in rural Chihuahua, he came to Ciudad Juárez as a boy to do two things: live rough and train as a lawyer, thereby proving his worth to his father, with whom he had a complex relationship. His mother's side of the family, he says, traces its ancestry in the United States to the eighteenth century. De la Rosa explains all this with disarming candour over an Italian dinner after his second day in exile in the USA – in flight from death threats by the Mexican army. After he qualified, de la Rosa became a labour lawyer, defending rights and conditions in the *maquiladoras*. But he was no soft touch: during the 1990s, he was appointed governor of Juárez jail, a formidable task and dangerous position for anyone. He brokered a truce between street gangs that confronted each other within the prison walls, and so presided over a period of peace, shattered only after he left, when, in March 2009, the riot between gangs led to twenty-one deaths, with reports that the authorities had sanctioned the *Aztecas* to attack the rival *Mexicles* affiliated to the Sinaloa cartel.[25]

In April 2008, de la Rosa was appointed legal director of the Chihuahua branch of the National Human Rights Commission, a rare institution of self-policing by the Mexican government. Established in 1989 by the Interior Ministry, the commission has independent judicial power and can refer instances of human rights abuse to the appropriate prosecuting authority, and this was de la Rosa's role in Chihuahua – in theory. Soon after the arrival of the military in Ciudad Juárez, during early 2008, de la Rosa began to open files on what he believed to be abuses by the military. From January of that year, he collected 154 complaints against the army, including 'allegations of house searches without warrants, arbitrary detentions, torture, abuse and even killings during the detention of victims'.

De la Rosa was on his way home from work on 4 September 2009, he says, when he stopped at a traffic light. A driver pulled up alongside him, rolled down his window, and imitated a pistol with his hand – 'like this', says de la Rosa, and he makes as though to fire through a barrel made of two outstretched fingers, with recoil. The motorist said: 'Quieten down, or we'll kill you.' When de la Rosa asked his own commission for physical protection, he was refused; indeed, his superiors in the state human rights commission headquarters at Chihuahua City ordered him to stop taking statements from alleged victims of army abuse. Soon afterwards, one of de la Rosa's bodyguards was shot dead. On 22 September 2009, de la Rosa walked across the bridge into El Paso, and exile. He stayed with his brother, resident in the US, and on Thursday 24, had lunch with his son and daughter in the restaurant of the century-old *Camino Real* hotel, downtown. After eating, he kissed his children and bid them goodbye that they may cross the bridge into Juárez and return home before dark. Then he sat down to talk.

He has an imposing stature, a wild mop of white hair and white beard – everyone, including him, says he looks like Father Christmas. But there is severity too, and in this circumstance even a certain vulnerability. De la Rosa talks about the notion of *limpia social* – social cleansing – going back a long way in Juárez, to the 1950s when, he said, undesirables and criminals 'would be taken up in aircraft, and simply thrown out into the desert'. De la Rosa does not believe that *limpia social* can account for all or even most of the deaths in Ciudad Juárez' war. But, he says, 'I believe the police know who the expert executioners are, who the people are fighting the cartel war at street level. I believe they know who is in the Azteca gangs, and who is in their assassination squads. When I was at the jail, the adminstration, CERESO, had a map in the office showing which *colonia* gangs affiliate to which cartel, and quite a lot on specific individuals, which means that when they affiliate to a cartel, they know exactly who the rivals are. The information that we have is that when the killings involve known members of the Aztecas, they are carried out by Guzmán's people, and vice versa. And as we know, elements of the police will themselves be at the disposal of one or the other.'

But, de la Rosa continues, ordering a fourth coffee, 'another group of killings, about four to five hundred this year, are of *malandros* – common delinquents, junkies, nothings – such as those in the rehabilitation centres, crack dens and abandoned houses, taking drugs. They are always people expelled from society: low-lifes, addicts, dressed shabbily, often homeless. They play no part in this war, beyond the fact that they are drug addicts, they have no affiliations and their deaths have no logical explanation. And they are killed in a different way to the drug dealers or informers. They are not ritually murdered or mutilated, and I don't think these killings are the work of *sicarios* for the simple reasons that I don't think anyone would want to pay the money the cartel *sicarios* charge in order to kill *malandros*, and the style of killing is entirely different. You would not need a *sicario* affiliated with Guzmán or *La Línea* to kill *malandros* who had gathered to try to clean out in a rehabilitation centre. Cartel *sicarios* either use a few bullets or fire sixty bullets accurately through a small area, like a car window. The *malandros* are also killed by experts in killing – but differently, in ways characteristic of soldiers or the police, in a hail of bullets, sprayed all over the place, mechanically but without regard to the amount of ammunition spent, as is characteristic of military commandos or death squads. The victims are nothing, but their murders are systematic and cruel. I don't have any hard evidence of this beyond ten homicides and fourteen disappearances, but they are all humble people, poor people, not narco traffickers, and I observe that this kind of mechanical killing of the *malandros* suggests training in the army or federal police. They're always after poor people in the poor *colonias*, breaking down doors, taking the young men away and if there's no young man, they take the father, and hardly ever a drug dealer or serious criminal – always *malandros*, low-life.

'I would say,' he observes, less forensically, 'that the army has come to defend the politicians, not the people. I said publicly that a culture of delinquency is growing in the army. My mistake, or my offence, was that I got involved in military matters. Let me say, though, I don't think the soldiers are necessarily directly responsible for many of the killings, but I am convinced that the assassination units are operating with their knowledge, or trained by them, and often you can see the killers working on one side of an army checkpoint, then on another. I notice this when killers go into the rehabilitation centres on some occasions, and more often into houses to kill maybe four or five people, day after day: they often do this within three hundred metres of an army checkpoint.'

'I am not able to pursue these cases,' continues de la Rosa, 'or any other that I have investigated.' The procedure is that he sends his findings to the state commission, which passes them onto the 11th district's military command, which should pass them on to the army's internal investigations division in Mazatlan, Sinaloa. 'I do not know which papers reached which destination,' says de la Rosa, 'all I know is that no proceedings have been brought on any of them.' After we have finished our seventh coffee and a glass of wine in El Paso, de la Rosa's main anxiety is to get to Las Cruces, New Mexico, to meet with Molly Molloy of New Mexico State University, who has been monitoring the threats against him – as part of her coverage of violence in Juárez – and rallying support for him in his flight. It gets even later; we put off the journey until the following morning. On the Interstate, de la Rosa makes a dark joke, saying that when in El Paso, he keeps being recognised by what he describes as the 'middle management' of the Juárez cartel, living on the US side of the border in flight from the violence. 'They ask me to come and eat in their restaurants,' he laughs, 'in just two days I've seen seven or eight of them – their *capos* are still in Mexico, but they're all over here!' De la Rosa has spoken to his office, and been told that if he does not return to work by 6 October, two weeks hence, he will lose the job he is being prevented from doing anyway. We reach Las Cruces, find Molloy in the *Milagro* coffee bar near campus, and de la Rosa orders muffins and coffee, showering the waitress with compliments. When I catch up with them later for dinner, de la Rosa is sporting a beige *Milagro Café* T-shirt.

As we drive back late to El Paso, de la Rosa asks where I am staying. The *La Quinta* on Geronimo Avenue, as always, I reply, nowhere fancy, but it's good and clean, with a fantastic view of Juárez. 'I'll come there too,' says de la Rosa, without so much as a toothbrush. 'The family and I will only get in each other's way; I need to be alone to think.' He checks in, half-recognised by the girl on night duty who comes from Ciudad Juárez, goes to his room on an upper floor and makes a phone call sitting on the bed. The news is not encouraging: an intermediary through whom de la Rosa communicates with General Loera urges him to stay away from the city. 'I must try and get hold of the general, then my wife, in that order, so I know what to say to her,' he says, shifting from the bed to the desk. This tower of a man seems suddenly vulnerable, still dressed in the *Milagro* T-shirt; these are clearly private calls, so the best thing to do seems to be to get him a beer from the fridge in that room of mine, number 262 on the other side of the motel. '*Negra Modelo* or Bud light?' I ask. 'Bud light', he answers quickly, 'with lime.' De la Rosa's room faces out directly onto Interstate 10, cutting virtually across the open doorway, trucks roaring by a short distance from where his head will be, with luck, sleeping. Mine, as always, is at the back, tranquil, overlooking the border and a panorama of Juárez by night, twinkling lights and belching smoke beneath my favourite balcony in America. I offer to get de la Rosa's room changed to the rear, in the interests of slumber and the view. 'No, it's fine.' He smiles as another truck grinds by his doorway. 'I prefer to look at El Paso.'

CHAPTER FIVE

The Human Junkyard

The procession of the possessed sets out soon after the quickening of the eastern sky, while the sun is still low, and meanders its way along the littered bank of dying grass beside Highway 45, as the road departs the raggedy outskirts of Ciudad Juárez heading towards Nuevo Casas Grandes. There are 113 of them: walking like marionettes, some mumbling to themselves, some shrieking out loud, others laughing awkwardly or else silently lost in fretted, crazy thought. They are patients of *Visión En Acción*, a rehabilitation centre and mental asylum on the chewed-up edges of the city, for people enduring the hallucinogenic horror of withdrawal from crack cocaine, crystal meth, heroin, methamphetamine, 'blue water' glue – and the rest. Some are just schizophrenics to whom no other place would open a door, who have found themselves in the company of the recovering addicts. And they all love this walk; they do it three times a week for exercise, and the outings are its high points. And no wonder: the patients spend most of the rest of their lives within the concrete walls and behind the iron doors of the rehab compound where the desert strewn with old tyres and garbage meets the gangrened urban outskirts, just past an army checkpoint and one last Oxxo convenience store before the open road. Some of them even live behind bars – in cages, padlocked, for the safety of others and themselves. Some are former killers, some are former nurses, some are former drug traffickers, some are former strippers – but almost all were drug addicts, now 'clean', but journeying through an inner landscape of nightmare and cold turkey. Indeed, it has been quite a night, punctuated by cries, screeching and laments piercing the still of the desert, and the rattling of metal bars against the chains and locks that bind them.

But night has passed now, its phantoms dispelled with the dew on the creosote bushes and discarded tyres. And as the caravan of the mad makes its way along the roadside, the walkers gesticulate wildly at passing cars, at each other, at thin air or whatever monstrosity or delight they see in their mind's wayward eye. Some motorists look aghast at this surreal parade, and swerve away from it, across the carriageway, lest something untoward happen at close range through the car window. Others, though, are regulars along the route and are acquainted with the procession and even some of the individuals. The driver of a white tanker carrying drinking water hoots and waves, and those walkers who notice the greeting wave back, and call out strange acknowledgements in return. Alejandro, wearing leather headgear and goggles for vintage automobile driving, bursts into a jog in pursuit of the truck, then stops suddenly, distracted by something in the distance that has caught his eye, or at least his imagination. He used to deal drugs, he says, 'all over the world – in China, Japan, and of course France'. There is Manuel, striding along – scary Manuel, who keeps trying to kill his mother, on advice from a rapper called Mr Bone, who visits his visions escorted by 'four little witches'. And there is Becky, 'Crazy Baby' as she calls herself, one of the team leaders and in high spirits this morning, singing '*Escucha la canción de la alegría!*' – listen to the song of happiness. A man called Antonio needs to wear a diaper, only it has come loose and flaps around his thighs as he walks, bare-legged, in a motion of semicircles in alternate directions, leaving a trail rather like that of a snake but occasionally barking like a dog. A twenty-one-year-old called Olivia arrived only this morning, and now tries to make what she can of her new circumstances, clutching at a doll. Crazy Baby Becky takes it upon herself to keep the newcomer company and make sure she feels welcome. Up on the road itself, at the edge of the tarmac, is Josué Rosales, the man who keeps *Visión En Acción* ticking over, day to day – a former heroin dealer and street gang fighter in Los Angeles, he now sees to the running of the refuge, and this morning must act as sheepdog, to ensure no one wanders onto Route 45 and under a truck. Like the one carrying groceries, a big one, which now passes by with a hooting salute to the parade that sounds like a great mechanical fart, and the more cognisant walkers call back, knowing this driver well: 'Señor Oxxo!

Hola, Oxxo!' – the name of the store chain emblazoned on the vehicle's side. But Marisela, once a topless dancer, prostitute and crack addict, lags behind in silence; she has had a hard time so far today, troubled by *'muchas memorias'* and had been tearfully worried that the pastor who runs this remarkable institution might be late, and the walk not happen.

But she worried needlessly, for there he is, up front, leading the way, José Antonio Galván, who established and directs *Visión En Acción*. He has a full head of silver hair which he wears 1950s style; he has his trousers tucked into his boots and carries a long wooden staff to steady his long stride, adding a biblical feel to this exodus to nowhere in particular along the road, 3 kilometres and back again. He, too, from time to time, breaks into a jog, then walks to talk awhile. 'This is the human junkyard,' says the pastor, with a sweep of the arm towards his flock. He was one of them once, a street-wise kid from Juárez who lived illegally in Los Angeles and El Paso, got deported, became a drug addict on the streets back home and 'hit rock bottom, man, the very bottom before I was saved by the Lord.'

'We are the people no one wanted,' he says with a kind of pride, 'cast out. This is where they send the trash that no one else wants. I run a recycling centre for human trash. I take the scrap people off the street, and treat them like human beings. When they come to us, they're not junkies or working women any more, they're not orphans, they're as much God's children as anyone. So just you think about this, brother: back there in the city, the *sicarios* are killing children, people are kidnapping and raping and killing young girls, and people are torturing other people to death, and people are cutting each other's heads off. In here, we're not doing any of that; here we are still alive, helping each other, not killing each other. Here, you can shout out loud, walk around naked with your diaper falling off, and no one will judge you or bother you. In fact, we'll hug you. We're crazy here, but we have love, and we have been saved.' All things being relative, the pastor has a point: in the human junkyard of Ciudad Juárez, the procession of the possessed is, in its peculiar way, a procession of the saved.

To drive south-west out of Juárez towards *Visión En Acción* is to journey through contaminated desert dust along boulevards of shopping malls, nightclubs and rooms-by-the-hour with names like 'San Judas Quick Motel', past more compounds of prefabs built to house labour fodder for the *maquiladoras*, sprawling *colonias* built from scrap and wastelands controlled by gangs. In the dust of early morning, the Boulevard Oscar Flores passes the so-called 'green spaces' that a civic forum of more enlightened business people called Plan Juárez wants to 'reclaim', on which football is sometimes played, but which are more often becoming *dompes* for trash. '*Di No A Las Drogas*' reads a large hoarding – say no to drugs. Another displays an emergency number, o66, which few citizens care to call, because the people manning the hotline are universally believed to be working for the cartels or the security personnel under their control. People joke that calling o66 is the best way to talk to the kidnappers in the event of the abduction of a relative. The road skirts a hillside into which a giant white horse is carved in imitation of that in Wiltshire. It was done by order of Amado Carrillo Fuentes, the Lord of the Skies. Through the outlying military checkpoint, one arrives at a half-built breeze-block structure in the middle of nothing and nowhere declaring itself in careful paintwork to be an '*Alberque Para Discapacitados Mentales*', a home for the mentally disabled – invariably for those fallen prey to drugs. On the wall beside the iron doorway are painted the logo of *Visión En Acción*, a sword breaking and a passage from St Paul's Epistle to the Ephesians, Chapter 6, Verses 11 to 17, which begins: 'Put on the whole armour of the God, that ye may be able to stand against the wiles of the Devil / Because we wrestle not against the flesh and blood, but against principalities, against powers, against the rulers of darkness of this world, against spiritual wickedness in high places.'

As the rust-coloured iron door is pulled aside by those who welcome us, it reveals what seems at first to be a courtyard of narco bedlam. People in various states of derangement and decay either cower and jabber to themselves, dancing around like puppets on strings, or rooted to the ground, just stare incredulously at the very air in front of them. Some come forward, as though propelled by electric shocks, to greet us. First is toothless Rebecca, in a red beret. '*Yo soy* Becky! Crazy Baby!' Then comes another man, diaper flying about his exposed not-so-private parts, with skin pitted by warts and scars. Then another, in a dirty track-suit top and shorts starts to talk, but whatever his story, which he tells in fits and starts, my Spanish is nowhere near understanding a word of it. But neither is anyone else's for whom Spanish is a native tongue. All around is the stench of tribulation, excretia, sweat, grime and a sense of miracle against all odds.

Pastor Galván, who founded *Visión en Acción*, has yet to arrive at this point. But the keeper of the lodge, Josué Rosales, starts to explain how these people came here. He has an inexplicable inner calm behind the intensity with which he speaks, in faultless American English, punctuated by Crazy Baby's contributions. 'Most of them have been addicted to drugs for years,' he says, 'crack cocaine, crystal meth, heroin; and some take stuff that can blow your fuse with just one hit. All of it made here in Mexico, intended for the US, but it only gets as far as the streets of Juárez. See that woman sitting over there, with white hair? She don't say much. She was a strip dancer in a club, got raped, got into crack, went to jail – but she's getting along better now.' Sometimes these people just roll up at the gates, some voice inside telling them they're desperately in need of help, 'which is why I live here', says Josué, 'to welcome them, 'cause they could come any time. Sometimes we find them on the street, talk 'em through it, and bring 'em in, to get 'em off whatever they're on, get 'em some food, attention, and get 'em off drugs. The hospitals, they don't want to know, and someone has to. I ain't got no medical training, but I need to know what to do with 'em, what kind of medicine to give 'em, how to book 'em in and calm them down if they're freaking out or having bad visions, before the doctor and psychiatrist come to check 'em out. Recently, we've had the Mexican consulate bring 'em in after they get deported, the police too – just bring 'em here, like junk, er . . . well, garbage, I guess I should say' – and Josué allows himself a smile – ''cause I'm a recovered heroin addict myself!'

So first comes Josué's own story, which he takes time out to tell, first on a rickety bench outside his little breeze-block and sleeping quarters 'office' on the outside of the heavy iron gates – a story he tells during four visits over a year. The pastor keeps a video of Josué arriving at the home on a stretcher, unable to move, heavily bearded and skeletal, his skin like dry parchment folded over his bones. 'Sometimes,' Josué begins, 'you can be on both sides. You can think you're fine, and go back over to the other side. You flip, or take drugs just once, and you're back in the dark. Me, I'm fine now. I think. I do my best. I do my very, very best, and I'm still here, on this side of them gates.' He gestures towards the door though which he arrived as a patient some three years ago; his veins swimming with heroin and flesh punctured by needles, his bones broken after a car crash. He was in death's waiting room. 'When Josué came,' Pastor Galván would recall later, 'he couldn't walk — he could barely move. I had to amputate his finger myself. I kept it for a while, to show him, but eventually threw it away.' 'I arrived on St Valentine's day, I later learned,' says Josué. 'February fourteen, three years ago next year [2010]. I've seen the video; I was dying. I was in a coma. I was one of *them*.' And he gestures across the yard, as afternoon deepens, and a woman who has just eaten asks where the line for food is. 'I'd had a car accident and I couldn't walk, couldn't move. I lay here for a year on a mattress in a corner with the door open, watching all these crazy people jumping around the patio, just like I'd been jumping around downtown. And a voice said to me, "Kill this person inside you who is destroying you." And the Lord told me not to go back to being one of them again. All I wanted to do was walk, and get my life back.'

Born in Ciudad Juárez, Josué went to the San Gabriel Valley in California, to live and work. 'But I grew up with heroin,' he says. 'Heroin is always the same thing, wherever you take it — Juárez, LA, it's always heroin. I used to do heroin in California, and deal it too. I did cocaine, angel dust and all the other stuff, too, but got stuck with heroin. And when you get stuck with heroin, you're hanging out with heavy fellas. Some of them junkies have big houses and nice cars, but some again they sleep in the trash and empty houses. For a while, I had a job in an auto body shop, and I used to lift weights. I had a '62 convertible and a 1946 customised truck. In 1982, I got first place in a low-rider show. But I was doing heroin, I got busted, I went to jail, and that's where I blew my mind. I remember thinking, I'm too young for this — 'cause jail is all about gangs. I was given a knife, and I was fighting. Jail is where I went crazy. When I came out, I knew every gang in east LA and the San Gabriel Valley, and after a while out, I knew every barrio. Serious shit, shit, shit.' And Josué lifts his shirt and sleeves to show the scars

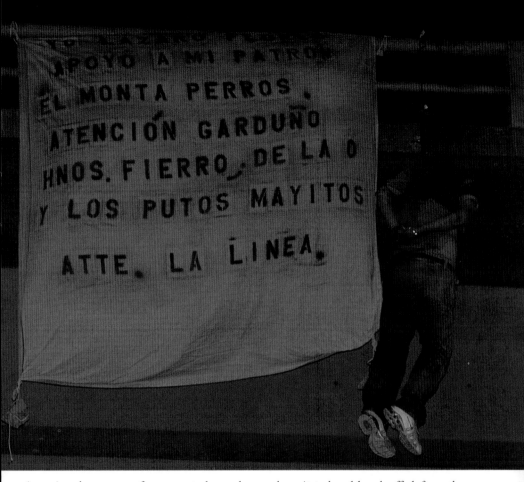

Amexica: the corpse of an executed man hangs, decapitated and handcuffed, from the Puente Rotario in Cuidad Juárez, known as the Bridge of Dreams, accompanied by a banner of warning – September 2008. (*Below left*) La plaza: Joaquín Guzmán Loera, leader of the Sinaloa cartel, known as *El Chapo*, or 'Shorty' – wanted and at liberty. (*Below right*) Osiel Cárdenas Guillén, leader of the Gulf cartel/Zetas – captured, extradited, convicted and jailed in Texas.

The devil's highway: migrants prepare to cross the perilous and deadly desert frontier, illegally, into the United States, northwards from the Sonoran town of Altar – after a briefing with the Mexican army.

Urban Frankenstein: children forage in the blood-strewn aftermath of the massacre of ten patients at the Anexo de Vida – Annexe of Life – drug rehabilitation clinic in Cuidad Juárez – September 2009 – one of many such massacres in rehabilitation centres.

Here begins the homeland: federal police and a helicopter arrive at the scene of another murder in Tijuana – the war in what was once a tourist destination rages between Guzmán and the local Tijuana cartel.

Urban Frankenstein the corpse of another victim of the slaughter in Juárez is hung by handcuffs to a chain link fence. Drug-related murders in Juárez make it the most dangerous city in the world.

The human junkyard: pastor José Antonio Galván, with patients at his *visión en acción* centre for recovering addicts and the insane, on the outskirts of Ciudad Juárez.

Wind of knives: women protest for peace in Ciudad Juárez. Since 1997, hundreds of women have been singled out for especially brutal murders in the city – a series of killings that has come to be known as the *feminicidio*.

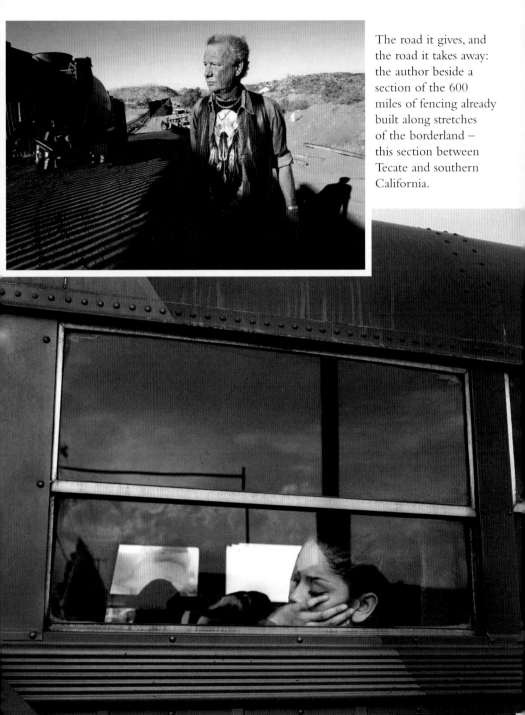

The road it gives, and the road it takes away: the author beside a section of the 600 miles of fencing already built along stretches of the borderland – this section between Tecate and southern California.

Eat off the floor: an exhausted factory girl leaves work aboard a special transport bus after a shift in one of the thousands of *maquiladoras* – sweatshop factories built along the border to assemble goods for duty-free export to the United States.

(*Above*) Gateway to the Americas: migrants prepare to jump and ride a train from Nuevo Laredo across the border into Texas. Trains and trucks carry $367.4m worth of trade through this crossing annually. The cargoes are often contaminated with drugs.

(*Left*) Amexica: in downtown Ciudad Juárez life goes on, the bars stay open, and cowboy hats and baseball caps remain in style. But soon after dark, the streets will be deserted.

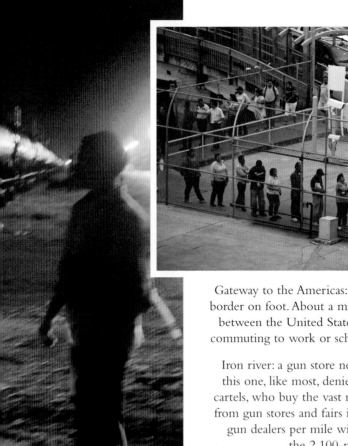

Gateway to the Americas: the daily line to cross the border on foot. About a million people walk or drive between the United States and Mexico every day, commuting to work or school, shop or visit relatives.

Iron river: a gun store near the border in Texas – this one, like most, denies selling weapons to the cartels, who buy the vast majority of their hardware from gun stores and fairs in the US. There are three gun dealers per mile within a short distance of the 2,100-mile border.

Tell them who you are: Santísima Muerte, most holy death, is the spiritual icon of the narco war, here kept company by an M1 carbine.

Tell them who you are: the Virgin of Guadalupe, Empress of the Americas – wearing the serpent of her Aztec alter ego, the Mother Goddess Coatlicue, deity of fertility and destruction.

from bullet wounds. 'That one happened in San Dimas, there was a battle in the middle of the night. A gang from La Susa shooting at us, but I got to take off, running right up the side of the highway, like that' – and he shoots a flat hand through the air, cutting.

Josué's recollection of his past keeps getting interrupted by reminders of his illness: patients. 'There are a lot of feelings in this place for me. I'm only the person I am now because I've been there and I know their feelings.' The narrative continues: 'I had to come back from LA because my mother was sick, but I kept taking the drugs – man. I was part looking after my mother, and part not looking after myself. By the time I got hit by the car, I was spending 250 pesos a day on heroin, that's almost a gram a day, five or six shots. I was in that scene; some of them got AIDS. Some got gangrene, like me. There's always heroin around for fifty or sixty pesos a shot, and you got people needing a fix, seeing other people carrying a load of money around and they're thinking, Hey, what's going on here? Hey, hey, hey – I can have some of that money if I shoot what I need and sell on the rest. That's what happens when you're totally hooked, totally fucked up. If you found some work and got fifty dollars, you'd spend it all on getting a fix. It was just: I've got to get fifty dollars so I can get fixed up.'

Even though this conversation happens in stages, months apart, Josué's narrative is punctuated by feral sounds from within the yard and dormitories looking onto it, sounds from some zone between a scream of pain and a peel of laughter. He continues: 'When a car hit my back three years ago next February, something else hit me too. I told myself that if I hadn't been using drugs, that car would never have hit me. I realised there was no one to blame, no one said 'hey, try this', no one pushed me. I'd done this all to myself. They brought me here and I just wanted to go to sleep for ever. But I didn't sleep for months, I just watched and listened to the people who were like I'd been, for days, nights, weeks and months – feeling the pain, and watching. Then really I woke up, something exploded, *gracias* to the Lord. I'm fifty years old now, and I feel better than I've ever felt. When I go downtown, I always see four or five of 'em. People I used to shoot up with. And they call me *Güero* – blondie – just 'cause I lived in the US. Then someone'll say, "You looking good, man! Wish I could look like you. Wish I could stop taking all these cocktails, shooting all this junk." That's when my life gets weird, man, very weird. So I get glad I went through that pain, so I can help the others.'

From Josué now comes the street-level explanation of what is happening in Juárez. 'The market now for drugs in Juárez – it's very tough competition 'cause the drugs are getting so much stronger – and you go round the houses: "Hey, mine's better!" they say, "mine's stronger", and people have so many options. And especially in Juárez. If you're somewhere else, you'll come all the way to Juárez to get the good stuff. That's what a lot of these people were doing. Most of these people were addicts, selling drugs to feed their own habit. But they never see the big fellas. They buy it off people one step up the line, and here, you don't need to sell pure like the stuff that crosses the border. They buy it cut with rat poison, fertiliser or whatever; take some then cut the rest again to sell on. Cut it ten times, you get ten times the money; sell it in the wrong place, you get shot. The big guys are nothing to do with this level, I know that. They don't even know what Juárez looks like. They just make the $250,000 a day, the next guy down $10,000 a day, and so on, down to ten dollars a day. You know who you buy from, and who you deal to, but you never know beyond that, or who is moving all that coke or meth into the USA. Only other folks know that, way above the street.

'Do you want to see where I lived on the floor for a year?' Josué asks. And we walk through the iron gates again, into the world that was his, and from which he is now separated by the thin veils of his conversion, his responsibilities and a wall. To say that the stench is unbearable is no insult, it is just to admit that there is nothing like the suffocating stink of misery. A man speaks, Manuel – a former but now part-time crack and heroin addict on a high wire between saving himself and the abyss. When he hears the voice of a rapper called Mr Bone, he explains, coherently, 'Mr Bone tells me to kill my mother. "Kill Your Mother!" he says. "Kill Your Mother!" He comes into my room, and tears fall from my eyes. And when I get with my friends and we smoke some, the four little witches arrive, and Mr Bone too, and they order me to fight with guns.' For four years, Manuel has been here to try to exorcise Mr Bone and the little witches, and exchange the drugs for religion, or at least survival. 'He's getting there,' says Josué, 'but he ain't there just yet.'

A man wearing a football shirt joins us, Luis Noreto. 'He was a problem for a while,' says Josué, 'tried to kill someone three or four times, and tried to kill his mother.' (It seems to be a rite of narco-passage, this matricide.) 'Yes,' recalls Luis, 'I hit some bad luck. My mother was praying for me with a candle, but I thought it was a sword, so I tried to kill her, and she brought me here.' Luis was on crystal meth, 'rock' (crack) and sniffing paint-thinner. 'But now,' he says, 'I listen to Josué and have found Jesus Christ, and when my mother comes to visit me, I see my mother. I want to stay here forever, and help people like I was, to be like Josué.'

So just as Josué modelled himself on the pastor, so Luis models himself on Josué. And now, the pastor himself arrives. There is a term in African-American preaching: the 'charismatic' style, and the pastor is its Hispanic mutation. Galván has little (earthly) backing for what he is doing here, hardly any money, but 'with love in our hearts, smiles and hugs, and holding them close to our chest, we do what we do in here', he says, by way of introducing himself. The patients call out: '*Papí!*' − Daddy − with excitement, run to him, and he clasps them to his breast, kissing them, heedless of their weeping sores, stroking their matted hair. He looks a bit like a movie star acting the role of a former street-wise kid from the barrios. Which is exactly what Galván is − the former barrio kid. He has a tattoo of an Indian squaw on one arm. 'I was born in Ciudad Juárez, it's my city and I love it. But I was fourteen years over there, from 1972. I was an illegal in Los Angeles and El Paso. Yeah, the wild years! Man, I was making money, operating a crane, hanging out whatever; there were drugs and babes to spend it on and that's what I spent it on.' He was jailed for a period − he implies it was for drugs − and deported. 'And after I got deported and I was back home in Juárez,' he says, echoing Josué and gesturing towards his patients. 'I was one of *them*, completely lost.'

Galván's conversion happened on the streets upon which he was dying, found by street missionaries just as he now finds others for *Visión En Acción*. '"The Lord Wants You," they told me. "Wants *me?*" I figured. "*Wants* me?" I used to tell those Bible people to get the hell away from me. "Get the fuck off my back!", I'd cuss 'em − but they treated me in a different way to how I'd ever been treated, so I started treating myself differently. Found a whole lot of needs

I didn't have before.' There were several spiritual and physical adventures, culminating in an experience that led to the founding of *Visión En Acción*, an echo of the Good Samaritan: 'I was driving through the cold one night, and saw people sleeping by the wayside wrapped in blankets of snow. That was when the Lord gave me this mission.' The shivering roadside outcasts were Pastor Galván's calling to establish *Visión En Acción*, which he believes to be his destiny. 'The task,' says Galván, 'is to dignify the lives of these people, and to return those lives to them. Sixty per cent of them have completely lost their identity. They don't know their own name, age, who they are, where they came from or why they're here. They don't know what they were doing before they came here, but many get very aggressive when they arrive. That guy there, the big guy, he was brought by eight cops, handcuffed by the hands and feet – he'd tried to kill a guy in the USA. That one there had a problem with heroin, his arms were all pitted with holes and all them holes infected. And when we go inside their heads, we find that no one ever loved them or hugged them, their mothers didn't care and their stepfathers hated them, they never went to school – they sold Chicklets and newspapers on street corners or worked in clubs if they were girls. They started out on glue and paint-thinner, then different drugs, more expensive and dangerous drugs, then they're hooked.

'But we show 'em the path, the way out, because we've been there too, we know where they are, and how to find the path. I was there; I was living on the streets, trying to work out where the next hit was coming from, and the next meal, looking for food in trash cans. Josué, too – the director of the hospital brought him saying: "I'm giving you this man to die." No, I thought, he's already dead but we can bring him back to life. Now he's my right arm here, and my greatest fear is he'll slide back and start taking drugs again. He says he won't, he won't even use tranquillisers, but we're all on the edge here.'

The pastor finds it 'weird that there are also people here who know me from my old life', he says with a strange expression of disdain, whether for them or himself. 'They've seen me on the street and lying in a bed, and some of them try to take advantage of me; at first I had trouble with a couple of guys and a woman – I could see into their thinking: We used to change this guy's diapers and spoon feed him and now he's a boss? But mostly now they see me as a boss — they have to learn that's what I am. There's a hierarchy here, there has to be for it to function.'

There is a man called Alejandro Valencia García with electric-blue eyes who washes all the cars parked outside the centre, obsessively — wiping them down, polishing them; the visiting relatives' cars, our car and especially the pastor's. He's the man wearing vintage driver's headgear, a leather cap with earflaps, and tells the pastor: 'You fool everybody.' 'Why?' retorts the Pastor. 'Because I'm the only one who knows that you're even crazier than the rest of us,' Alejandro replies, and walks away laughing. 'He was a big drug dealer,' says Pastor Galván. So it was true, what Alejandro had said, out along the highway, though maybe not about China, Japan and France.

One Sunday, they await the pastor again. The iron gate is open, it being the Sabbath, and the patients mill around in the shade of trees they have planted, surrounded by benches made of rocks they have set and painted white. And when the pastor's car pulls up in the driveway, they surround it, clapping. Others stream through the doorway from the courtyard calling: '*Papí! Papí!*' Others again, on the edges of the throng, wander and wonder, staring with a flicker of recognition, whis-pering confidences for themselves alone to hear. Because it is Sunday, the pastor is wearing a Zoot-style blazer in a paisley design, and black suede shoes. He looks as though he is about to sing 'Rock Around The Clock', but instead — once the multitude is settled — he gets out his acoustic guitar, sits down on the painted concrete bench in the shade of a mesquite tree and begins to sing. 'Who is your friend when you need Him? . . .' A woman sits at his feet, unties his shoelaces and ties them up again — a deranged but poignant echo of Mary Magdelen at the feet of Christ. '*Cristo Sí, Cristo Sí, Cristo Sí, Sí, Sí . . .*' The singa-long is extraordinary — uplifting and disturbing. Some sing beautifully, and in tune; others wail like coyotes in a fit of lunar-induced ecstasy. 'Crazy Baby' Becky bashes a tambourine hopelessly out of time but with feeling, singing louder than anyone else, while a lady with a black shawl and cropped hair and a smock stares into mid-distance, smiles, drops the smile and weeps. Becky puts down the tambourine, takes her head and lays it in her lap.

Pastor Galván sits down to talk about things that have happened in the eight months since my last visit. 'The big thing now,' he says, surveying the bedlam around him, slightly stilled by Sunday hymns, 'is synthetic labs, synthetic drugs: we're seeing people's brains getting fried by crystal meth and ice; it's easy to transport, easy to hide, but it's causing a lot of dead people, lots of orphans and widows, and a lot more people like you see here. There's been an invasion of addiction in the city – they're everywhere, like human cockroaches crawling around looking for synthetic drugs. Juárez – it's sinking under a flood tide, a tsunami of addicts, all crazy. They've been given video games if they're lucky, so they know how to kill virtually, and when they're out of their heads and need another hit, they'll take the money to go out and kill for real jus' like they learned in the games.'

I ask about Manuel, Mr Bone and his little witches. 'He suddenly recovers his mind, and suddenly loses it,' replies the pastor. 'When he's doing well, he knows who he is. Then he hears the voices, telling him to go and kill his mother, and starts masturbating all the time, in front of people. He's been doing it since he was seventeen years old and started on crack, and now he's twenty-five.' One time, says Pastor Galván, 'I took him to the store to get cigarettes, and on the way back we stopped at the checkpoint and as we descended he was at the soldiers trying to get their weapons so he could kill the people in his head, and when I told them I was a pastor, they said, "What are you doing with this guy, motherfucker?" They never want to see me with him at the checkpoint again. Yeah, a lot of problems, Manuel.'

Manuel is a heavy-set man who sometimes contorts his face as he speaks, and at other times smiles as though concealing a secret. It has been some ten months since he explained about Mr Bone and the four little witches, and now he talks quite lucidly, though the content follows his own logic. 'I don't have so many problems now, but I do want to go back and party and I still have a big problem with my mother about witchcraft. She also says I beat her, which I do; I like to beat her. My brother was attacking me with witchcraft, but I don't have the papers to escape to the US. My wife is in Texas, living with my sister.' ('Rubbish,' says the pastor.) Mr Bone, says Manuel, continues to 'use spells and magic against me. And he's very tall, as tall as I am. My new mission is Thai boxing.' Manuel veers into a new theme.

Can you box against Mr Bone? 'Hmm. If I recognised him and he made me angry, I could fight him. I'm dangerous when I'm angry.' And Manuel stops screwing up his face, and smiles that secretive smile. 'They gave me the weapons to do it, but I never intended to spray people with bullets.' We have to let that go. Manuel presses his nose against his face, squashing it, then pulls and stretches it – kneading it between his fingers as he talks. 'And then come the four little witches again, telling me I should go home, to have money and women.' Would he ever try to fight the four little witches? 'I want to fuck the four little witches,' replies Manuel. 'They look so sexy, they're *gringa* witches, blonde ones, Americans.'

We walk back, with the pastor, into the yard, the human junk-yard, the concrete quadrangle where the mad and the scared people roam. In a room off to the right, a man rattles the bars of his padlocked cage, growling in short bursts, then suddenly conversing in a winning way, feigning lucidity, asking for help to be let out to return home to his family. 'Don't get involved,' counsels the pastor, 'he knows how to manipulate, even though his brain's gone. He tried to stab someone, so we call him '*Cholo*', the gangbanger. He can get very violent,' the pastor continues relaxedly, a matter of inches away from the cage. 'And Josué's problem is that he's not that strong yet, and if he tried to intervene between *Cholo* or Manuel and one of the other patients, he could get killed. When *Cholo*'s in a crisis, it's ugly, hard to stop him, so we keep him locked up.'

Bounding across the yard comes Rebecca, Crazy Baby, who, says the pastor, is usually 'more than half in command of herself', and is thus a supervisor of the thirty-six women patients. You can see her taking to her role – that girl crying during the singing this morning, whom Becky rested upon her lap. 'Ah yes, Lety,' says the pastor. 'Lety and Elia – they're sisters. They were found chained up in an abandoned house. They'd been chained up all their lives, like dogs, ever since they were babies. Their parents were addicts and finally left them, abandoned.' We pass the line for food served by big Oscar, now a prefect for the men's wards, and we enter one of those for the women. The rows of mattresses and bodies stink noticeably less than the men's quarters, but the insects are just as populous and, as with the men, there is little distinction between being clothed and unclothed, although Becky's regime tries to keep things decent. On one mattress, Lety and Elia cling to one another. Both have shaven heads and wear long frocks. They speak – or rather, make squeaking noises – in fits and starts, staring hard and quizzically. They are like two little children, although they are in their early thirties. 'They're afraid of everyone,' says Pastor Galván. Apart from, it seems, Becky, who approaches them, and strokes their cropped hair. 'I take care of them,' says Becky, who is about the same age as they are, 'they are my little babies.' In this world, it matters not where affection comes from, only that it exists at all.

Becky has a deputy in her task as prefect: Marisol, who wears a woolly hat despite the September heat, and closes her eyelids when spoken to with a shy, childlike sweetness – and sadness. 'She was a waitress at a strip joint,' the pastor informs, 'a dancer, doing cocaine and smoking crack, and prostitution to feed the habit.' Now she sweeps the yard and cleans surfaces with a dirty rag, in silence. Marisol seems to know where and who she is, but keeps it all to herself. 'I'm jealous of Marisol,' says Becky. Oh yes? 'Yes I am, because she has a little baby, who they bring to visit her. I fell in love with him when he was three years old.' (Marisol's child is a girl.) Marisol also plays an important role here, adds Pastor Galván, organising the women's wards, their food, dressing and washing. 'But she's schizophrenic; terrible depressions, fits, loses herself completely. She had to be locked up for a year, she was so violent.' It seems unbelievable – this placid, timid, apparently crushed but gentle soul, but there is no such thing as a surprise in this place – only the threat of the worst surprise of all.

'Now we're in the firing-line,' says the pastor. 'Yes, us – mental hospitals, rehab centres. You had ten killed at the *Anexo* the day after the *Grito*; and seventeen were lined up and shot in August at the *Aliviane* – just little addicts, like we have. They're going round the rehab centres taking out people who had any business with the other cartels, and anyone else they take with 'em.' There have already been some 'funny phone calls', says the pastor, on another occasion – at dinner in El Paso, where he lives for safety. 'They called up and said they were the police – but that can mean anything in Juárez. Now we're in danger, we who run help for the addicts and crazy people, we're on the front line, just by being here and doing what we're doing. They could come for us any night now.'

Night falls over *Visión En Acción*, and the pastor has left. Josué – delegating some tasks to Oscar, Becky and Marisol – administers medication and shuts things down before retiring to his quarters. The darkness that falls is a deep one, out of which the pastor's fears of what has happened to so many other rehab centres loom larger than they do in daylight. The room, or rather the little cubicle of breeze-blocks, in which I am graciously hosted to sleep is, as Cardona points out as he leaves, 'right next to the entrance; the first they'd get to if they come tonight'. But the iron bed is already made up, and there's nothing for it but to settle in with Josué and chat away the evening by torchlight. We talk about Led Zeppelin and The Who. 'Man, they come from England? I never knew that. I used to love that stuff, but we don't get it in here.' He talks about his family, while we eat cold burritos, and about his cousin's husband, a US marine, who had 'fought in Afghanistan and against that other guy, Saddam Hussein – he kicked his ass too'. Josué makes as though to fire a machine gun: 'I heard from him all about those countries, it sounds like fun.' But Josué had recently attended his cousin's funeral: he died not in warfare, but 'in Pinkie's bar, having fun, you know [Josué shakes his hips, as though to jive], and in they came, looking for someone. Sprayed the place with bullets.' And Josué talks about his work and some of the people in his care. 'Look, what I do here is part of my testimony. A lot of people come through here, and we stare at each other in the eyes, and we can see the drugs; we know, yes we know we've been there. In that stare, I say it with my eyes that I've been even worse'n you are now. I say to 'em – staring hard with my eyes, 'cause they wouldn't understand if I spoke it – I say: "You've come through fire and water and so have I, so I know what you are doing here." And even though they're crazy, and can't hear a word, I think they kinda understand.' He lets on that the benign ones are not always what they seem. 'Becky can be real dangerous. Usually she's fine, but when she flips, she flips real bad, she's a violent one. When she gets angry with me she's threatening to kill me and all sorts. Oscar, he's desperate to make it. He really wants to succeed. But man, when he explodes, he explodes. He needs putting down real hard, real difficult to deal with.'

Josué wants to watch a home-view movie. He goes to his cubicle, next to mine, rummages around for his DVD player and sifts through the black wallet containing his collection. 'I got some titty ones, but, hey, how about this? It's about the crucifixion of Jesus, man, this one's gonna blow your mind; I saw it but not really properly.' It is Mel Gibson's *Passion of The Christ*, and into the player it goes. The bloodier the sufferings of Our Saviour get, the more Josué's devotion deepens. The flagellation is an especially savage and prolonged episode, Jesus lacerated to the bone. Josué is transfixed. The fiendish elders of Jewry and weakness of Pontius Pilate stir his wrath – 'Motherfuckers!' – and a pitiless depiction of Calvary makes Josué sweat with empathetic rage, so that by the time of Jesus' convulsions of pain on Golgotha, Josué's eyes are popping out of his head. Only with the storm clouds, and winds that rent the temple shroud apart, does Josué relax again, and prepare for bed. There is one last tour of the courtyard, under the stars. However haunted their slumber may be, those tortured in the mind rather than by nails to the hands and feet are mostly asleep. The occasional groan of anguish drifts from the dormitories, on the desert breeze, sometimes ascending into a whine. Josué shines his flashlight through the bars of *Cholo*'s cage – he is motionless, under a heap of blankets. All told, it feels as though some untamed animal is at rest, its afflictions abated a moment, by the quiescence of unconsciousness. There is quiet, but the smell still lingers, though even that is tempered by the chill hanging from the desert night. Josué makes his way back through the kitchens to our adjacent sleeping quarters, and we exchange good wishes for the night, so dark in these windowless quarters, with nothing but desert out there, that even with eyes-wide-open one is blind as a mole.

The occasional truck rumbles by towards Nuevo Casas Grandes or back into Juárez, but otherwise there is silence. Josué has been both disturbed and excited by the sufferings of his Saviour, and the dark feels darker just for the fact of being on the edges of the murder capital of the world with 113 recovering maniacs for company, and only Josué and a wall between us. But it is not the maniacs that constitute the unquiet in the night, what with the events at *Anexo* and *Aliviane* a few days beforehand, and the trick is not to think too hard about those bloody bootprints all over the courtyard back there, the sticky crimson pools in the infirmary or the pastor's fears about this place. So long as the door remains shut, one will survive the night. Sleep comes (with a little chemical assistance), but for the laments that pierce the black from within the dormitories – the wailing, yowling, winnowing sounds of visions disturbing the sleep of the mad.

Josué's shuffling heralds the day. Through a crack in the door, now ajar as he begins his duties, a first hint of silver-blue across the eastern horizon makes its entry into my cubicle. The hills to the west, into which the Lord of the Skies' white horse is etched, respond with a pink hue, and twilight arrives. And into the morning, as the sun rises, they emerge into the courtyard to begin another day; mumbling, grunting or singing but mostly silent as they depart the land of sleep. The first task is to deal with the excretia that night has generated, the stench of which is best removed before it is intensified by sunrise. This involves teams organised by Josué, big Oscar and others, swilling buckets of water across the dormitories and floors. Part of the same operation is to change the diapers of those who use them, mostly men. The afflicted are lined up in a row outside their sleeping places while those with an awareness of where to direct the body's rejected matter wipe them down and apply new nappies. Then, with the sun bolder, come the showers. There are two of them, attached to the courtyard walls, and all 113 people line up to wash, men under one waterfall, women under the other – the line therefore twice as long on the male side. They leave their clothes in a pile on the concrete slabs, stand under the cold water, and may or may not be scrubbed down by the team of prefects, Oscar and his male assistants for the men, Becky and Marisol for the women. Some, of course, have to be unlocked from their cages for washing down, and this is supervised by Josué himself, working in overdrive. Some of them rattle the bars and scream to be let out; others, like *Cholo*, just wait in sullen silence to be called and temporarily released for cleansing. When the bathers are finished, they clutch their own shrivelled, crinkly bodies against the cold, dry dawn with their clothes or a towel if they can get one, go back round to their underwear and pile of rags and put them back on. It all works estimably well and smoothly, there is order in the mayhem. All the while, the patients acclimatise themselves to morning, test their walk, stop, reflect, walk a little more, stop again, look around them and work it out, whatever it is. They may smile or they may cry at the conclusion they draw. A man called Julio has been completely blinded by the cocktails of drugs he has taken, and complains of cold and the noise the others are making. Josué, working like there'll be no tomorrow, now appears with a collection of brooms, which he distributes. Becky commandeers one and sweeps every corner of the courtyard she can reach. Others follow her, some just stand there, holding their brooms. Alejandro, the former drug dealer, has already donned his open-top driving headgear and started cleaning cars again – the only one parked here and others abandoned in the desert. 'See that radio over there?' He points to a car stereo lying in the dirt. 'I got that from the truck with a broken window. I'll tell you something,' and Alejandro draws near, his breath heavy with something smelly, 'it's not a car, it's a plane. It flies.'

The sun is risen, it is time for the walk along the highway, and the pastor is late. They gather outside the gates, sit under the trees and wait. *¡El Camino! ¡El Camino!*' they shout excitedly. Marisol stands alone, clutching a broom and weeping. 'If *Papi* doesn't come, we can't walk,' she sobs. Then she crawls back into her cave of silence. What's troubling you? 'Many things.' Memories? 'Many memories.' Bad ones? 'Very bad.' But the pastor will be here soon, and we can all walk! 'I just want to walk. It's so beautiful, the walk. My baby came to see me. But she's gone now. All I want is to have a nice walk, but *Papi* is gone too.' She cries again. 'It happens suddenly,' says Josué, 'you don't know what or why, just hurtin' inside.' But not for long, for a maroon car pulls into the driveway and here he is, pulling his staff off the back seat and off we go.

'We need money,' Pastor Galván cuts to the quick. 'People like you come and say they care, but we need money. What about you? Can you give us some of what you got?' We stride out to the highway, and Alejandro stays behind to wash the pastor's car. 'Let's go all the way to Argentina!' Josué shouts from the roadside as the procession of the possessed winds its way to nowhere in particular, Pastor Galván to the fore, trousers tucked into his boots and pounding his staff into the ground. Out on the road, they talk, even Lety, who amazes: 'When we were chained in the house, we were like birds in a cage. When we walk we are alive,' she warbles.

And by the time we return, 3 kilometres down the road and 3 back to the centre, big Oscar has supervised the creation of a plentiful breakfast. There are vegetables, fruits, beans and rice. There is water and there is singing, led mainly by Becky who has not stopped her '*Canción de la Alegría*', song of happiness, since halfway down the road. The sun is high, the air is warm at last, and another day of heterotopia in the human junkyard begins.

We agree that whatever one believes or does not believe, the bedrock of Christianity is a progression from Crucifixion, via Descent into Hell, to Resurrection – essentially: Good Friday, Easter Saturday and Easter Sunday. And that whatever is happening here is hopefully some stage between Saturday and Sunday morning. But by the time we get to this conversation though, impending night covers the land, the gloaming begins to fall, the witching time arrives, darkness is visible to the east. We say our farewells, and make to go, until the next time. 'You call this a mental institution, but when you get back to the city, you're in the real madhouse,' says the pastor, 'back in the real human junkyard.' But he is interrupted by a figure who has clambered out of the yard and is now lurking on the roof, leaning over the eves and silhouetted against the deep golden flare of last light on the desert horizon. '*Yo soy* Rebecca!' comes a voice between a croak and laughter. 'Crazy Baby!'

CHAPTER SIX

The Wind of Knives

In Aztec lore, life was a brief passage through a world of pain and malice, prelude to reunion with the ancestors after death. Beyond the boundaries of the world was a universe made from death, whence the winds blew from the four directions. Death had three realms: The House of the Sun, in the sky; a paradise on earth called Tlalocan, and Hell, named Michtlan. Most people – apart from those killed in battle or women at childbirth; those struck by lightning or lepers – began their journey in death through the underworld, in and out of Michtlan. The journey of the dead out of hell was a long and arduous one, across rivers and mountains, encountering devils demanding tribute. But it began with a voyage along a road guarded by a green lizard called Xochitonal, Sign of the Flower, and proceeded across eight icy deserts, through a wind so cold that the deceased needed to burn all his or her possessions – weapons, gifts of passage and the remains and clothing of any captives they had captured in war. The name of the wind was Izchecaya, the Wind of Knives.[1]

When the authorities finally gave Paula González back the medallion of the Virgin of Guadalupe which her daughter María Sagrario had worn around her neck, it was terrible proof of that from which Paula had been hiding some five weeks, refusing to believe that Sagrario was dead. Paula held the medallion in her hands and implored the Madonna: 'Where were *you* when they did that to my little girl?'

Paula and her husband, Jesús, had last seen their seventeen-year-old daughter when she rose for work shortly before 4 a.m. on 16 April 1998, at their gimcrack home in Lomas de Poleo, a shanty of dwellings sprawled across high desert. Sagrario worked, like hundreds of thousands of other local girls, at one of the new factories, the American-owned *maquiladoras*. Normally, Sagrario would leave for the afternoon shift with her father and elder sister Guillermina, but the CapCom company had changed her routine. Instead, Sagrario now took the lonely mile-long walk down unlit dirt tracks to the main route through another shanty, Anapra, where she would wait for the company-chartered bus to take her and her fellow factory girls to work. After Sagrario failed to return that afternoon, Paula went to the police. 'Did she like to stay out late?' they asked. 'Did she wear miniskirts and go dancing?' Paula, disgusted, made 2,000 flysheets: 'Missing Teenager. Please Help.' Eventually, she learned not from the authorities but a newspaper article that Sagrario's corpse had been dumped near her *maquila* on the other side of town.

There is a new word in the Spanish language as spoken in Juárez: *feminicidio* – femicide – the mass slaughter of women. There is no other word to describe the iniquity of a singular and savage phenomenon which appeared at first unique to this city at the heart of Amexica – mystifying and vile: some 340 young women found murdered between 1992 and 2001, when I first went to report on these events. Killed in different circumstances and varying degrees of sadistic savagery, with a further 180 or so missing. 'They have been dumped in public places, not even like animals; more like trash,' says Marisela Ortiz, from one of the groups campaigning to bring the killers to justice. The victims, she says, fit a pattern: 'they are poor, young, working class'. And when they are found, she says, some 'have been tortured, mutilated, bruised, fractured or strangled and violated'. 'The killers,' adds Marisela's colleague Rosario Acosta, 'take no trouble to cover up evidence. With these, the evidence is brazen, right there, every time. Whoever is doing this knows they are immune from the law.' 'When our search teams fail to find a body, one will appear next day,' says Marisela Ortiz. 'There's some code or language: "Just letting you know we are here."' One body discovered in 2002, that of Erica Pérez, was found with her purse strings tied around her neck and underwear around her knees. The authorities say she died 'of an overdose', but would not confirm the results of toxicology analysis. Another, unidentified, girl was found wearing clothes belonging to a different teenager whose body was found along with seven others in 2001. Another, Esmeralda Juárez Alarcón, shut down the little market stall at which she worked in January 2003 in order to catch her computer class. It was dusk; plenty of people to intervene, police officers to be seen around, including a special downtown patrol. But Esmeralda vanished. Gabriel Alonzo, her boyfriend, still works at the stall opposite hers: 'I watched her as she left that day to walk to the school.'

And that same month in 2003, I stumbled into further horror, and a more sinister implication of apparent official complicity: yet more bodies found, and either outright denials or silence from the authorities over their existence – as if there were something to hide; something worse than ineptitude. On a visit to Lomas de Poleo, only to say goodbyes and pay respects to Paula González and present flowers before leaving Juárez one time, there is news. It comes from E.P. (whose name must be protected), one of the vigilantes patrolling the area in the absence of any police interest. E.P. had found three more bodies in the hinterland behind the town a few days ago. Strange, because the official number of bodies recovered for that month, January 2003, was zero. E.P. puts on a cap reading *Jesús Cristo Te Ama* – Jesus Loves You – and heads out to show us the location of his latest, grievous find. We set out, accompanied by Sagrario González's remarkable sister, Guillermina, who has returned from work and is seeing to her mother, but for whom E.P.'s narrative is a recurrent nightmare and was once her work too. In rage and grief at her sister's murder, Guillermina had, she explained, established an organisation called *Voces Sin Echo* – Voices Without Echo – to mobilise search parties in the deserts above Lomas de Poleo, and pressurise the authorities. But, explained Guillermina as we left the shacks behind and drove up into the desert, 'we disbanded it as a formal group. We were being used by the media, by the NGOs [non-governmental organisations]; people were profiting from us, pretending to help, raising money which never arrived.'

We pass through a gate marked in Spanish 'Private Property', and out onto land known to have connections with the Juárez cartel and to contain an airstrip, says Guillermina, for light planes carrying cocaine heading north, as well as roads used by no one except the *traficantes*. In this desert expanse, *Voces Sin Echo* would comb the land day in day out, and E.P.'s tireless group still keeps watch for circling buzzards above a possible cadaver. He guides us to a bush to which plastic police ribbon has been attached, and demonstrates how he works, and worked last week, he says, pawing the fine sand: 'Suddenly there was a hand, then a severed arm.' The bodies were arrayed on their backs in a row, each in the shape of a cross, naked and recently killed, with two *maquiladora* uniforms strewn nearby. 'Their arms were chopped and stomachs ripped out,' E.P. says. 'You get used to finding them,' he adds. 'I've done this so many times.' E.P. radioed the police and fellow vigilantes, with some thirteen witnesses to his call, and the authorities duly arrived to take the bodies into official custody. 'When they came,' says E.P., 'they told us: "That's your work done. You guys can go now."' If we hadn't found them,' he insists, 'nothing would have been done.' As we leave the accursed terrain, a motorcycle rider who has left a plume of sand as he headed to cross our path, waits at the gate to ensure our departure. He wears a balaclava mask, says nothing – and nor do we. Just get out.

Marisela Ortiz, who founded the campaigning group *Nuestras Hijas Regreso a Casa* – may our Daughters Return Home – had asked the authorities about rumours of bodies found that January. 'They denied it, outright,' she reports. Marisela Ortega, a journalist from the paper *El Norte De Monterrey*, was told the same, also Diana Washington Valdez from the *El Paso Times*, across the US border. 'We will provide any pertinent information to the public . . . except for whatever is considered confidential,' Valdez was told. To me, despite instant cooperation from the prosecutor's office on other questions, and offers to respond any time, not a word – until later, when E.P.'s terrible find was admitted to – on this latest discovery. Only one thing emerged as certain from this rueful development: the authorities of Ciudad Juárez were, for whatever reason, covering up the discovery of bodies of murdered women. And so another word in the Spanish tongue came to be oft spoken in Ciudad Juárez during these days: '*el encubrimiento*' – the cover-up.

The *feminicidio* became a badge of Juárez: doctoral theses were published across university departments in the United States; films were made, including Bordertown starring Jennifer Lopez; many books were written, and the cause of the women and bereaved mothers in Juárez, trying to seek the truth against a wall of official resistance and suffering continual menace, became a rallying cause for the women's movement in America and worldwide. In the recent explosion of violence in the city – and implosion of the city – the *feminicidio* continues still; unfortunately, it never went away. Only now it is everywhere across Mexico, directed against all ages of women, subsumed into the hurricane of violence and yet a distinct strand within it. An investigation by *Proceso* magazine in December 2009 showed that as narco-related violence spirals, so too does the intensity and cruelty in the killing of women.[2] They are related: deeply and terrifyingly so, argues one of the leading Mexican-Americans currently writing on these matters, Cecilia Ballí. 'The murders of the women in Juárez revealed a certain *style of killing*,' she says. 'The fact that many of the killings were sexualised in some ways related to the broader wave of violence we're seeing now against both men and women. It has to do with an expression of power, and a particular form of masculine power.' Ms Ballí is descended from one of the formerly great ranching families of the Rio Grande Valley (as will feature in Chapter Nine). She has garnered recognition for her brand of narrative journalism and teaches in the anthropology department of the University of Texas at Austin. 'Some of the media coverage of the women's killings made me cringe,' she argues. 'It perpetuated this idea of Mexico as an exotically violent place; the idea that only Mexican men are capable of these terrible things. The truth is that people in Mexico are struggling as much as anyone to understand this chilling type of violence. I'm trying as an anthropologist to understand what is happening, what it means, where it's coming from. Not that violence always means something, but specific types of violence exerted on the body can serve as a form of communication. I think the message has more to do with the killers than with the victims, which is why I think the *feminicidios* ultimately signal a crisis of masculinity in Juárez, not a crisis with women.

'For me,' she continues, 'the killing of the women in Juárez is about power more than it is about sexual pleasure. The style of the violence demonstrates a specific kind of male performance and a complete domination of the other person.' 'Style' is not a word Ballí deploys lightly, and she will use it later to define the 'social performance' of the new generation of narco bosses and footsoldiers. 'Before, the violence in Juárez was merely functional, but now it's also meant to publicly display a specific kind of masculinity, and to reassert that male power at a time when the traditional forms of masculinity along the border are under threat. You see a similar thing happening between men; the way men are tortured by the military and police and by people in the drug world is often highly sexualised. So I personally see a relationship there between the two. Of course, since men and women's bodies and social status is different, the violence takes different forms and is experienced differently. But all of it is focused on violating the body and on displaying this kind of masculinity that is not simply what we usually think of as "machismo".'

As we have seen, it was the legitimate global economy that wrought fundamental change in Juárez, and provided raw material for the *feminicidio*: the arrival of the *maquiladoras* factories brought to town a workforce that was at the outset almost 80 per cent female. According to an undeclared stereotype, women's hands are more dextrous, and women can be paid less than men and be more easily exploited. *Maquiladora* work is relentless, concentrated and hard on the eye: tiny adjustments to microchip boards, under a searing artificial light. 'We cannot really talk because then you would slip behind,' says Cinthia Rodríguez, who works at the same *maquila* as María Sagrario González. Two visits to the bathroom a day, no independent unions and production lines demanding punishing quotas which are then slowed down when inspectors visit from US parent companies. 'But it's good work,' Cinthia concludes. The arrival of so many young women workers plays hard with the *machista* foundations of Mexican society. For within the enslavement of the *maquilas* was a liberation of sorts. Esther Chávez Cano (who passed away in December 2009) established *Casa Amiga*, the city's first and only centre dealing with sexual and domestic abuse. She explained: 'Men found themselves no longer the breadwinner. Women exchanged subordination at home for subordination to the factory boss, but this offered a certain independence; they could buy clothes, leave their abusive boyfriends, wear mini skirts, go out alone. And, with middle-aged men unemployable in Juárez, this created frustration, a backlash against women exhibiting independence for the first time. Being financially independent and wearing a mini skirt, however, is not an invitation to one's death.'

'The *maquilas* provided meat for the killers,' says Dr Arminé Arjona, trying to gather evidence of the slaying. 'They bring girls from all over, and they're easy to get hold of, for whatever purpose.' 'From the *maquilas*,' says Marisela Ortiz, 'comes the culture of dispensability that underwrites the murders. The *maquilas* see women who work much as they see our city, as something expendable. So what if a woman is murdered? Ten, or a hundred? There are always plenty more.' 'If you want to beat, rape or kill a woman, there is no better place than Juárez,' Esther Chávez told me. 'There are thousands to choose from, plenty of opportunities and, thirdly, you can get away with it. The lives of women, especially poor women, have no value. They are faceless.'

The wind, cold as a wind of knives, whips up sand on the main road though the desperately poor *colonia* of Anapra, which lies beneath Lomas de Poleo, and to the edge of which the dirt road leading to the city arrives. When daylight comes, this road will be heaving with buses and trucks, kicking up the dust; but in the hours before dawn, the shadowy, huddled figures of young women emerge from makeshift homes, moving through the side streets and down to await the special buses which transport them en masse to work. It was down such a road that María Sagrario González walked after saying her last goodnight to her family. Along these dark pathways, many a young woman has disappeared, to be found, weeks later, violated and lifeless, in the scrub beneath the mountain, now a hulk against coming sunrise. At first light, three women from Veracruz explain that they are not even going to work; rather, they get up every morning and go to the *maquilas* in the hope of doing so, having been laid off by a company that went to China, where labour is even cheaper and more compliant. Another, Rosa López Contreras balks when approached by two males, then explains how she never waits for the bus alone now, preferring to stick with friends or else her dog, trained to raise the alarm. These women have forgotten the names of most of their murdered workmates, but María Sagrario González rings a bell. 'I remember her,' says Rosa, 'everybody knows her mother.'

Paula González has a singular, disarming way of talking about her daughter's murder; she moves her eyes across mid-distance and a strange, distant smile crosses her face when reaching the most heartsick passages of her narrative. The González family arrived from Durango in 1995. Jesús had worked in a sawmill, but 'we wanted to come to Juárez to make our lives', says Paula, 'although of course the reality is different. After all, the boss of a *maquila* is like a government official; not a normal human being because he has everything he needs. All he cares about is that you arrive on time and work. That's all.

'This area is famous,' proclaims Paula. 'People say, "Oh, that's where all the murdered girls come from!"' It is a place of hutches on borrowed land; there are spirited little *abarrotes* – basic stores – here and there; Paula has managed to open one of her own. After her daughter was killed, she retreated even from the neighbourhood she had made home: 'My first reaction was to close off completely, thinking only about Sagrario. Her father was in a terrible state; awful physical problems. But then some mothers from the neighbourhood asked me to be their representative, and to act. And I did.'

From somewhere, somewhere remarkable, Paula drew insistent strength. The resultant 'Committee of Neighbours' meets every Sunday. Rather than dwell on the murders, it seeks to find 'ways to protect the living'. It has forced the authorities to install a few electrical lines, some water pumps, and even a kindergarten school. Not that the authorities had much to do with the latter, exactly: merely to give Paula a registration licence number. She found a teacher, and men of the neighbourhood built the little hut to which children are brought at 9 a.m.

'When I deal with the police about my daughter,' says Paula, 'I never know whether I am dealing with a criminal or a cop – probably both. But I feel they have the obligation to tell me what is going on. It's hard to go there every day and see how bored and hostile they are. We don't expect help from the authorities any more. All we can do is awaken the citizenry.' Along the main *Ruta Anapra* are painted black crosses on a pink background – 'Less to commemorate the dead,' says Paula, 'than to warn young women that they are in danger. I do everything for Sagrario,' she reflects. 'Sagrario was in the chorus at church and taught catechism class. She gave the children sweets, therefore so do I. From Sagrario . . .' And Sagrario is staring out from the photograph overhead, with serious, dark eyes.

Paula wrings her hands. There is little point in asking for the big things, so we fight for the normal things in life.

'Only one thing,' laments Paula: 'I would love to have taken Sagrario back to Durango so she could have seen her roots. It is so beautiful there, and she was only fifteen when she left. But now it is impossible even for me to go alone.' Why? 'Because of Sagrario I cannot go. We're a tight family, and they always insisted that if I went back to Durango, I would take Sagrario with me. So that if I returned alone, she would have left them.'

'Everything still astonishes me,' said Esther Chávez at the domestic abuse crisis centre. 'Even though I have been fighting this for ten years.' Chávez had returned from Mexico City to her native Juárez to look after her sick mother, intending to leave again. But her mother lived until the age of 102; Chávez established herself, in Juárez, worked as an accountant, wrote a column in the *Diario* newspaper and opened a dress shop. As she heard about the lives of women in the city, she set up *Casa Amiga*. When the *feminicidio* began, she tried to push the authorities for answers. The official response was to advise women not to dress provocatively, avoid walking the streets and: 'if you are sexually attacked, pretend to vomit. That will be repulsive to the attacker, and he will probably flee'. The unofficial answers came in a more distinctive tone. For a girl to go out alone is 'like a little treat', said former prosecutor Arturo González Rascón. 'Like putting a candy at the entrance to a school.' The former deputy state attorney general, Jorge López, remarked: 'When a young woman goes missing, more often than not, the parents will tell you that she was practically a saint! But then we start making enquiries and find out that she was out dancing every night.' The mother of one girl murdered last year was appalled to find her daughter's clothes tossed, some mornings later, over the fence of the back yard. When a police officer came to collect them, he remarked: '*La chavana andaba da cabrona*' – roughly: that slut was asking for it. 'You must remember,' Chávez had counselled in 2002, 'that this is a state in which wife-beating was not a criminal offence until a year ago. Not unless the wounds were "visible for longer than fifteen days". And even since then, we have failed to get one conviction, because the cases are always said to be too "complicated".'

The tragic farce of the authorities' professed attempts to find the killers began in October 1995. Abdel Latif Sharif, an Egyptian former *maquila* engineer, was arrested and accused of seven murders. Despite a record of sexual violence, he pleaded innocent. The case hit problems: one of the women he was accused of murdering, Elizabeth Ontiveros, turned up alive. The police forensic expert on the case, Irma Rodríguez, said that the bite marks on his alleged victims did not match Sharif's teeth. Police then arrested a group of nightclub workers belonging to a gang, *Los Rebeldes* — the rebels — charging that Sharif paid them to kill seventeen women while jailed. They were accused of seven murders, including that of María Sagrario González, while Sharif's conviction for a single murder was overturned in 2000. The case against the rebels also collapsed, but the authorities claimed another break in February 1999, when a peasant opened his door one night to the sight of a fourteen-year-old called Nancy González, blood streaming from a wound above her eye. A bus driver had violated her, tried to strangle her and left her for dead. The abuser, Jesús Manual Guardardo, and other members of his gang, the Toltecs, were arrested and accused of fifteen murders, to which they admitted but later withdrew their confessions — extracted, they said, under duress and torture. Subsequently, the bus driver Guardardo was convicted and jailed in January 2005 for his part in the murder of 113 women in Ciudad Juárez, along with nine other members of the Toltec gang, two others were also bus drivers.

Events then twisted along a strange course. On 13 May 1999, Sharif's lawyer, Irene Blanco, received a strange telephone call saying there had been a shoot-out between narco gangs and a victim, Eduardo 'Blancas' (an error in the name). She went to the hospital to find her son, severely wounded from three gunshot wounds. He had been driving when the would-be assassins opened fire. Injured, he stepped on the gas, making it to the emergency ward. While he was being operated on, agents from the state police arrived to ask the doctors whether he was dead or alive. A month after the attempted murder, a newspaper in Mexico City, *Reforma*, published the account of a whistleblower from the Juárez police, Victor Valenzuela. Valenzuela had gone to his superiors saying that he knew who was behind the murder of scores of women in the most horrific and sadistic circumstances: people close to and members of the Juárez cartel. The group was, moreover, protected by the police and government officials, including two police officers on the Sharif case. The *feminicidio* in Juárez appeared to include a statistically small but, in Ms Cecilia Ballí's terms, 'stylistically important' number among the 300-plus murdered women killed with a sadistic and sexualised brutality, and allegedly with official sanction.

They stand silent and spectral in the light of dusk: a rose-coloured hue in the sky reflecting the colour with which eight upright crosses are painted. They were placed in what was once a cotton field, now a dumping ground for old tyres, chemical drums, and stinking flotsam and jetsam. On the crosses – by contrast – sweet, fresh flowers are attached. Names are painted in careful script: Claudia Yvette, Brenda, Barbara, *Desconocida* (unidentified), Laura Bernice, Lupita, Esmeralda, Veronica. They are the names of eight women whose mutilated bodies were found here on 21 November 2001. The land is exposed, at a busy road junction; rows of windows on the upper storeys of houses in a walled community overlook the site. No one wanted to see, or tell about, whoever left these cadavers.

Yellow police tape is still strung out along the ditch behind the crosses and there's another cadaver, that of a dog. The stench of rotting rubbish fills the air, along with the evensong of birds and hum of traffic. But whatever message those who dumped the bodies wanted to deliver, there is one from those who erected these crosses: they do not only mark and mourn, they stare, hush as death itself, in accusation, straight across the scrappy land to the cylindrical offices of the *Asociacion de Maquiladoras* – the bonded factories' employers' fedration. In the evening, the pink paint becomes luminous, reflecting the light of the building, and that of the twilight sky. During another dusk, on Mexico's Day of the Dead in November 2002, women from the movement for justice gathered here in tribute 'not just to the eight, but to all the dead women', as Marisela Ortiz said. Two torches were lit and planted in the ground. A cross made in stones was carved into the dirt and surrounded by candles. Flowers were strewn and the Requiem Mass said by two priests: 'Lamb of God who takest away the sins of the world, grant us thy peace . . .'

'It is,' says Marisela, 'a funeral rite, a dignified burial for all of them.'

After years of little headway, prosecutor Arturo González held a sudden press conference, declaring that he had cracked the case. Within five days of the 'cotton-field' discovery, two bus drivers were arrested: Victor Javier García Urbe and Gustavo González Meza, and charged with all eight murders. Confessions to rape, killing and dumping the bodies were quickly secured, videotaped and shown to the press, with a suspense movie-style soundtrack. The drivers said they had been tortured, the authorities retorted that the wounds were 'self-inflicted'. The drivers retained counsel, Sergio Dante Almaraz and Mario Escobedo, ready to prove the procurement of invalid confessions under duress. On the night of 5 February 2002, Escobedo found his car being tailed by the police. He was on the cell phone to his father as the shooting started; the old man heard his son being murdered by a burst of automatic fire. The police insisted that Escobedo was mistaken for a dangerous fugitive and had shot first at their officers' car. There were bullet holes in the police car to prove it. Co-counsel Dante Almarez says he was advised, meanwhile: 'If you do not drop the case, we'll kill you the same way we did Escobedo.'

'It was an execution,' says the man at the heart of the case, Oscar Máynez Griljava, former forensic chief for the Chihuahua state assistant attorney general, who handled the case of the two drivers. Máynez, having resigned in disgust at the end of January 2002, holds one of the few keys to this serpentine story. He is a young, curiously puckish man who, for all his passionate involvement, talks with the professional's air of detachment when we meet in the lobby of what was then the Holiday Inn. As tutor of police cadets and later chief forensic scientist, Máynez was the first to alert his own masters about the likelihood of a powerful consortium of killers behind the slaughter: he connected fifty-six murders between 1993 and 1999.

Máynez says the supposedly self-inflicted cigarette burns to the bus drivers' bodies and genitals were twin-pointed injuries made by two-pronged electrodes used by the police. As regards the Escobedo shooting, Máynez noted that bullet holes in the door of the police car allegedly fired by Escobedo were on the *other side* (the driver's side) to that which was supposedly attacked, and on the other side from the wreckage of the lawyer's car – making it a defiance of physics for Escobedo to have made them. And anyway, adds Máynez, 'whoever shot those holes in the police car, they were not there immediately after the incident. Pictures, even those in the paper, clearly show no holes'.

Máynez points to no specific culprit, but he is lucid on that about which he is certain, even as far back as 2002. One: that 'the authorities and business interests in Juárez have been thoroughly 'narcoticised'. Big drug cartels are a force you need to deal with if you go into government. You can't fight that, and – more important – you are able to make a lot of money out of that.' Second: 'I think behind many of the murders lies an organised group with resources. There are big, powerful forces behind this. The only certain thing is that fact, and that they will continue killing.'

The eight bodies in the 'cotton field' were a last straw for Máynez, even before the torture of the bus drivers. When he checked their DNA, in only one case did forensic evidence give a positive identification (the others either misidentified or the samples contaminated). Five of the bodies, moreover, were covered in 'big pieces of concrete rubble. I thought inevitably possible connections to the construction industry, heavily "narcoticised", with concrete easily traced. But those leads were never followed up. After two days, "case closed".'

With Oscar Máynez gone, the forensic burden fell upon Irma Rodríguez Galarza, who examined body after body, and even spent time roaming the streets under cover. But on 25 July 2001 – two years after she had forensically discarded the case against Sharif – Dr Rodríguez was preparing a lecture in Mexico City when someone asked her if she had seen the news: 'They shot up the family of some forensic scientist in Juárez.' Irma's daughter, Paloma Villa Rodríguez, and her husband, Sotero Alejandre Ledesma, had been gunned down on the porch of the family home in a brazen execution by men firing AK 47 rifles from two vehicles. The authorities expressed regret that the pair were caught in the crossfire of a drug-related shoot-out. No suspects were identified or interviewed.

* * *

There is one case that particularly disturbed Oscar Máynez, as it did his opposite numbers at the FBI in El Paso: the killing of seventeen-year-old Lilia Alejandra García Andrade, abducted on St Valentine's Day 2000 outside a television shop, her body found a week later. The murder, says Máynez, bears the same signatures as those of the women in the 'cotton field'. An FBI report on Andrade's killing was leaked to Mexico City's *Reforma* newspaper based on the testimony of three witnesses who, failing to gain a satisfactory audience in Juárez, crossed the river. Lilia was abducted by hit men working for the Juárez cartel, said the report. The television store was known to be used as a conduit for cocaine dealing and among the attackers was a certain 'Raul', known to the authorities. After the girl was bundled into a white Thunderbird car, sounds of a struggle were heard, and a lookout disappeared into the shop. Taxi drivers parked on the other side of the street looked on, said the witnesses, doing nothing. 'Someone must have seen something,' says Norma Andrade, Lilia's mother, 'and the only people who could possibly get away with this is someone who had some connection to the police.' The FBI document was dismissed by Juárez authorities as 'erroneous'. But across the river, the *El Paso Times* newspaper reported that people in Juárez, falsely claiming to be FBI agents, were knocking on doors in search of the witnesses.[3] Lilia's body was dumped 300 yards from a *maquila* factory owned by the ProMex company. She had been held alive for an estimated five days, raped, tortured and strangled. Forensic reports suggested she had been bound by police handcuffs.

Norma Andrade is a wounded but formidable woman, in stature, gesture and courage. 'What kills me,' she says, 'is that the people who did this are out there somewhere, maybe doing it again to some other girl. But I am sticking with my determination that whoever did this be punished. I am fighting impunity, that the authorities are allowing this to happen.' Over the years there have been endless suspicions as to who is behind the malefaction of Ciudad Juárez. There are theories about narco-cartel 'Juniors', male heirs to big landowning and *maquila* management families, about police cadres, common domestic violence, snuff videos and occult connections. There is even a constituency of academics in the USA that argues that the deaths have been the subject of undue attention, since more men were being killed than women, meanwhile. 'Only one thing is certain,' presumes Norma Andrade, 'that whoever is killing is killing for pleasure.'

A primary school teacher, Norma lives on the southern edges of Juárez in a house so nearly joyful, filled with the sounds of playing children; children of neighbours, nieces, nephews, and Lilia's own two children, Jade, now three, and Kaleb, aged two. They call their grandmother 'Mama', while their real mother's portrait sits on a shelf, inquisitive, gentle, bespectacled. 'The authorities never bothered to call,' recalls Norma of the day they found her daughter's corpse. 'I heard from someone out of the blue, and went down to the morgue. Even now, they never call me. I feel they have lied to me about my daughter's case. They said she had been tied with shoelaces, but I believe it was police handcuffs. They said there were no marks of strangulation but I know there were. It's up to me to go down there and pester them. If I didn't, I'd never hear from them again.' Lilia's murder has been categorised as a 'crime of passion'. Her (separated) husband was accordingly interviewed and struck off any suspect list – but the crime not re-categorised. 'He wouldn't have the trousers to do it anyway,' sneers Norma, allowing herself a hollow laugh. 'It's hard to think too much about it.' She exhales a deep breath. 'The facts speak for themselves. She had been dead thirty hours when they found her, but had been missing a week. My life has totally changed,' she reflects. 'You know, I was so happy; I enjoyed everything. But I saw the world through rose-tinted spectacles. Now, I trust no one. I could count them on one hand. Only two, actually, Martha Cabrera at the school where I teach, and Marisela Ortiz.'

After Lilia was murdered, Norma went to her daughter's former high school teacher, Marisela Ortiz, to urge her to become involved. An elegant woman who hides rage beneath a bushel of civility, Marisela founded *Nuestras Hijas* in the belief that 'it's time to challenge the entire order here, and meanwhile try to take care of the mothers; and the children who are orphaned. Many of those are now growing up to be drug addicts, or gang members.' Marisela has herself become the target of harassment. One night recently, she was driving home, trailed by an SUV. It followed her bumper-to-bumper, until she gave it the slip. 'I was terrified,' she says. 'I . . . well, it was a clear signal.' But it is not threats, says Marisela, that deter her. Nor even the response of the authorities, whom Marisela believes to be complicit anyway. Rather, it is the response of the *maquiladoras* that 'takes away our hope'.

Three thirty in the afternoon: shift change at the *maquilas*. The buses line up outside each factory, waiting to take their load downtown or back up to the *colonias*. The girls emerge from the fluorescent-lit world within. Some stay to chatter, one young woman simply boards the bus, sits down, rests her head against the pane of the bus window, closes her long eyelashes and sinks into sleep. Half an hour later, up the *Ruta Anapra*, the buses grind in convoy, kicking up great clouds of dust, old American schoolbuses, marked *'trans-porte de personal'* and household names: Philips, TDK, Delphi, Lear. Occasionally, they pull over, fart a puff of exhaust and drop off workers who then weave their onerous way home between the shacks climbing the hillside.

The silence of the *maquila* companies over the slaughter of their employees was perhaps loudest in the case of seventeen-year-old Claudia Ivette González, one of the eight found in the cotton field. She had worked for Lear, but was sent away one morning for being three minutes late, having missed the works bus. That was the day Claudia, turned away alone, disappeared. The company's official response to her subsequent death was that 'González's murder did not happen on Lear property'. In response to the attempted murder of the fourteen-year-old bus rape survivor Nancy Illaba González, her employer said only: 'It is not our policy to hire anyone under sixteen.' The company even filed legal papers against the family for helping Nancy to forge false identification.

Outside the Juárez offices of the Chihuahua state authorities, a forest of little crosses was planted in a scrap of lawn, no longer there. Each cross, beginning in 1993, bore a name, starting with 'Ivonne Estrada Salas'; one for each recovered corpse, and towards 2003, they bunched for lack of space. Many were unidentified because, explained Rosario Acosta of *Nuestras Hijas*, 'so many girls came alone from the south, and have no one here that knows them'. Inside, there are frosty hand-shakes with the head of the special office for sexual homicides, young Ángela Talavera, in a smart skirt suit. She is happy, she says, to answer questions. 'Many were seduced by men who . . . took advantage of the situation. Most were seduced, but others taken by force. There is no fixed pattern.' Ms Talavera gets little opportunity to speak, as most questions are answered in perfect American English by a bullish, discomforting man, former head of the unit, now an aide in charge of 'liaison'. The aide details the categories of sexual homicide, and statistics involved. There have been 229 during the period under discussion, of which, he insists, 163 have been solved, leaving 66 ongoing investigations. Of these 229, 70 were sexual homicides, of which 24 have been solved, with 46 pending. The other categories include 'argument related', 'accidental death' and the largest, 'crimes of passion'.

I ask about the case of Lilia Andrade, categorised as a 'crime of passion'. When we talk about this particular subject, he says only, with contempt, 'her mother always misinterprets what we are saying'. On the recent 'overdose' case of the girl with panties pulled down and handbag strings round her neck, Ms Talavera pitches in: 'It is true her pants were slightly above the knee, and her handbag on her arm close to the neck. The medical examiner did the autopsy on the body. She did not have any type of sexual assault on her.' Oscar Máynez finds the argument laughable: 'I have seen no end of overdoses; they do not have panties halfway down their legs and purse strings around their necks.' The question of possible connections to weighty families or to the authorities is quickly dismissed. 'When I was in charge of this unit,' the aide buts in again, 'we did have information about a specific powerful person. It didn't lead anywhere. It was one of these powerful people, but that didn't stop us then, and it wouldn't stop us now.' And the murdered lawyer, Escobedo? 'He wasn't the attorney,' snaps the aide. 'The attorney was his father. I don't know how it transpired, but unfortunately the younger lawyer was killed. However, it had nothing to do with the bus drivers.' 'Mario Escobedo *junior*,' affirms Oscar Máynez, 'was the registered attorney for one of the bus drivers. That is in the records.' The meeting concludes with an assurance from the aide that only three of all the bodies recovered between 1993 and 2003 were mutilated. The FBI, he says, is welcome in Juárez, 'for training' – but not to help with investigations. Meanwhile, the movement butside is preparing to act above the heads of the prosecution team.

* * *

A year later, Rosario Acosta came to Washington DC for the first hearing at the headquarters of the Organisation of American states, as *Nuestras Hijas* endeavoured to consider legal action through the OAS Interamerican Court of Human Rights, sitting in Costa Rica and established by a Holocaust survivor, the formidable Thomas Buergenthal, now the presiding judge representing the United States at the International Court of Justice in The Hague. Rosario's journey turned out to be a first step down a long road, but when we met for lunch in Starbucks amongst the glass and steel of Washington, the pellucid light in Rosario's eyes was already fading. 'It is a desolate landscape now,' she says. 'There's no one to turn to in Mexico any more. While this game goes on, more women die. No, that road has ended now. We need to play a bigger game, or nothing. This can only be solved if we challenge the mechanism whereby the law is enforced. What drives me,' she says, 'is not "activism" any more, it is rage and sorrow. Sometimes I feel the organisation is full of women working together, sometimes that we are just a few, and sometimes that I am totally alone.' Rosario talks not only about the crimes, but their impact after ten years on Ciudad Juárez – and this in 2003, four years before the outbreak of the present narco war: 'This is a decomposing society. We are witnessing its destruction – women in pain who cannot turn to society, suffering cancer through stress, children to take care of, and domestic violence against women rampant.' The battering of women in Juárez is through the roof, she says: even those rare instances reported to the police increased by 300 per cent during the month after the eight bodies in the cotton field. 'It's logical,' says Rosario, 'if they can kill women and get away with it, then why shouldn't they beat them close to death? It's common now for men to taunt their wives: "If you tell on me, I'll dump you in the Lote Bravo"' – referring to a canal where a number of bodies were found.'

'This message of complete impunity is having terrible effects in all directions,' said Esther Chávez at the crisis centre around the same time. 'It is now so bad that women come to me who cannot do anything about being beaten because their husbands threaten to kill them. What can I say if a woman says, "I can't come again, because he says he'll dump my body in the cotton field?" If the police would only intervene in these cases, we might start to break that cycle of impunity.'

Back again at Norma Andrade's lovely but poignant home. As Shakespeare would say, she 'bears it out even to the edge of doom'. 'I'm proceeding with my own investigation,' she insists with foursquare resolve, 'looking into that *narco* television shop.' Down at the police station, 'their attitude gets worse and worse, but I won't let this go, whatever that means for me'. She slams the palms of her hands onto her knees, and turns her attention to Lilia's children, sticking pieces of yellow paper onto a stencil drawing. 'My husband doesn't like what I am doing. "Think of the children," he says. But that's the whole point. I do it for the children. So long as they look at me and call me *Mama*, I have Lilia with me, and a reason to get up each day and fight on.'

In December 2009, The Inter-American Court of Human Rights ruled against the Mexican government in three test cases involving murders of young women in Ciudad Juárez. The court found that Mexican authorities failed adequately to investigate the murders of Claudia Ivette González, seventeen, Esmeralda Herrera Monreal, fifteen, and Laura Berenice Ramos, twenty – all killed in the 'cotton field'. The report, running to 167 pages, also said Mexico failed to protect the victims, and that the government must publicly acknowledge its responsibility, publish the sentence in official government records and build a monument in memory of the victims. Authorities must also investigate the murders and bring those responsible for the slayings to justice. The case was without precedent, the first time the court has ruled against Mexico on a human-rights complaint, and the first ruling to recognise murder according to gender – whereby women are killed only because they are women.[4] Benita Monárrez, the mother of Laura Berenice, had petitioned the United States for asylum such were the threats from police officers and government officials menacing her to drop her case. The ruling came just as mothers of some of the victims and their supporters set out on a march from Ciudad Juárez all the way to Mexico City. Two months previously, however, in mid September, President Calderón had undertaken a cabinet reshuffle, and appointed Arturo Chávez Chávez as attorney general of the Republic to replace the outgoing Eduardo Medina Mora. Chávez was formerly the lead prosecutor of Chihuahua state, a post he held during the 1990s, when investigations into the murders of young women went nowhere. 'It is like sending a wolf to protect the lambs,' said an opposition parliamentarian. In testimony before a Senate committe, Chávez had acknowledged failings by his former agency, but said he did his utmost as state prosecutor to investigate and prosecute the slayings.[5]

'This year, however,' Marisela Ortiz reflects, two weeks before the ruling in Costa Rica, 'the number of murders of women is higher than in the previous year, and that was an increase on 2007. We have had more than two hundred this year now; the violations and killings are of a different kind, many kinds – in the home, on the street, on the way back from work, and some directly connected to narco trafficking. But one thing is consistent: there is always a reason for not investigating. The police will always find a reason to wash their hands of the crime.' We meet in Sanborns, as we almost always did over nine years – only this branch is in an outlying shopping mall, not downtown, because it is evening. 'I can't get safely to the one we went to before,' she explains. 'I had to move out here, because of all the threats.' Marisela is dressed elegantly and exudes resolve and charm, but she looks exhausted. 'The state has found a way to be a little less offensive about the killing,' she continues, 'there are not the same insults about the girls inviting the kidnaps and tortures with their dress.' But 'we are still having to investigate all the cases ourselves, and they're different from before, more varied. Some are university students taken off the street, some are even of school age. Most are taken when they go downtown looking for work, especially since the recession, because that's where all the buses go, and they have to change buses after dark. They're not always raped, sometimes killed in the style of Mafia executions because they have something to do with narco traffic. Others are abducted and killed while selling sexual services to the federal police; they get into difficult situations if they accept very high fees for gang sex. But to be honest, it's not important to me how a woman is killed; what is important is WHY: and the fact is that these men kill women because they are women, and because they can.' And she echoes Cecilia Ballí's point: 'The killing of the women here was an indication of how things would go. That men would think this was a way to exert their power, to overwhelm women and other people with such violence, until such point as that kind of violence spreads like cancer and becomes a part of the culture. So you end up with this madhouse:

there was an execution across the street from where I teach in September, and the *sicario* came to pick up his child so it could watch the execution.'

Marisela's own life continues to be threatened. 'My car was shot at twice, from a black vehicle with tinted windows, but I wasn't hurt,' she says, switching from coffee to a modest liqueur. 'I had to move house, and live apart from my daughters to keep them safe. And I have a couple of escorts, but they work indirectly to Arturo Chávez, so that since he was ratified as attorney general, my enemy is protecting me! Maybe that should make me doubly afraid. But I can't stop. The day I stop means that I have accepted that this is the right way.'

I revisit Paula González near Christmastime, and she has a model nativity scene laid out on the floor. A centre for children in Anapra, which was merely a gleam in her eye and a piece of cleared desert scrubland in 2002, has been completed, thanks to private donations, and named after Sagrario. A sign of restored faith? 'Maybe,' replies Paula pensively. 'At the beginning, I prayed a lot, and I still do. Not in church, but here at home, to the Virgin of Guadalupe. I have always been a very religious woman, and believed in the resurrection and miracle of Guadalupe. But I never really recovered my faith after that moment, when Sagrario's Virgin came back to me, the one she wore around her neck. Maybe with time, I will get it back.' Her deep, comfortless eyes move across the photographs of her dead daughter, and back to mid-distance. 'Because justice is what I crave. Justice against her killer, and against all of the killers. There is no justice in Juárez, so I have given up on that. I have my work to do here, meanwhile, and wait for the justice of God.'

The Road It Gives and the Road It Takes Away

'What do the coyotes mean when they yodel at the moon?'
Edward Abbey, Desert Solitaire

I had always wondered about those people who sit next to motel pools that are only a couple of hundred yards from an interstate. But I did just that, after a long stay in Juárez, for a whole four hours, applying factor 15 and listening to the clamour of trucks thundering down Interstate 10 at very close range. The more exhausting Juárez gets, the more wonderful it is to sit by the *La Quinta* pool inhaling aromatherapeutic emissions from the chemical smokestack just over the border, embarrassed by hard-working cleaners, and soaking up ultraviolet, it feels like near wild heaven. This was the last day in El Paso for a while, and that before an evening with the singer Tom Russell, whose music I played after towelling down, on my way to Cowtown Boots and the Luccese factory outlet – and continued to play during the next several thousand miles, in various loop-de-loops across the Texas borderland on one side, Chihuahua, Coahuila and Tamaulipas on the other. One song made me especially sad and another made me especially happy. The first went:

> Then he finally got married and he had two little girls /
> But he didn't see 'em much cause he had to see the world /
> And the lie that he told 'em is I'm like most men /
> It's always down the road that the dream begins /
> And the girls grew up to be pretty and wise /
> They said 'you could've seen the dream by looking in our eyes"

And the second:

But we'll sing 'Hallelujah!' – we'll sing it in the morning /
And thank the Lord for giving one more day /
For ones who passed on through, we'll sing this one for you /
For the road it gives, and the road it takes away[2]

Next morning after dinner with Russell and his wife, Nadine, I left
El Paso an hour before sunrise, right in my face along Interstate 10,
heading into the eternity of Texas, which accounts for the entire
eastern half of the United States side of the border, the Rio Grande's
left bank, all the way to the sea. From El Paso to the mouth of the
river and the border's end is 645 miles as the crow flies, but as the
Rio Grande flows it is 1,254 miles, and eight times that by automobile, if one is zigzagging to and from the hinterland on either
side. Driving alone in America, the car radio is one's companion,
channels changing of their own accord as one proceeds from one
signal range to another. So that without touching the dial, one is serially accompanied by classic rock, apocalyptic fundamentalist Christian
soothsaying, country music, pulsating *Norteño* and windbag talk radio.
Every now and then there's a public broadcasting station, discussing
health care or playing Sibelius (why it's always Sibelius, I don't know).
Channel-surfing is achieved not by flicking the dial but by one of
the main themes on any journey through Amexica: boundless distance.
The kind of distances film directors can only measure with receding
telegraph poles by day; the kind of distances to which private cars
surrender after dark, their drivers tucked up in motels, so that one
shares the night highway almost exclusively with trucks and the
coloured lights with which each teamster makes his sixteen-wheeled
monster distinctive. Distances across which the endlessly long, thrilling
freight trains rattle and surge so that sometimes in the desert night,
I would pull over just to wonder at their thunderous passing – a
highly erotic, industrial excitement that never wears off – 'Nine
hundred thousand tons of steel' – as the Grateful Dead song goes –
of which an iron horse of the Santa Fe, Kansas City Southern or
Union Pacific is made, virile, all-conquering, ploughing and hooting
through the desert night.

For the Aztecs, Tezcatlipoca was the supreme God of the sky. He
was a 'Smoking Mirror', and no wonder, for the Aztecs made their
mirrors of gossamer-thin obsidian, and obsidian is black. It is at

night, heralded by the sumptuous colours of sundown and twilight, that the sky comes alive above the desert. In the skies over Amexica, one can attempt to learn the ancient Native American art of stargazing. I remember seeing Indians sitting alone in South Dakota, staring skywards for hours – and envying them. So I bought myself a metal chair from Walgreens for eleven dollars to try it myself. I parked, walked, and kept walking – although no landmark butte or rock seemed to get any closer, such is desert distance – until the dark blue band that is the earth's shadow opposite sunset rises and fades into the mauve light above it, which is that of the sun illuminating the atmosphere. After dark, there are three fundamental rules: 1, Wait at least fifteen minutes until you really start looking into the depth of the constellations of so many stars like God is throwing sugar at you from the deep; 2, Never forget that it is all moving (or rather, as Galileo realised and for which he was excommunicated, you are moving) and that you can watch this happen by keeping your eye on the horizon; 3, Always take your empty beer bottles with you back to the car. There is nothing more depressing than finally finding what one thinks is a spot of mystical isolation, only to discover that frat-brats and *cholos* have already turned the place into a venue for Miller Lite drinking contests and/or a landfill for the disposal of condoms and Burger King packaging.

Somewhere near Coyanosa, Texas, I recalled my father telling me as a child that many of these stars were extinguished millions of years ago, yet the light they emit continues to reach us, and there are only 350 million years before we in the Milky Way collide with our next-door-neighbour Andromeda. It all seems to make sense in the desert, as though the universe was almost as big as Texas itself. The endlessness of Texas: where there is nothing like the feeling that one is entirely alone – until suddenly, behind the constellations, fulminate the sounds of the creations of man: the roar of fighter planes and sometimes even a sonic boom. Or, after hours of nothing but signs by the roadside warning, with a gratifying existentialist twist, that 'Dust Storms May Exist', frantic lights flash ahead, where the border patrol has pulled someone over and has him pinned, spread-eagled at gunpoint, against his vehicle. Above all, after nightfall, there are the coyotes, the prairie wolf whose name derives from the Nahuatl word *coyotlinaut* – an Aztec diety whose followers wear the animal's fur – and is the jester and 'God's dog' of a thousand Native American stories. The trickster whose resilience has defied all erosion by modern man of its habits and habitats, by outwitting him at every turn. The jackal of America which unleashes its flesh-creeping range of haunting sounds across the desert night: howling, yipping, yapping – sometimes almost laughing. Their chorus, whether it is sung for territory or for fun – no one knows – seems to bring the night to a standstill, unless there are domestic dogs around, which can be sure to go into a frenzy, knowing something deep down about these wild cousins with whom they have so much – though so little – in common. But keep going, until daybreak – for the loneliness can be sublime when a lilac light of dawn fades the constellations in the vast sky, by way of fanfare for the golden desert sunrise, like firelight across the land.

Turning off I-10 at Van Horn, via the truckers' travel centre, the railroad and Highway 90 run hand-in-hand back towards the border through scrub and grassland. An incongruous roadside shrine at the entrance to a ranch containing and advertising for Prada shoes gives some idea of the upcoming arty settlement of Marfa, south of which the landscape changes dramatically. Suddenly it is huge and isolating again, with horizon after horizon, layer upon layer, of mountain ridges ahead, turning green to blue to grey into the distance, as the frontier comes back into view. After miles of savannah and scrub, the first ocotillo since Arizona appear again, and buttes rise against the skyline.

If only TV teenaged soaps hadn't kidnapped the word 'awesome' – for that is what these mountains are, such is the dread, southwards along Highway 67. Only the awe emanates not just from nature; it has also to do with the arrival at dusk in the most remote of the twin towns along the border, clinging together and surrounded by an expanse of mountainous wilderness and what feels like infinite nothing: Presidio on the Texas side and Ojinaga over the river. Although they live as one, clinging together in the emptiness, Presidio's clocks are an hour ahead of Ojinaga's, which often leads to confusion. Here, the Rio Grande ceases to be the trickle that divides El Paso from Juárez, its waters back there plundered by the farmers of New Mexico, for it is now joined by the Conches river and a lusty current. In fact, what is from now on called the Rio Grande or Rio Bravo is almost all water from the Conches. Presidio by night is a place of mobile trailer homes to which cling canisters of butane gas, a place lit by isolated fluorescent lights against the glow from over the river of the larger Mexican town, behind which rises a steep, impassable escarpment.

It was that mountain slope on which the joint US and Mexican operation against drug baron Pablo Acosta was banking, for it gave him no way out. What the SWAT teams on the American side did not know was that the operation over the river was in part arranged and paid for by Acosta's trusty lieutenant, 'Lord of the Skies' Carrillo Fuentes, who needed to be rid of his mentor in order to reform the Juárez cartel under his authority. The history hangs heavy in the deep valley, into which a mist rises from the river after the sunrise.

Perhaps surprisingly, behind the corrugated iron Subway sandwich store in Presidio is a small villa with a diplomatic plaque above the portico and cloister within, up the walls of which bright flowers climb, with a fountain in the middle of it. This is the Mexican consulate, where Héctor Acosta Flores presides, supported by his tireless aide, Elsa Villa, who busies herself with 'a massive workload, mostly protection of Mexican nationals, their documentation, what they need to present themselves to the US authorities, birth certificates, ID, labour rights, family rights – the everyday machinery of Mexican life on the border'. The office handles 300 cases a day and covers eighteen prisons, to which it organises visits for the Mexican families of inmates. 'We had to get involved in riots recently,' says Acosta, 'in Pecos jail – most of those involved were Mexican. The rise in numbers detained for deportation, or with cases pending, adds to convicted criminals – it's a lot of work. But we did manage to have nine independence *Grito* ceremonies in nine jails this year – that was quite something!' In Presidio and Ojinaga, it is Health Awareness Week, which Acosta is helping to organise on both sides of the river. Today's business opens with a seminar in Ojinaga on health and migration, for which we, of course, arrive an hour early because of the time difference we both forgot, allowing for a breakfast of sickly sweet cakes. There follows an interesting and edgy exchange in which the director of the Ojinaga hospital (also called Acosta) and some of his paramedics quiz a man from Mexican customs called Porfidio about delays in getting the migrants home once they have been deported, leaving them stranded in Ojinaga.

'If they don't have any money, how are they going to get home?' asks the director. Apparently there is a plan afoot to help, but 'I know of no such plan', grunts the customs man. 'How many millions of dollars do these people send back to Mexico?' protests a paramedic called Clara, lambasting the 'functionaries', while Consul Acosta looks a little shamefaced, adding: 'I am arguing that the government do all it can to help.' There's a Woody Guthrie song called 'Deportee' about the nameless people made to 'ride the big airplane', but the truth is that they don't get their names back when they reach the borderland of their own country either.

Apart from the migrants who roam the streets looking to earn a fare home, Ojinaga is one of those places that looks entirely normal, and probably is 'unless you're here on bad business', says a man called Raul in Kick Ass Pizza. The bar and pizzeria – one of many here, pizza clearly a favourite in the middle of nowhere – is quiet and friendly, with curiosity getting the better of suspicion. Raul is keen to talk about melons and onions, for which the surrounding area is famous, and about the annual onion festival held in town, rather than any illegal form of commerce. A random compliment along the lines that because of Pablo Acosta, famous Ojinaga is where it all started is greeted by silence, a swift change of subject to The Beatles and, oddly, a peel of laughter from a man at a table in the corner by the pretty lace curtains who then buys me a shot of tequila, insisting to the barman that it be a good one, and leaves.

As we had returned over the bridge to Presidio earlier, Mr Acosta the consulate explains that his is an 'itinerant consulate', meaning that its constituency includes two towns away from the border, but very much part of Amexica: Midland and Odessa – the names rang a bell after covering the Bush administration for several years, for these towns were the New England dynasty's western colony, cradle for its recent money and the place where of its most recent political sons, Jeb and George W. were raised. Odessa and Midland require a detour north, through a landscape of desert mountains that cast a blue shadow over the heat, then becomes a barren scrub across which dust devils fly and trains rumble like iron snakes. I took a walk towards a railroad line, just to watch them forge a way through the now crepuscular light, their own lights visible and the sound of their hooting audible at least ten minutes before reaching a deafening crescendo as they thunder by. I stayed until way past dark, then on into the country of apparently humble origins in which the Bush dynasty entwined with the energy barons of Texas. America likes to think of the Bush era as distant past already, whether with regret or relief, but until recently, a member of the Bush family had for half a century occupied the White House, a Senate seat or governor's mansion and the family continues to fascinate here around its fortress in this corner of the Lone Star state's wild west, nowadays very much part of 'Amexica'. It was here that a young pilot back from the Second World War called George Herbert Walker Bush was sent by his father, Senator Prescott Bush, to a trainee job with the International Derrick and Equipment Company. Derrick was a subsidiary of Dresser Industries, controlled by the Bush family and selling more oilrigs than anyone in the world, later absorbed by Halliburton, of which future Vice President Dick Cheney became chairman, keeping things in the family, so to speak. The Bush family settled in Midland, although the workshop of the area was scrappy Odessa, where the White working class live on one side of the tracks, Blacks and Hispanics on the other.

The world did not hear much about Odessa until one fateful day in December 1998 when George W. Bush was governor of Texas and the sky turned black after an 'upset' at the Huntsman chemical plant which was literally on the wrong side of the railroad tracks it shares with poor housing, where the Mexicans live. (An 'upset' is an unplanned accident releasing pollution, not part of the plant's normal running procedure, and which does not count in its regulatory tally.) Lucia Llánez, whose family came from Tabasco and thereafter the border, lives in this tightly knit community of bungalows squeezed between the chemical plant and the railroad. She will never forget that day: 'It was dark all over; cars on the Interstate slowing down and putting their lights on because they couldn't see, though it was day. There was a rumbling like trains that rattled the windows, and people were going to hospital for watering eyes, allergies and problems breathing. The cloud stayed two weeks.' In Odessa, where Mexico came to live on the Bushes' doorstep, I ate one of the best fajitas I had eaten along the entire road, found a motel with a room looking straight across the parking lot at a railroad line and – by now a hopelessly addicted trainspotter – sat propped against

the wall drinking beers and watching them crash by, dividing
Mexican Odessa from white Odessa, until turning in and allowing
the rattle and hum of Union Pacific to hammer me to sleep.

Next day, I hear the story of how Huntsman goes back to the days
of George Herbert Bush's arrival, when Odessa was a town of what
retired fireman Don Dangerfield calls 'wildcatters'. In the forties, the
US Air Force bombed deep holes in the giant Permian oil basin in
a search for oil, which then attracted a stampede of speculators who
would, recalls Dangerfield, 'spend the nights in a hotel, the End of
the Golden West, and gamble their lots in rooms so thick with cigar
smoke you could hardly see'. Among them was a man he remembers
well: John Ben Shepperd, a former attorney general of Texas and
member of the White Citizens Council come to seek his fortune out
west by setting up the El Paso Products company, later Huntsman.

George Herbert Bush landed in this mayhem but quickly
decamped 20 miles north to Midland, where new millionaires like
him established a country club, a Harvard and a Yale club, met at
the Petroleum Club and played golf on irrigated lawns. Midland
was, at the time, one of only two towns in America (the other was
Los Angeles) with its own Rolls-Royce dealership and more millionaires per capita than any other town, out here in the dusty desert.
This was where Bush Senior built his oil fortune, launched a political career on its shoulders and raised his sons Jeb and George W.
in the art and language of power, which the latter feigned to speak
from the White House over two terms. These were decades during
which the Mexicans arrived to work the chemical pipelines in Odessa
and water the lawns and golf courses of Midland, so that now more
people speak Spanish in Odessa and Midland than English.

Driving back to Presidio and the border, I parked up at that same
spot from which I had walked to watch trains roll through the twilight
two nights before, only to find that I was walking against the tracks
of my own still perfectly indented footprints, coming at me in the
opposite direction, as though walking backwards against time. It was
the strangest feeling out there in forever, Texas, and not out of place,
for in this desert, time and space curve into their own endlessness.

Southbound from Presidio, Highway 170 leads to one of the most
famous and famously spectacular natural monuments in America,
Big Bend National Park, but there are lovelier and less crowded

wonders to behold on the way, past Redford in the less celebrated Big Bend State Park, and a stretch of border at once baffling and gratifying. Past Palo Amarillo Ranch, the winding road, deep in a valley, runs right alongside the bubbling brook that the Rio Grande has become. Here, you could play a game of catch between the United States and Mexico, and no one would see or interrupt you. There is no fence, no border patrol, no sign of any sensors, but that could be a trick. If a child kicked a ball across, you could kick it back, or you could bring as much cocaine or as many Salvadoreans as you wanted. Of course, the roads north are no breeze, but you would be inside the United States. At the Coronado River Access Point, the Rio Grande flows by like a pleasant pastoral stream in which you could wash your face (try doing that in El Paso). The only fence is a wooden one put up by the state parks service, and the only signpost is that instructing: 'Do Not Block The Boat Ramp. Pets Prohibited. By Order.' On the far bank, 20 feet away, rocks rise to a small hill, and that is Mexico. The road passes red-headed buttes at the foot of which red-headed vultures pick at the carcass of a desert fox by the road. It climbs, and overlooks the great ravine that is Madre Canyon, where a picnic area looks across the running water at Mexico on the other bank, with toy teepees instead of parasols for shade and tables set for a riverside snack. Then, to stay on course (for this is no tourist trail to the Big Bend), my route swings north towards Alpine, Texas, and into a moonscape, a flat horizon punched by Kokernot Mesa and the 5,000-foot peak of Hen Eggs Mountain. Along these liberating stretches of road, not only is there no phone signal, but the digital 'radioset' channel-surfing function just whizzes through the numbers which it thinks locate a radio station, finding nothing. Heading east between Marathon and Sanderson, even the railway track is like an oxbow lake left behind by a river: cut off, going nowhere, home to an abandoned, idle row of freight boxcars painted with graffiti in the rust.

The destination is not a butte or a mountain, it is one of the very few people to whom one can talk and who can say they met Pablo Acosta and the Lord of the Skies himself, Amado Carrillo Fuentes. Don Henry Ford farms a ranch at Belmont, near the agricultural centre of Seguin, Texas, once the high, arid plains have become grassland through which runs the Guadalupe River. Ford was a dope smuggler from near Fort Stockton, a way north from Hen Eggs

Mountain. It was a trade he chose, for which he was jailed, escaped and was jailed again, and about which he wrote a book called *Contrabando*. His meetings with the drug lords over the river were both remarkable. The first with Carrillo Fuentes, during his years of apprenticeship to Pablo Acosta in Ojinaga, was part of an attempt by Ford's smuggling partner Oscar to get into the big time. They meet in a motel room for negotiations over mountains of cocaine, during which Ford has the temerity to say he prefers not to get into any business that involves killing people. He and another smuggler are left, but then returned for, taken out into a parking lot stark naked, interrogated and then into another room where Oscar is in the process of being beaten senseless by Carrillo Fuentes' men. 'I had no idea then how powerful Carrillo would become,' says Ford. The meeting with Acosta comes later, while Ford is on the run from prison and guarding a stash of marijuana, is spotted and taken by Acosta's men, then recognises the man himself. 'Don't look into my face,' snaps the drug lord. Ford is interrogated, held, and in an extraordinary exchange asked by Acosta whether (and why not) he had never killed a man. The dialogue is knife-edge tense, Ford pleading only for his life – which he is granted, Acosta also insisting that he take his load of marijuana 'as a gift from me', even though Ford has said he would rather leave without it. 'Yes, sir,' agrees Ford, when Acosta presses the offer.[3]

The gateway to Ford's ranch is open, flanked by the Lone Star flag of Texas. The access road winds through the green, deepened by a day of steady rain, past a lake, to the house Ford and his wife have only recently completed. There is no one there at first, just a noisy greeting by a pack of dogs and countless cats and kittens. Eventually, Ford arrives, in his old pickup, the gentleman cowboy farmer, with a difference. Quite a few differences, actually. It is afternoon, and a grey one, and there is a quick glance around the immediate vicinity, with a full tour of the property promised for tomorrow. Ford also breeds, and loves, racehorses at a stable near Seguin, from which a horse he feeds in a field here has retired. 'He can't race any more, this old sack of shit,' says Ford. 'But he's a good man, gentle soul, so the kids love to ride him.'

If there is one thing Ford does not want to talk about over the three days and two nights he graciously hosts me at his ranch, it is his book and his life as a narco trafficker. But we have barely finished our first cup of tea at the table in his great kitchen before he begins to talk about the CIA, cocaine and Iran-Contra, and about his own second work, *Ruminations From the Garden*, which he has been unable to publish commercially but has had printed and bound. He writes: 'I have had a hard time convincing people that I dislike revisiting my past. I did write a book about it, I'm not looking for pity. I chose my path then and now.' In conversation, Ford does, however, reflect on the old trade, as darkness falls and we eat spicy stuffed jalapeno poppers to die for. Leah Ford and I drink beer, Don is teetotal, and prefers tea. 'The area I was living in, that was south-east of Ojinaga, you kill someone, and that makes you Somebody. But the thing was, I never ran cocaine. I refused to run cocaine. It's a fucker, and I wouldn't do it. I put that in my deposition, my plea, but they edited it out of the tape. The cops were trying to turn me into this coke dealer, and I said no, I'm against hard drugs. But they didn't want the judge to see that. No mitigation ... Yeah,' Ford reflects, without much relish or even interest, 'I still meet some of those people. I met someone recently and I said: "Who do you work for?" and he said: "I don't work for no one." He was just like the Mexicans you meet in my yard. He said he'd love to go back, but couldn't take the risk, back into the middle of it all now. They can kill you just because you were once a name they knew.

'Look,' says Ford, leaning across his kitchen table, 'I know the business I was involved in. You hear about all these people back-packing across country with the dope, but that's all shit. That stuff is going right through customs, I know it is. Taxi drivers going back and forth, the same cars getting waved through every day by people on the US side who know. And as for the trucks − Jeezus Christ! All you have to do is get paid to do what you'd do anyway, wave ten per cent of the trucks right on through. I've heard that if you have the money and you know the Zetas, you can get anything you want into the United States − you can get it waved through, and they might even ship it on up for you in a nice fucking border patrol vehicle.' Ford remembers: 'In my day, a place like Ciudad Acuña was run by *Chapo* Guzmán, but now it's all Zetas. And it's not just drug dealing. You got taxis sit there all day, and have to show one hundred per cent occupancy even though they haven't taken a single fare. The taxi firm works for the Zetas, the Zetas launder their money, and the driver registers busy all day without driving anywhere.'

This being a dairy ranch, Leah churns butter in a big porcelain jar as we talk. It is turning slowly, and Ford takes the bowl, and talks about the cash paid for all these drugs crossing back into Mexico. An investigation by the Associated Press in December 2009 found that only a fraction of the river of cash flowing through the border was being intercepted.[4] During 2008, the customs and border patrol in El Paso alone confiscated $2.8 million in cash, but most of it was in a single, massive $1.9 million load heading to Ciudad Juárez from Kansas City, Missouri.

'I read that two hundred million dollars is crossing the bridges,' says Ford. 'That's two hundred kilos of cash if it's in hundreds, 'cause a bill weighs a gram. If it's in twenties, that's a thousand kilos. How are you gonna spend that in Mexico? You can't get rid of that kind of money! They say there's five hundred billion dollars a year in this business. Dammit, there's only eight hundred billion dollars of currency circulating in cash at any time, so am I gonna believe that five-eighths of that is drug money? Of course not. So how does all that money get back into circulation? It does through legal funds, don't it? How else? Or am I just dumb? But, you can't bank all that cash. You can't roll into a bank and say, "I gotta deposit a truckload of dollars, quick". You got to find someone who's gonna launder that money and take a cut, you got to find someone who's going to re-introduce it into legal channels. If you've got a semi-articulated truck full of cash, you go to Mexico City and you find the representative of a big-assed American bank to do you a favour for a big-assed cut. And the money's gonna go via that representative to some even bigger smart-ass on fucking Wall Street. How else is it gonna work? You gonna find guys driving round Mexico spending cash out of a semi truck? I don't think so. It's Bob Dylan, ain't it: 'Steal a little and they put you in jail / Steal a load and they make you a king'.'

But what compels Ford now, and the real subject of his book, is self-sufficiency. Like many Americans electing to live and farm in reclusion, in enviable quarantine, from the hullabaloo. 'When I came out of prison, after five years surrounded by the constant noise, stress and confusion of a federal joint, I found the idea of living alone in a forest kind of appealing,' Ford says. But he is watching hard; watching the oil run out, what he believes to be the guzzling of a finite resource by the planet generally, even by his own peers 'turning too much diesel into too much of the wrong kinda food, with bigger

and bigger machines. Well, if all this breaks down, I'm gonna ▎
prepared. I'm gonna be able to feed myself, my family, my children
and even a few of my favourite people. We receive an inheritance,
and, God willing, we get to leave a legacy.'

Morning starts especially early for Ford as a farmer, and he begins
the day with darkness outside and a scour of his overnight email
before we go out through the misty chill smelling of moist, fresh
earth, Jack Frost underfoot, and milk the cows, which Ford does by
hand, into a bucket, squelching. After breakfast – a warming bowl
of rice, egg and the freshest, creamiest milk I've ever tasted – we
prepare to go to Gonzales, the nearest town.

There is word again of Texan secession from the union, as is the
formerly confederate Lone Star state's constitutional right. It never
happens, but is much discussed in these parts, on a cyclical pattern
depending on who is in the White House and especially since the
election of Barack Obama. Before that, the secessionists had quietened,
not least because one of the guiding characteristics of the Bush presidency was the fact that George W.'s team was led by his father's
Texan men of steel, Karl Rove and Dick Cheney, the heavy hand of
Texan big oil, and many who had served Bush's governorship – the
idea being that if Texas has to be part of the union, then one might
as well forge the union into being Texas. But it's not like that anymore
– Obama is not only black and Democrat, he's a Yankee. And so the
language and threat of secession now re-enters Republican politics,
and the battle for the party's nomination in gubernatorial elections.
And as the lexicon of secession that accompanied the Clinton years
resurfaces, Ford's neighbourhood becomes the secessionist heartland.
This is logical: Gonzales is where in 1835, the first battle of the Texan
revolution against Mexico was fought. The Mexican army asked for
a cannon it had loaned the Texans to fight off Apache raids be
returned, to which the Texans retorted what became a legendary
taunt: 'Come and Take It.' When the Mexicans tried to do just that,
in Ford's words, 'they got the shit shot out of them'. So as Ford and
I drive to Gonzales to pick up cattle feed and deal with the bank, we
pass a flag flying from a ranch gate with a Lone Star, a cannon and
the slogan written on it: 'Come and Take It'. 'The government can
say whatever it fucking wants,' spits Ford. 'We're all disaffected, we're
too far from Washington DC, we feel left out of the equation and

over-taxed by too much federal government.' Only Ford is wary of the 'redneck secessionists'. 'I sure ain't one of them,' he says. 'I don't go to things like the secessionist Tea Parties they have – they got over five thousand people to that.' In American political parlance, to be left wing tends to entail a sympathy for federal government, while right entails libertarianism. Ford, though, produces an ingenious four-way 'political compass' quiz whereby one answers questions about various issues and is then placed on a grid between left and right on a vertical scale, and 'authoritarian' and 'libertarian' on a horizontal one. He comes out in the bottom left-hand corner, a left-wing libertarian, and while that stakes out a vertical difference between him and his anti-government neighbours, it binds him to them on the horitzontal scale. Ford's other distinction is his fluent Spanish, and deep love for Mexico; Ford is a horseman and man of the borderland, he is not unlike the principal character in Cormac McCarthy's *All the Pretty Horses*. 'Over on the other side, you got people who are as far away from Mexico City as we are from Washington, and that man is our neighbour. What I see is that we end up with a bunch of counter-cultural rebels on both sides of the border with more in common with each other than we have with the capital cities.' Ford wants to hear some of that counter-cultural rebel stuff, so we head off to see a young singer-songwriter whom Ford has taken under his wing somewhat, scheduled to play a gig in New Braunfels, over the other side of Seguin, Ryan Bingham. Bingham's songs have become the soundtrack to the whole stay, two discs Ford and Leah play over and over again. 'Found him on the circuit here, playing to just a bunch of people, and wrote him up in a cowboy music magazine I contribute to. He's the real thing. Parents ran a roadhouse in southeast New Mexico. He grew up sleeping in the same beds where prostitutes worked. His uncle was a rodeo rider and he was riding competitive rodeo in Mexico by the age of five, but got thrown by a horse, messed his hands up. Now Ryan writes songs, sounds a bit like Dylan and making a name for himself.'

It's a drive, the night is cold, the support acts endless, the crowd small when the boy comes on, in a Dylan 'rolling thunder' white hat, a Dylan voice and Dylan looks. The songs, sung in a small yard under an avenue of pecan trees, are poignant, deep-felt and of the frontier ground they come from: 'Tell my mother I miss her so', sings Bingham;

Ford leans over and whispers: 'His mother died just recently.' Bingham swigs from a can of Shiner beer, fairy-lights wink from the branches of the pecan trees, the frat-brat audience is barely listening, but he sings on: ''Cause hard times they come and they go / Most of the time they're in the middle of your road'[5]

One can feel Ford's tough love for this boy; immersed, it appears, not only in the young singer's music, life and words, but also his own youth, after a fashion – there is more than a faint echo of the dope-smuggling cowboy in this son-of-a-roadhouse on stage, assailing his acoustic guitar and straining his larynx, even for these jocks with their beers and bimbo blonde girlfriends. These jugheads should get work as speed bumps lying the road: they have no idea what they are listening to, giving an authentic cowboy rocker like Bingham the pronged-horn metal rock salute with one hand and raised Bud can with the other as he sings a heartbroken but gritty song called *For What It's Worth*. And as we leave, which has to be early if the cows are going to get milked in the morning, the young man begins to sing 'The Times They Are A-Changing', written by his muse in 1962 when his father was probably younger than Ryan is now. 'I can't say I don't worry about Ryan,' muses Ford. 'There's a side of him that stays detached, then there's a side of him that's like Jim Morrison, auto-destruct. Be interesting to see how he handles success. Funny thing, capitalism: takes a protest song by a poor boy and turns it into big business. Bit like the Church, I guess, taking something as revolutionary as Christianity and turning it into a religion.' And he thinks back instinctively to his own past. 'Drugs are a symptom, not a cause. Ask the addicts, they'll tell you. What the hell happened, and why? What's the root cause of that stuff I was smuggling?' He leaves his question hanging from the night as we drive through the gates of the ranch.

The sun beats down, next afternoon, through bigger, older pecan trees than those around Ryan Bingham's stage, with older, venerable trunks. There's been a bumpy ride around the now luminous meadows and woodland, refreshed by rain. Now the sun is out and down by the lazy-rolling Guadalupe River, Ford's foreman on the ranch, Manuel García Guajito, and his assistant Abraham are cutting dead branches. They take a break as Ford applies the brakes and alights to chat. For some reason the conversation turns from wood clearance to the Zetas, about whom Manuel has things to say. 'I don't think the Zetas are bad people,' he asserts. Why? 'Well, they're not. They're good. My brother was driving a bus in Tamaulipas once, which broke down. And the Zetas helped him, they got help, and helped him fix the bus.' After this eccentric account of Zetas as an emergency roadside service, there's also unusual word from the underworld of migration, a steady current through these parts as reliable as that of the Guadalupe River. 'In the old days', says Manuel, 'when the *coyotes* brought people over, there was always trouble. They got robbed by the *polleros*, the women were violated, everything was trouble. Now, the Zetas have taken over, and it's all under control. Everyone coming through says the same. They take more money, *claro*' – certainly, of course – 'but it's much safer. You keep your things, and the women keep their honour.' But the surface of things is of little interest to Manuel García, who has worked with Ford many years and whom Ford respects greatly, 'good a land manager as you'll ever find'. What interests Manuel are the happenings and phenomena in the extraordinary world he inhabits while he runs this ranch, seeing not the beauty of the pasture and wildwood, the shafts of sunlight that shine through and illuminate the leaves of oak and pecan trees, nor hearing the mellifluous singing of birds. For Manuel has his visions.

'I saw gold and silver mosquitoes,' he relates, 'and others of fluorescent colours, biting people and taking out their DNA. Taking our DNA elsewhere, bit like Noah's Ark. But there was no ark, they were taking each of us, and every animal, to another time, or another place.' Some might nod politely and leave Manuel to his chopping, but on a long afternoon, Ford and I stay rooted to the spot and wait for more. Ford is a man with a short bullshit endurance fuse, and he not only wants to talk more to his foreman, but says this: 'He said he'd seen a tornado of eagles, going round and round, upwards. And the funny thing was that two years later, there was one. Most far-out Godamn thing I ever saw: like a cyclone of eagles, swirling in a circle towards the sky, just like Manuel said.' Now Manuel continues: 'I've seen a lot of people walking down the highway there. Their clothes are all torn, and they're hungry, and we offered them some food, but they didn't know what to do with it. They were walking like zombies, right along the road.' And he sweeps his arm towards Highway 80 and the distant border. 'Thing is, I'm not afraid of dying, what I'm afraid of is being alive and not being able to help these people out on that road.'

CHAPTER SEVEN

Eat off the Floor

In May 2000, shareholders of the giant Alcoa aluminium company assembled in Pittsburgh, Pennsylvania, to hear their chief executive, Paul O'Neill, for the last time. O'Neill had served the company well and those who had invested would be sad to see him go. On the other hand, there was a great honour awaiting him: President George W. Bush would soon announce O'Neill's appointment for the post of Treasury Secretary in what the business community regarded as a powerhouse administration, at the commanding apex of his economic and financial agenda. Alcoa and its subsidiaries had plants all over the world, including a number of *maquiladoras*, mostly automotive assembly plants and joint ventures just inside Mexico. One of those was in the city of Ciudad Acuña, opposite Del Rio, Texas, which made electrical distribution systems for light and heavy vehicles – 'electrical octopuses', as the workers call them.

The twin cities of Ciudad Acuña and Del Rio are the first in what now becomes the eastern third of the borderland, after the deserts and mountains descend in altitude towards rolling Texas ranch land and the vast Mexican state of Coahuila. The land becomes greener, semi-tropical and on the US side more densely scattered with towns and industrial settlements from now on, to the sea. On the Mexican side, the cities of Acuña and, a little further downriver, Piedras Negras have been transformed by the arrival of *maquiladoras*, an industrial revolution in what was horse and cattle hacienda country, now assembling the contents of America's supermarket shelves and auto-dealerships. Ciudad Acuña was, until the recession of 2009, the fastest-growing city in the country.

Reports of protest against poor conditions and wages had emanated from Alcoa's plant in Acuña since two chemical exposures in 1994, one of which had caused a three-day shutdown with 179 workers sent to hospital for evaluation. Despite a reputation for concern with workers' safety, O'Neill had reportedly brushed these whispers aside at another shareholders meeting in 1996, saying that conditions at Alcoa's plants were so good the workers could 'eat off the floor'.¹ But at that meeting in 1996, also in Pittsburgh, a shareholder rose to speak. He was no ordinary shareholder: his name was Juan Tovar Santos and he was himself a worker for Alcoa in Ciudad Acuña. Tovar Santos addressed the assembly with a bulletin from the shop floor of the *maquiladora*. He spoke about intoxication of the air by materials used in the factory. He spoke of relentless working hours and pittance pay. He described punishing production quotas and the iron regulation of breaks – to rest the eyes and fingers, to eat, even to use the lavatory. He spoke about discrimination against pregnant women, and workers having to leave after industrial injuries without compensation. Matters had become so bad, said Tovar, that riot police had had to be called in to quell a demonstration in the factory yard with tear gas.

The intervention had been carefully and long planned. The clutch of shares enabling Tovar Santos to speak had been bought by a support network for workers in the *maquilas* led by the Quaker American Friends Service Committee, and a group of Benedictine nuns in San Antonio led by one extraordinary Sister Susan Mika. Both teams worked in concert with one of the most impressive and cogent organisations along the border, the only one of its kind, the *Comité Fronterizo de Obreras*, Frontier Committee of Women Workers or CFO, based downriver from Acuña at Piedras Negras. The committee had come to represent men, too, and Tovar had been one of the driving forces behind it. The CFO is not a union but a pressure group and cadre of people working in, or sacked from, the *maquilas*, and devoted to harassing, educating, agitating, inciting, motivating, fomenting, prompting and blandishing. In Mexico, trade unions are traditionally affiliated to the central *Confederacion de Trabajo México*, the confederation of labour or CTM, a vast bureaucracy. The CTM-affiliated unions are known by democratic currents and militants as *charros*, for which there is sadly no translation other than the literal 'horseman' – 'union hacks,' perhaps, or even 'scabs'.

Such institutionalised organisation of labour is a legacy of the seven decades of power invested in the PRI, which proclaimed a veneer of sympathy with organised labour, not unlike that of the Peronist system in Argentina, with unions ceding a measure of control to the corporatist state. The PRI President Salinas Gortari talked about 'the indestructible historic pact between the Revolutionary government and the working class', sealing it with the union leader Fidel Velásquez in 1988.[2] When the *maquilas* were brought to Mexico by the PRI, there was little changing the notion that a union is not there to rock the boat. Quite the reverse, it was from now on there to keep the PRI's industrial peace, even with the new wave of investors from north of the border. In Ciudad Acuña, however, even this is luxury: the city boasts itself to potential investors in North America as being the only one along the border in which the *maquilas* are entirely 'union free', which is music to the ears of boardrooms across the USA but is a red rag to the bull of the CFO. In the post-modern, globalised marketplace, just as in the post-modern drug war, there is little place for the old lexicon. In the world of globalised production, the idea of structures to negotiate pay and conditions sits uneasily within a doctrine of profit free from restraint which carries a big stick whereby if the Mexicans get too difficult, an employer can simply move to China, or some other place where the wages are even lower and the workers docile. Only it takes longer, and costs more, to cross the Yangtzee into Texas than it does the Rio Grande, and for this reason, *maquilas* are spreading south within Mexico, into the interior, where the decrease in wages payable on terrain of abject poverty more than offsets increased costs of trans-port. In his excellent book on *maquilas*, Alejandro Lugar found that 'the life of working-class people at the US-Mexico border is so fragmented, and yet so systematically inspected, that a culture of rebellion, or of class mobilisation, was not found . . . The ruthless working conditions, the cutthroat competitive performances among workers, and the struggle over decadent tools of production often led to the unmaking of class.' His conclusion, based on years of work on and in the factories, no doubt describes the landscape accurately and in justified despair.[3] Strangely, though, the arrival of a new workforce on the border worked in two directions. On the one hand, the generally rural agricultural population that came north to work in the factories had no experience of unions or organised labour when they confronted their new transnational employers. On the other hand, the new workforce 'undermined old spaces of union control, while opening up a space for non-PRI militant unionism', wrote Altha Cravey in a study of *maquila* labour.[4] Into that space, the CFO emerged to try to ensure the basics of decency and fairness at work; that the endangered species enshrined in its slogan, 'Dignity, Justice, Solidarity', were not banished entirely, as the employers avowed, from the globalised industrial landscape in borderland Mexico.

Juan Tovar Santos has now left the border and settled in Torreon, at the southern tip of Coahuila, of which Acuña is the far north. But I caught up with him two years after a second visit to Pittsburgh in 2000, tending to the engine of a car propped up on blocks of wood and concrete outside his home in the *Colonia 28 Junio* on the edge of Ciudad Acuña. 'I'm a mechanic now, and have been since they sacked me,' he said, with both wariness and a hint of humour. 'I was never an activist before, I just came here from Zacatecas to work in the *maquila* eleven years ago, and was hired the following day – the wages were one hundred and fifty pesos a week in 1991, about fifteen dollars; they were seven hundred when I left, about fifty dollars, but worth much less in the shops.

'We'd all come from the same farms in the south of the state, we knew each other and had had enough shit from landowners during the privatisation. There were nine of us in a local factory committee, and we started trying to get direct meetings with the managers.' The things he remembered best about the Alcoa plant were the poisonings and untreated industrial injuries, the sacking of workers after being injured, the lowest wages in Ciudad Acuña and 'having to apply for toilet paper, being allowed one piece per go, only being allowed to go to the toilet twice a day and not being allowed to spend more than a minute about one's business in there. It was particularly hard on the women'. There was only one thirty-minute break for lunch and two five-minute breaks in the nine-hour working day. Tovar and his committee 'tried to talk to managers in the factory, but no one wanted to listen. Then we had an idea that we would try and get the board itself, in the United States, to listen. The CFO got involved; they said that if we wanted that, they could make it happen, with their contacts.' The CFO, he says, had been contacting workers inside the plant since 1994: the shares were duly bought by the AFSC and San Antonio nuns and the plan laid to attend Mr O'Neill's shareholders meeting in 1996. 'A number of people were invited to go to Pittsburgh,' says Tovar, 'but they were too afraid to do it, so I said okay, I'll tell the boss what's wrong in this company. So with Sister Mika and the Quakers we wrote down a list of complaints, they brought translators and off we went, to an old hotel downtown, I don't remember its name. We went to the new company headquarters and had a great time – our problems were back here, not there. Only when I stood to speak, there was an argument between O'Neill and the chairman of the meeting, and the chairman said the people should hear what the workers have to say.'

Once Tovar Santos had spoken, Alcoa's response was immediate. The following week, O'Neill fired the chief executive of his Acuña plant for failing to inform headquarters about the intoxications in 1994, and made sure that toilet paper and soap were available across all eleven of his Mexican borderland factories. 'The week after we got back,' says Tovar, 'the Alcoa human resources people showed up. They offered us a choice to work in all different places, any shift we wanted. They asked how much we wanted just to leave all this alone. I said that didn't interest me. A man called José Juan Ortiz offered me 100,000 pesos just to quit, and I said no.' O'Neill was eventually replaced by a tough new CEO, Alain Belda, but negotiations through the religious shareholders continued. Alcoa promised, says Tovar, that 'nothing would happen to those of us who had campaigned for better conditions'. However, he says, 'those conversations occurred just a few weeks before the attacks on 11 September, so that no one was really looking when the company turned against us. I was accused of sabotage,' Tovar says. 'Almost immediately afterwards they sacked the ringleaders involved. The plant was locked down tight so that the CFO could hardly get a foot inside.' Tovar has a brother in Dallas – 'and I'd like to go across. I tried to get a visa but there's not much chance of that now! My brother says to try and cross as a wetback and I'm thinking about it, but there's an issue with my mother and father. So I earn my living this way now, fixing cars. I'm quite good at it, actually; I don't have anyone to boss me around like in the *maquila*; if I work hard I can operate my own bonus scheme, if I fix up a car for myself I have a travel subsidy, the days off are more generous and I can wipe my ass as often as I want.'

On New Year's Day 1994, the same day as the Zapatista revolt at the other end of Mexico, the North American Free Trade Agreement came into effect, evaporating duty barriers and tarriffs between Canada, the United States and Mexico. As the great historian of Mexico, Enrique Krauze, writes: 'Even coming up with the idea of the North American Free Trade Agreement was a violation of the Eleventh Commandment of official Mexican mythology: Thou Shalt Not Trust Americans.'[5] Barack Obama is the first president since 1994 to show any sign of wanting to 'upgrade' NAFTA, in other words tighten the flow in favour of some protectionist measures aimed at protecting American jobs and manufacturing. His mention of the possibility proved to be a sticking point during a meeting the week before Obama's inauguration with President Calderón.[6] NAFTA was a boon to business and free trade, a blow to jobs in America and transformed the economies of Mexico and the border. For the narco cartels, NAFTA was a gift: the perfect cover for their traffic, which multiplied overnight while the bureaucracy required to ship it diminished. But it had all started with the *maquiladoras*, three decades beforehand. Although they are now the emblem of the NAFTA treaty, the *maquilas*, which defined the border's new economy by bringing the millions north (and now define it in reverse, as recession and competition from Asia cause depopulation), were NAFTA's pilot scheme, and symbol of Mexico's subjugated but dependent relationship to the US economy.

In 1961, after thousands of former migrants returned across the border when the United States ended the Bracero Program, Mexican president Adolfo López Mateos, followed by Salinas Gortari, drew up the PRONAF, or *Programa Nacional Fronterizo*, seeking to lure American corporations to northern Mexico. It offered loans, tax concessions and free zone status for the import of goods into the US. The United States was hardly going to spurn the occasion to enjoy bargain-basement Third World wages and industrial costs on its doorstep, and the US Border Industrial Program was duly drawn up on the American side, and put into effect in 1965. Mexican fortunes could also be made, leasing to the North Americans, and jobs created in a 'developing' country. As we saw in Juárez, the necklace of *maquilas* was accordingly built along the border, where cities burgeoned with those come to seek employment, but little or no attempt was made to create infrastructure capable of sustaining the new labour force – neither water nor roads, electricity nor adequate housing. As profits soared, the wage gap and that in family budgets between workers on either side of the border widened, thus antagonising relations across the frontier in 'Amexica'. The early *maquilas* thus became a scale model not only for NAFTA but for the global economy, staring the First World in the face across the Rio Grande. While the *maquilas* paid wages close to slave labour by US standards, people in the impoverished villages of the south and interior – Oaxaca, Zacatecas, Chiapas or Durango – viewed them as money indeed. Whole communities in the Mexican interior were left as ghost towns as their populations headed north, not to try to cross the border, but to work on the Mexican side, creating not only an explosion of trade, but also the busiest border on earth and work that is both comparable to factory labour around the world but also unique in its way. The collective edifice of the *maquilas* is calculatedly impregnable. The factories are architecturally ugly and soulless, homogenous and monolithic, reflecting the toil undertaken within them and the human condition required to perform it. They are invariably surrounded by fencing, barbed wire and security lodges or gates manned by guards, not so much to protect as to control. They are collated into 'parks', the ambience of which could not contrast more strikingly with the cluttered streets from which most workers commute: sterile, colourless, angular and clean. The 'parks' throttle the towns to which they have moved, built around their edges in locations that bring fabulous wealth to those who own the land, and strangulation to everyone else.

The only spoke in this wheel of production – wheel of life, indeed, as envisaged by the transformation of the borderland by the *maquiladoras* – is that the human race, and especially the Mexicans among it, has not quite yet been reduced to the automaton this cybernated model demands. Even in the *maquiladoras* of Amexica, these servo-system feeder plants of globalisation, little irritants are at work, such as unofficial lotteries, under-the-counter cosmetics sales, jokes about line managers or flirtation during stolen breaks. Dangerous in different ways to the new corporate uniformity is the questioning of this bludgeoned order by the CFO, and the indefatigability of a woman called Julia Quiñonez.

Of all the big cities on the Mexican side of the border, Piedras Negras, 60 kilometres downriver from Ciudad Acuña, is to date the easiest to be in and the safest. One can stay at the *Autel Rio* with families in transit and walk out at night to eat or relax in bars where staff are fully clothed. Tourist shops are open, and a few Americans still browse the bric-a-brac. The name of the city means 'Black Rocks', but, says Julia Quiñonez, who runs the CFO from its office some twenty benign blocks from Bridge No. 1 over the Rio Grande, 'though we are Piedras Negras, we are also called the *Frontera Blanca* — the white frontier. For some reason, touch wood, the narco war has not greatly affected us. No doubt they are here, but not in our everyday lives.'

Julia Quiñonez is on one hand effervescent, with her ready laugh, boundless energy and mischievous fun-poking, but also resilient and indurate when dealing with her subject matter — abuse of the rights of labour and human beings — and pretty tough, too, when dealing with her own people. After nearly a decade of visiting Piedras Negras, it is always wonderful to find her again, not a volt of her energy gone, nor a jalapeno sting from her severity — though she has developed a sparkly smile that was missing from the earlier days of struggle. From its humble office, and with its stretched resources, the CFO has had an influence against all odds and entirely against the zeitgeist. For instance, says Quiñonez, at one point in 2004 during the dialogue with Alcoa, the company said it needed to make cuts to wages and extend working hours by trimming benefits. Such measures, it claimed, were necessary to avoid a decision to move the plant to Honduras. The CFO organised a ballot, asking workers which they preferred between two options: to accept the changed conditions or to refuse them and challenge the company to leave. 'We called their bluff,' says Quiñonez. 'Of those that voted, eighty-nine per cent told them to go to Honduras. Part of the company did go to Honduras, but it came back again.'

In Mexico, 'it had always been the men that worked', says Quiñonez, yet from the outset 'the *maquilas* employed mostly women.

The idea was that women were more careful, with smaller delicate hands. Of course it was also thought, but not said, they were easier to manipulate in the workplace. This caused social disruption and resentments – men unused to looking after kids were staying at home cooking while their wives were out at work – often harassed at work by male supervisors.' The proportion of female workers was at its highest during the 1970s, she says, when the first generation of *maquilas* were built as assembly plants. A next generation would produce more complex products, such as electronics and electrical auto-parts, and a third, latest round would involve 'new technologies and computer chips'. The CFO, she explains, was originally formed in 1979, in the state of Tamaulipas, backed by supporters in Edinburg, Texas, knocking door to door in the sprawling new *colonias*, collecting information and offering advice on conditions, hours, pay and domestic disruption. Although CFO was not a union as such, union branches affiliated to the CTM found themselves unable to accept wage cuts and quota increases because of pressure by the CFO.

In 1980, aged fifteen, Quiñonez took her first job in the Piedras Negras *maquila* operated by Johnson & Johnson, sewing hems for medical fabrics and bandages. 'We had a union,' she recalls, 'affiliated to the PRI and functioning in the interests of the company.' She was paid by productivity, and after five years 'I was exhausted, and fed up with always having my finger punctured by the needle on the machine and pulling it back so the needle tore even more'. Julia was seventeen when the CFO organised its first assembly workers in her plant, suggesting that they vote on whether to accept a wage cut. 'I thought: Why don't we always do this?' In 1986, Quiñonez joined the new CFO regional committee covering the states of Tamaulipas and Coahuila, and the following year established a local CFO organisation for the two cities of Piedras Negras and Ciudad Acuña – made up 'mostly of women', she says. 'Our first aim was to give the workers a voice of their own, not through a union which was beholden. Our second aim was to make workers aware of the law and their rights and the third was to work in the *colonias* to support people, and stop their lives being like a parade of ants to and from work. The *maquila* depends on us being machines and the CFO was formed here to tell the workers they were human beings, and the first thing that makes you a human being is knowing what your rights are. At first, there was no hope, complete apathy. But we started by talking about sexual harassment by the managers, and taking up cases. Then we took the logic of that into the *colonia*: if it's not okay for the supervisor to yell at you and abuse you, it's not okay for your husband to do that either. So we became a force in the *colonias*, and the more that happened, the more we became a force in the *maquilas*, talking about wages, health and safety, pregnancy and conditions.'

With time, the CFO moved its headquarters to Piedras Negras, and Quiñonez became its primary, later full-time, mover and shaker. Guided by the CFO, an unprecedented series of thirty face-to-face dialogues began between employee representatives and Alcoa, after Tovar Santos' intervention. They were deftly handled by the man who had always led the initiative for the Quaker American Friends Service Committee, Ricardo Hernández, and more enlightened managers at Alcoa proved willing to venture to the Mexican side of the border for seventeen meetings – seven in Acuña and ten in Piedras Negras – for discussion about hours and conditions, on which some important agreements were reached over renewal of protective clothing, sexual harassment, holidays and injury benefits. 'The workers were speaking directly to the company, says Hernández, 'prompted by the CFO, though the CFO organisers weren't allowed themselves to come to the meetings. The workers were there, I was there, Sister Mika was there, but the CFO did all the work.'

The Colonia Luis Donaldo Colosio in Piedras Negras is a shanty town made up of one long street, a continuous strip of wooden shacks built with planks and tarpaulin roofs tumbling into one another and sharing each other's back yards. The *colonia* is sandwiched between the Airport Industrial Park and the main railway line, along which freight trains roll through from Mexico City and Monterrey so that, Julia Quiñonez says, 'children quite often get run over and killed'. The estate has been so well located that it suffers from regular flooding whenever there is heavy rain to turn the dirt that makes up the street and most people's flooring into mud. In addition to houses tucked behind the slat-wood fence that runs parallel to the railway line, there are corrugated-iron *bodegas* selling household basics.

A roll-call of the industrial park and its neighbour, the *Parque Industrial Piedras Negras*, reveals a backyard production line making the icons that adorn the temple of America. The Mex-Star factory makes wrapping for straws in McDonald's. Another factory, Southwest Manufacturing de Mexico, makes wiring for Harley Davidson motorcycles. Dimmit Industries, which closed in 2001, made jeans for Levi's. And there's a factory called FAMX, formerly the Fujikura half of Alcoa's interest, which makes the electrical circuits that keep America switching on the ignition.

Three thirty in the afternoon: and it's shift change again, in another town. Rows of school buses past their sell-by date north of the border line up outside each factory, waiting to take their load downtown or back up to the *colonias*. The workers emerge from their windowless, fluorescent-lit world within, down a flight of steps and into the forecourt, blinking into the sunlight. There is a crush waiting to get through the chicane of an exit, everyone dressed in either a blue or a green tunic, patient, but anxious to get past the security fence that is supposedly to keep people out – but that's unconvincing – and the guards. Some girls pick out a waiting face, and blow a kiss at a boyfriend through the chainlink before taking a walk, arm-in-arm. Others chatter amongst themselves as they board the buses; others again stare, hypnotised with fatigue.

It is here in Colonia Colosio between the factory and the railway that Leticia Ramírez lives, and here that Leticia works. She takes some finding – four visits before she is finally home. She works so hard: all the overtime she can get, and her house is a four-generational revolving door of two visiting sisters, their children, Leticia's daughter and her children, other relatives come to visit, and her mother from Zacatecas trying to have a holiday with the brood – plus the dogs chilling out in the dirt. She has a striking appearance: flame-red hair, a skin condition which has affected her face, the figure of a sixteen-year-old even though she is forty and a grandmother, a lambent smile and vice-grip handshake. Leticia has the aura of Semtex or some compressed plastic explosive. She was with Alcoa for eight years until 2003, and now works at the Elektrokontak factory from which she has just returned, the rear wall of which is visible from the yard where her teenaged nephews are sitting around barefoot, countless girls tend countless babies, and old Mum takes in the evening sun in a rickety chair wanting dinner, so we cannot be too long and we're lucky to have caught Lety at all. 'I was involved in the CFO right from the start,' she affirms. 'I was like Julia – asking questions, challenging them: "Why should you take away a day's wages if I'm five minutes late?" "How can you reduce my bonus just for talking?" I was always asking the CFO for advice, and soon people were coming up to me for tips on how to get round this problem or that. What we did was to know our rights and educate the others, house-to-house in the *colonias* mostly. There was knowledge to learn from books, and there was the question of confidence at work. The managers have these two big problems: they think they're smart and they've convinced themselves you can't resist their masculine charms. Both are nonsense, so if you have your wits about you, you can run rings around them, or at least put up a fight, even if they win in the end. They started talking to us, granting better benefits, but I was blacklisted, and left. And things started to slip back after we, the CFO crowd, had left the factory. We need to be on the inside and the outside. Right now, we're campaigning on Mex-Star over there.' And she waves at another stark wall enclosing another factory within view. 'The McDonald's straw place – it's dangerous,' she claims, 'something they use in a glue to make the plastic that wraps the straws.'

Now, says Leticia, finally in work again after five years on the blacklist, 'I get better pay, but only because I work longer hours.' Her ten-hour shift is 7 a.m. to 5 p.m., which brings home 600 pesos, about $50, for a five-day week. 'I work as late as they will let me every evening [as we know, she is never there when we call] and at weekends if possible. I have to, to feed everyone. I'm a mother, a grandmother and a daughter – families to feed here, parents to feed in Zacatecas.' The *colonia*, she says, 'is quite a place to live. We're all on top of each other, as you can see, and there's not much sleep with the trains two metres away – they're on their way from Mexico City to Kansas, and even Canada.' Two little boys idle on the rail tracks, torturing a frog. 'You!' shouts Lety. 'Get off the line! Idiots, they're always getting killed.'

There was one creepy *maquiladora*, says Julia Quiñonez, 'which gave me the spooks when I visited it. They made body bags for the American military. The ones they use to bring the dead soldiers back from Iraq and Afghanistan. There was a problem, they closed it. It was the strictest of all: no chewing gum, no music. No wonder: the boss was an evangelical Christian.'

By 2008 and 2009, the *maquiladora* landscape has changed in Piedras Negras since my early visits here nearly a decade previously. Although gains had been made at Alcoa, the company responding to the CFO's initiatives, a new arrival in Piedras Negras, the Lear Corporation, has brought with it new problems, says Quiñonez: 'paying wages under a new "flexible architecture" management model, of $46 for a fify-hour week. Among the lowest of all,' says Julia, 'in terrible conditions. We are having to work with victims of serious industrial accidents and injuries with no recourse to compensation.'

And there is further turbulence for those employed, or formerly employed, by Alcoa in both Acuña and Piedras Negras. Alcoa's interests had been in part a joint venture with the Japanese Fujikura company. But in 2009 Alcoa, wanting to divest and focus on aluminium production, sold its share of operations in Ciudad Acuña, Piedras Negras and other borderland cities to a California-based company called Platinum Equity. One immediate problem on the ground in Piedras Negras and Acuña is that the AFSC and Benedictine nuns in San Antonio were, as Hernández says, 'owners of stock in Alcoa, using those shares to speak to the company and bring the workers to the table. Now, there's a whole new board of directors, of an equity company without stakeholders, so we no longer have a formal platform for discussion.'

Piedras Negras' appealing architecture after crossing from Eagle Pass dissipates as one progresses into the miles of drably uniform INFONAVIT housing, built and mortgaged by the government to *maquila* workers, designed either deliberately or by happenstance to be without character. In one such forlorn terrace of cuboid habitations, Dora Luz Córdoba lives in a relative's house, rain lashing the leaking roof. She has a pink streak in her hair. It's a gesture of defiance, in its way, and she needs to be defiant, unable to work after suffering an industrial injury at the new Lear factory, and laid off without compensation, she claims. 'I only got to work there two years,' she complains, though it wasn't much fun. Her job was to operate a machine punching nails into a metal plate, only one day last year the nail punched into her hand. You only get gloves, she says, 'so as not to contaminate the circuits', and she didn't qualify for a pair. 'I suppose I have myself to blame, but I'm angry that no one trained us, just put us in front of that machine; it was never explained how to use it. And I'm angry that they didn't give me any protection for my hands, especially after a man near me lost his finger.' The accident happened at 2 a.m., and Dora was bundled off to an emergency doctor chosen by her employer, though she was made liable for the taxi fare. She claims she was told she was fine and could carry on working, though she had lost the use of a thumb, and laboured on with one hand. It was her personal doctor who insisted on an appointment with social security, but Lear declined to accept that Dora's injury was an industrial accident, as she claimed, and no benefit was forthcoming. 'So now I do what I can. I clean, mostly, people's houses, front yards, or I mind kids, anything.' Quite often while doing the rounds in Piedras Negras, one will come across Dora, in one neighbourhood or other – sweeping, scrubbing, wiping, polishing or dusting like an outdoor scullery maid with a shock of pink hair in a town where everyone works for someone else.

Dora is from Monclova in the south of Coahuila. She came here to work in the *maquilas*; she is only in her early thirties, but looks wearier. She recalls the main meal breaks, described in most *maquiladora* contracts as something to be 'enjoyed' – *disfrutar*, it says in the workplace rulebook – as especially stressful. 'If the workers exceed the thirty-minute limit, they will receive disciplinary action,' reads the rulebook.[7] 'It's supposed to be half an hour,' says Dora, 'but okay: you have to line up to clock your card out, then you line up to use the bathroom if you want to wash your hands before eating, then you line up for the food and then line up to clock back in again. That leaves about five minutes to bolt your food. Everything has to be done to the second, even your meal break. If you're late back from lunch three times at Lear, you lose a day's wages. The managers are always on your back, inspecting you, checking you, throwing their weight around and, of course, trying to make a pass. All we could do to get rid of the stress was dance. Every Friday. I'd go out with the special people I bonded with at work, the ones I had friendships with, jokes and sometimes romance. And I used to lose myself in the music and a drink, and in a dance club you could take it out on the ones who were sneaks, sucking up to the bosses. I'd work all evening, come off a shift at 2 a.m., dance all night, and sleep all next day. It was heaven.'

If there's one thing worse than Dora's *maquila* working life, it is being thrown out of it. For how different is the life of young Sara González Noriega, in a similarly tiny but well-kept house on *Calle Mar Muerto*, Dead Sea Street, making racks that enable car seats to recline. The shift, from 5 p.m. to 2 a.m., pays her 700 pesos (about $55) a week, plus the $6 bonus she keeps to spend strictly on herself, for treats or outings with friends. 'I don't like the job, but I like going to work,' says Sara, 'because I get bored at home now that my son is in school, and I like the jokes we make about the bosses, the *jefes de línea*. They're mostly vulgar, but not always. There's one who really fancies himself, always flirting and bossing us around, but he's so short and we call him *Dobico*, after a dwarf on TV. We do it every time he passes, and collapse laughing.' The managers are mad, she says, 'really insane: they have to regiment everything, enforce a strict dress code – no bracelets or anything. They might let us chew gum, but if they make us stop, we squash it into the machines! If you miss a single day, they dock twenty dollars' pay, nearly half the week. I have to start at five but there can be problems leaving my son, only if I am five minutes late, they dock a whole day's wages. You have to sign this form accepting whatever discipline they give you.'

'Article 107 of the Labour Law,' interjects Carmen Luria Vidal, a CFO organiser who accompanies us, 'prohibits arbitrary fines for workers, whatever the reason – did you know that?' 'I do now,' replies Sara, flashing a smile. 'Only sometimes people are scared to talk about things like that, in case they get sacked. When they find out that a worker is studying their rights, they ask: "How do you know? Where did you learn that?"'

Men were at first a minority of 25 per cent of the *maquila* workforce along the border, which is now about evenly balanced. Reynaldo Bueno Sifuentes is part of that equation, after thirteen years with Alcoa and now at AEES, the acronym name of the factory owned by Platinum Equity, with his baseball cap on backwards, buzz cut and red T-shirt, and piles of breeze-blocks propping up a car on which he is working in the front yard. He earns 'the same pay as when I started', about 940 pesos ($80) a week including overtime if there is any, and is happy to be driving a forklift truck stacking crates rather than on the production line. But even that is insufficient for a young family – who soon join us, his wife and two children – and so Reynaldo joins the procession over the bridge each weekend to Eagle Pass to sell plasma and raise extra cash. 'I go twice, for sixty dollars says Reynaldo, 'two-thirds of what I earn all week at Alcoa. It pays for small things and extras, details, fixing up the bathroom and car, toys for the kids. But you have to be careful selling plasma. I've seen people who don't eat right or sell too much, and they're dizzy all the way home. I've seen them falling over on the bridge coming back.' Reynaldo's dream, he says, 'is to be a mechanic. In the *maquila*, though it's much more dangerous than driving, and eventually for myself, just fixing up cars back there.' I think of Juan Tovar Santos, the original troublemaker, fixing cars and wiping his ass whenever he wants. Reynaldo was part of the CFO dialogues with Alcoa executives, and one of the plant delegates nominated by the *charro* union leaders. As such, he was supposed to attend what Ricardo Hernández calls the parallel 'pantomime negotiations' supposedly to prepare the workers' positions and brief the union leaders who would themselves negotiate. In reality, these meetings were held so that workers could be briefed on what the leadership had decided, and says Reynaldo, 'when the time came for the contract negotiations at the Alcoa plant in Piedras Negras, which is unionised, no one would tell me when the negotiations were happening, because I'm with the CFO and I know the book of labour law. So how was I supposed to brief my shift if I can't go to the negotiations? So I'm walking a high wire now – there are threats, but only verbal ones so far. The snitches'll say: "Let's kick this guy in", right in front of the manager, to please him. So we'll see, but I ain't backing down.'

Behind Julia Quiñonez' offices, there is a *maquiladora* run by the CFO with a modest workforce of eight. With a difference, as one might expect: the *Maquiladora Dignidad y Justicia* – of dignity and justice – employs women sacked or retired from the jungle *maquilas* out there, working to timetables that fit their lives, making goods for sale on the Internet, made of organic, 'fair-trade' materials. 'Once,' says Julia, 'we got an offer to make holsters for guns, from a company called Maverick Arms. We turned it down because it was part of the arms industry. Shame, we'd have made them much better holsters.'

Two ladies have come to work at the CFO's *maquila* this morning: Sonia, who made Levi's for eleven years at the Dimmit factory, and Herlinda, who worked as a seamstress for Barry Industries in Ciudad Acuña, making slippers for America's favourite family mall mega-stores. Where will America be without them? Who knows, but both ladies have meanwhile been retrained by a third woman, Ofelia, suggested by Julia Quiñonez. Sonia and Herlinda remember the days of the twelve-hour *maquiladora* shift that has now been reduced to nine by most employers. Twelve hours from 6 a.m. to 6 p.m., that is, punctuated by a ten-minute break at 9 a.m., thirty minutes at midday and another ten at 3 p.m. Sonia was eventually promoted to quality control, 'inspecting miles and miles of fabric, having made it myself for many years. They got more and more strict "do it quicker, do it quicker" – so there's a chain of pressure, which I had to pass on. There was one we called Jalapeno, because he was always stinging us. The twelve hours got you five hundred pesos [$42] a week; you had to work weekends to get the extra two hundred. Eventually, I had to leave because I lost my eyesight from concen-trating all day – before, I could see like an eagle, now I'm blind as a bat – and because the bones in my ankle got all messed up from standing for eleven years. I'm not a small lady,' she laughs, 'and I started having trouble walking.'

Herlinda spent twenty-two years making slippers, seven days a week. 'Sometimes we had to increase production because there was an emergency, like when the buyer first started ordering them by the thousands, and if we didn't complete the order in time, the buyer might go somewhere else.' Interestingly, to wrap a straw for McDonald's is a much slower process than stitching a slipper. Herlinda would sew a base figure of eighty-four slippers a minute. In a day of 720 minutes minus 50 minutes for breaks, that is 56,280 slippers per day and 393,960 slippers in a seven-day week. This level of productivity paid a basic wage of 600 pesos a week – 0.0015 pesos (0.00011 cents) per slipper. 'But we could earn an extra three hundred pesos a week if we increased our productivity by an extra thirty slippers a minute, which I learned to do,' says Herlinda – 114 slippers per minute, totalling 76,380 slippers a day, or 534,660 in a seven-day week. Herlinda almost certainly didn't do this, but if she had worked at the higher rate for all her twenty-two years, and not accounting for any days off she must have taken, she'd have amassed what in baseball would be called a career total of 613,331,400 – well over half a billion – slippers, over a career average of 27,878,700 (nearly twenty-eight million) slippers a year. But that was not enough, not fast enough, not cheap enough. Suddenly, says Herlinda, 'the factory closed. It went to China, and after twenty-two years I lost my job. But everyone kept talking about this Julia, who had helped the workers and was retraining specialists who had lost their jobs, so here I am.' And she beams through her spectacles, a woman now in her forties, with the fingers of an eighty-year-old, but nimble as a child's as she serves herself from the aluminium trays containing a hearty lunch of fajitas that Julia has brought from a *taqueria* round the corner.

Of course, this workshop could not begin to try to compete in the service of America's appetite for slippers. But it is a going concern, it has its catalogue and its business: T-shirts, tote bags, handbags, sweaters, blouses and shirts. 'My dream is to grow this workshop into an export business,' says Ofelia, who was herself a seamstress but self-employed in her house, 'because I had six sons', making school uniforms and habits for monks and priests and once, even, the bishop's robe. The CFO *maquila* has carved itself important partners like the Minnesota-based 'North Country Fair Trade', and a high point came when the Mexican fashion designer Juan Pablo López asked the women in Piedras Negras to realise his designs for various haute couture shows in Paris. The ladies take an intake of proud breath at the very thought. 'We made a summer and winter collection,' purrs Ofelia, 'all fair-trade materials, all organic: blouses and dresses for the women, and some shirts for the men. And there they were on the DVD, on a catwalk in Paris, paraded by models!' López' design drawings are on the wall, garments named after and reflecting the planets and their qualities. 'Earth is men's stuff, as you can see,' enthuses Ofelia; 'Mercury is a lovely blouse and Mars this sexy mini-dress. Jupiter's very pretty, a blouse with big baggy sleeves, but look at Pluto, a frock with a high waist, hem above the knee and designs from *Chiapas*.'

A hard few days in Piedras Negras end with a get-together in a dimly lit room at the back of a house in another shanty town, Colonia 28 Junio where Juan Tovar Santos lived, of buildings made of wood and this one, belonging to the Ozilla family, of concrete. The walls of the room are covered by the Virgin of Guadalupe, Club America and children's drawings, and it is hard to tell which of the people dangling their legs from both storeys of bunk-beds and sitting across the floor are Ozillas and which are family, friends or workmates. This is a social occasion, not another collective gripe, though the two tend to overlap. Arturo and Luis, two of the old guard, sing the praises of lotteries that operate in most *maquilas*. Arturo says that tickets for the official state-run lottery sell for less in the *maquilas* than they do on the street, but with the same prize money, because the salesman's commission is lower. To be caught selling tickets, though, 'gets at least a four-day suspension, and usually the sack'. Marginally less risky are the sweepstakes held, and odds offered, on horseracing and football. 'I won fifty pesos on a nag running in Torreón last year,' says a man called Adrian, 'for a stake of only five, though I've probably spent another hundred since.' Gabriela and the girls are dependent on thriving cosmetics markets that operate unofficially in the *maquilas*. 'The older ladies who can cross to Eagle Pass buy them in bulk and bring them back to sell in the toilets. The only snag is going into the bathroom two at a time to check out what they've got without being seen. Usually, the sales and raffles are on pay day, but it's getting easier now to pick up your winnings or perfume after work.' 'Better to go to Eagle Pass to buy cosmetics,' says Julia Quiñonez drily, 'than to sell your blood.'

The old baseball stadium in Ciudad Acuña is a rickety but precious one; the kind of ground that would melt the heart of an ageing American aficionado of the game who feels out of step with electronic scoreboards and a thumping disco beat through the seventh-inning stretch. The Acuña stadium didn't make it into Ken Burns' series on the history of the game, but it reminds one that this is still a pastoral game, though invented in the city: there are little windows in the brickwork through which to buy tickets, scuffed concrete steps into the stands off which the paintwork has been worn by decades of boot heels. The crowd is arraigned on wooden bench seats without numbers; *Krakejak* is on sale from an ad-hoc stall for ten cents and Tecate with lime and salt in a can for thirty-five cents instead of the seven dollars that Americans pay for Bud Lite in plastic cups. This afternoon's game is a Coahuila state cup knockout fixture between Acuña's Atleticos and Saltillo, and the crowd is full of piss and vinegar with Acuña winning 8–1, sitting pretty with bases loaded at the bottom of the eighth. A third strike collapses the chance to go 12–1, but the standard is high, the signalling and second-guessing sophisticated and at the close range afforded by this stadium, you get to savour those moments of sudden acceleration and deceleration, after the tension of carefully calculated nothing. Across the scrap of land outside, a market is in full swing, selling *ropa usada* – literally 'used stuff': second-hand clothes brought from Del Rio across the border – knock-off CDs and very unofficial soccer kit: those in Acuña who are not fans of baseball tend to be devoted to the *Santos de Torreón* soccer team. Boys accordingly play football in the dust wearing either local green or Club America yellow, and a crowd of tambourine-bashing evangelicals sing on a corner, '*los Hallelujas*', as they are jokingly called. Jehovah's Witnesses – *Los Testigos de Jehovah* – are more commonly known as *Los Testiculos de Jehovah* (which shouldn't need translating), jokes Oscar Gonzáles, our companion.

In June 2009, after the sale by Alcoa to Platinum Equity, the workers in Ciudad Acuña supported by the CFO, uncertain about the future of their forum for dialogue with company executives, made a decision: they would seek recognition to a trade union – that of Mexico's coal miners – a fly in the ointment of the city's selling point north of the border. This is not a shift away from the CFO, which is not a union and cannot legally organise a workplace. Quite the reverse, the CFO is as usual part of the plan. The CFO's office in Ciudad Acuña is located at the end of a dusty stretch of road along which a *pulga* (literally: flea) market sprawls, blaring music by our *narco-corrido* friends Los Tigres del Norte (Julia Quiñonez is a big fan). And inside the CFO office, on two consecutive September afternoons in 2009, groups of mischief-makers meet to discuss the progress of the idea to organise the first union in the city's *maquilas*, before moving on to work their shifts. These were all members of the dialogue forum, the legacy and tribe of Juan Tovar Santos and his day out in Pittsburgh. A man called Juan Carlos Palomino remembers the riot back in 1999 in the parking lot: 'they came in with guns, attacked us by force'; he feels his blood rush even now. 'People were fainting from the tear gas, women too, they didn't give a damn about the women.' And 'after they sacked 240 people, they thought the problem had gone away – ha ha! All they'd done was steel our nerve and spread 240 people to fight in other *maquilas*!'

The group on the second afternoon included Sergio from Veracruz who works in plant 2 of AEES, with a red T-shirt and ruddy face, and Javier from Tabasco with a pony tail pulling back the hair from his handsome face and a baseball cap on back to front, leaning forward, elbows on knees throughout the discussion. 'There were numerous advances as a result of our meetings with the executives,' says Sergio, citing a few: deals over pregnant women and protective shoes, time out for medical emergencies and recognition of grades and differentials. 'But there's been a change since the company was sold by Alcoa, noticeably by supervisors and managers, going back to the old ways.' The men use the term *prepotencia* – prepotency, throwing their weight around. 'We're worried about the recession, but especially the way they respond. Laying people off, increasing the quotas, constantly repeating the threats to leave for Honduras or Asia, whether that comes from the top or not.' The uncertainty takes a social toll on Acuña as it did Riberas del Bravo in Juárez, Javier talking about 'people returning to Veracruz or the south of Coahuila, nine out of ten of the empty homes left being invaded by gangs and addicts. It all helps organised crime sink roots into the *colonias*. Kids don't go to school, and things disintegrate socially. It's not Ciudad Juárez, but we're on the road to Ciudad Juárez.' The fact that things are quieter here, and the CFO's minds are on other things, does not mean the Zetas are any less active. Joe Morales, a former security coordinator for US and transnational companies investing in *maquilas* across Piedras Negras and Ciudad Acuña, said that the narco traffickers were 'in complete control of the streets and get very little resistance from those they extort. It's every citizen for himself if they are confronted by the drug lords. If the drug dealers need to kill someone, they take them outside Acuña so they don't attract attention of the Mexican federal officers or the military.'[8] In 2007, the Zetas organised a street party for children's day, with food, cakes and drinks. A banner was posted: 'Happy Day to All, from Osiel Cárdenas.'

'Because of who we are,' says Javier, 'we think the solution to all the problems has to start where the problem starts: in the workplace. We need to improve the quality of life, and that starts at work. It all begins with that.' Hence the aim to create a union branch, but why the miners' union? 'Because it's a strong union,' says a man called Nicolás Rojas Romero. 'It's less *charro* than the others, doesn't kiss the boss's ass and has a history in Coahuila – the coal mines in the south of the state were always well organised.' Ciudad Acuña's promise north of the border was that such a thing would never be tolerated. But contact has already been made with the miners in Mexico City, which is now ready to recognise a local branch of the union across the AEES plants belonging to Platinum Equity, in union-free Ciudad Acuña. How Platinum Equity will react is anybody's guess. 'It feels like back to Pittsburgh!' laughs Juan Carlos Palomino, like an old trooper called back to the front after too long in the rear echelon.

Once past the usual ring of Pemex stations and Oxxo convenience stores that flank any Mexican border town, and the Colonia 28 Junio where Juan Tovar Santos lived, the road out of Acuña and back to Piedras Negras crosses flat land reaching towards the border, through groves of mesquite trees and nopales cactus, wholesome and delicious with beans, and the pretty little town of La Purisima – the most pure. But before reaching the most pure, there is a sudden jolt. A white-painted chapel stands on the south side of the road, alone. Julia Quiñonez presumes it to be just another Virgin of Guadalupe and pays it no heed, puzzled at my demands we pull over.

The skeleton within is shrouded in a cloak of colours, the spectrum of the rainbow. In one bony hand, her right, she holds a globe – the earth, the whole world, the sphere of continuum and eternity. In the other, the left, a bunch of white flowers someone has placed there, roses and lilies, the flower of purity presented by the archangel

Gabriel to the mother of Christ. At her feet, candles burn in glass holders bearing her image, only in the pictures, the cloak is hooded and black and she carries a scythe. Also on the ground, in homage, offerings of oranges, Tecate beer, ashtrays full of cigarette ends and scratch cards. An iron grille across the face of the chapel is locked. To partake in this homage, in this petition for protection and blessing, one needs access to a key, one must be initiated. On the side of the chapel is painted an oration which reads: You who await the exact moment/ To extend your hands to me/ To enter the time ordained/ Protect me from evil and all memory.

The skull of *Santísima Muerte* – most holy death – is unadorned. This is rare. She is usually crowned, at least with flowers, if not a mitre. She stares north, with her hollow eyes. And the black light of her gaze stares through those eye sockets of bone towards the river, the Rio Bravo, Rio Grande – call it what you may, under this gaze it matters not a fig. The river: the flowing border, its waters now moving towards a new chapter in this war, a new terrain – that controlled by the Zetas, where all the rules change, the landscape changes, and the air itself is heavy with the cartel's power, deadly and, until very recently, intact. The skeleton's eyes stare towards the river as it winds now towards a bridge called the Gateway to the Americas, where the war began.

CHAPTER EIGHT

Gateway to the Americas / Pax Mafiosa

The headlights aimed along Highway 85 coming in from Monterrey throw bedazzling beams through the dust kicked up around truck stop *Veintiseis* – Twenty-six – so that the encampment of drivers, roadside cafés and police officers at their checkpoint is coated in a thick, illuminated mist of powdery, pulverised dirt. Although the trucks are parked up like a military column, many of their drivers have kept the engines loading so the granulated dust is also heavy with noise and fumes, chugging Volvo and belched Pemex diesel. There is no daytime or night in the truckers' world, only daylight and darkness; there is no clock apart from that which measures pick-up and delivery times, delays. North of the border, the commandment is set in stone and monitored by tachometer, an accord between the Teamsters and haulage companies: after ten hours' driving, you rest ten hours. But this side, in Mexico, things are more flexible. Or maybe not so flexible, there's just a different kind of rule: you drive all the hours God gives, pep yourself up with chemical cocktails to do so and make as much money – that is, drive as many kilometres – as you are physically capable of, Devil take the consequences. But even a Mexican trucker must eat, sleep a little and do other things while off the road.

Veintiseis is the name given to the truckers' republic that has sprung up around the customs post and police checkpoint 26 kilometres south of Nuevo Laredo, the city that, with its twin on the US side, Laredo, makes up the gateway to the last, industrial, leg of the border journey. The bridge between the two downtown areas of each city is called the 'Gateway to the Americas', because this is the border's commercial fulcrum, at which you arrive either by freeway up from Monterrey in the south or down Interstate 13 from Dallas to the north. Or, of course, as I did: along the flat border road from Eagle Pass, Texas. The railway bridge and three other road bridges between these cities form the umbilical cord of trade connecting Mexican and Latin American freight, and Chinese exports, with North America. Forty per cent of all trade between the US and Mexico – totalling $367.4 billion – crosses the Rio Grande here every day, loaded onto thousands of rail cars and 8,000 trucks crossing daily in both directions, converging from all over the US and Mexico to transfer their payloads to shuttle-trucks at vast freight-forwarding yards on either side of the border. More than twelve million barrels of crude oil a day cross the line here, along with 432 tonnes of jalapeno peppers, 11,000 ATM cash machines, 16,000 television sets – all this and more through a town that on the Mexican side didn't light the streets until recently and on the US side was a sleepy cowboy town famous for the song, 'The Streets of Laredo'. Now, neither side can mix concrete fast enough. *Los Dos Laredos*, as the twin cities are called, form a commercial DMZ full of freight containers as far as the eye can see. There is charisma and excitement in the whole thing – trucking – in both these twin cities.

Laredo, Texas, is the fourth biggest port – and the biggest land-locked port – in the USA, after New York, Los Angeles and Detroit. Some 5,000 trucks a day cross north, and 5,000 south, over the busiest bridges in the world. But here's the rub: although 97 per cent of the goods transported is legal, an estimated 3 per cent is contraband – invariably drugs northbound, guns and cash southbound – making this the principal crossing point for narco-cartel exports. And these drivers are their witting or unwitting transporters. The cartels' war – which began here in earnest in 2005 – was for the prize corridor, the most important Plaza of all. The authorities' war is against a simple logic: the more trade that comes through *Veintiseis* and across the border, the more drugs come with it.

Behind the rays of the headlamps at *Veintiseis* are other lights, the pale yellow or bright fluorescent lanterns of the *comedores*, places to eat, each marked with a hand-crafted sign. Approaching night, the place is all bustle and hustle. Exhausts farting, brakes screeching, reverse gears grinding and the drivers checking out the deals in the *comedores*. In the middle of this arcade is a little chapel, lit from within by flickering flames of candles burning on its floor and in alcoves in the side walls. On the back wall are painted the images of the Virgin of Guadalupe and San Jude Taddeo, beneath whom is written an oration: *Pros mi por San Judas Tadeo / Dame la mano firme y migrada vigilante / Para que llegue a mi destino / Sin accidentarme ni danar a los demas / Librame de los conductores brigandos y agresores.* Grant me a firm, vigilant hand to lead me to my destination, without hurt to myself or the others – and deliver me from bandit and aggressive drivers – for thine is the eternal ribbon of asphalt, for ever and ever, Amen.

In the *Comedor Johanna*, two drivers sit on red plastic chairs at a red plastic table eating fajitas. They are Juan Gabriel Morales from Tabasco, driving a load from the Pacific port of Lázaro Cárdenas, and Alfredo Cornelio from the gulf port of Veracruz, hauling a container from a depot outside Mexico City. Juan Gabriel has two front teeth missing from the upper tier, a chest thick with hair and a ring with a crown of thorns on it. Alfredo wears a Chivas T-shirt and shorts despite the damp drizzle. Neither is told what their load is nowadays, they complain. Both men are exhausted and glad to have made it. 'The road gets harder,' says Juan Gabriel, the older man, 'more checkpoints, more delays, more *mordida* [bribes to pay along the way.] 'It's crazy,' says Alfredo, 'there's more work than ever, but more hassle on the route – because of the problems.' Their friend Jorge emerges from the gloom of the desert and backyard behind *Comedor Topo Chico* next door, zips up his flies and re-clasps his belt buckle with a hand of four Aces on it. It's too late to eat, he says; he'll have breakfast in the morning and a beer for now. Jorge looks the part: black pony tail, Durango boots with a harness and buckle, tight jeans.

Beyond the banter, no driver wants to get into an involved discussion about anything until morning, that is to say in five hours' time, at 5 a.m., same place. There are things to talk about, says Juan Gabriel, the older man, with glasses, but for now we'll just exchange team news between Chivas and Liverpool, and talk about Barcelona. Barca's following in Mexico and among Mexican Americans is ubiquitously passionate, not least because the Mexican national captain, Ráfa Márquez, plays at left back for the Catalans. But the issue now is to find somewhere to sleep, not having available the cabin of a truck personalised with religious articles and pictures of women wearing only cowboy hats and boots. The first hotel on the northbound carriageway was the *Campo Real*, but the din and squealing from the adjacent Bar Jaguar, from which one presumably adjourns in company to bed, made us U-turn back to the 8km line and the Motel California, with courtyard walls painted ochre yellow with a touch of pastel green to give the chipped cement that south-west adobe feel. The man at reception gives us the keys to rooms 05 and 07 in exchange for 200 pesos each and asks, how long we want them for. 'For the night,' I reply and his reaction says it all: part shrug, part compliment at the prowess entailed by a rental longer than an hour.

The world over, truckers sleep in the cabins of their juggernauts to save money (though Europe and the USA have different facilities that offer a driver a bed). In Mexico, where every peso counts, there is only one reason why a trucker would spend good money on an iron bed and clammy sheets. Come to think of it, the *Comedor Economico 'La Sirena'* back at *Veintiseis* had been exactly as it proclaimed itself, some of the yellow tables occupied by *conductores* tucking in, others by groups of sultry ladies chain smoking and crossing their legs in skirts so short, for all the chill of night, there was little left to the mind's eye. And before long, that one reason starts assembling in reception and sure enough there's a knock at the door. I feign sleep. Knock, knock again. Towel round my waist, I answer the door to say, '*Desculpe, pero—*' 'You like my hair?' which is beautifully permed for sure, but not the first thing you'd notice. 'Twenny dollar, thirty for my fren' join us,' the visitor continues, all this in passable English. 'Thank you but no, I just need to sleep.' It seems rude, so I say it again in Spanish, out of some weird sense of etiquette: 'No offence, er . . . thank you, no.' It is enlightening to learn what kind of real woman a Mexican trucker prefers to spend his hard-earned wages on cuddling up to, for all the size-zero, snake-waisted pin-ups wriggling around the walls of their cabins. Some of these buxom behemoths patrolling *Veintiseis* and the Motel California would weigh in at a tonnage above some of the sixteen-wheelers themselves.

By 5 a.m., *Comedor Johanna* is in full swing as ebullient *Veintiseis* gears up for another day of NAFTA. Of last night's company, only Jorge from Puebla, looking chipper in a clean Wrangler shirt with embroidered horseshoes, has kept the 5 a.m. rendezvous. 'So you stayed at the Motel Californicada!' he growls with laughter, raising a thick eyebrow as though to ask: And how was she? Jorge calls hookers not the usual *putas* but *arañas*, which means spiders, and reports that the ones at *Veintiseis* are particularly *garrapatas*, literally ticks, meaning pushy. 'Not my type,' I offer, trying to sound more macho than prudish. 'You should've stayed in my truck and put me in the motel,' retorts Jorge, who says he's fed up with the food at *Johanna's* so we take a stroll across the pitted roadside tarmac through a battleship-grey dawn to the first eatery inside the line drawn across the highway by police inspection booths.

Jorge started driving after losing his job as a mechanic in Córdoba, south of Puebla. 'The Mexican driver,' says Jorge, 'is the best in the world because he has to be. It's not like the USA – there's no job protection, no guaranteed rest, no limit on the time you can drive. The company will never pay for a second driver, so it's all down to you. The pressure comes from both the company, and the other drivers. The crazier they are, the crazier I have to be. We set our own pace, always driving further to make more money, always stretching it, pushing it.' Jorge has been driving trucks the length of Mexico for eleven years: 'I know every metre between here and Monterrey, Monterrey and Mexico City, and down from my town to Guatemala. I know every trick – ha, and I know every *cachimba*.' That's a new one. It means literally fireplace or hearth, but Jorge means the kind of roadhouse where you can get fed, drunk and laid – and score drugs – all in one. 'In Zacatecas and the south, you get everything money can buy whenever you want,' assures Jorge. One hardly needs to ask how Jorge and his comrades perform these miracles of itinerant sleeplessness over weeks, months, years, for they are not miracles. 'How much do you get paid for this?' I ask. Jorge looks around him, checks that the cook is stirring eggs, and pulls out a plastic bag full of pills and little packets of silver foil. 'This much.' He smiles with a grimace.

At that moment, Juan Gabriel comes in and orders coffee. Juan Gabriel being a family man, Jorge explains that we're just talking about driving, a lot of driving. And Juan Gabriel has seen the highways change, he says, especially of late, since the drug war began, in 2005, here in Nuevo Laredo. 'The timing is stressful. You have your load, your deadline and delivery date. If you fuck it up, you don't get paid. After five years, I think I know every trick, and suddenly: new checkpoints, new hassle. And it gets scary,' though Juan Gabriel seems ashamed to admit it, for Mexican truckers are supposed to be unacquainted with fear. 'You're coming out of San Luis Potosí towards Saltillo and there's a checkpoint that wasn't there before. You've no idea who it is. If it's the army, you can usually talk your way out of it, even if you have to pay. But what if it's the police? Or the police working for the bad guys from here who are big in that area?' (No one utters the word 'Zetas', we shall see why.) 'You just have to get the papers out and give them what they want – you can try, but the company won't pay it back.'

What both Juan Gabriel and Jorge want to talk about more than anything is the moment that, as it happens, first brought me to Laredo in 2001. In a narrow window of time between his election and the attacks of 11 September that year, George W. Bush, as former governor of Texas and devotee of free trade, had made the first overtures of his presidency to Mexico. Vicente Fox was the first foreign head of state with whom he met and President Bush proposed the unthinkable: he wanted to admit Mexican trucks into and throughout the United States. Instead of a drayage system of forwarding yards and shuttling loads across the border, the long-haul trucks containing goods from the south and from China via Lázaro Cárdenas would simply line up for inspection and roll over the bridges. The proposal drew flurries of reaction from all sides and in all directions. US haulage firms accelerated their already substantial financial stakes in transporters based in Mexico. The Teamsters union was outraged: jobs regulated by years of negotiation were threatened by drivers working to timetables that were recklessly non-existent. Ironically, the left and right swapped sides: the former isolationist and the latter wanting to tear down the border while environmental groups joined the fray with dire warnings about Mexicans, the trucks they drove and the way they drove them. In the event, the proposal was scotched by 9/11, but it had begged all kinds of questions about not only NAFTA and the vagaries of free trade but about the border itself. It sent particles of interest flying about like those in a nuclear reactor, smashing into one another from all directions.

At every truck stop in Mexico, the passing moment fuelled a conversation that will never end. 'Let me drive to Chicago!' enthuses Jorge, eating breakfast like a bear. 'We could beat those *gringo* truckers' asses off their cabin seats!' Juan Gabriel says, with more deduction: 'If they let us cross the border, that would change everything. We'd make more money than the *gringos* even though their wages are higher, just because we'd drive so hard. We'd drive them out of a job with equal competition. That's why it'll never happen. But I respect them. They're doing what we would do − I wish we had the Teamsters instead of a *charro* union. They're drivers, we're drivers, we're the same people. If I was a Teamster, I wouldn't want crazy Mexicans driving everywhere, popping pills.'

We walk back to the parking area, past the police checkpoint, behind a very different eating joint which amalgamates Church's Chicken, Subway and Daily Roast. Along the way, an entire village has been built up around the *Veintiseis*, with houses where *comedor* owners, cooks, dishwashers, waiters and waitresses, used-clothing dealers, prostitutes, engine repair mechanics and their children live, and yards where rangy dogs, cats, cows, goats, pigs and rats cohabit with them. The *Comedor La Güera* − the blonde − also operates a full service market for detergents, shaving gear, batteries, penknives and knock-off audio and video entertainment, while the *Restaurante Jalisiense* is attached to a *Yonke La Maroma*, fixing up cars and exhausted engines. And all along the way, the ground is littered with discarded little aluminium packages that once contained pills, the overnight dosage of downers to sleep and amphetamines to get you going again. There are hundreds of them strewn across the dust, but they are only the slightest micro-shaving off the great block of narcotics pulling up at *Veintiseis* and moving on through. The drugs are aboard the trucks, in bulk, heading straight into the United States of America. There is no reason why, if 40 per cent of cross-border trade moves through here, 40 per cent of the drugs shouldn't either, if not more. That is why the drug war began in Nuevo Laredo, and that is why the Gulf cartel and Zetas made sure to win it.

The battle for Nuevo Laredo was the beginning of the current phase of Mexico's agony. It announced a new level and a new kind of violence: some 2,000 were killed in 2005 across the country. The Sinaloa cartel sent a lieutenant called Edgar Valdez Villarreal, aka *La Barbie*, to lead its siege of the Laredo trade route, who used the Internet to show videos of four Gulf cartel killers being beaten, and ending with one being shot in the head. Valdez got his nickname because of his pale complexion and blue eyes.[1] After one firefight late in 2006, the dead 'lay in pools of blood flowing into the Rio Grande', after which men with assault rifles 'picked up the bodies of the victims, threw them in the back of pickup trucks and headed out of downtown.'[2] In June 2005, President Vicente Fox sent in a token military force, which he called Operation Secure Mexico, but as a commander of the police department, Enrique Sánchez, said when asked by journalists where the solders were during the fighting: 'That's a good question. Where are they?' It was a barbed remark, with Mexican federal officials at the time briefing that the Nuevo Laredo's police department was at the disposal of the jailed Osiel Cárdenas, leader of the Gulf cartel and creator of the Zetas. At the same time, Alejandro Domínguez Coello, a former federal law-enforcement official and president of the chamber of commerce, became chief of police in Nuevo Laredo. He was honest, unaffiliated to the cartel – and assassinated seven hours after taking office.[3] Within days of the police chief's murder, the US government closed its consulate, comparing Nuevo Laredo to Baghdad, a city of 'bazookas, grenades and machine guns', said a businessman after watching a twenty-minute battle.[4] Throughout, the cartel hung their *narcomensajes*, one reading: 'What Else Could You Want? The State of Tamaulipas, Mexico, The United States, The Whole World – Territory of the Gulf Cartel.' Another promised that the Zetas served 'Better Food Than Noodle Soup', the standard fare consumed by serving soldiers.[5]

But the war has now abated. Nuevo Laredo is calm, or has the appearance of calm that could blow at any moment. When the human rights campaigner Raymundo Ramos Vásquez shows off a narco villa in the exclusive Madero neighbourhood whose owner switched loyalty to the Sinaloa cartel five years ago – attacked with bazookas, incinerated and still empty – he does so as though it were both a cautionary tale and a tourist attraction. But Nuevo Laredo lives the peace of the tomb, or what in Italy would be called *Pax Mafiosa*. 'There has been a truce,' says Ramos. 'I don't know the details, and I don't want to know, but the Gulf cartel has won, the Sinaloa cartel has lost, and they have reached an accord. I can only guess that Guzmán pays some kind of tax to use the corridor, if he uses it at all. The Gulf cartel controls the corridor again, and the federal army patrols every block of the city, twenty-four hours a day, 365 days a year. Apart from a new presence, *La Familia*, this has had the effect of stopping the war.'

It has also had the effect of producing a society in which no one dares speak the word *Zeta*. In every town under their control, the Zetas have another name in everyday parlance, a codeword used as a vain insurance policy by the few who dare speak of this subject; here it seems to be *El Pirámide*, or just the generic 'bad guys', as everywhere else. It is an absurd charade − anyone who talks about the Zetas is at risk whatever they call them − but the shying away from the word is fundamentally important. It shows that the faux-mystique of the Zetas works and intimidates; that their name has become an evil talisman, and to avoid uttering it is a primal act of superstition. To speak it, on the other hand, feels like self-condem-nation. Ramos talks about the Gulf cartel, but never uses the 'Z' word. There are, though, exceptions of insane courage.

Driving back with Raymundo Ramos into town one day, there was an extraordinary coincidence, speaking of brave people. I asked after a mutual friend of ours, Elisabeth, and Raymundo said he hadn't seen her for nearly a year, since the three of us were last together, in fact. At that very moment, in a little street behind the Church of the Holy Infant downtown, there she was. Elisabeth was once a leading attorney in town, fighting domestic violence, as a public defender for five years and four years in jails on cases of wrongful conviction. She was the first woman from Nuevo Laredo ever to volunteer for national military service. But in this city, her curriculum vitae makes Elisabeth unemployable, a transgressor of the values that sustain this society (which she is). No *curia*, tribunal or court will touch her, though she still carries her resume round every forum in town.

In her hurt and rage, Elisabeth is another rare soul who testifies to what is happening, but unlike Raymundo she does so with a Devil-may-care fury heedless of consequence. After the joy at the serendipity of the meeting, we adjourn to a friend's house in an alleyway behind the church for coffee and incautiousness. 'I watch them control every-thing, different people but always the same interests. First the police, then the Zetas − let's call them by their name [she is the only person who does] − beating the city into silence. They control everything in this town, everything that moves, every particle of our lives.' Shouldn't you be careful, saying all this, Elisabeth? 'It's driven me mad being careful. If I am so dangerous, let them kill me. If they do, at least I'll die with a clean conscience.' People know Elisabeth, as we walk around and towards the church. They greet her from underneath the parasols that shade their taco stands, but make sure not to tarry too long talking, lest someone see or hear.

On the back of a truck, there is a sticker of *Santa Muerte*, and the words: '*Dio mi guía, Ella mi proteja*' – God guides me, she protects me. 'Just look,' spits Elizabeth, 'there's a cult of death across this town. It is sick, dying from within.' We enter the church and breathe the musky air with relief. Elisabeth caresses the feet of the saints with fervent exhalations. 'Here, I am safe,' she says beneath the figure of the *Virgen del Carmen*, and the words: '*En la vida protejo / En la muerte ayudo / Y despues la muerte salvo*' – in life I protect, in death I help, and after death, I save.

Nuevo Laredo's peace is a hideous, precarious but browbeaten calm, yet it serves as a model which the Mexican government, or any future Mexican government, keeps on as an option, especially if the PRI were to return to power by beating President Felipe's Calderón's PAN party out of popular exhaustion with his war. Put starkly, and in the extreme: Mexico's choice may one day be between the implosion in Juárez, where the war grinds on, or the *Pax Mafiosa* of Tamaulipas. The only problem is that a national *Pax Mafiosa* would be entrusted to Guzmán for safe keeping, so what deal to cut with the Gulf cartel, and/or Zetas? (These latter two were synonymous – until 2010, when an as yet unresolved internecine power struggle exploded further downriver and at the time of writing was about to arrive in Nuevo Laredo.)

When I return to see Raymundo Ramos a year later, in 2009, the 'peace' is one year older, the town almost buzzing, such is the façade of the *Pax Mafiosa* and the determination of these people to live as best they can. Raymundo and I convene in the front room of the house of a friend of his. He is an intriguing man – secretive about his life, but boldly forthright in his utterances and analysis. He runs the beleaguered Nuevo Laredo Committee for Human Rights, working as a *rapporteur* to the United Nations human rights commission, but his casework mainly involves complaints against the army – he stays well clear of problems caused by the Zetas. 'The difference between here and Juárez,' he begins, 'is that there, the Plaza is still contested – a battle between gangs, cartels and the army. Here, we don't have that problem. The Plaza is tranquil, it's peaceful now compared to three years ago. Here, there's one cartel and the army. But the volume of traffic going through Nuevo Laredo doesn't change. All it means is that the accord between narcos at the highest level must be holding, between the Gulf cartel, Guzmán and the *Familia*.' But, he warns: 'Laredo is the main crossing point for trafficking throughout all the USA, we're right in the middle of the distribution network here, and no one wants to give it up entirely. The Gulf cartel and Zetas hold the terrain, and anyone else must pay a tax. The army is here, but that doesn't effect the traffic either: you notice that President Calderón is fighting a war against the narco traffickers, but not the narco traffic!' And he echoes Ignacio Alvarado in Juárez: 'It's a strategy to control the traffic, not to erad-icate it. Calderón's war is a political flag, a battle against the impunity of the narco traffickers. He's lowered their status in society, but it has done nothing to interfere with the economy the narco gener-ates, the transportation and delivery networks that come through here – a structure that remains intact – and the infrastructure that has been established to launder money. All that is untouched. So the drugs cross over, and then what? The supply chain is in Mexico, and the distribution and demand chain is in the US, where the infra-structures are also intact. The US wants to try and stop the drugs coming over, but like Calderón, they don't go after the money or the infrastructure. Laredo – San Antonio – Houston: it's a seamless supply chain, and a seamless financial system.' And here in *Los Dos Laredos*, the essential link in the equally seamless transportation chain, 'the smuggling is closely tied to NAFTA. We supply the US with goods, and we supply the US with drugs, through the same corridor, aboard the same trucks.' The more goods, the more drugs, the percentage is consistent. 'The US has friends, and it has inter-ests,' says Raymundo. 'In the cases of both goods and drugs, Mexico is not a friend, we are an interest. Depending on who you are in the USA, Mexico produces the goods and delivers the drugs.

'But things have changed,' he goes on. 'Before the war, and during the PRI time, the narco was granted impunity, so he thought he was the boss, but actually the politicians and the police were the bosses of the narco. Now, after the war and with PAN, the cartel in

Tamaulipas has become a parallel structure; they are not subject to the political parties, they are a parallel government. Before, the policeman and politician were the bosses of the narco. Now, the narco is the boss of the policeman and politician, and does what he wants.'

The changes have also generated a domestic market in Nuevo Laredo, though nothing like the scale of Juárez. 'Almost all the drugs here pass on through,' says Ramos. 'Before the war, you didn't find drugs here – it wasn't like Juárez or Tijuana – because this was the gateway to America, the border was wide open and there were only twenty federal police here to fight domestic dealing. The addicts even had to go over to Laredo, Texas, to buy drugs and smuggle them back! Now that's changing, there is a domestic market. But it is smaller. Again, the difference with Juárez is that here even the domestic market is hardly contested, it's controlled by one cartel. In Juárez, it is out of control and proliferates; here it is under control, and they don't want it disrupting the exports.'

Ramos was once a journalist for the local paper with a reputation for fearless reporting on the narcos, *El Mañana*. But, he says, 'I just couldn't carry on. It became too dangerous to be a reporter here. What would be the point risking it? The papers can't publish the news – it's too dangerous for them to do so.' In imploding Juárez, people banded around the words '*Línea*' and 'Guzmán' with relative ease in public, for all the raging violence. Here, barely anyone speaks and in the local press, nothing.

As any visiting reporter trying to cover Nuevo Laredo – and all Zeta or Gulf cartel territory – knows, this terrain is harder and more frightening than Juárez. Juárez has a functioning, albeit assaulted, mass media; a visiting journalist has reason to be there. In Juárez, there are press conferences, interviews and articles about the violence. The tabloid arm of the *Diario* newspaper, PM, makes a point of getting to the latest atrocity first, for a gory front-page photo. In Nuevo Laredo, the opposite prevails – the press has been bludgeoned into silence by the Zetas.

Nuevo Laredo is one of those towns in which the local paper is a local institution, as is the family which owns it: one of the most prominent and respected in the state, along the border indeed: the Cantú family, the head of which is Heriberto Ramón Cantú, with his wife Ninfa Deánder as its matriarch. The executive editor of the paper, and others the family owns, is their son Ramón Cantú, an impressive man, something of a good-living rake, charming, clever, forceful and unreliable in his appointments. But the doors of his newspaper are protected by a bullet-proof, bomb-proof screen, atop which is an understated memorial plaque commemorating an attack on the paper by the Zetas with grenades and guns in February 2006, targeting and injuring a veteran journalist investigating narco smuggling and conditions in the *maquiladoras*, Jaime Oscar Tey. Two years previously, in March 2004, the editor, Roberto Javier Mora García, was stabbed to death in his SUV, outside his apartment. The case developed a gruesome momentum of its own, after the arrest of a homosexual couple living in the apartment above Mora's, one of them a US citizen, Mario Medina. Both were convicted for the murder, and Medina himself stabbed to death in a hallway in Nuevo Laredo's state prison. He had accused the Tamaulipas police of torturing him, and gave an interview the day before his death to *El Manana*, saying he was confident of being proved innocent.[6] And it was not only in Nuevo Laredo that journalists were being attacked and killed. In January 2010, Mexico's National Human Rights Commission published a tally of fifty-six reporters killed over the previous nine years, with eight missing and seven newspaper offices attacked.[7] In most cases, the assailants were narco-trafficking cartels hitting reporters investigating drug traffic, corruption or crime, said the report. But the *susurro* in Mexican journalistic circles is that in a few cases, reporters put themselves at the disposition of one cartel, or had been threatened into doing so, and were thereby targeted by another. The Committee to Protect Journalists has assiduously traced the attacks, and in its report for 2008 came up with a lower casualty figure, and damning indictment of the Mexican authorities: 'Powerful drug cartels and escalating violence made journalists in Mexico more vulnerable to attack than ever before,' read the report. 'Most crimes against the press remained unsolved as Mexican law-enforcement agencies, awash in corruption, did not aggressively investigate attacks. With no guarantee of safety, reporters increasingly turned to self-censorship to protect themselves.'[8]

Ramón Cantú defends his ground with estimable tenacity, though takes care to do so on the US side of the border, on the public occasion of a 'War-on-Drugs' conference in El Paso. In private, he confides, 'I'm sick of the whole thing. I want to talk about something else, about the future of this place, trucks and trade.' But on the conference podium he bites the bullet: it was made clear, he says, 'that we should not use the word "Zetas". And I took the view that the lives of our staff are more important. This war is not going to be won by a newspaper or magazine. We have to be aware of our safety as well as benefit the community. We spend a lot of time looking out for our own safety so as to avoid more complicated situations . . . We're censoring the newspaper, because we have to get our children to school. If we get some anonymous tip or call, we have to decide what's correct and what's incorrect. These people' – he reminds his audience in case it urge him to brandish the sword of truth at all costs, as many do – 'they just kill you. They don't make up a slander that you're having an affair, or taking money from the Mafia. If they don't like you, they kill you. We have to be very calm. Yes, I've received complaints: "Why don't you publish this or that?" And I try to explain that I feel bad that we're not doing our job, and then: a lady calls, and we must report something. Next day, THEY call and tell me that two of my reporters have been kidnapped, and advise me to keep silent. I'd like to say I had a bit of courage, but these are innocent reporters covering social affairs – what am I going to do?'

Other journalists in Nuevo Laredo do speak what they cannot write – off the record. One editor says of the crossings into the United States: 'The Mexican government can put all the money it wants into the customs and inspections posts, it's all useless. A customs officer is as afraid of organised crime as anyone else. What are they to do when a convoy of fifteen Suburban SUVs pulls up at the forwarding yard or even at the bridge? And men get out wearing paramilitary uniform and ski masks, carrying AK-47s. If it's a forwarding yard, they're told to open the truck. If it's on the bridge, they're told just to let a truck through across the river. They're not asked, they're told. What do they do? They move to one side. They open the door. They let the truck cross, they don't ask or say anything. They just look the other way. Who wouldn't? This is a military unit; they wear hand grenades in their vests. They don't need to ask people to cooperate. This is what happens here, this is how it's done.' He hypothesises: 'How can you deal with a military formation? You can militarise customs instead of having civilian law enforcement, and have regular shoot-outs on the border bridge, but I can't see that – you'd be having battles all day. You can check every truck, but what happens to NAFTA if you check four thousand trucks a day? The line would go all the way to Chiapas!' We are talking late. There's an edition due. None of this can be broadcast locally. 'When the truck reaches the US side,' he continues, an impeccable source, 'they have their corrupt officers among the honest ones. They are approached, offered money and threatened. You play and get paid or you refuse to play and pay with your life; they're bought the old-fashioned way.'

At the end of a street running through the Colonia Victoria and down to the reeds along the riverbank and the border is a migrant shelter called the House of Nazareth, run along similar lines to the CCAMYN in Altar, catering mostly to desperate Central Americans waiting to cross, or else deported back. Over the road is a blue wall tagged with graffiti, not of gang names but those who have died. '*El Veracruz* RIP' – the implication being that this was a migrant from the state or city of that name who perished in the desert. Wrong.

A posse of lads is shallying around the wall, apparently nonchalant but watching over the stretch of land between the end of the street and the border. Presuming them to be something to do with the migrant shelter, and the priest in charge not available, I saunter over for a chat. 'No,' says a rapscallion youth in a grey zip hoodie and jeans. 'They died here in accidents, in this *colonia*.' 'That's my brother,' says another, in perfect English, pointing at a name on the wall. So you're not migrants, then? 'No, we're from here.' These boys need to be spoken to, but carefully. 'Antonio' lived in Houston awhile. 'Came back after a few years – got deported.' So these people were killed? 'Yeah.' So the Victoria *colonia* was bad during the war. And when I ask where's a place to eat, Antonio talks about a restaurant called the *Esquina*, now a shell, which 'closed during the killing and never re-opened because the owner was shot'. A slim boy is standing on the corner wearing nothing but a pair of dirty shorts, a red baseball cap on backwards and expensive new sneakers. He has said nothing so far, but suddenly a walkie-talkie in the pocket of his shorts crackles to life. He takes it out and walks away round the corner to talk. There's a feeling that I'm not supposed to be here while this communication takes place, so we shake hands and I leave, saying I'll come back to see the padre.

I return a week later, to find Antonio speaking to a friend at the Fox motorcycle service station near the memorial wall, to which we walk back together, talking about Houston and his deportation, past houses made out of wooden slats. I am alone – probably not a good idea, but being a clueless *gringo* can be a form of protection, as is the proximity of the House of Nazareth, where I feign an appointment for which I have been stood up again. I am therefore obliged to wait around. I thought it might help to be European, which apparently makes me a *gabacho* rather than a *gringo*, and wear a Barcelona shirt with 'Marquez' and a number 4 on the back, the Mexican captain's shirt. The fact that it is official merchandise is worth twenty minutes of valuable conversation, which rolls along sufficiently as to have me slouch up to the *Abarote El Brego* for some beer. We pour down a couple of cold ones as the sunlight sweetens and deepens, and I take a risk. I ask the boy wearing the hoodie if they might be able to sell me something '*de la buena*', some '*trueno verde*', green thunder. There's a frisson. Antonio looks at the boy with the walkie-talkie. My move: It's your work, no? Silence. 'Maybe, yeah,' says Antonio, 'but we don't do weed.' *Coca?* '*Chiva*', heroin, he replies immediately in Spanish, 'but not us, other people. We watch.' And in English again: 'For export only.' And he laughs. The boys address each other as '*carnal*', a form of 'bro', but apparently thicker since it implies common blood. If these are not smugglers, they are *halcónes* – falcons, lookouts. Well, I say, respects and God bless your brothers, and cross myself looking over at the names on the wall. 'It was heavy,' says Antonio. 2005? 'Yeah.' Guzmán's people? Silence.

Next day, the shelter is shut so I tell the boys I have to wait. They don't believe me, nor do they want to talk about Barcelona. Okay, I ask, but getting nervous: tell me just one thing and I'll go. Do you work for yourselves, or are you part of the pyramid? Antonio screws up his face as though he has just eaten a jalapeno too far. Then he stares back. 'Kind of connected,' he says in English, 'everyone is.' The walkie-talkie crackles in the young boy's pocket again, and I leave for the last time.

On the outskirts of another town, he balances his weight in the shade of a walnut tree, through which dappled sunshine falls. 'Oliver' is a big man, with a belly and a second one beneath it. He moves slowly, and wears a yellow T-shirt and grey track-suit trousers. One would like to be able to say that he had the keen, darting eyes of an executioner, but he hasn't. Like him, they are slow but not languid, they are considered. They do, however, have a certain extinguishment in them. He was, so his employer had said, a member of a gang affiliated to the Gulf cartel, and a *sicario* – an executioner – though Oliver doesn't like the word. He prefers *asesino*.

For all its importance and size, Nuevo Laredo lies in a far northwest corner of the state of Tamaulipas, the Zetas' home territory, but it is not their bastion – that lies further downriver. And it was in Nuevo Laredo that the war showed how little sense of brotherhood there really is within the cartels, happy to kill out of factional greed within the same organisation. Guzmán's attack on Nuevo Laredo in 2005 was an opportunist push several years after the arrest and extradition of Osiel Cárdenas, but the arrest led also to an internal struggle within the Gulf cartel, as the seizure of a *capo* often does. Cárdenas' power base was Matamoros and his soldiers were the Zetas he founded, with Nuevo Laredo far away and run by an old guard in the Gulf cartel, some of them loyal to Chava Gómez, whom Cárdenas killed to assume supremacy. They had their own deals with the local police and, crucially, with the haulage industry, and needed subjugation by the Zetas from down the valley. Oliver's gang served a network which the Zetas from Matamoros needed to bring to heel, but his faction fought its ground. (There are reports as this book goes to press that a sudden burst of violence across Tamaulipas in early 2010 is a resurgence of this internecine battle between the Zetas and the Gulf cartel's old guard.)

Oliver won't say for whom he worked, only that he was one of *Los Tejas*, which he sometimes calls *Tejanos* – Texas and Texans. It was, he says, 'a gang' ('*pandilla*', he calls it), 'on Calle Leona and Calle Vicario in the Victoria *colonia*. We carried out tasks for the organisations in this area of Tamaulipas, in Nuevo Laredo; it also has connections over the river.' Oliver had been a truck driver in the United States, and a drug addict – he is now a born-again Christian. 'I looked up the *Tejas* guys there in San Antonio while I was trucking over there,' he says. 'I was taking some heavy stuff, and suffered mental problems. I got deported.' Back in his home town of Nuevo Laredo, in need of work,

Oliver hooked up with the gang again, by now formally affiliated to the Gulf cartel. The 'truck driving', it seems, had involved distribution of drugs. 'We were in the *colonia*; we were safe in the *colonia*, but only in the *colonia*. Outside of that, you don't know who you're dealing with. You don't know who's armed and who isn't. So you work for the organisation and they work for you. First, they get you dealing. Then they get you dealing a little more. But if you're good, the real money is in killing.' How much? Silence. Oliver stares back, waiting for another question. He could just get up and go, but he doesn't, he just sits and waits. There are other people around; his boss isn't far away. It's not easy to talk – Oliver is on probation for promotion at work – back to a post he held, but lost. He wants it back a lot more than he wants to talk to me.

How did it start? 'It started with fights against the gangs from other *colonias*. They were creating problems. We got told they were shaving the product, or going over to the guys from Matamoros who were coming in [the Zetas]. I killed one guy in a parking lot, between Victoria and the *Puente* 2. I shot him.' And? (There's no point in asking those daft 'how did it feel?' questions, Oliver would probably knock my head off with a flick of his finger.) 'And he died.'

Until 1994, says Oliver, 'the organisation was straightforward. I wasn't involved in smuggling. Most of the drugs were going through the POEs, and they were taking care of that, but some of the gang would organise for distribution with people we knew on the other side in San Antonio. What they needed to make things run smooth was enforcement.' What's enforcement? 'Enforcement is getting problems off the cartel's back.' There's another silence, which Oliver finally fills of his own accord, heaving his huge frame from one side to the other and rolling his eyes. 'I killed a guy on orders – he was *drogado*.' Here the slang kicks in: in border street talk, *drogado* can mean 'in debt' as well as 'drugged'. 'He hadn't paid, he was moving stuff and he wouldn't pay back what he'd sold. He died.' Where? 'In his house.' Why? 'For the money he owed the cartel.' That is all.

The reason I am at this place, a medical institution, is not to talk to Oliver but to his employer and manager about the wonderful work he does with drug addicts – of which Oliver was one. Oliver was doing well, and about to become one of the manager's top assistants, but rescinded back to his friends in the gang, and to drugs again. Then he returned, like the prodigal son, desperate to get back to where he was, said the employer, 'But it had to be on my terms: "I'll take you back," I told him, "but you'll have to start at the beginning."' 'It's hard,' Oliver says softening, almost confiding, 'always that temptation.'

After 2003 and Osiel Cárdenas' arrest, 'there was more to do,' says Oliver, 'just more to do. Now I know it was because the people from Matamoros didn't like my people, and my people didn't want the people from Matamoros moving in. I never tortured anyone. I beat the shit out of people. But I never tortured anyone, like they do now.'

Oliver speaks in short phrases; his breaths do not accord with the beginning or the end of a sentence. As he speaks, he rolls his heavy head back, and adjusts himself and his weight on the metal seat around the tree-trunk. 'I ran a guy down with my truck,' he says, 'I made a big mess.' There is no point fishing for details. 'This'll only stop when people stop taking drugs,' says Oliver. The body language is a strange mixture of sloth and strength, like a drowsy animal that can become dangerous in the blink of an eye. 'I was never part of the people who were cartel and police,' he goes on, at last exhibiting some pride in himself. 'We were on the street, in the *colonia*. The cops didn't trust us. I was in it for the *territorialita* [defence of the turf]. That's why we were trying to stop the guys from Matamoros. I'd seen my friends die, I was doing it for the *Calle Leona* and for my brothers [*carnales*] in the gang, and because it paid.'

Oliver says he played no part in the war between the Zetas and Guzmán between 2005 and 2007; he had begun his road to recovery from drugs and endeavoured to live his new life by then. But memories are long and the danger remains, says his employer. 'He's a threat to us all. He was a *sicario*, he was one of the gang affiliated to the Nuevo Laredo faction, and the Zetas could come for him any time. Which is very dangerous for all of us.' 'I was not a *sicario*,' insists Oliver, 'I was an *asesino*. I didn't kill enough for a *sicario*, and I didn't get the money a *sicario* gets. I did other things. I was an *asesino*' — an assassin, but not an executioner.

One of the things the editors and reporters on *El Mañana* are eager to talk about is the 97 per cent of merchandise crossing the river that is legal. Not just because it changes the subject, but also because 'trade is the only viable solution to the problems', says Ramón Cantú, 'good jobs and a strong economy for the city'.

The four road bridges that make this the Gateway to the Americas are: the Colombia Bridge to the east over the Nuevo Leon state line; the World Trade Bridge towards Laredo, which carries the bulk of traffic; the Gateway to the Americas itself (also known as Bridge 1), which connects the two main streets downtown and has a pedestrian pathway, and Bridge 2, a short way east. A fifth is planned. The railway bridge or *Puente Negro* runs between the Gateway and World Trade bridges, owned by Union Pacific, which charges the other principal user, Kansas City Southern, for its use. But with Kansas emerging as the new rail hub of the United States, the muscular KCS line, which had bought into Mexico's network during privatisation, is masterminding plans for a second rail bridge, its own, connecting Lázaro Cárdenas to Laredo.

'It's been a flag of this paper as the voice of the city: Get the New Rail Bridge,' says *La Mañana*'s editorial director, Antonio Martínez Santoyo. 'It will complete the infrastructure we need to cope with future traffic. It's now more than just trade between Mexico and the US, it's China, too – some of the goods not even destined for the United States: a route has expanded over the past five years bringing goods from China, through Lázaro Cárdenas, up through Laredo and out through Galveston or New Orleans to Europe, by sea and train. It's quicker than coming through the Middle East, and the new 'Post-Panamax' generation of ships are too big to get through the Panama Canal and sail the Atlantic. So it all has to dock in Mexico and proceed by rail. For now, trucking is the bedrock of this town, and Laredo over the river. Every one of those truckers and workers in the yards has a relative who works in freight over the other side. However, there'll come a time when the fuel situation will change, making sea and rail the future, and we can be part of that. The whole thing is a lesson of history. For centuries, Valparaiso in Chile was the stepping-stone between Asia and Europe, then the Panama Canal, and now it can be *Los Dos Laredos*.' It can. But for the problem: Nuevo Laredo is a place in which almost every business is shaken down by extortion rackets run not by the local *cholos*, as in Juárez, but by the Zetas and their '*pirámide*'. Bigger business needs protection by a bigger stick, but the Zetas' attention to detail is thorough.

In the maze of alleyways behind the border parking lot downtown, a group of ladies engage busily in one of the most established businesses throughout the borderland, *ropa usada*, used stuff – or clothing. They are called *chiveras*, and they work in every city on the Mexican side, going over to the US to pick up second-hand clothes to bring back for sale – which is, unbelievably, against a Mexican law forbidding the import of used clothes for retail.[9] Nevertheless, in every Mexican border town, garden fences and roadside railings are lined with jeans, shirts, blouses, baby wear, skirts and frocks for sale.

In Laredo, on the US side, in a low grey building with a brick-red sloping roof, a team of women and girls overseen by an Anglo manager sort mountains of *ropa usada*. The warehouse is one of many along Santa Isabel Avenue beside the Union Pacific railway sidings and inspection yards. It is hot, hard work, which the women undertake with genially high spirits: piles and piles of clothing, tied together in bundles, are sorted according to type, thrown into canvas containers marked with labels like '*Mujeres* Leisure', 'Western' or 'Teen'. There is even an Amexican word for this process, a verb: '*clasear*'.[10] The ladies are helped out by their daughters after school's out. Rick, the supervisor, is wary of any conversation that gets too detailed, but the money is fair, and the labour done with gusto. Then the problems begin.

Over the bridge in Nuevo Laredo, a woman cooks chicken and corn for her daughter and friends in a little house near the bridge car park. All these ladies know and visit the warehouses and sorting depots along Santa Isabel Avenue from which they collect *ropa usada*, and bring it over the Gateway to the Americas bridge, in big zip-top bags. Some of the women then sell their loads to people who retail it from their fences to boost the punishing family budget. Others sell directly themselves, but none escape the tap on the shoulder. Unbelievably, the Gulf cartel – an international criminal syndicate dealing drugs into the USA and to Europe worth billions of dollars – has the *ropa usada* ladies firmly in its sights. Of the women in the whitewashed room, none pays less than one peso in ten as a tariff on the sale value of what she brings across the bridge from Laredo, most pay two pesos and one pays three, probably because she sells direct. This is not a street-corner crew of teenaged thugs, this is *El Pirámide*, the Zetas, though of course not even the boldest-speaking of these women, wearing her headscarf would consider using the word. 'The customs is right there in the parking lot,' she says with a dry laugh. 'And if they're not on duty, they come to the place where we distribute. That's how it is. What's the point of arguing? I need the work to get the money that's left to eat and send my daughter to school.'

But this is just the small fry. Raymundo Ramos and I are driving through the horizons of forwarding yards and containers, when the strangest thing happens: a sudden storm of little moths fill the air as far as the eye can see flying into the windscreen like hailstones. They almost eclipse the pale, hazy sun, and make the panorama of haulage and rungs of yellow cabins behind the chicken wire, dust and dirt even more surreal. Still, we keep passing the yards, at a slower pace: ALA, Cargo Consolidada, Trasportes Mineras de Coahuila, Fletes México, FEMA, Aeromexexpres. Ramos chooses his words carefully, alternating on and off the record with meticulous attention to what he is saying. We have been talking about 'the cartel' levying *cuotas* or *mordidas* (bribes) from local businesses. Do these freight companies pay the *cuota* – extortion money – as well? 'Everyone,' replies Raymundo. To who, the police or the cartel? 'The cartel.' Is that on or off the record? 'On the record.' Are you sure? 'Yes.' Is that normal? 'It's totally normal. It's the system. Those who get killed in Nuevo Laredo now,' he says, 'are not part of any turf war; they're usually businessmen who have problems with the cartel. But none of this has had any impact on the drug traffic or the *cuota* that everyone must pay.'

On another occasion, the line of shuttle trucks waiting to cross the busiest bridge in the world, *Puente Comercio Mundial*, No. 3, a couple of weeks later stretches back for miles, the truckers expecting at least a five-hour wait today and alighting for coffee and breakfast tacos at the roadside buffets. A group snacking at a little roadside stall called *Takos Kora* have just been hauling plasma TV sets and domestic white goods from Korea and China. They complain that enhanced security makes two runs a day more strenuous to complete if not impossible. They object to the amount of tracking devices and checking the shuttle companies are now obliged to carry out to make sure the load goes straight from the forwarding yards to the bridge, not via some other place where the load may be tampered with and a little extra put on board. 'If there are drugs in the container,' says a driver called Luis, 'they'll have been there all the way, and you'll know nothing.' And anyway, says another man, these new seals they put on the containers are all very well; 'but the bad guys know how to break the seal, do what they want and put everything back looking like nothing had happened'. The conversation, already a bit awkward, winds down. Then a driver wearing a brown bomber jacket and smoking silently until now says: 'Sometimes, the bad guys just come into the yard in a *troca*, and just say: "open the container." There's nothing you can do but turn away, wait, get in the cabin and drive.'

Thirteen miles north of the border, Bill Sanderson shoots a dart of spittle through his front teeth onto the tarmac and points his cowboy boots towards the entrance to the Pilot Travel Center. A Teamster of twenty-three years, Sanderson was born in southern Missouri, raised in Little Rock, Arkansas, 'but now I live in Carlisle, Pennsylvania, 'cause it's the crossroads of trucking and it makes life easier. I get to see more of my wife and kids that way, if I'm living right on the depot.' Crossroads it certainly is; Carlisle should be twinned with Laredo: I remember interviewing Jimmy Hoffa Jr. there once in a diner at 3.30 a.m., president of the International Brotherhood of Teamsters made famous by his father, who is believed to be entombed within the concrete of a bridge over the New Jersey Turnpike. 'I love it,' says Sanderson without hesitation, 'doing this job. Right amount of freedom, right amount of home. I can say I know every mile between here and Dallas, Dallas and Little Rock where my parents are, Little Rock and Nashville and Louisville, and between Louisville and Pennsylvania pretty much every inch. I know just where to stop when the hours are up and the clock's gonna catch me out. But it's always different: different weather, different time of day. And there's always an adventure, up to Montana, always some place you don't know yet.' Sanderson wears a great T-shirt: 'Born Free. Taxed to Death.'

This is Port Laredo, the truckers' lair, US equivalent of *Veintiseis*, 13 miles north of Laredo up Interstate 35, the spinal freeway that connects the freight yards with San Antonio, Houston, Dallas and all stations north. And it could not be more different. You can choose

between McDonald's and Subway to eat right here, or any number
of other chain favourites within a couple of miles down the 1-35
business loop. If you don't care to eat in, your meal can be ordered
and your number called by loudspeaker into the forwarding yards.
You can buy special phone cards called 'Truckerbucks'. You can buy
a T-shirt reading: 'Christ is the ROCK ON which I stand'. A voice
comes over the Tannoy: 'Shower customer number 114, your shower
is ready. Please proceed to shower ten.' There are slot machines and
a bewildering range of scratch cards. 'Pumpkin Spice Capuccino
is Back,' says a sign, as though it ever went away. Sanderson acknow-
ledges a man wearing a fluorescent orange jacket and combat fatigues;
he is travelling with his wife and child, in defiance of the lonesome
trucking stereotype, but Sanderson leaves him to his itinerant family
Sunday lunch. 'There's places I'd rather be than Laredo,' says Bill,
who is down collecting a mixed load for Yellow Freight. 'But it's an
interesting enough town, on the edge, kind of thing, seen a few
problems but that don't affect me. People is kind, that's for sure,
though I can't say I like the food. Some of the boys like it, and used
to visit over in Mexico, too. But you never caught me going across
there, oh no, not even when it was quiet. I'm a family man, got
responsibilities; far as I'm concerned, you kiss goodbye to all your
rights as a human being soon as you cross that border.'

In the old days, says a driver called Mitch from Springfield, Illinois,
a taxi would take you in a group of four for $25 each, over the
border to what is called the *Zona de Tolerancia* in Nuevo Laredo –
'he'd wait for everyone to finish their business and bring you back.
Only twenty-five bucks, and you didn't spend much more'n two
times that over there,' says Mitch. But, happily for the Mexicans,
that caper has ended since war started – one of its few welcome
beneficial side effects. Maybe it is coincidence, but since I was last
here, a new building has risen over the road from the Pilot Travel
Center: the multi-storey 'City Limits Adult XXX' complex. This is
an air-conditioned hypermarket for sex aids, S&M appliances, blue
DVDs, the lot – open twenty-four hours, with dark reflective glass
and an ATM machine. On a sweaty Saturday afternoon it is fairly
well patronised: on a Saturday night, it's teeming. 'They hang out
in the motels around the Howard Johnson's down there,' Mitch had
said. 'You'll see a bunch of guys parked up at the 610 truck stop on

Santa Maria next to the movie theatre and that's them. The pussy's all Mexican.'

The Dos Laredos freight system works like this: once past the *Veintiseis*, Mexican long-haul truckers take their loads towards the border and fan out along the two great *Anillos Periféricos* ring roads that circumvent the south of the city. From these yards operates the system of 'drayage' – the Mexicans have adapted the word to '*Drayaje*'. Shuttle companies – some locally and independently owned, others belonging to the big long-haulers – operate smaller, usually older, cabins to which the containers are affixed and which take the merchandise over the river, via a long wait, as becomes clear, skirting the edges of a city to which 10,000 men have come to live as shuttle truckers in the freight yards that extend the length of the Airport Boulevard, Pan American Boulevard and the giant ring roads mile after mile of stack upon stack of containers waiting to go; row after row of little cabins returned having just handed over their load north of the border or else waiting to go. And row upon row of bigger, newer cabins also parked, ready to head back through *Veintiseis* to the south or Lázaro Cárdenas, pick up another container, bring it back and do it all again. At any time, there are 30,000 containers in Nuevo Laredo awaiting transportation, and easily tampered with, loaded with freight that does not appear on the ledgers. Once through customs and on the US side, the drayage drivers take the load over the flyovers and overpasses connected to the international bridges and deposit them at any one of the miles and miles of forwarding yards on the US side, flanking Mines Road, officially known as FM1472, to the west, and Port Laredo to the east of the freeway. Even the street names on which the yards are located have ambitious names like Inter American Boulevard, Pan American Boulevard and Trade Center Boulevard. Many of these yards are US-owned with names like Swift Transportation, but an increasing number are Mexican, like *Despachos del Norte*.

Aldo Fernández has the rare distinction of being a trucker who actually lives in Laredo, among these yards where Pan American Boulevard meets Mines Road. 'Right in the middle of them,' he says. 'You'd never know there was residential housing in here.' He does so not only because he comes from Nuevo Laredo, so that this is home, but for reasons similar to Bill Sanderson's: 'If you live near the depot, you get more time at home.' Employed by Tri-National, or just 'Tri-Nat' as the drivers call it, of St Louis, Missouri, Aldo is a committed Volvo man. 'This is 2009,' he beams, 'best truck I ever drove.' His usual route is to Oklahoma City, but last night he came back from Detroit, and tomorrow, he's going to Canada, 'where they open the border at eight a.m., so you have more waiting around than here, but less paperwork. I see the whole of America, but I know how it works here.' There is 'total camaraderie between truckers', Aldo says. 'I'm Hispanic and I speak Spanish on the CB, someone else may be black, someone else may be white, but if you're a trucker, you're just a trucker. When you get into trouble, the nearest guy helps you out.' However, there is 'no camaraderie between the long-distance *gringos* and the drayage drivers who bring their loads over from Mexico. The Americans never speak to them when they switch the loads cause they're just in little four-wheelers. It's more like "hey, motherfucker, out the way!" when they're backing up.' But they need to be careful, watch their language. 'If you come to Laredo and talk shit about Mexicans on the CB, that's not a good idea,' says Aldo. 'There was some guy a couple of years back talking all that wetback stuff and hairy Mexican women. He was doing it on the CB radio and parked up. Only his truck didn't move from the truck stop, and six days later they had a look inside and found him stabbed to death in the cabin.'

In Laredo, too, there is no avoiding frequent offers to transport smuggled drugs from cartel contacts in the forwarding yards. 'You get offered money according to how far you'd go,' says Aldo. 'So much to take a load to San Antonio, more to New York. It's a dumb game to get into — a couple of my friends are in jail for that. They get the offer, think it's easy cash, get caught.' Are the drugs loaded up in the Mexican forwarding yards, or do they come all the way? 'Usually they've come all the way,' replies Aldo, preferring to change the subject, since this is a social dinner with a friend from Nuevo Laredo over for the evening. He takes us down by the river to show us a trick the drayage drivers play. Beneath the Gateway to the Americas bridge connecting downtown Laredo with its Mexican neighbour, they have parked their cabins overnight. 'They walk back across the bridge, get drunk, sleep in Mexico and walk back across to start from this side and avoid the morning rush-hour line on the bridge.'

* * *

The Czech composer Antonín Dvořák wrote his greatest string quartet
– No. 12 in F major, op. 96, 'The American' – in a little town called
Spillville, Iowa. He had gone there by way of a retreat from New
York, where he was not always happy, knowing that he would find
there a community of fellow Czechs. It was a blissful summer: Dvořák
would take a bucket of ale down to the banks of the Turkey River
at five each morning and compose, so that moments in the quartet's
molto vivace third movement replicate in music the exact notes of
the birdsong to which he listened. No piece of music ever written
evokes the lightness and lyrical serenity of America's open spaces
more than the quartet's mellifluent *lento* second movement. The
arrival in Laredo of the internationally acclaimed Bellas Artes Quartet
of Mexico City to perform Dvořák's masterpiece one evening in
October 2009 was hailed in a series of speeches as a cultural high
watermark in the city's long history. 'A wish come true,' said the host,
the provost, in the hall of Texas A&M university campus. The freight
business elite of the Gateway to the Americas made sure to be there
for the occasion, resplendently dressed. Many spoke Spanish, and
continued to do so through the music, although the woman next to
me who asked out loud, as we approached an especially lovely moment
in the Allegro: 'Why is everyone being so QUIET?' did so in broad
Texan. Sitting in the front row was Laredo's first citizen, who looks
like an FBI agent with his quarterback frame, spivvy suit and shaven
head; probably because he was an FBI agent. Raul Salinas's position
keeps him so busy that he is obliged to look into his computer screen
and tap away throughout most of our interview, but this is a man
who can chew gum and walk at the same time, for he makes a salient
point about 'the high wire we're on, between needing to keep goods
coming through, and stopping that illegal percentage. We've had
problems on the border, sure. We have crime statistics that tag us.'
When Salinas qualifies this by insisting that 'bad news sells, and
that's been our problem' and that 'the drug and violence situation
has been exaggerated', he sounds like a bad salesman. But when he
insists that 'I won't accept a compromise in the fact that we and our
Mexican neighbours need to support each other as cities and keep
the bridges open', then he sounds like a mayor. 'We can't slap our
neighbour then ask for his help – that's a mistake we constantly make
with Mexico. We're the number-one inland port in America, and we

don't need a damned wall between us and the number-one inland
port in Mexico.' He says that 'it's more difficult being mayor than
an FBI agent. As an agent, you investigate crimes and send people
to jail. As the mayor, you gotta run Laredo.'

In Mayor Salinas's city hall, an estimable diplomatic system operates: an office is occupied by a consul from Nuevo Laredo, a Mexican
ambassador from the twin city, Gerardo Lozarno. Born in Laredo,
Texas, raised in Nuevo Laredo and educated in San Antonio, he would
appear perfect for the job. He also talks straight, less convinced about
what Mayor Salinas called the 'exaggeration' of drug trafficking.
Lozarno puts it the other way round: 'Amazingly, the narco war hasn't
affected trade. More traffic is arriving in Nuevo Laredo than we have
the infrastructure to deal with, and that's our great challenge – to
build and provide it. But it hasn't affected drug smuggling either.
Let's say that only three per cent of the merchandise is illegal, that's
probably about it, despite all the technical devices. But three per cent
is three per cent of whatever's coming through. Imagine: if eight
thousand trucks a day cross the border, and three per cent of what
they bring is contraband, that's a hell of a lot of contraband.' But
Lozarno's crusade now is to ensure for Nuevo Laredo the fourth road
bridge, the implications of which are being weighed by Miguel
Conchas, director of Laredo's all-important Chamber of Commerce.

Conchas keeps the figures, and they are staggering. Truck crossings: 0.6 million in 1990, 3.2 million in 2008. Rail car crossings: 90,000
in 1990, 335,000 in 2008. Percentage share of all US-Mexico Trade:
in 2007, Laredo, 39.8 per cent, all other ports, 60.2 per cent. In 2008:
Laredo, 40.9 per cent, all other ports, 59.1 per cent. US-Mexico total
trade: Exports in 2007, $136.5 billion-worth; in 2008, $151.5 billion-
worth. Imports in 2007, $210.8 billion-worth, in 2008, $215.9 billion-
worth. Total trade: in 2007 $347.3 billion-worth, in 2008, $367.4
billion-worth. Conchas ponders: 'The problem is always one of logis-
tics – how to ship it all, and to ship it fast enough. That will be
Laredo's task as long as the Mexican long-haulers are prohibited from
coming over. The recession has affected us slightly, but the amount
of cargo will grow now that Kansas City Southern have bought the
railway line from Lázaro Cárdenas to Nuevo Laredo and we're getting
the new bridge; that'll mean a big increase. It's part of talk we're
hearing about a super-corridor – bringing less in through the US ports

like Long Beach and New Orleans, deepening the Mexican pacific ports and bringing it all straight up through here to Dallas and Chicago, cheaper and faster. We're on the brink of that.' This 'Super-corridor' is much discussed, with its potentially cataclysmic impact on the US docklands and other jobs in the service industries that support them. 'But just as all this is happening,' says Conchas, 'business is confronted by the major problem of the drug trade. Legitimate business knows that you can't always guarantee what your drivers are bringing across.'

If the Rio Grande, which unites and divides Amexica, has a living human son, his name is Keith Bowden. Bowden navigated the watery borderline by kayak, from El Paso to the sea, as war raged through Zeta country in 2005. He was trying to experience the beauty and power of the river in the wake of the loss of his young wife to slow and painful cancer. Bowden kept and published a record of his voyage, which he called *The Tecate Journals*. There is an intensity, an existential solitude, about Bowden which draws one in rather than orders one away. He is strikingly good-looking, and physically trim – a sports coach as well as a teacher of English at Laredo Community College. On the wall of his windowless office is a photograph Bowden took of a moment in the river's flow as it rounds a colossus of red rock along the Big Bend, on which one inevitably comments. He takes it down and says, 'Have it.' Although Bowden is more afraid of rapids than of Nuevo Laredo, he speaks as someone who knows the narco footsoldiers well, as a baseball coach in Ciudad Acuña and in Nuevo Laredo, where he could hardly avoid the young men's other interests and activities. 'In one year,' he remembers, 'I lost fourteen ex-students or players. Kids I'd coached or taught.'

Among the young baseball players he coached was a boy named Ricardo who 'made a swift descent into the Nuevo Laredo drug-trade underworld, and his transformation from innocent adolescent to cold-blooded killer was total'. Ricardo's uncle was a standing member of the FBI's Ten Most Wanted list, and Ricardo bragged to coach Keith Bowden one day that he used the baseball team as cover to smuggle 'a hell of a lot of loads. The last time I saw him', writes Bowden, was 'a chance encounter at the same Nuevo Laredo baseball fields where we were once team-mates – he boasted that he was killing fifteen people a month "as part of business". I assailed his barbarism as "chicken shit" and demanded he explain the logic . . . "People with babies and mothers and little sisters. That's what you do. You kill people and you brag about it. I can't accept that." Ricardo buried his head in his hands and wept like a child.' Bowden never saw Ricardo again. 'A rumour surfaced that he had been hacked into five hundred pieces.' The body of another student, Alicia, was found dead beneath a construction site, to which police were led by yet another boy who studied with Bowden. He likewise vanished; 'his specific instruction leading to the discovery of her corpse were the last words he ever uttered'.[11]

Between this world and his, the river, says Bowden, 'there's a kind of oblivion, even hostility, towards the natural elements. Nature's a hard sell to people on both sides of the river. By the time people are five years old, they dislike it, distrust it, they're afraid of it — they're told it's filthy and polluted, it's something migrants cross, it's where bodies wash up . . . Only when you're out on the river for days do you get a sense of it, both as nature and as the border.' So one gets a strange view of a war from a kayak. 'When I came through here, it was during the crazy time,' he says of his river passage between *Los Dos Laredos*, 'the middle of the war, wondering whether I'd see bodies floating on the river. But what really worried me were things like currents, things I had to have a sense of and could do something about. My fear did not come from people, it tends not to when you're trying to kayak through Big Bend or facing down a charging mountain lion. The person who could do me the most damage was myself, by making one tiny mistake.'

In days not long ago when the *Houston Chronicle* was one of the great newspapers in the world, it carried weighty, definitive supplements on a burning issue of the day in western America, one of which, in October 1993, was about the Rio Grande. The supplement followed the river from its source to the sea at Brownsville: 'A Clean Start in Colorado, A Filthy Finish in the Gulf', ran the opening headline. But there was beauty and poetry too, as the Rio Grande, 'like any river, it keeps trying to shed itself of the filth dumped into it. Given enough time, enough water, enough air, any river can remedy many pollution problems'.[12] But if one talks now about a river full of metal as the Rio Grande flows into its final, tropical stretch of borderland, people will not think you are talking about pollution. A river of iron, in these parts, means something else.

CHAPTER NINE

Iron River / Tell Them Who You Are

Metalwork and metalware strewn across every table, stretching all the way to the back of the hall — weaponry of matt, gunmetal grey. The guns are expertly made, all of them — although it is much easier to feel affection and admiration for the venerable collector's items with worn wooden butts, or the latest hunter's shotguns, than it is the wholly inorganic steely weapons that only make sense in combat. Quite apart from what an AR-15 is designed to do so effectively, its steely, glaucous grey emanates a sombre foreboding all of its own. Apart from the fact that a Czech vz.58 Military Folder Polymer is said to be among the best-value variations of a Kalashnikov, its leaden slatiness commands menace in itself. Apart from the full-time rimfire boasted by the new Colt M4, its griseous coldness is itself intimidating, just to look at — even before it is picked up, sized up, deftly handled and wiped down by a hefty-framed man demonstrating his sure touch of familiarity with the heavy weapon's ways and whimsies. But one must not apply European squeamishness to a gun show in Texas. It is a citizen's right to bear arms in America, and the Sunday-afternoon crowd here in the Convention Center at Pharr, on Highway 281, is for the most part made up of families and couples come to browse; farmers protecting their livestock and duck hunters come to stock up on ammo; collectors hunting for bargains, and kids who just want to shoot rabbits, blast away in a quarry or punch holes in the back of road signs or BP hoardings, as happens since one Gulf oil disaster. That's America, whether you like it or not. Matter of fact, this gun show at Pharr in October 2009 is far less brazenly militaristic than another three times the size held a few weeks back at the Pima County fairgrounds outside Tucson, Arizona. There, the Blackwater Company – some of whose guards were acquitted late in December 2009 of murder in Iraq, where they opened fire on a crowd – had a stall abundantly stocked with tactical combat gear, night-vision equipment, body armour and other stuff you need for all-out warfare rather than duck-hunting. There, it wasn't just a matter of the AR-15 semi-automatics being lined up for sale as here in Pharr. There was a banner hanging from the ceiling beckoning buyers to a wide range of the deadliest weapons available on the open market, at reduced prices.

But there are nevertheless a couple of twists to holding a gun show in Pharr during October 2009. The hall is about six miles from the Mexican border and eight miles from Reynosa, Mexico, fortress city for the Zetas and scene of ferocious fighting a few months later, in spring 2010. Back on New Year's Eve 2008, three off-duty police officers were enjoying a celebration drink at the El Booty Lounge in Pharr when a man lobbed a grenade into the bar. The explosive was traced to Monterrey an hour across the border.[1] In March 2009, seven months before this gun show, the first coup in President Obama's then week-old offensive against gun-running, Operation Gun-Runner, was a haul of semi-automatic barrels, firearms accessories and gunpowder crossing from Pharr into Reynosa aboard a tractor-trailer. A seller at the Pharr gun show called Billy – a courteous and friendly man with a pony tail – is extolling the virtues of the body armour he has for sale, the intensity of the fusillades it can withstand, the specific kinds and calibre of ammunition. He has an especially rare weapon on his stand: a Heckler and Koch M3 Super 90, but made under licence by Berelli in Italy. 'There's not so many of them out there,' assures Billy, 'I got it off a guy was ex-military. Just shows how badly the armed forces need these weapons – must've been Heckler and Koch were running to max capacity, so they got 'em made under licence by Berelli.' Billy talks me through the advantages: he likes this thing called an 'annular knurled ring', which would enable me to 'switch to the semi-automatic recoil system' thereby moving from a manually operated pump-action mode 'to being able to fire full-power combat loads in rapid semi-automatic mode'.

There's an 'underbarrel magazine', which can hold 'eight rounds for police or military versions. That's a rare piece' – a snip at $1,300.

Another man takes me through the benefits of an AR-15: 'the ultimate urban rifle', adaptable to thirty-round Magpul magazines, as
used by 'our troops in the Middle East'. A new model he has on the
table has a forearm design enabling the shooter to 'fit rails at all
twelve-clock positions', he says. I tell him I'm not a US citizen, so
there's a problem. He gives me his card and says to call so we can
'work something out'. Just as one must not be Euro-sanctimonious
about guns in Texas, one must not engage in racial profiling. But
what do those Mexican lads over there with shaven heads and tattoos
on their scalps want with an SHF R50 magazine-fed bolt action .50
BMG rifle with a 22-inch barrel? How many farmers and antelope
hunters really need, from the same stall, an ASA M4A3 Top 16
.223 calibre carbine machine gun, a *Santa Muerte* wallet and an
ammunition pouch adorned with '*Arriba Tamaulipas*' – Go
Tamaulipas – a favourite Zeta slogan on YouTube?

At the back of the hall, up a small flight of steps, is a bookstall.
In amongst the many perfectly innocent catalogues and trade volumes
are US army manuals on counter-insurgency warfare, with tips on
bomb-making, how to blow up bridges and other useful things to
know while hunting deer. For $25, there's a *Militia Battle Manual*,
with a second chapter on 'Combat Operations'. 'An ambush is an
active form of a defensive position,' it counsels. There are sections
on 'Bounding Overwatch', 'Immediate Assault' and 'Urban Assault':
'when entering an enemy building, always throw a fragmentation
grenade first'. In the section on 'Acquisition of Military Equipment',
the manual says: 'In this section we are talking about the theft of
military equipment from military bases. Sounds hard? Well, it isn't.'
There is, of course, a section on explosives and how to blow up buildings, and diagrams like that showing 'Electrical blasting cap attached
to car battery'.[2] It is hard not to flashback a moment, to the night
of 19 April 1995, the year *before* this manual was published, when
I landed in Oklahoma City. The killers of 169 people, including
nineteen children, in the Alfred P. Murrah federal building in
Oklahoma came from this constituency of militia manuals and they
were not lone wolves, they were part of a fomenting culture –
Americans killing Americans in the name of America. Now, here's
a variation on that theme: Americans selling guns that arm the
cartels that kill each other so as to peddle the drugs that kill

Americans. The cartels' guns of choice are the AR-15 and AK-47. The automatic versions, of course, the sale of which is illegal in the United States. But what are these manuals, selling for fifteen dollars a copy, six miles from the Mexican border in Pharr, expertly written and cheap at the price? With a white cover is volume one of the *Full Auto* manual series, telling you how to 'modify' your AR-15. 'The purpose of this small book is to clarify and explain the procedure and parts needed to convert a semi-automatic AR-15 assault rifle to be a selectable, fully automatic weapon.' In figure 11, it reads, 'an auto sear is being inserted into the pocket of the lower receiver where the take-down pin engages the lug of the upper receiver. Figure 12 shows the auto sear fully installed.'[3] Also for fifteen dollars, with a blue cover, is the conversion manual for the all-time favourite *cuerno de chivo*, the AK-47. Step six is 'Reassembly' of your fully automatic Kalashnikov: 'You are now ready to check the timing of the bolt with the movement to auto sear, which should release the hammer.'[4] But there are waivers. In the AR-15 manual, the publisher affirms that he 'produces this book for informational and entertainment purposes and under no circumstances advises, encourages or approves of use of this material in any manner'. The AK-47 booklet advises that 'all conversions must be done by a licensed Class II manufacturer'. Zetas: Do Not Try This At Home.

Since the election of Barack Obama, discussion of the flow of weapons from the United States to the cartels has found a place on the US political agenda, become a recurrent theme for the Mexican government and almost de rigueur in media coverage of the border crisis. But all this is recent, part of President Obama and his Secretary of State Hillary Clinton's final acceptance of some 'co-responsibility' for that crisis – as Mrs Clinton put it on her visit to Mexico City soon after taking office in 2009. Until very recently, however, such a suggestion was almost taboo. Certainly, gun-running to Mexico and 'co-responsibility' for the drug war had played no part in Mrs Clinton's husband's agenda when he was President between 1992 and 2000. President Obama is pressing the Senate to ratify the Inter-American Arms Treaty, which was to be fair, signed by President Clinton in 1988 but stalled on Capitol Hill, and which seeks to crack down on illicit firearms with a regulation of the import and export of weaponry across the hemisphere, and to increase cooperation

between law-enforcement agencies. To gun lobby hardliners, even
the discussion is seen as yet another attempt at creeping gun control;
while others who support the Second Amendment's guarantee of
the right to bear arms nonetheless recognise that gun-running to
Mexico is a separate discourse. President Obama has made no effort
though to reinstate the domestic ban on semi-automatic weapons
imposed by Bill Clinton in 1994, but which expired in 2004, just
as the war began in Nuevo Laredo. As recently as 2008, Raymundo
Ramos was a near lone voice making the point that while 5,000
truckloads a day were crossing from Nuevo Laredo to Laredo,
5,000 also came back, and that this counterflux current of goods
exported from the USA into Mexico involved smuggling in the
other, southerly, direction: not of drugs, but guns. The few US
law-enforcement agencies taking the threat seriously call that
counterflux 'the Iron River'.

'It's obvious,' Ramos said on that occasion, 'that without the drugs,
there would be no war. We all know that. But without the guns, there
would be nothing to fight the war with.' It is indeed obvious, but
apart from the US Bureau of Alcohol, Tobacco, Firearms and Explosives
(ATF) and a report by Lora Lumpe, well ahead of its time, in *Covert
Action Quarterly* in 1997, few people north of the border realised
it as an issue. Lumpe's work demonstrated that the Arellano Félix
brothers' weapon that killed Cardinal Posada Ocampo in Guadalajara
had been smuggled from the USA.[5] Not too many in Mexico made
much noise either, though the Iron River did gain some diplomatic
traction after the appointment of a forthright ambassador to
Washington, Arturo Sárukhan, in 2006. But Ramos was able to say
as late as 2008: 'I've been campaigning for five years now for tougher
action against smuggling guns. I raise the matter every time I meet
with the authorities on either side of the border. The Americans
don't see it as a major problem; and the Mexicans? Every time they
find an arsenal, they act all surprised! For the Americans, it's a
billion-dollar business, and the Mexicans do not have the political
will to get serious with gun-running.'

It is of no disadvantage to the narco cartels that the four states
bordering Mexico – Texas, New Mexico, Arizona and California –
cherish the lore of firearms as part of their heritage and identity.
It is of no disadvantage that they are among the states in which it

is easiest to buy weapons. Speaking to a conference in El Paso in August 2008, Michael Sullivan, then acting director of the ATF, said the US and Mexican governments were cooperating in an effort to trace weapons seized in Mexico's narco war, finding – to no one's great surprise – that between 90 and 95 per cent of them originate in the United States – 'mostly from the four south-western states. Two-thirds of them were traced back to Texas.' That year, 90 per cent of 20,455 weapons seized by Mexican authorities for which traces were requested showed a purchase in the US, with Texas, Arizona and California accounting for most of them. The irony and tragedy was that they had also already been used. The gun smugglers were described by the prosecutor in one case involving a gun dealer in Arizona shipping hundreds of Kalashnikovs as operating 'like a parade of ants'.

Ironically, too, the ideological right which stands so firm on people – and, of course, drugs – crossing the border northwards also opposes restrictions over marketing the hardware the narcos need to shift southwards, and the frequency with which they can buy weapons. Although the Justice Department brands the narco cartels as a 'security threat' to the United States, there are more than 6,700 arms dealers within half a day's drive of the border – three dealers per mile of frontier. One of them called X-Caliber, a distance away in Phoenix, was shut down in spring 2008 for allegedly dispatching hundreds of AK-47s and other weaponry to Mexico. The dealer, George Iknadosian, won a reprieve, however, when in March 2009, a judge threw out the case against him, finding no evidence of fraud or illicit dealing, even though some of the 700 weapons he was accused of selling to smugglers were identified in a shoot-out in Sinaloa in 2007 in which eight police officers were killed. The state of Arizona was appealing the decision at the time of writing.

Known as 'Straw Buyers', agents for the narco cartels and gangs cruise gun stores and fairs to buy the weapons. Court records from innumerable trials tell the story of the iceberg of which they are but a minuscule tip: Adan Rodríguez, aged thirty-five, was struggling as a carpet-layer in Dallas when he was tapped by two men called 'Kati' and 'César' from the Gulf cartel. They came up with the idea, with $12,000 cash up front, that if he went around telling gun dealers he was a private security employee and showing them his ID, he might need the 112 assault rifles, Beretta handguns and other weaponry he managed to procure for them. All he had to do was take the hardware to a safe house in Dallas and pick up a commission of between $30 to $40 per gun, in cash, with marijuana stored between the bills. At the time of his arrest, Rodríguez's contacts were hoping to upscale their order to include hand grenades and rocket-launchers. 'The temptation got over me,' Rodríguez told the judge in Dallas who sentenced him to five years in jail in 2006. The ATF's special agent in charge in Arizona, Tom Mangan, had said candidly: 'Gun shows have become particularly troublesome. You see the Sinaloan cowboys come in, you see them with their ammunition belts, and their ammunition boots. You can see the dollies being rolled outside to their cars. Why do they need high-powered guns? Because the Mexican military is armed too, and they need to pierce that armour.'[6]

In June 2009, the US Government Accountability Office published a report that left no rational room for doubt: 'Many of the firearms fuelling Mexican drug violence originated in the United States, including a growing number of increasingly lethal weapons.' The agencies responsible for combating gun-running 'do not effectively coordinate their efforts', said the GAO, 'in part because the agencies lack clear roles and responsibilities'. Moreover, 'agencies generally have not systematically gathered, analysed and reported data that could be useful to help plan and assess results of their efforts to address arms trafficking to Mexico'. The GAO notes that for the very first time, the National Southwest Border Counternarcotics Strategy only recently includes a chapter on combating arms trafficking and that 'while US law-enforcement agencies have developed initiatives to address arms trafficking to Mexico, none have been guided by a comprehensive, governmentwide strategy'. While the violence in Mexico 'has raised concern, there has not been a coordinated US government effort to combat the illicit arms trafficking to Mexico that US and Mexican government officials agree is fuelling much of the drug-related violence'.[7]

From Laredo eastwards, deep into Zeta country, the border becomes tropical and urban, palm trees and concrete. The road on the Texas side of the river winds its way through the town of Zapata, where, appropriately, the local auto repair shop is called 'Guevara's Garage' but where many humble Mexican-American residents suddenly found themselves to be rich, after oil was found on their patches of land. The next town is Roma, where – the Vatican will be pleased to hear – the Church of the Holy Family is full to bursting on a Sunday morning, only next door there is a raid by five flashing police cars on a branch of Mr Pollo's fast-food chicken. Next comes Rio Grande City, where the popular, moustachioed Starr County sherriff, Reymundo Guerra, was taken out of his office in handcuffs and pleaded guilty in May 2009 for using his position as a law-enforcement officer to help the Gulf cartel. Guerra was friendly with an operative for the Zetas called José Carlos Hinojosa, and took money in exchange for giving Hinojosa tips on the movements and tactics of his colleagues, information on upcoming raids on stash houses and closing a case against one of Hinojosa's associates.[8]

On the Mexican side, the same Highway 2 that left Tijuana for Tecate way back west now finds a way through tropical flatland beneath a huge sky, and a daunting town called Miguel Alemán, where every pair of eyes seems to follow a stranger. Now the borderland reaches its most easterly and most southerly terrain, the tapered southern-most tip of the United States, from which Mexico City is only 470 miles. The Rio Grande Valley on the Texas side and tropical Tamaulipas on the Mexican right bank combine to weave the border's richest historical narrative and most complex social tapestry; it is a land apart and a special place, fiercely proud of its heritage and identity astride the border, past and present.

On the Mexican side of the valley, the road heads towards two cities: Reynosa, which has become a bustling industrial centre, and Matamoros, which despite industrialisation has held true to its roots in estate ranching and commerce. The Texas side is also dominated by a pair of cities, McAllen opposite Reynosa, and, facing Matamoros, Brownsville. They could hardly be more different: both are poor, but McAllen has sprung from almost nothing in no time, a sudden player threatening to rival Laredo with a proposed second trade corridor from Reynosa into the heart of Texas, along a new Interstate 69. Brownsville is seeped in epic history and for all the strip-sprawl along the highways is at heart sedate and unarguably the most charming city along the border, enchanted by laden, lush palm trees and ubiquitous ox-bow lakes known as *resacas*, left behind by the slow-winding river as it strolls and slouches its way out to sea. McAllen is new money, Brownsville is old, and each rather resents the other for it.

The observances, remembrances and rites begin early on the Day of the Dead in Reynosa, in the Church of Our Lady of Guadalupe and in the main Plaza into which its steps descend. Last night in McAllen, Mexican-American children had celebrated Halloween like any other American children, dressed in their ghoulish best, and out for a treat at *Taco Palenque* dressed as Count Dracula, his brides and victims. The Day of the Dead in Reynosa, however, is unchanged, uncoloured by orange and black bunting, even on the border. Inside the church portal is a special exhibition of *Los Mas Famosos Santos Incorruptos Méxicanos* – the most famous incorruptible saints – but not all saints, only the Mexican ones. The stories of their lives and martyrdom are told along with the guarantee that 'Death is not an entity / It is a simple transition from the elemental life to the celestial homeland'. But in Mexico, the dead are never far from the living, especially after the night when the veil is drawn back. In Reynosa of late, the Reaper has been given a helping hand by years of violence. Today belongs, however – though the menace is never entirely dispelled – to everybody's departed ones; the sky is deep blue, the special bread of the dead is baked, and it tastes good.

Outside in the square, altars are being built and decorated, the first thing being to lay thousands of petals in patterns on the flagstones, of flowers called Zempazuchitl ('flower of a hundred petals'), representing the rays of the sun illuminating the path to a celestial home, and *Garra de León* – lion's paw – so that the sidewalk is ablaze with white, representing the sky, golden yellow, representing the earth and resonant purple, the colour of mourning. Around the bases of the altars are abundant offerings and ritual matter: incense, sticks of cinnamon, bowls of rice and of carefully chosen minerals, semi-precious stones and common pebbles. The food is 'to nourish the soul of the dead', explains Patricia Espinoza, aged fifteen, and the water to 'quench their thirst'. The cross symbolises not the crucifixion but 'the four directions'. On the ground, salt is scattered so that the bodies of the dead will not rot, and candles arranged to light the way of their souls. Twigs and sticks are included so that the dead can bat away malicious spirits.

An especially splendid altar has been made by the Antonio Repizo high school, steps made of cardboard flanked by tables like wings decorated with skulls sculpted out of newspaper, flour and water. The steps are covered in offerings – dolls, bottles of tequila, dancing skeletons, books – and a New York Yankees shirt – atop which is a framed photograph of Guillermo López Treviño who lived from the 10 January 1907 until the 18 July 1983. 'He was my great grand-father,' says Lorenzo Martínez Rendez, aged fifteen, in broken English, 'a cowboy, farmer and very worker. He is my hero, he is always with me.' 'It's important to all of us,' says his schoolfriend, Mario López Villarreal. 'It's a celebration of those who bore us, to thank them and heed their advice. We've made the shrine to Lorenzo's great-grandfather, but he represents all of our ancestors, so we feel part of a chain.' 'This is not superstition,' says their teacher, Ana Teresa Luebbert, helping to arrange bowls of spices on the tarmac. 'The eyes of the dead are always upon us. They watch everything we do. If the young can reach them, they will be guided – though I sometimes wonder what the ancestors must be thinking now, with all that's going on.'

By now, it is mid-morning, and buses out to the cemeteries on the edge of town are filling with families, couples and ladies carrying flowers, mementoes, picnic chairs and children's toys as offerings to those who died in infancy. Everybody carries a bunch of little mauve-coloured flowers special to this day, called *Jesusuitas* – literally, little female Jesuses. There is piped music aboard the retired American school bus, not the local, lilting *ranchero* dance music one might have hoped for, but grinding *soca* from the West Indies. 'It's specially for the *Dia de los Muertos*,' says my companion Mario Treviño, a man with many strings to his bow, on both the city's dark and bright sides, working for a human rights office dealing mainly with depor-tees, and on cultural events in Reynosa, such as poetry readings here in Zeta country. The bus pulls up on a stretch of land between the baseball stadium and Reynosa's largest complex of cemeteries, on which a multitude is assembled, a great throng in the dusty heat, making its way to the headstones past stalls selling floral arrange-ments of every kind, and *pan de muerto* to eat.

In Reynosa, like everywhere else, you live by status and wealth
– and here you are buried that way too. Our souls may arrive as
equals to be either admitted through or turned away from that last
pearly border checkpoint in the sky, but the corporeal remains are
interred according to the ducats you left behind with them. First
comes the resting place for those at the bottom of the pile – blessed
are they, for they shall be buried here in the potter's field. Around
the modest headstones of the *Panteon Sagrado Corazón*, cemetery
of the sacred heart, families hold something between a dirge, wake,
party and grave-cleaning. Bands of musicians hawk their services,
playing mariachi music, local *ranchero* and traditional ballads of the
departed, depending on the mood. The Hernández family sits in
silence and the girls cry as musicians sing '*Amor Eterno*', usually
reserved for a departed mother. Another group over in the corner is
whooping it up – the ladies tapping their feet to the music while
sitting on deckchairs beside the graves, the men and boys standing
with their beers, and every so often pouring a few drops into the
earth under which Manuel Ramos López is buried, that he may
whet his lifeless lips as he used to. The Morales family is serving a
meal for eleven people around the memorial stone to its matriarch,
Lucia, which is draped in a pair of dungarees. 'She used to sell *ropa
usada*,' explains a daughter, 'so each year we bring some to put on
the grave.' The girls are studying a flyer for the special *Día de los
Muertes* celebration at Frida's Disco Club later on.

Those leaving behind a slightly bigger stash of mint leaves are
laid to rest in God's mid-ranking acre. Here families hold picnics
too: some pensive and restrained, others exuberant and vivacious.
Two musicians accompany one family sitting in silence, and sing a
lachrymose but soothing ballad of remembrance by a famous
Argentinian singer Alberto Cortez called '*Mi Querido Viejo*', My
Dearest Old One. And finally, we reach the *Panteon Espanol*, the
Spanish cemetery, 'where the business families are buried', says
Treviño. Here is respite from the clamour. Once inside the gate, one
is greeted by girls emerging from a gazebo. They're dressed in smart
air-hostess-like uniforms only with a higher hemline and appropriately black neckscarves, shoes and stockings of mourning, and they
asked if one would like to participate in a raffle to win a voucher
towards the funeral of a relative. Elegantly dressed people walk with

decorum through the Jardín Juan Pablo II, wherein perfectly pruned roses climb wire latticework. The lawns of the Jardín Padre Nuestro and Jardín Navidad – Christmas garden – into which the cemetery is tastefully divided, are impeccably manicured. No one wants a raucous *ranchero* band here; instead there are silent uniformed ushers and 'sanitary officers'. At the rear are mausoleums and family vaults as would line a big Italian cemetery containing centuries of the deceased, in mock monumental classical design. But even this is not the executive class of dear departed. There is yet another cemetery, says Treviño, 'for the very rich'. It is out of town, beyond the reach of the *soca*-rocking bus. 'There, the people we don't want to meet come to mourn, and who don't want us there today. It's where the top bad guys go, and the police, to be buried and settle their accounts.' We have no car, but I express a foolish interest in going, somehow. 'If you go, you're going alone,' says Mario, suddenly firm. 'Not me. They'll spot you right away: "What are you doing here, *gringo*?", they'll ask.' I'll tell them I'm reporting on the Day of the Dead. 'And they'll tell you no you're not, you're DEA, and they'll find a place for you to stay in the cemetery.' Mario is a much braver man than I, and this is his town, not mine; this is also a moment to defer to local knowledge rather than to arrive at the pearly checkpoint ahead of schedule, on 1 November of all days. Instead, we eat delicious *chiles rellenos* from a stall manned by a friend of Mario's, find a bus stop, and head back to town. Mario also buys a bunch of *Jesusitas*, and on the bus back a lady explains in detail how he must put them in a vase and let them dry until 24 June next year, the day of St John the Baptist, then bury them – and they will grow again in time for next year's Day of the Dead.

In the covered market downtown, the Dark Side store stands out from the others, selling food, magazines and tourist bric-a-brac (though there are no tourists, not even today). It is a Goth shop, at first sight of the kind you would find in New York's East Village or a city in Lancashire. The owner, Zombie Raul, wears long, jet-black hair, mascara and a black leather coat. His wife dresses in black lace and violet chiffon, and wears black nail varnish. Apparently even their child wears Goth baby clothes. All of which takes mettle and feistiness in a place like Reynosa. So we talk about the local Goth scene, for which *Día de los Muertos* is a keynote day in the calendar.

It being Sunday, Raul's shop is the only one in his arcade that is open, lest anyone be caught short, on this important festival, of a Metallica T-shirt or a pair of fingerless gloves with luminous bones. I ask about the cultural ancestry. 'No,' he says, 'not so much Iron Maiden, more Sisters of Mercy and Beethoven.' Well, so be it, and we have a terrific time talking about how Wagner's Niebelungs hammering on their anvils really was the first great heavy-metal riff, and as for that big double-punch in 'Siegfried's Funeral March', say no more. Raul was not a music student, he had studied the visual arts, 'but when I heard that stuff, I knew it was part of what I believe in'. Which is not strictly Goth, he hastens to add, it's Dark Side. 'It's a way of life, being aware of the beauty of things, and that all things are transient and must die, so obviously we're engaged in the Day of the Dead, but in our own way.' The Dark Side people in town are, he says unsurprisingly, 'the educated people who can think for themselves. We like to think beyond this culture in Mexico, we're open to new ideas, horror movies and different kinds of music.' This is an extremely refreshing young man to meet on the Day of the Dead, but how does all that go down in Reynosa? 'It means we have to live in our own world, but that's okay – because the fact that we refuse to participate in the compartmentalisation sets us apart from all that shit.' All we need to do is exchange a glance to know what 'that shit' is. There is one point over which that shit intrudes, however: *Santa Muerte*. 'They took our iconography. The hooded skeleton, the scythe – that's ours; that was metal and Goth long before it got to be anything to do with that shit.' Mario Treviño's tour of the marketplace, arts centre and historical museum inevitably leads to some discussion of what his Goth friend Raul called 'that shit'. We adjourn for food and coffee, over which he speaks coura- geously while carefully looking over his shoulder, and stopping when- ever anyone comes within earshot. 'What you see on the bridge is a circus,' he says. 'The soldiers standing there – it's a farce. Everyone knows the drugs go north and the guns come south across the bridge all day. People who earn hardly any money can get a hundred dollars cash for bringing a gun over for the Zetas. The region is a hub for guns all over Mexico. They're supposed to be illegal in Mexico, unlike the US, but everyone here has a gun, some people have six guns. They get them from the army, too – the soldiers are poor, and for too – the soldiers are poor, and for ten thousand dollars they let the bad guys in, and they take what they want.' A man selling *Pan de Muerto* for the *Drogadictos Anónimos* counselling service on Day of the Dead, had said: 'But the army's good, we can trust them. The police, they're just the troops of the Zetas. They tell them where the soldiers are going. You see them on the corner, waiting, watching the troops go by, then radio the movements through to the Zetas, so if they ever had a chance of catching anyone, it's too late. The only way they ever get them is with an inside tip-off.'

That is what the Zetas presumed to have happened in November 2008 when federal army troops arrested one of the founding commanders of the Zetas, Jaime González Durán, aka *'El Hummer'* (as per his preferred SUV), after a fifteen-minute shoot-out in Reynosa. The paramilitary unit that took *El Hummer* also hauled 428 guns of every kind and capability (including 288 assault weapons, and automatic or semi-automatic machine guns), anti-aircraft missiles, 287 grenades and bombs, and half a million rounds of ammunition. With the betrayal said to have come from within, the Zetas went on a rampage of violence.

Within weeks, the bodies of a long-time Mexican army general and two of his associates were found executed beside a road into Cancún. General Mauro Enrique Tello was the highest-ranking military scalp to be claimed by any assassination thus far; he had been methodically tortured, driven to the jungle and shot in the head. A week previously, he had been appointed by 'Greg' Sánchez, the mayor of Cancún, a Caribbean vacation playground, to face down the penetration of the tourist economy and transport routes by the Zetas, which threatened the ability of Mexico's number-one beach destination to attract visitors.[9] The general had led the initial military crackdown in December 2006 against *La Familia*, and now Mayor Sánchez wanted him to organise a hundred-strong armed unit to confront the Zetas. Anyone who feared the worst in Cancún was on the right track: within a week of the general's murder, federal agents had arrested Cancún's chief of police, Francisco Velasco, known as 'The Viking', and six other officers, and flown them to Mexico City for interrogation about their alleged roles in the general's murder. Federal prosecutors compiling the case still pending against Velasco estimated that as many as 1,700 of his officers in Cancún's police force were working for the Zetas.[10] He was known locally for driving around in his black Nissan Armada SUV playing *narcocorridos* glorifying the Zetas; his favourites were said to be 'Z Dynasty' and 'Pact Of Honour'. Although painted with police logos, the vehicle had been reported stolen in Mexico City in 2006. A week after the murder of the general, police arrested a cell of seven Zetas from Tamaulipas who had set up stall in Cancún.[11] The Zetas accelerated their operations against the Sinaloa's cocaine routes in central and Southern Mexico, arriving suddenly and horribly in places like the small, lazy agricultural town of Ixtlahuacán del Rio near Guadalajara, where five decapitated heads were found in beer coolers with messages such as 'I'm coming for you, Goyo'.[12] The Zetas' offensive had meanwhile hit neighbouring Zacatecas, with the most audacious prison break since that by *Chapo* Guzmán in 2001. A convoy of seventeen vehicles backed up by a helicopter approached Cieneguillas prison. Thirty men alighted, most of them dressed in police uniforms, marched into the jail, where they rounded up and freed some forty prisoners affiliated to the Gulf cartel.[13] The Zetas escalated their war in Central America, too, killing ten Guatemalan agents in an attempted police ambush on a Zetas drug consignment in April 2009. When the killers finally fled, they left behind a truck containing 700 lbs of white powder and – perhaps more significantly – an arsenal of eleven M-60 machine guns, a stash of claymore mines, a Chinese-made anti-tank rocket, more than 500 grenades as well as uniforms, bullet-proof vests, commando uniforms and thousands of rounds of ammunition.[14]

The Central American front is crucial to the Zetas for many reasons: it secures control of a land route for cocaine from the producing countries, it provides a strategic outlet for smuggling to Europe and Africa and it is the source of another Iron River, weaponry of a different, heavier, calibre. Although the Iron River's deepest flow is from the United States into Mexico, an investigation by the *Los Angeles Times* showed what amounted to an arms race between cartels in military-grade weapons from Central America. The attack by the Zetas on the Independence Day celebrations in Morelia used fragmentation grenades – a weapon of war. In Mexico itself, industrial explosives plants are robbed of material that can be used to make car bombs and roadside ambush devices. Grenades used in three attacks in Monterrey were linked to a single warehouse in the city, reportedly belonging to the Gulf cartel and raided in October 2008. Much of the cache seized on that occasion was made in South Korea, including fragmentation grenades.[15]

As with Raymundo Ramos upriver, it is abuse by the army and the concerns of migrants and deportees which most preoccupies the organisation for which Mario Treviño works, the *Centro de Estudios Fronterizos Y Promocion de los Derechos Humanos* – centre for border studies and promotion of human rights, run by Rebeca Rodríguez. Ms Rodríguez directs her rage not at the Zetas specifically but at the circumstances that have turned the town into 'a combat zone, in which the human rights situation is critical; a war between the military and the criminals, in which the civilian population has no stake but is held to ransom. The first human right to be trampled in Reynosa is the right to feel safe when you take a bus ride, or walk the street. Look at my hands: we don't wear jewellery, we don't wear expensive clothes – if you do, you could be kidnapped. In other countries, when a crime is committed you go to the police – but we daren't do that, because we have no idea who we're talking to. In February [2009], we had a shoot-out in an elementary school, between the soldiers and organised crime, innocent children caught in the crossfire. We live in fear of organised crime, and equal fear of the military.' The battle in the Felipe Carrillo Puerto elementary school happened on 20 February after men driving an SUV opened fire on federal police attempting to stop their vehicle. Soldiers took positions on the school patio and inside its low-walled compound for a shoot-out, lasting two hours with grenades exploding in the street and teachers ordering pupils to lie on the floor while they stacked desks against the windows to trap stray bullets. 'The bad guys feel they are lords of the streets', the sixty-one-year-old principal Martha Aguirre, had said.[16] The battle was but one of many spasms of fighting between the army and Zetas. In February 2009, there were running gun battles at six points across Reynosa, the Zetas commandeering vehicles to block roads and create a stockade. One battle lasted an hour, with the Mexican government claiming six dead among the narco gunmen.[17] As this book goes to press in spring 2010, there is a sudden spate of further fighting as the Zetas and army stand off. Other reports are of revived internecine fighting between the Zetas and the Gulf cartel old guard from which the paramilitaries, led by Osiel Cárdenas, seized power. Armoured cars are reported by *El Universal* newspaper to be cruising around town painted with 'CdG' for the Gulf cartel or 'XX' for the Zetas. Eight journalists disappear, of whom two are released by their kidnappers, one tortured to death and five, at the time of writing, remain missing. Mario Treviño sends a message which reads: 'Reynosa is in mourning . . . For the moment, the city is a no man's land . . . the caravans of death rolling through the streets.'

Ms Rodríguez echoes the arguments of Gustavo de la Rosa in Ciudad Juárez: 'The cartel is growing and expanding, and increasing its weaponry. But you can't fight crime with crime,' she says of the army's record of 'state torture and murder' in Reynosa. 'They don't protect us: they are around our houses, but they are not around the houses of the narcos. If you say that out loud, you're the fifth column – they call me the fifth column. But the worse the army, the more the criminals will organise the people against them.' There have been large demonstrations against the army here and in Matamoros, downstream, which the cartel has been suspected of organising – blockades by taxi drivers, for example, known to be under their control. In February 2009, demonstrations against the army blocked nine bridges connecting Ciudad Juárez and various towns in Tamaulipas to the United States, with federal authorities accusing the Juárez and Gulf cartels of paying the demonstrators in order to mobilise them. In the same month, anti-army demonstrations mobilised by the Zetas extended to the state capital of Nuevo León, Monterrey, blocking the centre of the richest and second biggest city in Mexico.[18] Although Monterrey is seen as too cleanly built of glass and steel, too much an embodiment of the new Mexico, too peppered with sushi restaurants, to be a proper Zeta fortress, an investigation – the only one of its kind – into the city's undergrowth by Tracy Wilkinson of the *Los Angeles Times* found the Zetas to have sunk deep roots in its poorer barrios like that of Independencia. The barrio's long history of small-time drug dealing has allowed it to be penetrated by the Gulf cartel, which paid residents to stage huge demonstrations blocking the roads.[19] The '*tapados*', as they were called, were paid small amounts of cash (about $13), or with cell phones and even school knapsacks filled with domestic supplies, to turn out against the army. Meanwhile, back in Tamaulipas, came a warning from the US and Mexican authorities: the Zetas were said to have procured forty bullet-proof vests emblazoned with the letters FBI and DEA.[20]

Monterrey, though, is the centre for what one might call the underground of artists that exists in cautious defiance of the narcos – a group of remarkable bravery and innovation. One is Francisco Benitez, who collects (or takes) photographs of the *narcomanta* banners hung in public places, also making his own, in protest or pastiche. He is fascinated by the new, perverse literacy of the *narcomantas*, of which he says: 'they are, in their own way, messages. Some of them are directed at the civic population, in order to spread fear, showing a certain bluff of power over these official authorities. It is a means of telling everyone that they own these territories, that there is nothing to do against them.' Benitez collects his photographs into a book/installation that has become almost a historic archive of the strange, vile, macabre humour, menace and obscenity of the *narcomantas*.

Except that Francisco also makes his own, by way of pastiche and comment. 'My *narcomantas* are a reflection on the situation that exists in Mexico,' he says. 'Some of them are black – black thread embroidery on black material – because they are related to the black flag of anarchy.' One of the embroidered messages reads: *Soldados de Plomo y Policias de Paja* – tin soldiers and straw cops. 'It used to be a common line on the *narcomantas* messages a derogatory way to indicate the authorities,' says Benitez, 'and in a certain way, it happens to be true. Any kind of crime committed by the criminals goes unpunished. The authorities do nothing but co-operate with the criminals More than a message for peace, this work is a critique of the whole situation.'

Benitez adds: 'Personally, I think the *narcomantas* reflect several social situations that have not to do just with narco cartels, but with issues of basic education, employment and social indifference,' especially among, he says, quarters of the artistic community. Though sometimes, the real thing can blow horribly close, as happened to one of Benitez's students. 'I teach at several institutions and workshops,' says Benitez, 'and one day I took a call on my cell phone. It was one of my students asking how to spell a word correctly. I told him, and he asked me for some other word. No word in particular. So I was curious, and asked him what he was doing, and after an odd attempt to explain, he told me that someone knew he was studying art and asked him to make a *narcomanta*. For good money. The student already knew this person, and tried to avoid problems, because this was an offer he couldn't refuse. Fortunately, he heard no more from this guy.'

Benitez works alongside a friend, Tomas Hernández, who carves reliefs in wood, in a constructivist style. One especially graphic one shows two pipelines, one dripping black oil, the other red blood. 'It's hard to find artists or artwork that challenges these issues,' he says. 'Sadly, the artistic community avoids them, or the references are shy and lateral.' Not Tomas, however, who collects 'discarded pieces of wood and cardboard from squatter ghettos. My materials were part of improvised houses abandoned by their inhabitants, and by this means I try to give the materials a second chance.' Of his pipelines relief, called *Hole In The Ground*, explains Tomas: 'A machine gun cannon targets the viewer and in the background we can see stylised veins, one of them drips oil, and the other drips blood, and in the meantime, everything is consumed in flames. It is about economic interests, and neo-liberal politics combining together to perpetrate chaos everywhere.' Tomas picks up on the themes of post-industrialisation in Juarez: 'what is happening here in Mexico is post-political and post-industrial. I choose the constructivist aesthetics for my artwork so as to relate to the idea of an industrial world. Monterrey is a post-industrial city, but the common people are still attached to the values of the nineteenth century. It generates despair when people don't understand why they cannot have work as safe as their grand-parents had – and in this awful war, teenagers make up the death squads, the consequence of lack of education, and social failure.' As this book got to press, Hernández reports a terrifying episode outside his parents' house: two black trucks arrive, firing machine guns, returning two hours later to dump two bodies, one of a teenager sliced in two at the waist.

Third in this trio of bold innovation in Monterrey is Jessica Salinas, whose work is starkly and shockingly terrifying. It divides into two categories: one shows portraits of beauty queens crowned, ensnared and killed by narco gangs, their posed bodies fading into decorative wallpaper, which is what they were. The others are assertively grotesque sculptures of machine guns and pistols with erect phalluses for barrels. Jessica works, she says, 'with the subject of criminality out of control, and its collateral damage from a feminine perspective – pieces intended to graphically portray the phenomenon of cartel beauty queens as trophies for the capos, until such point as women take the cartels under their own leadership, flashing firearms all the time. It is a situation I portray by relating the male anatomy to machine guns and firearms.' She certainly does, with such sculptures as *Anatomic Plates: Missile Gun and Smith and Wesson* – handle, trigger, then stretched back foreskin and all.

'So we're balancing here,' says Ms Rodríguez back in Reynosa, 'which is a difficult task.' She discusses the cartel with extreme care: 'They're doing what they are doing for the money, for the girls, the lifestyle and the power of money. But they have become a military formation, not a social formation.' The sage Treviño has been listening, and says something simple, but of importance: 'They're doing it for the money, yes, but more than that. They're doing it for kudos, to show they can wear this T-shirt by this designer worth this much money – instead of that one that the other guy is wearing. It's like stripes on a military uniform – corporal, sergeant. You walk around and everyone knows what rank you are, because your T-shirt is worth three hundred dollars, or your sneakers. They're doing it for the money, so they can show off the things the money can buy. It's a system of rank: if you have this T-shirt, you get a cute girl to show off; if you have an even more expensive T-shirt, you get an even cuter girl. But you can't be seen in the T-shirt you wore last year, which has gone out of style – that would mean you hadn't climbed the ladder. Same with the cars, gadgets and haircuts. They're disgusting people, high on amphetamines, but in Reynosa they can wear the uniform of their rank, and they're somebody.' It is a simple, but crucial and cogent analysis.

Meanwhile, 'the economy has become dependent on illegal money', asserts a lawyer working in Reynosa who prefers to remain anonymous. 'Drugs, guns and people-smuggling: it's a cycle of illegal money.' In contrast to the criminal anarchy in Juárez, 'if you work on the domestic drug market, just selling a little on the street, you

pay a commission to the narcos. If you are in legal business, you pay
a quota to the narcos. They control the police, so the police don't
protect you, then the narco comes to you and says: "The police
can't protect you, so we will."' (Or as a businessman over the river
in McAllen puts it: 'They say: "We'll protect you from us, if you
pay us to do so."') 'That way,' continues the lawyer, 'the narco is in
total control of the economy. Likewise the political parties: there
are elections between the PRI and the PAN, but they are no more
than a matter of Calderón and the army supporting PAN, so the
narcos back the PRI. You have the army on one side, the narcos and
the police on the other, and the middle – the economy, education,
political life – collapsing, normal communication broken down.'
Although the spring of 2010 saw a sudden and ferocious internecine
conflict between the old guard of the Gulf cartel and Cárdenas'
military wing, the Zetas, 'our problem', says Rodríguez, 'is not like
elsewhere. In most places, there is a war between different gangs.'
Despite the internecine tensions, 'this has always been the territory
of the Gulf cartel. Reynosa is a one-company town'.

Not only a one-company town, but now an insurgent one-
company town, at all-out war with the Mexican state and only
lately, with itself. If it was ever the determination of the Mexican
government that the crisis should be solved by the restoration of
the PRI's old narco order, under one strong cartel with tacit licence
to operate from the government, such a strategy has now been
overtaken by events. If, as the *susurro* has it, *Chapo* Guzmán was
– or may one day be – intended to be that one licenced monopoly
cartel, then the plan has failed, thrown off course by collapse in
Juárez and the ferocity of the Zetas. The Zetas can be bought off
– anyone can in this game – but at what price? And if the Zetas
are to preserve the *Pax Mafiosa* in this territory, what price
Guzmán? The mysterious treaty in Nuevo Laredo offers a tanta-
lising but terrifying answer: an uneasy arrangement between the
cartels, with the loser paying a tax to the winner, and the price of
peace being the kind of public submission Ms Rodríguez and the
lawyer describe, of society and the economy to the cartel.

The word 'Zetas' is conspicuously absent from this discourse in
Ms Rodríguez's office, although it has gone well beyond what most
people in Reynosa dare to speak. Another human rights worker in

town who cannot be named says it privately: 'We call them The Last Letter of the Alphabet; we don't call them Zetas – it's too dangerous to acknowledge their existence or use their name, which is mad, since they're so proud of who they are, and boast it around all the time themselves. It is like this: if someone crosses them, they pay the price, either in cash or with their life.'

Around the centre of Reynosa is a system of canals built partly for irrigation and partly to channel floodwater from the Rio Grande. Along the canals are banks of grasses, and over them are bridges with yellow railings. To have a city surrounded by a system of moats is warfare's most tried and tested defence – as the Zetas realise only too well. The activist speaks of displays of strength of which no word has hitherto escaped Reynosa: 'it was February thirteenth [2009] when they did it for the first time,' she says. 'They just sealed off the city centre, as a gesture of intimidation, with road blocks at the bridges. To show they can do what they want, and to show the army they can do a training excercise. They did it again on the seventeenth – this time they hijacked buses across the bridges over the canals: boarded the buses, ordered the drivers to swing them round and everyone to get off, then took the keys. Usually they do it for two or three hours at a time, but once the buses stayed there for fifteen hours, no one dared move them; the city felt in a state of siege.' Some days later, a woman dared to speak, if only briefly, about being on one of those buses: 'We jerked to a stop. There was banging on the door and four men jumped on, shouting at the driver. They wore balaclava masks, but we all knew immediately who they were. They ignored us; it happened quickly: they shouted at us to get off the bus, quietly and no one would get hurt. One lady insulted them because she was late, but nothing happened. A few stayed and watched the driver steer the bus across the road. He got down and was sent away. They just left the bus there, empty, in the rain.'

'One time it happened,' said the activist, 'a male friend of mine was getting married, and his bride couldn't get to the church! She was coming downtown when the Zetas shut the bridge, and everyone got worried, especially my friend, because his bride arrived so late for the wedding!' Over the bridge in McAllen, Texas, the narrative of the Zetas and the bridges becomes even more serious: it is not only those into downtown Reynosa that the narco militiamen are blocking in their shows of strength; they have another audience to impress, which involves a more audacious display across other bridges: those into the United States. 'It was a bad day here, about April or May [2009]. They blocked several bridges, the international bridges into the US. It's never happened before, they just shut 'em down.'

The businessman in McAllen talks on condition of anonymity, as well he might. But his knowledge and veracity are unimpeachable, and what he knows has never been leaked. 'They called us here at the company, and they told me that whatever I got to get over, I had to get it over by 2 p.m. Just get your stuff across, they said, 'cause we ain't reopening for a while. They said it would be peaceful, they were just making a point. And boy were they. What they were really saying was: "We're running the show." These are people who roll up with rocket-propelled grenades, and can stage a four-hour shoot-out with the military. When they roll up to close a bridge, people do what they say. The only bridge they left open was the one over from Progreso, because of the tourism that still crosses there.' No word of this ominous manoeuvre was spoken by US authorities at the other side of the bridge, or the local Texan politicians or press.

McAllen is becoming a city that looks north as well as south, turning in the direction the trucks will one day be going, it hopes, past the signs posted along Highway 281 towards Houston reading 'Future Interstate 69'. Which is also the direction that the genealogy of businessman Sam Vale's family has taken: his ancestors are from Reynosa, but his office now sits atop the only tower in McAllen from which Spanish language news, football and showbiz feed into almost every household in the Rio Grande Valley. Vale is director for the region of the Mexican Telemundo televison network and also owns the ultimate piece of Amexican real estate: a border bridge – that between Camargo, Tamaulipas, and Rio Grande City, Texas, for which each crossing vehicle pays him a toll. Mr Vale, who typifies the new, muscular McAllen, tells the story with gusto: originally the bridge was co-owned with another businessman, Vale's father holding a minority 40 per cent, but through a series of clever manoeuvres, threatened law suits and hard-faced verbal duelling, each episode increasing the stake by increments, the Vales secured majority and then sole ownership. All other bridges across the Rio Grande are the property of the federal government, apart from one other, whose owner's name happens to be Sam Sparks, says Vale, 'so that to own a bridge, you gotta be Sam, Sam or Uncle Sam'.

Vale's office is decorated with artwork and antiquities from Mexico's recent and distant past: paintings, religious artefacts and carvings. 'They're the result of what I call the Mexican way of doing business,' says Vale. 'You see something you like, you name a price you know the guy can't accept, then you ask: what else you got?' The family, however, was Mexican ranching and later commercial aristocracy from another world. 'My grandmother used to send her dresses by steamship to be cleaned,' says Vale, 'in Paris.' He is a man of presence, wears a full moustache, an open shirt and gold jewellery, talks entertainingly and with ease. He is Tex-Mex, big on the Tex, is generous with his time and believes passionately in McAllen, Texas. Throughout the family's rise in the real estate business, he says, it had been surrounded by 'people who wanted South Texas to be California – but hell no, I always said, we are what we are – that was the first principle'. The second was that 'whatever we do, we do with Mexico, rather than spend billions of dollars building a damned wall, like this is Israel and Gaza'. Laredo, he says, 'always had that integrated mentality, and did well out of it'. And he looks at the sweep beneath us, out beyond the heavy oak desk in his top-storey office. 'When I was in high school, all this was fields.' It sounded lovely, compared to the vista of concrete sprawl and the strip mall next door shared by Country Omlette, Viva Life Christian Booksellers, The Armory Guns 'n' Ammo, signs on stalks advertising AutoZone and a hoarding that reads: 'Your Wife Is Hot. Tint Her Windows'. But that is not what Sam Vale means about the fields; he means the opposite: build all over them.

'McAllen lives or dies on the basis of international trade, starting with the fact that forty per cent of retail in this town is Mexicans coming over here to buy stuff.' But that is not where it ends. 'We have people sitting there working out how to make money for this city. What next? What else? This valley is churning big time,' says Vale. 'The city must be part of the action that Laredo's part of,' and establish its own inland port along its own trade corridor. 'Laredo has a system it likes, but we can make it cheaper by letting the Mexican long-haul truck come straight across to the point of delivery, cutting out the shuttle.' No drayage trucks here: this will be the boys from *Veintiseis* crossing over as far as the Pilot Travel Center – the mind boggles.

Vale has no illusion that 'all the money is lily-white, because it's not. But around here, the cartels only affect you if you're involved in some way, you owe them, or sold them computers. The people who pay the cartels on this side have a part of their business that's illicit, some extension of the system over there, where no one can function without agreement with the Zetas.' And, of course, there is the Iron River: 'The biggest industry the cartel is involved in this side of the border is the import of guns from the US. You've got a family – you get the Gulf cartel six to ten weapons at $500 per gun – that's good money. A lot of people, myself included, have been clamouring for the ATF to be given more resources in this region. The government talks about sending a hundred more – dammit, we need a thousand – we need people working undercover on the other side, we need men on the ground who can root out the people selling the weapons around here, and the gangs who are buying the weapons and getting them to the cartels. They're buying up parts and assembling them on the other side of the border. But all this hardware has to be stashed somewhere, it has to be taken to Mexico one gun at a time. There has to be a collection and distribution network, and it's got to be broken.'

But the Zetas' penetration of the legal economy runs deep. One astonishing story, told by an attorney in McAllen with good connections, affords a rare insight into the world of Zeta Inc. It involves them stealing condensate from oil terminals belonging to the Petroleos Mex company, and exporting it to the USA. The scam was said to have been personally overseen from jail in Houston by Osiel Cárdenas himself. 'They got the contacts inside the Petroleos Mex company,' says the attorney, 'and were literally siphoning off the condensate, bringing it from Monterrey to terminals in the US, with all the correct paperwork. Coming up through Pharr, up to Houston. How do we know this? Because something happened: a man called Manuel Gómez was found decapitated.' The background to the murder, says the attorney, swearing inside knowledge: 'Gómez was working with the cartel to provide transportation. He never used his own vehicles, always smaller trucking companies. He was responsible for hauling these tankers to refineries in Houston, for use in jet oil products. He even had a name in their circles: '*Manolo*'. After a while, the cartel operatives on the receiving end in Houston 'started to notice a shortage of product arriving at the refineries; a shortfall in the cartel shipment. And what did they find out back in Monterrey? That Gómez was siphoning off his own stash. They figured it out, and cut his head off.'

According to one assessment of the Zetas, in a briefing by the DEA in 2009, such is the extent of their criminal empire that only 20 per cent of the syndicate's turnover is now generated by drug trafficking. This can be seen as a terrifying corruption of the economy, but Vale insists it can be looked at another way. 'If the economy is right, they'll condemn themselves to respectability. They'll realise that the big money is mainstream. As things are, the Zetas and cartels are infiltrating the US side – they're in Houston, they're in New York City, they're all over the Indian reservations. But these gangsters are going to have children and these children are going to have to learn legal business. Of course I'm not saying we make agreements with them, but you wait for them to condemn themselves to legality, then instead of fighting about it, you find some way to settle it. At the moment, you have a battle over an illegal product, with the profits going into semi-legal business. It's painful, and we have to face that down. But it's a growing pain, they can't fight for ever. They're already buying up houses on South Padre Island like the British do in Spain, and when the war is over it'll be like the waterfront in New York – they'll start doing things in a more licit way, then go legal.'

In defining McAllen as the town figuring out how to make money, swashbuckling Sam Vale had said: 'Brownsville, by the way, doesn't think like we do, it's more old fashioned.' Such generalisations will always need to surrender to exceptions, but they are not without their grains of truth, and Vale's remark defines the curtain that divides the two cities on the Texan side of the valley, connected by the sprawling concrete overgrowth along Highway 83 or, running parallel right along the borderline: the big sky and long story of the Old Military Highway. It is one of the great roads in America, not because of the curious border towns it passes through, or the sweeping palms and tobacco fields that line the way, not even for the fact that Mexico and the river are never more than half a mile away, and sometimes a few feet. Indeed, if there is anything that makes the highway surreal, it is the border fence, cutting like a gash across the landscape, and often across the back of people's gardens. What makes the Old Military Highway so richly agreeable to travel are the Historical Markers erected by various institutions at various stages along the way. It was an Indian trail used by Spanish explorers in the sixteenth century, initially established to connect settlements to one another; later a military road connecting the Texan and US forts at Laredo and Brownsville during the Mexican wars; then a stage-coach, mail route and inland supply line for cotton during the Civil War.

By definition, the narrative followed by an eastward journey along the Old Military Highway to Brownsville is not a chronological one. Past a glorious avenue of palm trees to the south, one arrives at the site of Toluca Ranch, founded in 1880 by Florencio Cano, on land owned by his Spanish ancestors, once covering 10,000 acres. There is high drama at the next marker, Rio Rico. In 1906, says the plaque, the Rio Grande Irrigation Company dug a canal that 'altered the natural course of the Rio Grande', abandoning 419 acres to the south of the river, in Mexico. After a treaty of 1884, says the marker, the 'popular gambling community of Rio Rico, which flowered in the 20s and 30s, became subject to Mexican jurisdiction'. Later, in 1970, the USA ceded the communities of Rio Rico and El Horcon to Mexico, starting an eight-year legal battle that ended in the granting of US citizenship to 200 natives of Rio Rico born prior to 1970. Nature's border does not always coincide with mankind's, and the river knows best.

As one nears Brownsville, the road is marked by the site of the *Rancho de Santa Maria*, commandeered as a military sub-post by Fort Brown, and a mile further is the site of Villa de Reynosa, built by Juan Miguel Longoria (1815–1875), who fathered seventeen children with three wives, the last of whom was Teresa Guerra, one of the great 'matriarch ranchers of Texas'. Two miles further along, two markers and a cannon stand together. One plaque marks the route taken by Spanish general Alonso de León, fighting French incursions in 1685. Another marks the spot where 'American blood was shed on American soil. April 25th 1846. Here, Captain Philip Thornton and 62 dragoons were attacked by Mexican troops.' The cannon, aimed at the border, was placed there in 1846 by Lt. Thomas

Barlow Chapter, against the Mexicans. Three miles (and eighteen years) later, 'Col. John S. Ford of the Confederate Army defeated the Union forces. June 25 1864'. Now the border fence almost touches the road, passes through Garco's construction yard, then behind a car wash and auto sales outlet in La Paloma and back right up against the road, which then runs past Dark Side of the Moon Tattoo and into Brownsville.

One marker along the way had located the Battle of La Bolsa, fought in 1859, which ignited a conflict that was named after the man who fought here, Juan Cortina. The Cortina Wars witnessed the only seizure by land of US territory in the nation's history. In 1859 and early 1860, reads the plaque, a 'series of raids led by Juan N. Cortina (1824–1894) led to skirmishes with companies of Texas Rangers and US soldiers.' Here at La Bolsa, it says, 'a battle occurred between Cortina's raiders and Capt. John S. 'Rip' Ford's Texas Rangers'. Cortina, a Mexican from north of the border, led a raid on Brownsville in 1859, occupying Fort Brown with 200 men and hoisting the Mexican flag from its ramparts. He was eventually thwarted by a mobilisation of Texas Rangers.[21]

'*Diles Quíen Eres*,' says Dr Antonio Zavaleta, special assistant to the provost at the University of Brownsville – Tell Them Who You Are. It was the title of a paper he gave to a conference on border identity, and a *dicho* he heard in childhood – as well it might be, for Dr Zavaleta's paternal great-great-grandfather was General Juan Cortina. His academic post is therefore all the more apposite because the university campus occupies the site of the old Fort Brown captured by his ancestor.

Dr Zavaleta's office is a museum to both his ancestry and his imagination. The room is a wonder: if Sam Vale had wheeled and dealt his way into a collection of artefacts, Zavaleta has accumu-lated a treasure trove. He works surrounded by totem poles, icons, painted panels, carvings and masks representing deities, saints, spirits, sprites and banshees – presided over, of course, by the Virgin of Guadalupe. Here is a roomful of the syncretism – mumbo-jumbo, if you prefer – of multiple and multilayered faiths that has defined the border's history and the road, and infused the air it breathes even more than the violence. It has done so all the way from the demol-ished *Santa Muerte* chapels above Tijuana to this room: a council of the incorporeal at the border's far Eastern edge end. General Juan Cortina looks down with a commanding and perfectly somatic aspect from a portrait by the window – *'Diles Quién Eres'* indeed.

Zavaleta is captivated, personally and professionally, by what he calls 'folk Catholicism', as believed and practised by the people of Mexico and the border, rather than the kind issued in Papal bulls and edicts. Folk Catholicism retains elements of pre-Colombian faith, which have remained as part of Christian iconography and practice in Mexico, whether it please the Vatican or not. Zavaleta is an expert in a central part of this overlay of faiths: *'curanderismo'* – the work of *curandero*, faith healers – as embodied by the *'Niño Fidencio'*, who practised in and around Espinazo, Nuevo León, during the 1920s. And when I arrive to talk, by coincidence, copies of a new book have just been delivered: a selection by Zavaleta of petitions sent by email to the *curandero* healer Alberto Salinas, an acquaintance of his, almost entirely from Mexican Americans, together with the *curandero*'s responses. They range from requests for advice on schoolwork to that on demonic possession, from injuries to a baby by a lunar eclipse to dancing with death and, inevitably, in pursuit of deliverance from the power of *Santa Muerte*. Most correspondents, one infers, are young.[22]

'I went through over seven thousand emails,' says Zavaleta, 'and noticed a subliminal pattern that had a lot to do with very traditional *curanderismo*. They had come to this through word of mouth, at home, in schools, villages or churches, and what they sought was a subtle mix of spiritual, artistic and scientific or medical treatment and advice, a holistic process. We could only choose 190 of them, but they are 190 lives, very particularly expressed in a way that was modern to the eye, but ancient.' He makes the connection by waving an arm around the room: 'All this is pervasive in our culture. It's in every being on the border. This stuff' – which seems either distant or exotic to the modern eye – 'is very real to people, every day,' says Zavaleta. 'Dancing with the devil, feeling the eyes of the dead upon you, the patron saints of your home or travelling, saints' days, magic numbers and colours, protective talismans – it cuts deep and is always close to the surface. It plays a role in your life and community. These are poor people, but throughout, there's this deep understanding, even in the world we live in, of forms of faith and belief that go way back, from which the healing and magic traditions of all religions in Mexico including Catholicism are drawn.' Zavaleta has a professorial air, for sure – but there's something more than that: this is not academe, this is a life's faith as well as a life's work, ever since, he says, 'I was raised a Catholic in Brownsville, Texas, but of Mexican ancestry, and educated by a priest from Ireland.[23]

'I know priests who admit that it's not a problem if people don't believe what they're doing, so long as they keep doing it,' says Zavaleta. 'But we're not like that – folk Catholicism is something primal that never leaves you. It doesn't leave even people who go off to become born again evangelicals. They sing in chapel, they go to Bible classes, then they come back, to their roots in the primal mystery. They'll take in the great work – food stalls in the barrio, soup kitchens, all good. But then they come home. To not wanting to disappoint their patron saint, feeling unlucky at the eye of a certain animal on you – not Bible class, but *this*!' And again, a sweep of the hand across the room, past the dancing skeletons, the plumed serpents, the bright birds – and mesmerising figure of the Virgin of Guadalupe, standing atop the new moon. 'It's like asking someone on a beautiful warm evening,' says Zavaleta, '"what would you like to drink, a cup of coffee or a nice cold beer?"'

Zavaleta's book contains the case of a boy who feels trapped by a pledge he has made to *Santa Muerte*. He petitions the *curandero* Salinas 'as a matter of life and death', fearing that *Santa Muerte* will 'collect on a broken promise'. 'He knows there's a payback,' says Zavaleta, 'and is afraid it will be with his life. He's terrified, and reaches out for help in a desperate way, but one which understands the deep history of what he is doing.' And at last, here is the conversation I have been waiting to have since that fearsome afternoon above the dam with the F-150 truck drivers guarding the ruins of *Santa Muerte's* chapel in Tijuana. '*Santa Muerte* was resurrected in Mexico City twenty-five years ago, in the poor Tepito neighbourhood. And was adopted by the narcos – that's what everybody knows,' says Zavaleta. 'It's a huge cult now, among the young – it's become a way of identifying with power, with easily accessible evil. For the narcos, it's obviously something more sinister and dangerous, but it's them who've mutated *Santa Muerte* into this image. She's been made into a pop saint by the drug traffickers to sublimate their cult of death.

'If you go back, *Santa Muerte* was not evil. She was, strictly speaking, the representation of a folk saint to which a woman prayed to get her wayward husband back – of course she means more than that! She represents a holistic relationship between life and death, a cycle and totality. The image of the reaper is inaccurate. That's something new – if you see *Santa Muerte* as a black-hooded reaper on the back of a car, it's more likely from Tamaulipas than Mexico City. *Santa Muerte* originally wears not black but the colours of the rainbow. It's important that she represents the universality of the colours. Originally, she holds not a scythe – that's another narco creation – but the world, the globe. Her power is that she holds everything in her palm.'

The appeal of the cult to young people, says Zavaleta, 'reminds me of when, as a fifteen-year-old, I brought home a copy of Aleister Crowley's satanic bible and showed it to my mother. And I can see that sentiment everywhere now. The gold standard in folk religions is to see what's selling – it's as true now in the marketplaces as it ever was with the sale of indulgences and relics. Now, you'll find shops broken into and the only thing missing the thieves wanted to steal is a statuette of *Santa Muerte*. There's been a rash of these thefts in the valley. Here in Brownsville, you have little kids in elementary school third grade who are doing *Santa Muerte*, they wear the gold chains, they talk to the statues, and it's obvious that their fathers are drug dealers; if you talk to them, they'll tell you their fathers work for the cartel. This is serious, and dangerous, but our reaction is different to that of the mainstream Church.' How so? 'If you ask someone who practises *curanderismo*, they will distinguish between this new cult of *Santa Muerte* and her original meaning. But the Church will not – they'll give you a blank look, dismiss it all and offer you God with the right hand or the devil with the left – that's the way it is. If you ask someone who believes in *curandero* healing, they'll grapple with it, engage in cognitive discussion, go back to the original meanings of what is really happening, understand them and find a way out.'

Where does '*diles quíen eres*' come from? I ask. 'My grandfather said it to me once, in Spanish. I was about twelve years old. I asked him what it meant, and he looked at me sternly: 'Tell them who you are.' I asked him to tell me the story, of this Juan Cortina I was descended from, and he did. I felt like a new-born child.'

Elizabeth Street in Brownsville, running a block north of, and parallel to, the border, is a destination point for shoppers from across town, of course, but also the north-east corner of Tamaulipas. Cross-border shopping is a theme that defines the frontier, and as in Calexico, as in Laredo and everywhere in between, there is this delicate balance between what is more affordable (or less unaffordable) on the US side and on the Mexican side. Quite apart from which side the bargain might hide, or the little luxury that doesn't appear on the list prepared in advance.

The Signature store is a cavernous adventure, miles of fluffy bears, zip-up bags for *ropa usada*, marker pens, Tupperware and cutlery, towels with designs of Sylvester Stallone, Marilyn Monroe or Club America to choose from, flashing antennae and model New York yellow cabs. El Toro Sports is stacked with perfumes, soccer shirts and bags with Mickey Mouse or the Dallas Cowboys' star on the back. And in this marketplace of essentials, little luxuries and junk, stands the temple, HEB. A Texan supermarket chain that strides the frontier, with consulates in every Mexican border town, HEB is an institution. The parking lot in Brownsville is a social scene at sundown, a gossip exchange, a chat-up opportunity, a place to compare phone applications and bets on horses. About half the car plates are Texan, the other half from Tamaulipas, while over in Matamoros, the percentage is about two-to-one in favour of the indigenous Mexican shoppers. Over in Matamoros, the HEB is more department store than supermarket: an array of electronic goods more expensive than in the US, sofas and armchairs at much higher prices and a spectacle of cheap chilli and jalapeños without rival. But the pièce de résistance is over in the corner, the *Pastelitos*, the bakery. Here, at apparently reasonable prices, is a fanfaronade of cakes decorated electric pink, yellow or blue. This is the cake department to end all cake departments: cakes shaped like racing cars, Spiderman and Cat woman, Mickey and Minnie Mouse, with inscriptions in sugar icing like '*Machito*', in blue, for little boys and '*Florita*', little flower in pink for girls. A corpulent man in a chef's hat who looks quite like the pastry he is baking heaves a humungous cake over the counter covered in sugared Technicolor, received with difficulty on the other side by two girls – this is Brian César's birthday cake, personalised in turquoise icing.

At the end of the row of shops on Elizabeth Street back across the border is a Pandora's Box of a shop. Written above the door: 'AZTECA: *Yerberia*. Gifts Dolls *Regalos Muñecas*. *Se Leen Las Cartas*' – Herbshop. Gifts. Mannequins. We read cards. Azteca is an omnium gatherum of spiritual, religious and magic accoutrements and a child's dream made real. Hidden among flowers or lined up on shelves are dolls of every kind. There are white plaster statuettes: of Venus, of fine ladies in ball gowns, of the three Magi, amorous cherubs and mischievous putti as well as Christ both in manger and on cross. There are shelves of remedies for every ailment of the mind, body or soul: herbs, oils and essences of cactus. Four shelves are devoted to devotional candles to every saint, angel and archangel, including *Santa Muerte* in all her incarnations. But guiding and presiding over all of this – framed, sculpted, painted onto candles, cast in silver, gold, plaster and plastic – is the figure who oversees it all, and everything along the border, standing on the moon: the Queen of Mexico and Empress of the Americas, the Virgin of Guadalupe.

The first of many prayers offered on Saturday 12 December 2009 in Brownsville was spoken through a megaphone and chilly, damp fog hanging from the dark sky – unusual for a tropical night in America's poorest neighbourhood. But the people of Cameron Park had awoken and converged nevertheless, in the parking lot behind the Church of San Felipe de Jesus on the outskirts of town to prepare for the day of Our Lady the Virgin of Guadalupe. And they did so, they knew only too well, along with tens of millions of others across Mexico and along the borderline. As the Christian world prepared to commemorate the Nativity, Mexicans – including twenty-eight million Mexican Americans and probably the same number of Mexican citizens living legally or illegally in the US – celebrated what is for them a more spiritually cogent and enchanted day. 'In the name of the Holy Virgin Mary, Mother of God and *Nuestra Reina* [our Queen],' implored Father Hector Cruz down the megaphone, 'and please keep to the side of the road': three years ago a drunken driver ploughed into the parade, injuring three pilgrims. Accordingly, behind a pick-up truck leading the way, they set off, just after 3 a.m., in pilgrimage to the Church of Our Lady of Guadalupe, on 12th Street downtown. We walk at a pace, for this is no stroll and there is a way to go. Pounding those three hours through the dark are mostly young people, couples in hoodies holding hands, fathers with little children, women and girls clutching bunches of roses in December (for such was one of the Virgin's miracles when she first appeared) and the striking image of the Queen of Mexico standing on a crescent moon among the rays of the sun. A young man called Luis walked – he now has to commute to work as an ironworker 'way north in Alabama and Georgia' because there were no jobs left locally, his wife four months' pregnant; he had returned specially for this pilgrimage. A young woman called Gabriela Méndez had two weeks ago been laid off by HEB; she is now wondering what next, only glad to be able to concentrate better on basket-making class. Wearing a splendid 1994 World Cup Mexico bomber jacket, Alfonso – a steward keeping the parade in line – had been on all thirteen *Guadalupana* pilgrimages from Cameron Park since their inception, but just lost his job as a chandler in the harbour at nearby Port Isabel. 'This', he insists, however, 'is the day of *esperanza* [hope] for us all, and for all Mexicans.'

Cameron Park was until recently a Mexican-American *colonia*, which simply means 'neighbourhood' but on the US side means that it was too poor to be 'incorporated' and granted services such as lighting, running water or paved roads, because it raised no tax revenue. A movement by civic groups in the 1970s, later spearheaded by the remarkable man who was until recently parish priest at San Felipe de Jesus, Michael Seifert (he has since left the priesthood), registered Cameron Park's residents as voters and won the attention of the city, county and even the state of Texas, so that the trailer homes gradually grew permanent extensions and the oil lamps became electric light.[24]

The area remains in many ways a Mexican *colonia* as we walk first along pitted byways past little *bodega* kiosks which are windows of private homes, past guard dogs barking at the pilgrims as they wander the empty streets like a spectral procession towards the city. Then out onto the main artery into town, Ruben Torres Boulevard, past dark stillness on the *resacas* – the ox-bow lakes left by the winding Rio Grande – past deserted Wendy's and golden arches unlit, we are joined by tributaries of other pilgrims. It is strange and welcome to see this city becalmed at night: in motionless abeyance and wrapped in damp darkness, depopulated but for our muffled steps past mute buildings and dwellings. A twenty-four-hour Valero gas station is lit and open, though, selling famously good breakfast tacos, which tempt a few folks in search of nourishment and warmth to tarry behind. All along the way, the pilgrims sing; in fact, the choir on the back of the truck is not deemed good enough and as we pass Coffee Port Road, the hooded, anorak-clad choristers are ejected and stewards appeal to the now several hundred pilgrims: '*Quién canta?*' – Who can sing? – in search of substitutes. The special hymns duly continue, with greater glow: '*Y eran Méxicanos*' – 'They were Mexicans', goes the hymn – to whom the Virgin de Guadalupe appeared in 1531. Past Don Quixote Street they walk, alongside the freeway, and even that is deserted. After three cold hours, the procession enters a bath of fluorescent light, the church resplendently decorated for Mass, which begins during darkness at 6am. There is a justifiable sense of authenticity among those who walked, even if the best seats have been taken by others who drove. The altar is gleaming white, the choir dressed in bright indigenous Mexican colours and the priest has the image of the Virgin embroidered on his cream-coloured robe as he reads, apocalyptically, from the Book of Revelations. Drummers wearing lambent golden Aztec costumes and dancers in head dresses of peacock feathers perform, presided over by the icon of Guadalupe.

Icon of Mexico in the deepest sense, the Virgin of Guadalupe is at once dynamic, mystical and omnipotent. She appeared to what is commonly referred to as a 'poor Indian' – a Nuahatl peasant baptised as Juan Diego – in a number of encounters in 1531, during which she tasked Juan Diego to convince a doubtful archbishop to build a sanctuary in her honour.

But the Virgin of Guadalupe is much more complicated than that. After Mass, there is a hearty breakfast of *huevos a la Méxicana* with a man who has thought, preached and spoken about the image of the Empress of the Americas and the Virgin Queen it portrays in his former parish of Cameron Park. 'Cameron Park is in, but not of, Brownsville,' he says. 'Surrounded on all sides by one of the poorest cities in Texas, Cameron Park is so poor that not even Brownsville wants to have anything to do with the place.' It is pertinent, then, that the Virgin of Guadalupe appeared to a peasant in the cotton fields. 'She is the cry of the poor and the redemption of the poor. But it is not that straightforward: the poor Indian was from a warrior caste, vanquished and converted by another warrior caste [the Spanish conquisators] and in this, the Virgin is the child of rape, but pregnant − both queen and outcast, pregnant with the mixed-race Mexican *Mestizos* people, after what was not an immaculate conception. So the Virgin of Guadalupe is both spiritually and ethnically syncretic: a *mestizo*, icon of both pre-Columbian and Catholic spirituality, and of the indigenous and Spanish people. Indeed, in one of the great works of Mexican literature, the Nuahatl-language *Huei Thamahoicoltica*, or *Great Event*, she is defined only in terms of pre-Columbian, Mexica lore − an echo of Coatlicue, Goddess of the Aztec pantheon, who lived among the moon and stars, and gave birth to the primary god Huizilopochtli after being impregnated by a 'brilliant hummingbird feather carried on the wind', and who, like the Virgin of Guadalupe, had her sanctuary on the mountain of Tepeyac.

'And the Virgin of Guadalupe,' says Seifert, 'is also a symbol of defiant hope in the dark days of now. She is a social lament, and helps us in our resistance. She is what stands between places like Ciudad Juárez and total despair. And unlike any other Madonna, she is standing. If you look at her left knee, she is even dancing.' It is an extraordinary proposition. Yes, says Seifert, she is 'a young woman, dressed as an Aztec Queen, we know this from the colours and the style of dress, from the sun and the moon and the stars. This cosmic princess is standing, while amongst the people of those days, royalty sat, always and especially in the presence of the lower classes. [As do portrayals of the Madonna in European art.] She is, of course, pregnant, as we can tell from the way her robe stands forth, and from the dark sash, and she has her hair down. But she is in a dance, as well, her knee lifted forward.'

Equally unexpected is Seifert's sudden about-turn: 'Then I think to myself: Is it all opium? Opium of the people, to keep them servile?' What a thought − heresy on 12 December from a former priest − and what a terrible moment for Seifert to have to leave. His wife, a paediatrician, has arrived and they must record pictures of a newborn baby to send by internet to grandparents in Mexico, who cannot get papers to cross the border and visit. But some weeks later,

Seifert sends further thoughts on the Virgin of Guadalupe. He goes back to the Nuahatl equivalent of her name, 'Coatlaxopeuh', pronounced 'quatlasupe', which he constructs as 'Mary Who Crushes the Serpent'. 'At the heart of the Spanish conquest,' concludes Seifert, 'is rape. I don't mean the figurative rape of the country and the culture, but the rape of Indian women by Spanish soldiers.' And the child of that rape, he argues, 'would be a bastard, in the harshest technical sense of the word — a child without a past, without a people, for she is not an Indian, she is Other. This child, however, would be the most lasting reminder of the first, violent encounter between Europeans and the Aztec nation. She was Mexican, and she and her brothers and sisters would become yet another nation, another great people, a new people. In the humiliation of rape, a new race was born, a *mestizo* race, the Mexican race.' *Diles Quién Eres*: The Virgin of Guadalupe, telling Mexico who it is.

In the sign of peace at the end of Mass after the pilgrimage from Cameron Park, there is flesh-creeping poignancy after a year of violence across and along the border. But a woman in the front row shatters any rip-tide of thorns with a cry of redemptive defiance: '*Viva La Virgen de Guadalupe!*' '*Viva!*' roars the congregation, as the sky quickens outside. '*Viva San Juan Diego!*' '*Viva!*' they respond, as grey dawn breaks. '*Viva Cristo Rey!*' — Christ the King — '*Viva!*' comes the reply. Sitting in a pew on the nave is the writer Cecilia Ballí, who has narrated the trials and triumphs of poverty and resilience in Cameron Park. 'You notice,' she says, 'how today, Jesus Christ comes third, after the *Virgen* and Juan Diego.'

The Rio Grande Valley was ranched and farmed by a small number of great families before the border was drawn across it: two of which were the Ballí and Hinojosa dynasties from whom Cecilia is descended — great ranchers and owners of land. In many ways, both grandiose and bitter, the history of the valley and the border is the history of the Ballí family, which once owned — but was swindled out of — Padre Island, and proved so in a lengthy court case, a judge in Brownsville ruling in favour of the extended family in 2000. Ms Ballí wrote in the magazine *Texas Monthly* that the victory 'was for all of us to relish. In a way, its story is universal. For it is a story about how some people are washed out of their own histories.' Even more important, though, was the 'deep sense of pride and rootedness that these families share'. Cecilia's father had 'died sick on a hospital bed, and other than a little bit of pride and lots of love, he couldn't leave us much. He was a cab driver with cancer. He was forty-one. But he left us a special last name, and there lay the treasure.'

Cecilia Ballí and I drive across the land her own immediate family comes from, south of the border, stretching like low polder under an expansive but leaden winter sky towards the sea. We pass a small store – 'That belongs to a relative,' she says – then a huddle of green houses where her mother was raised, and further down the ranch where her father grew up. Along a fence beside the road, a man wearing a straw cowboy hat has hung a particularly up-market selection of *ropa usada* for sale, with a fine old Wrangler shirt to buy. 'I remember your grandfather,' he says. 'I drove a tractor on his ranch; I pasteurised and sold milk.' Past a gas station and the inevitable Oxxo store on Highway 5, a road leads off to the left. At its entrance are a buvette selling beer called Minisuper Bisby and three parked buses. It is not a road down which one turns, says Cecilia – it leads to the ranch where Osiel Cárdenas was raised. The ranch along that road itself constitutes a kind of wayside 'historical marker' in the narrative of Mexico's narco-cartel culture. Ms Ballí argues that it helps explain a shift in the social composition of the region's drug cartel, which she believes perfected the style of violence now seen in all of Mexico. 'Osiel Cárdenas comes from a very poor family that lived just on the fringes of a Mexican border city, literally and metaphorically. His predecessors in the Gulf cartel tended to be businessmen and to come from the middle-class, or at least from well-connected families. Osiel didn't initially have the same kind of access to politics and politicians. His way into the business was by becoming a federal cop. He represents the poor urban underclass that the Mexican government has always neglected, whose men basically have two options to genuinely climb out of poverty: go work on the other side of the border or join the trade.'

And what happens to these poor young men coming into the business for the first time? 'They finally get to experience power, what it is to be respected, and they're not as invested in the old social networks or political debts, in the old way of doing things. They don't just co-opt, they confront. The first thing Osiel did to become the boss was kill his associate; that's a departure from the past. People talk about him being particularly violent as a person, and once his enforcers, who came to be known as the 'Zetas', formed, they began branding a new style of violence, and it's a style that other cartels in Mexico have learned to match.' 'Style' is not a word Ballí uses lightly; she develops her own point in Chapter Five about the murders of women in Juárez. 'People say this is all about money,' she notes, 'but I think it's about money and something more. It's a social performance, a show of power, a very masculine form of power. They are saying, "We are somebodies," in a country where that was not supposed to be possible for men of their class. I think in some ways, the willingness of Mexico's rich to ignore the poor is coming back to haunt them. This isn't the poor's revenge on the rich; they are simply finding their own way to wealth and to social recognition. Especially since the old avenues for becoming a man in Mexico – you got married, found a job and supported your family – are shifting. Some men are now opting to establish their manhood this way, and this is hurting everyone.'

And yet even the cartel forms part of this narrative, of heritage, place and identity, argues Ms Ballí. 'The cartel here does still have ties to the community. People here know their names, they know who they are. Maybe they grew up or went to school together, or married distant relatives. And although they've gone national and international, their leadership is still from north-eastern Mexico and they're proud of it. They celebrate its music, its language. Regional identity is extremely strong in Mexico, and these guys like to assert the fact that they're from Tamaulipas and from the border, a place the rest of Mexico has always shunned. You see this pride displayed on the Internet, in YouTube clips extolling the Gulf cartel and the Zetas, and in the way they decorate their trucks. We like to talk about 'imagined communities' in academia, and I think the Mexican cartels have done an impressive job of harnessing those regional and communal identities, so that people almost root for them the way they would root for their soccer teams. And so when we talk about their struggles to retain control of their territories, we're not just talking about drug routes; we're talking about their ability to say, "This is our place." I think this is something that distinguishes the Gulf cartel from others. Aside from *La Familia* in Michoacán, the other cartels are made up of people who have moved around various states in northern and north-western Mexico, many of them originally from Sinaloa. The guys who took over Tijuana were from Sinaloa, not from Tijuana.' *Diles Quién Eres*: the Zetas, too, are telling who they are.

'People here don't condone drug trafficking,' says Ms Ballí, 'but they understand where it comes from. I think we're at an interesting crossroads now, though. The community is more silenced than ever, and everyone understands that something has been lost – something pretty big has been lost. The cross-border life that was so special about this place is changing every day.'

There's a joke they tell in Matamoros: first day of term and the schoolteacher welcomes the new children, supervised by the principal. 'All children with names beginning A to M sit over here,' says the principal, and they do. 'All children with names beginning N to Y sit over there.' And they do. 'What about children with names beginning with Z?' asks the teacher. 'Oh, they can sit wherever they want,' replies the principal crossly. The alternative, more sinister ending goes: 'Children with names beginning with what?' replies the principal, terrified.

The claw marks of artillery shells that pock-marked the walls of Sarajevo or Grozny do not usually form part of the landscape of the narco war, but in Matamoros they do, at the site of a shoot-out between the Zetas and the army during Autumn 2009, beside a construction site and *Tacos al Vapor* stand on Primera Street in a smarter neighbourhood of town not far from the river, nor very far from army headquarters bunkered down in a storage depot, with its heavy gate, security lodge, sentries and visible fleet of parked jeeps. According to eyewitnesses, the shooting lasted two hours after the army tried to stop a car, which then ran the soldiers' roadblock. The Zetas, apparently already in position to cover the car, reportedly took nine casualties, according to the unconfirmable *susurro*, the army admitting to none. After the incident, the Zetas are said to have sealed off the area and – giving tactical purpose to the exercises in Reynosa – boarded buses, ordered passengers off and took the keys.

I talked for a while, sitting on a wall, with a man called 'Arturo', from Monterrey, now living in Matamoros and the only person I met there prepared to discuss the Zetas. If they call them the '*Pirámide*' in Nuevo Laredo and the 'last letter of the alphabet' up the road in Reynosa, I asked him, what are they called here? 'We just say "The Letter",' said 'Arturo'. 'Half the town works for The Letter one way or another. The only way to avoid them is do things like make sure that your car insurance is in order, because some day either you're going to get hit or someone'll make sure you get hit, and there's a fifty per cent chance that the owner of the other car will be working for The Letter. You better make sure that any damage gets paid off quick, with full third-party insurance because you don't want to be owing anything to anyone in Matamoros. Because they won't just come for your car, they'll come wanting your house, every-thing you have, and *you*.' The Zetas, he confirms, 'shake down everyone in town. From big business to the small vendors, the taco stands, the mariachis. They all need to commit to The Letter people, nothing happens in Matamoros without them. So there's no war here, apart from between the army and the cartel, though for a while it was between the cartel and The Letter. Now, The Letter people have the police on their side, and I don't think the army can ever really beat them.'

The PRI mayor of Matamoros, Erick Silva Santos, graciously agrees to meet me and a colleague – Dudley Althaus of the *Houston Chronicle*, for whom this is familiar terrain – without an appointment. He talks in detail about his initiatives to combat organised crime with educa-tional opportunities, social and economic policy, and confirms – in a usefully coded remark – that 'there are no street gangs, as such' in Matamoros, 'you will see no graffiti on the walls'. It is true, almost (apart from a rough-looking estate along *Avenida Manuel Cavazos Lerma*: everything is under control). Mayor Silva insists: 'We are not in a war zone. This is a conflict between the government armed forces and a group of narco traffickers,' who, he concedes, 'have very sophis-ticated equipment and weapons'. But, he says, 'I have nothing at all to do with this fight. The law does not permit us in the municipal city hall to intervene. The law does not permit me to mobilise the munic-ipal police to intervene in narco traffic.' How very convenient. We ask if he has any information on the shoot-out that week down by army headquarters. 'I have no authority to ask the army to give me infor-mation on casualties or anything else.'

After this encounter with a man really grappling with the crisis, Althaus and I adjourn for lunch at a restaurant that is a silent

Matamoros landmark. Only Althaus can remember why, from his days as a reporter on the *Brownsville Herald* over the river. The simmering violence in Matamoros was inevitably part of his beat, and Althaus covered the murder of a gangster called Casimiro Espinoza – reportedly on orders from the Godfather of the old-time racket in town, Juan N. Guerra. 'This was nineteen eighty-four,' remembers Althaus. 'We heard the news and came right across – it was my first ever story in Matamoros. "*El Cacho*", they used to call Espinoza [the horn]. He was the only other serious gangster in town that was anything like a threat to Guerra. And Guerra made sure to rub him out. I think that was when we first heard the name of Juan García Abrego, who was said to be behind the killing: he was Guerra's nephew, and ran the Gulf cartel until ninety-six, after which Osiel took it from there. Looking back, that killing of Espinosa was when they consolidated power. Félix Gallardo was still running the federation down in Guadalajara, but that murder was, with hindsight, the birth of the Gulf cartel. This is when the old man Guerra used to sit at the back of this restaurant, holding court, and talk horse-racing.' The restaurant has thus been renamed 'Don Juan's', and the sign represents his favourite horse, riding crop and hat. The real hat hangs from the wall inside. We eat well, the service is polite, only the man behind the bar fixes us all the while with dead, unshining eyes, cold as steel and ice.

Back from the sentry posts leading to Osiel Cárdenas' ranch, Cecilia Ballí and I sit at a beach café on a windswept winter afternoon, the sun throwing spears of light, which children call 'ladders to heaven', onto the sea from behind battleship-grey clouds, creating ponds of light on the ocean's indigo surface. The rain comes ashore, and clusters of Sunday trippers bring their seafood, fries and chowder beneath the shelter that was built to be shade from sunshine – this is Padre Island, proven by the court in Brownsville to have been the rightful property of the Ballís. 'There are special dynamics on the border that you don't find anywhere else,' Cecilia says. 'For instance, there's a different sense of time along this part of the border. These communities in the valley, especially the ones on the Mexican side of the river, date back to the eighteenth century, which in Europe may not seem old, but in the United States means a lot. We've been here almost as long as the Thirteen Colonies.

'But ever since Mexico lost this region to the United States, Mexican Americans in Texas have always been made to feel like foreigners, even though this has been their home – our home – for generations. After the border was drawn, we began to psychically experience a gradual process of separation from Mexico, though of course culturally and socially some of the ties remained. Because Mexico is right there all the time, there's always that sense of threat of the "Other", and Mexican Americans constantly have to prove that they're American enough. When I was growing up we were made to feel embarrassed that our parents didn't speak English, even though most people in Brownsville were Mexicans. That's changing now with more immigration and the rise of a public Latino identity in the United States, which allows us not to have to hide who we are. The valley itself has changed a lot; now you hear Spanish regardless of where you are. But there's still that double movement happening. There's a cultural and emotional connection with Mexico, but most people live it on this side of the border, with other Mexicans who are here. Those of us who actually cross the border back and forth are statistically a minority. So here in the valley, Mexican Americans are becoming both more Mexican and more American at the same time, if that makes sense. I always wonder: Why are people so surprised when they come to the valley and find that Mexican Americans are really patriotic? That all our kids are signing up for the army? Well, if all your life people have questioned whether you belong, you find yourself having to *prove* that you're an American.'

One of the ways for teenaged boys to prove their American-ness has been to play the all-American game better than the Anglo-Americans – high school football. The book, film and television series *Friday Night Lights* was set in Midland and Odessa back in west Texas, but nowhere is Friday-night fever for the local team fiercer than in two small, poor towns joined at the hip in the Rio Grande Valley, Elsa and Edcouch. Sam Vale had said: 'The problem with Elsa is it's too far north from the border, too far east of McAllen and too far west of Brownsville.' But he was talking about the town's battered economy, not about the Yellow Jackets football team.

Indeed, Elsa is not on the way from anywhere to anywhere in particular. Most major employers, apart from the school district, have left or gone bankrupt – but the place has a sanguine, resilient feel to it; it is gladsome and vivacious. There is no way a visitor is going to get in and out of the Valero gas station or Stripes store without an affable interrogation, and the boys at the Elsa Body Shop fixing up cars that most garages would give up for dead are happy to carry on a companionable chat about the Yellow Jackets, even when they are lying back under the vehicle, spanners in hand.

In the Gladiator's stadium at Roma, the home stand is sparsely populated, for all their cheerleaders in mini-togas and a march-past by male pupils dressed as legionnaires and centurions carrying plastic imperial *fasci* and standards. The away stand, though, is another matter: packed, the brass band giving it what for, cheerleaders waving golden pom-poms, crowds whooping and yellow-and-amber flags waving, with pictures of bees on them. Roma is a good ninety minutes' drive from Edcouch-Elsa, but it feels like half the population has made the journey, even on a Thursday evening. Among the crowd are four generations of the Montalvo Flores family, from seventy-seven-year-old great-grandma Ida to little Deena, aged six. 'I graduated from Elsa high school in nineteen fifty,' Ida rasps above the noise, 'and hardly missed a game. I watch 'em wherever they go. You got to support the kids. We're such a small town, and we may be poor, but we're rich enough to buy our season tickets.' Her eyes glint from behind her spectacles. 'I'm sorry about my ugly *gringo* name,' she offers out of the blue, though Ida had sounded just fine to me. 'My mother's best friend was the midwife and my mother promised to name her baby after her.' An additional excitement is that one of the family, Isaac Prado (it is too complicated to work out how he fits genealogically, there are twenty of them in the party) is playing his last game before graduating. 'It's hard to take,' says his father, Enrique. 'He's wanted and waited to play for years and years, and so have we all, and this is the last time.' Isaac's girlfriend is a cheerleader, now sitting with the family.

So this thing between the cheerleaders and team stars isn't just a myth from *Friday Night Lights*, I ask my host for the evening, José Saldívar, who has driven all the way and will drive all the way back. 'Oh no,' says José, 'it's almost a requirement.' He hastens to add that he married a librarian. His father, also named José, has come with us, also a fanatic, season-ticket holder since he moved to Elsa in 1988. 'I could count on one hand the games I've missed.' Mr Saldívar fixes up classic and vintage cars for a living; mounted on bricks in his front yard. 'I'm working on a 55 Chevy right now.' The Edcouch-Elsa team for which José played in the 1990s is the envy of the valley, 'even though our town is not,' he says. 'Everyone resents us and everyone wants to beat us because we have the best record.' Elsa has won six district titles and made the state play-offs sixteen times, a tally unequalled by any team in the valley and for which the Yellow Jackets became more widely known as *La 'Maquina Amarilla* – the yellow machine.

Elsa and Edcouch, says José, were agricultural communities dating back to the 1920s; Elsa once boasted the largest fruit-packing shed in the world. In the 1970s and 80s, however, the fruit-picking and packing, and industries related to them, went into decline. In the period since, 'unemployment has been high and opportunities are scarce – the school district is the biggest employer, and they let two hundred people go last January [2009]. We're said to have the highest teenaged pregnancy rate in Texas. There's a lot of alcoholism even amongst the kids, a lot of drug abuse – a couple of my friends are in jail for dealing.' (In 2006, a mother in Elsa was targeted and killed in front of her children. In revenge, members of her family went in pursuit of the murderers and killed them. 'Zeta business,' says José.) 'But the more this defines the town, the more passionate it has become about the football,' he says. 'The nineteen fifty-nine team had been a legend during the good times, but now it's obvious why people are so enthused – football is all there is. *Friday Night Lights* was a story that needed to be told – we here just think it was told in the wrong town!

Tonight, *La Maquina Amarilla* prepares itself for the sack of Roma – another 100 per cent Hispanic team, but Roma has never beaten Edcouch-Elsa and although 2009 has not been a good year for the Yellow Machine, 'even on a bad season, it's a big thing to beat Elsa'. A scrappy game fails to impress either José or his father: 'It ain't the team it used to be,' laments José. Final score: Roma 14, Edcouch-Elsa 21. On the radio driving home, Elsa's famous sports show host Hugo de la Cruz hits the airwaves, reading the scoreboard as on any show, but diverting for a build-up of fanfares and *corridos* before announcing that from Roma tonight. A lady named Helen calls in and accuses Hugo of bias in favour of a team that didn't play that well. 'We're not supposed to diss the kids,' retorts Hugo. 'Anyhow, who won?'

'It's interesting that it was American football,' José says, at the wheel, Dad in the back, as we pass through Rio Grande City on the way to the game. 'The town is poor and Mexican American, and soccer is the Mexican sport, but it never really got hold in Elsa, and in the valley only as first-generation migrants arrived. The people that were born here grew up with American football and wanted to play American football.' In the mid '80s, Hugo de la Cruz began doing commentaries of games on local radio – 'He became an institution across the valley,' says José, 'a must-hear for all football fans, but everyone knew he was Elsa through and through so he got people pissed, and the more he got people pissed, the more they wanted to hear his show – it was a bit like the team.' But beneath this burning sporting ambition cuts a rip-tide of ethnic identity. 'Our town is one hundred per cent Mexican American,' says José. 'Our team was always one hundred per cent Mexican American and one hundred per cent working class. And I can remember the coaches being pretty up front about it, when we went to play teams that were Anglo and more affluent. We wanted to beat the pants off them, being who we were and where we came from. One coach in particular used to tell us in the dressing room: "Come on, guys, do it for the *Raza*", for the race. He'd say it even if there was only a handful of white kids in the other team! And oh man, we wanted to beat them so bad; there's no doubt it made us play harder. In the 'fifties, playing football was a way to prove that you were an American, to break the segregation barrier. I've heard about Mexican Americans walking into the chemistry class and being told to 'get out to your cotton fields where you belong!' – and that's where it started, needing to prove yourself on the football field. But it carried on after desegregation. So long as you were Latinos you were made to feel foreigners in your own country, and playing the Anglos, you were going out there to make a point and beat their ass. It helped, to be honest, that the game is physical – who's the toughest, who can beat up who. It was a way of knocking someone out legally, without getting arrested.'[25]

José Saldívar now teaches at Harlingen College, at a midway point between McAllen and Brownsville, a town very much in the Rio Grande Valley, but at its portal. When you turn your back on Harlingen and drive north, the palm trees thinning and eventually disappearing into the great flatlands of south-east Texas, towards the metropolis of Houston, you leave the border behind you, but not the borderland.

* * *

There is a perverse beauty in the landscape arraigned below the iron bridge where Highway 255 strides the Houston Ship Channel: great towers of light and fire as far as the eye can behold; sinewy steel piping, plumes of smoke and flame twinkling into a Texas night wrapped by a shroud of pollution hanging from the sky. It has long been said that, as the author Sam Quiñones puts it, 'Los Angeles is Mexico's culture factory.'[26] And that the gangland style and 'pseudo-romantic culture of drug trafficking' are in many ways exports from Los Angeles to Mexico.[27] This is no doubt true. But in the new landscape, according to the new and altered maps since war broke out first in Nuevo Laredo and then across Mexico in late 2006, the Mexican narco capital of the United States has moved to the citadel of oil: Houston, Texas. As the Tijuana cartel collapses, and arteries of the narco transport routes into the heart of America follow those of trade, Houston becomes the gateway, the hub of the wheel. If LA is the old Imperial seat of Amexica, Juárez/El Paso its fulcrum, *Los Dos Laredos* its spinal cord, the capital metropolis of Amexica is now Houston.

In April 2008, Special Agent Carla Mayfield of the Bureau of Alcohol, Firearms, Tobacco and Explosives testified to a court in Houston about an investigation into serial purchases of 328 weapons from two branches of a gun dealer called Carter Country by a circle of twenty-two people, notably one John Philip Hernández. Hernández was an unemployed machinist, arrested a few weeks beforehand, with most of the rest of his ring still at large. According to Special Agent Mayfield, twenty-eight of these firearms – purchased for a total of $352,134.04 – had been recovered in Mexico and Guatemala. The case was only the tip of an iceberg, but one of the very few that documented and illustrated the flow of the Iron River from Houston to the Zetas – for once, named in open court. Hernández had himself used his Texas driver's license number 15436960 to buy twenty-three firearms costing nearly $25,000. One reappeared in Puebla, 'during an incident in which a businessman was kidnapped and murdered'. Another emerged in Oaxaca, 'during an incident in which Los Zetas . . . opened fire on the Mexican army'. A weapon Hernández bought on 12 July 2006, read the court papers, 'was recovered in Acapulco, Guerro (sic) Mexico. This incident is commonly referred to as the "Acapulco police massacre", due to the fact that more than a dozen armed assailants attacked two offices of the state attorney general and executed four police officers and three secretaries.'[28] In November 2009, another case came out of the sting at Carter Country: a windscreen repairman called Christian Garza was charged in Houston – and pleaded guilty – with a role in a wider conspiracy to traffic more than 300 weapons across the border to the Zetas.[29]

In 2008 alone, 200 indictments were issued against straw buyers working for twelve arms-trafficking rings along the US border with Mexico. Border checks of southbound vehicle crossings have been stepped up by both US and Mexican customs. But there remain elements integral to US national gun law which militate against effective action. A ban on assault weapons passed by the Clinton administration in 1994 expired in 2004, with no attempt by George W. Bush to re-impose it and President Obama shying away from a confrontation with the gun lobby. There is no computerised national gun database or registry in the USA – investigations and convictions depend on a paper trail. Records of gun sales remain with dealers, so that it is up to the ATF to take the initiative if a gun is recovered at a crime scene, or the dealer if he or she suspects a buyer – indeed, the system depends on tips and audits, with most dealers happy to cooperate with the ATF.

'All our investigations show that Houston is the number-one source for firearms going from the US into Mexico, number-one source in the country,' says the man in midstream of the Iron River's flow, Dewey Webb, Special Agent in Charge of the ATF's Houston office, which covers a vast tranch of east Texas and the borderland as far as Del Rio, opposite Ciudad Acuña – in effect, the territory controlled by the Gulf cartel and Zetas. It is the largest ATF region and the easternmost on the border, neighbouring those run from Dallas, Phoenix and Los Angeles.

Webb is an interesting man, a Native American from Oklahoma City (he wears his ATF ID on a tag round his neck made of turquoise jewellery). He has devoted his life to the Bureau, having joined in the 1970s and worked all over Texas. He is a large man and chooses his words carefully but talks with estimable transparency and honesty about the scale of the problem facing him, and with that mixture of moral contempt and professional respect for his quarry that makes

the difference between a good and a great cop. He turns a scheduled one-hour briefing into a three-hour conversation on a wet
December afternoon in his unmarked office near Houston
Intercontinental airport. In the reception area are plaques honouring
the four agents the ATF lost in the siege of Waco up the road in
1993.

Webb opens, against the received wisdom, by saying that the smuggling of arms to Mexico is now more commonly achieved by buying
from licensed dealers than from gun shows, and that the Ports of
Entry used by everyone else far outstrip consignments across open
land. Smuggling guns, he says, is an entirely different kind of operation to smuggling drugs, demanding different expertise, 'mainly
because a gun just weighs so much, and it's so bulky', needing to be
dismantled, taken through the border in parts for reassembly. When
he first joined the service, Webb recalls, the drug gangs were serviced with 'occasional trafficking from the US. People would call
relatives to get weapons, and there were arms going down for political unrest in Mexico.' Often, weaponry would be trafficked by boat.
Recently, though, 'we've seen an upsurge in this war, fighting for
territory and needing the weaponry to fight for territory, and I've
seen both a surge in the volume and a change in the nature of the
weaponry: we're now looking at high-calibre rifles, high-quality
equipment – AR-15 rifles and a couple of dozen variations. They
want the top of the line, very high-quality weapons.' Some of the
guns are bought in Houston, he says, but 'a lot is carried down here
to Texas from places like Chicago, Minneapolis-St Paul and Michigan
– Washington State was always a hot spot. This happened after we
put a lot of effort into this area after it started off in Laredo in
2005. So Houston is both source and hub city, while in the Rio
Grande Valley it's a smaller fish bowl and easier to see what's going
on, the flags get raised quicker.'

It is not Webb's job to comment on gun, or gun control, policy –
not least because he relies in part on the cooperation of the vast
majority of honest dealers and to an extent on the industry. Besides,
no one knows guns better than he does. But he asserts clearly: 'So long
as we in the United States make it easy for these people to buy weapons,
we will be the easy touch for these criminals. Texas has 8,000 gun
dealers, and in the city of Houston, there are 1,500. The pattern we're

seeing is that they'll go to the shows to buy ammo and supplies, combat gear, and so on, and to the dealers to get their weapons, using straw buyers for fifty dollars per gun, on up. They come, and they just keep coming back . . . It's simple because we make it simple. There's no black market in the US, the guns are not being stolen – it's all legal: you can make fifty dollars a day going to two or three dealers. But there are still red flags: when a woman goes asking for a large rifle or if the dealer just asks the right questions.'

'Don't Lie For The Other Guy' is a campaign Webb's agency has launched as it starts to punch into the straw-buying networks like that run by Hernández, along with the National Safety Shooting Foundation. Webb needs to work with gun-owners and users, not against them. Yes, he concedes, much of the military-calibre hardware comes from Central America: 'If they need a weapon, and they can't get it in the US, they'll get it from somewhere else.' But, he insists, 'the bottom line is that the United States is the nearest, the cheapest and the easiest place to buy – for the cartels to get their weapons. But there is at last a wind of change, for the better, says Webb. 'For one, the agencies on our side are on the same page.' Secondly, 'we're working with the Mexican authorities in a more proactive way, we got more people in Mexico, running more agents'. The vetting procedures for Mexican hires have improved, he says, gratefully. And accordingly: 'we're getting more results', and understanding the cartels better: 'They're very smooth in their operations and the way they do business. They're managed like corporations, until it gets to the violence. Sometimes they want a gun because they want a gun. We're seeing them wanting the best: Mac 10s, Mac 11s, AR-15s, 9mm pistols – they want high-quality weapons. They want better weapons than I've seen in thirty-three and a half years. But then sometimes they want a gun because they saw it on TV. Then they get kind of like a wannabe Scarface. Then there's the fact that they all have the same trend: they have to defend their territory. And for that, they are busting each other's heads, and I know for a fact that it's costing them dear.' The cartels, says Webb, 'are also looking for alternative sources of income: human trafficking, kidnapping for ransom, and I've seen the cartels involved in oil'. But in the end, it comes down to the drugs. 'If people were not buying the dope, they wouldn't have the money to buy the guns, that's the bottom line.'

So far, Webb's efforts against the smuggling from Houston itself have focused on three cells, including Hernández', and 328 traced weapons taken across the border by them alone. In January 2009, the authorities in Houston also arrested ten members of a gang called Tango Blast Houstone, indicting four more on the run, for distributing marijuana and cocaine for the Gulf cartel from Houston. The arrests highlighted the position at the centre of the wheel of Houston's gang culture and gangland in the business of the cartels, using their contacts across the state, and thence the country, to distribute drugs. The arrests followed an investigation by both Webb's agents and those of the FBI – who noticed important differences between this new gang and those to which they had become accustomed over time – markedly the old-guard Texas Syndicate, established across jails in Texas and California during the 1960s. The differences between the two gangs echo the changes between the 'classic' and the new wave narcos across the border. Behind the glass façade of its new headquarters in Houston, FBI agents involved in busting both generations of gangs talk about the varied ways in which they put themselves at the disposition of the cartels, with very different structures. The agents give their names, even present business cards, but prefer not to be named. The expert in the Texas Syndicate – we'll call him 'James' – is chisel-jawed, terrifyingly fit with a vice-grip handshake and as courteous as he is direct. The agent who masterminded the bust of Tango Blast is more quietly spoken and considered, and we'll call him 'Mark'. There is also a woman at the briefing, who studies gangland patterns, movement and psychology, by the name of 'Angela'.

The Texas Syndicate, says James, 'has a leadership structure, its members have ranks – the *Sillón* or chairman for each region, like a lieutenant, and soldiers called *carnales*. It's blood in, blood out – you kill to join, and you can never leave. You wear the tattoo and the gang is your family, even if you get old, leave jail, go into business or have a proper family. Many of them live a low profile – they'll be family men in regular houses who hold down jobs, don't draw attention to themselves – some of them are middle-aged by now. They'll hold *Juntas* – meetings and assemblies – where they hold votes or discuss disciplining members.' The Texas Syndicate, which grew in response to the power of other criminal gangs in

California's jails, fits into the national network of gang affiliations and rivalries which an annual report by the Justice Department monitors in its role as distribution network for the narco cartels. James says that sometimes, 'if there is a business opportunity, you'll see the gangs put their differences aside.

'It's historical,' continues James – 'formed in California and grew in Texas, and they have been major dope traffickers over the years. Some are very big drug dealers indeed – and they are killers.' Tango Blast, however, is a bigger, wider, looser organisation. 'It's more fluid than the Texas Syndicate; a bit like Facebook,' says Mark. 'The gang changes according to what you need that day, from who, to do what. There's no blood in, blood out, no initiation rite that we know of, no set rules. One day, you need a guy who can bring in five kilos, so you deal with him, and make the contacts you need to get it where you need. Next week, you need to pick up and shift twenty kilos from someone else, and you may use different contacts. That's what makes it the biggest gang in Houston – we estimate about twenty thousand members in the city of Houston, a lot of people doing different criminal activities, that don't necessarily know each other like in a traditional gang structure. It's part of the time we're in – they're kids, they have no code, no rules.' Sometimes, says Angela, 'you'll get kids committing crimes just so they can get sent to jail to find the gang, and join. We're seeing a lot of young guys trying to join, it's the cool thing to do, the in thing to be. So in addition to the gang members, you get a lot of wannabe gang members who then become criminals, go to jail, and become gang members. There's a lot of prestige, there's the opportunity to make money, there's a intimate sense of belonging to a brotherhood – knowing that if I would kill for them, they would kill for me.'

Ironically, 'the tight structure of the Texas Syndicate makes it possible to plan strategies against them, dismantle cells by filling in the spaces', says James, while, 'the fact that Tango Blast doesn't have that kind of structure makes it harder to catch them', says Mark. 'Only the thing that makes it a little easier, is that they don't know how to hide. Not like [James] said about the Texas Syndicate keeping a low profile. When we bust these guys, they had luxury cars, Bentleys, Maseratis, diamond jewellery.' One of the men this team is most eager to find is one Raul Madrigal, who taunts them from file photographs: basking in a bubblebath, posing on a beach and even sticking up a finger – all from Mexico. Madrigal allegedly made so much money helping the Gulf cartel pump marijuana and cocaine into the US through Houston that the FBI has sequestered £18 million in assets and nine luxury cars, including a Bentley Sedan and two Maseratis, and a three-wheel motorbike with ostrich-skin seats.[30]

Dane Schiller of the *Houston Chronicle* monitors the city's underworld connections to the cartels across the border as both a job and a personal fixation. Schiller's work locates the narco hub of Amexica firmly in Houston – not just for the distribution of drugs and cash, and the procurement of guns, but for killing. Killing like that of Santiago '*Chago*' Salinas, a Gulf cartel operative shot in the head at point-blank range in 2006 at the Baymont Inn and Suits on the Gulf Freeway, three weeks after his brother-in-law was found dead, charred in a barrel of diesel near Monterrey across the border in Mexico. It had been the third attempt on Salinas' life in one year – he had been left for dead after the first, in Mexico, when a bullet intended to kill him went through his jaw. According to Schiller, the person believed responsible for that first shooting was Daniel 'Danny Boy' Zamora, who had grown up in Houston and was part of an enforcement crew for the Sinaloa cartel – himself later killed in a shoot-out in Mexico. A second attempt on Salinas' life was made in 2006 at a Mexican seafood restaurant in Houston called *Chilos* – also on the Gulf Freeway, only this time the spotters got the wrong man, killing a maintenance worker in front of his family. But the third attempt killed Salinas, as he answered the door of room 142 at the Baymont: this time the killer was believed to be Danny Zamora's younger brother, Jaime, a former employee of the Houston Parks Department – accused of the murder and that of the innocent man in the seafood restaurant car park. Jamie Zamora has since pleaded guilty to trafficking in cocaine and awaits trial in Houston for capital murder, to which charge he pleads not guilty. In another case, a married couple were found tortured to death in their home on Eastwood Drive in north-west Houston, 220 lbs of cocaine found in the attic, and the nephew of Osiel Cárdenas himself, Pedro Cárdenas, was left dead in a ditch in nearby Madden County.[31]. What intrigues Schiller most, though, are two things: how the profits from all these drugs, the spoils of this war, vanish into the economy of the United States, and the figure of Osiel Cárdenas himself.

In 1999, Schiller learned, two agents from the FBI and DEA were escorting an informant around Matamoros in a jeep, and were surrounded by Zeta troops. Cárdenas appeared, and — thinking better of executing all of them — demanded that the informant be handed over. The agents argued: 'If you do that, it'll be Kiki Camarena and Félix Gallardo all over again. They'll fight you to the bitter end.' Osiel Cárdenas let the convoy go. At every hearing of Cárdenas' trial, which ended with his conviction in February 2010, Schiller was there and at every hearing, he was asked to leave. 'It happens every time: there I am, the only person in the public or press gallery. And every time, the marshal comes and tells me to go and wait outside. So I wait, and then it's over and time to go. It's all being done in secret again, and it's getting kind of interesting that everything is being done in secret,' says Schiller of the days before the conviction. 'That whatever plea bargains Osiel Cárdenas is being offered, he must be giving them something pretty good in return. If this man is who they say he is, and what they say he is, then he's in a position to answer quite a few questions in front of the jury box. But it never happens, and it's incredibly frustrating. This man holds the secrets of what is going on, this unlikely Al Capone, and they're making damned sure to keep them from us.' Finally, on 23 February 2010, Schiller got to write this story: 'Behind armed guards and locked doors — in a secret hearing of judicial privacy not even given to some 9/11 terrorists or east-coast Mafia dons — Osiel Cárdenas Guillén, one of the most feared drug lords in history, was sentenced to twenty-five years in prison Wednesday. In a Houston courtroom sealed to the public, he also was ordered to forfeit $50 million, a small slice of his estimated earnings.[32]

'The famed drug lord has not been seen publicly since he was ushered in shackles into a Houston courtroom in 2007 to be read his rights when he arrived in Texas,' wrote Schiller. 'Despite a protest from the *Houston Chronicle* on Wednesday that the public had a right to be present for the sentencing of one of the most hunted men in recent times — in a case that has cost American taxpayers millions — US District Judge Hilda Tagle kept the hearing closed without explanation.' Which brings Schiller to his other point. 'Where does it all go, the cash?', he asks rhetorically, over breakfast in a diner next to a Shell gas station west of downtown Houston. During Spring and Summer of 2010, as this book goes to press, the unimpeachable Bloomberg financial news service dropped two bombshells into this discourse – and those leading to it with Lee Morgan the former customs officer and Don Ford the former dope-smuggler – opening the door to a staircase leading to the next level of Mexico's war. Bloomberg reported an admission to federal prosecutors by the Wachovia Bank, now owned by Wells Fargo, that it had failed to stop the laundering of at least $110 million of cartel money through exchange houses it operated in Mexico, and failed to monitor a staggering $420 billion in transactions through the so-called 'Casas de Cambio' in Mexico, between 2003 and 2008 – the crucial years in Mexico's bloodbath. Wachovia, bought by Wells Fargo at the end of 2008, paid $160 million to resolve a criminal investigation into how drug dealers used Wachovia accounts to buy planes, at least four of which had been seized by US and Mexican authorities, loaded with more than 20,000 kilos of cocaine.

In the US District Court in Miami, Wachovia admitted 'serious and systematic' violations of the federal Bank Secrecy Act, while Jeffrey Sloman, US District Attorney for the Southern district of Florida said the bank's 'blatant disregard of our banking laws gave international cocaine cartels a virtual carte blanche to finance their operations'. A further Bloomberg article quoted a former director of the bank's anti-laundering unit in London, Martin Woods, as saying that he quit the bank in disgust after executives ignored his warnings of laundering by drug cartels. 'If you don't see the correlation between the money laundering by banks, and the 22,000 people killed in Mexico, you're missing something', said Woods. (Wells Fargo co-operated with the investigation, and prosecutors said they had no evidence that the now parent bank's anti-laundering programme is deficient.)[33] 'The fifty billion dollars' profit from dealing drugs into America. I'm no accountant, but it blows my mind. Or am I crazy? What I'm thinking is: If you, the United States, are not lying to us, then where is this money? Where are these people handling the money? Who are they? I know that the guys on the ground in law enforcement in this town want to go through that door. They know this is the centre of things now, in this war, and that's where the answer lies. But that's a hell of a door to go through.'

El Negro Sol –
The Black Sun

In ancient Mexican lore, there lies behind the sun that shines, a Black Sun which leaves this world to shed light upon another, beneath. The Mexica believed the Black Sun was carried by the god of the underworld, and was the maleficent herald of death, though not death as finality. The Mexica lived in a condition of expectation of calamity and catastrophe, yet their preoccupation with death was a blend of fear and devotion to the moment of reunion with their ancestors, in the land upon which the Black Sun shines. And behind the sunlight of the deserts of Amexica – which turns to fire during eventide – there is some maculate, black light that gives nothing back; unshining behind the eternities of space and sky, or the bustle and music in all those labyrinthine streets lined with hot peppers and freshly gathered pistachios tumbling from every open storefront.

And one feels the rays of that dichotomous black sunshine especially after talking to Dr Hiram Muñoz, of the forensic autopsy team back in Tijuana, where all this began. This is a man who sees the world very clearly, from the slabs on which the saprophytic corpses are laid for inspection. Dr Muñoz defines his work as: 'spending my life trying to scientifically interrogate people who cannot talk,' he says, 'who have suffered terrible pain, but now feel nothing. They can only communicate silently through the terrible things that have been done to them. I have to look for a cause, not a result. I have to rewind the movie, work out what was done, and why.' Why did he choose this job? 'Because I love medicine, and I love the law. And because I lost my father when I was eight years old, and in his last words, he told the doctors: "Whatever you do, do it freely, but with exactitude."'

Muñoz is a man of courtesy and exceptionally good humour. After discussing the various mutilations and their significance, he says that 'the principal message is to the other cartels. They want respect, they want to say "this is what we do", and sometimes they say it in written messages, too, perhaps a joke, like the emergency number to call. There's also a message to their own people, of course: "Toe the line, or we will do this to you. The more brutally we get you to do things, the more brutally they could happen to you."'

But there are gradations within these barbarities, and this is what fascinates Dr Muñoz. 'Sometimes they are done by a medical student, sometimes just by a butcher. It is the medical students who have something to say. They are the ones trying to speak to us. I look at a cut-off toe. How was it done? Was it done well? Was it done from the left or the right? If it was done well, exactly between the bones, the person is more dangerous. If the finger was wrapped up tight before it was cut, we know we are dealing with the medical student, employed by the cartel hierarchy. If it's just hacked off, we're dealing with a *mana*, a street thug. You need to cut it properly if you are going to send it to the victim's family, or the police.'

'That Alejandra girl,' he says, 'the model and cheerleader, I really don't think that was the work of someone working for *El Teo*, as we're told. There was nothing one could do with fingers broken that crudely. When we see women and children mutilated, that is very serious – it's probably not a direct target; they're doing it to show someone else they know how to do it, and to drive them mad.' Decapitation, 'as I told you last time you were here, that is another matter. Again, it is significant how well it was done. If it is done badly, it shows nothing more than savagery. But if it is done well, it's a primal message: "Not only are we going to kill you, we're going to cut you in pieces." It's a message to all of the kind from which the victim came.

'The difference is this: in what I would call normal times, I kill you and make you disappear. Now, they are shouting it, turning it into a kind of grotesque carousel around their territory. In normal conditions, the torture and killing is private, now it is a public execution using extreme violence, and this is significant, I think. We need to say one thing first, however: these people are drama queens. They think what they do makes them powerful, masters of the universe.

But they're not. Ultimately, what they do is pathetic. We have to remember that. They keep saying they're poor people – well, they're poor in culture, that's what they are. They have no culture. The narcos in the old days had been to school. They knew that to be king-pins, they had to provide light, hospitals and schools. That way, they could keep a low profile, win respect, and protect themselves. Félix Gallardo was a businessman, using the same commercial acumen as Carlos Slim, the mobile phone man. If you play by the rules, I leave you alone. If you cross the line, I destroy you. These new people just want luxury, power and more power until they get arrested or killed. That is why they are doomed, and that is why they say so much about our society. They reflect a society without values. I don't even think they are against our society, I think they're products of it. People without culture or values in a society without culture or values. A society that has gone from Frank Sinatra to that Fifty Cent man I see on television. They're both associated with criminals, almost everyone is if they really want to make it – but look at the difference between them! Fifty Cent is the new role model for the narco, Sinatra is old school – I know which I'd rather have. The new narcos are like Fifty Cent – he says it all, product of a society that's lost its way. Money and power are what counts.' Muñoz sees this point as reason to let out a raucous laugh. He is a big man, demonstrative. Can one be nostalgic for the golden age of corruption, I ask? There had been so much misplaced nostalgia for what Julián Cardona called the 'classical' era of narco cartels. Dr Muñoz retorts with another question: 'Do you prefer it like it is now?'

Dr Muñoz considers what this war means in historical terms I had not expected this conversation to comprise. Or maybe I had, when we met briefly and made sure to talk properly, later. 'Consider how all the great civilisations fall, the marks of their last days.' He cites ancient Rome, and 'the terrible nature of public execution in its final phase'. Torture and violent public execution had also marked, he says, 'the end of the Middle Ages and the Spanish Inquisition, as they gave way to Renaissance and science. There are these great moments of civilisation, of science, but they try to be bigger and better than they are, and when they fall, they resort to grotesque public execution. And I think we are now in a moment of crisis, in the culture of global business.'

Muñoz refers back to what he calls 'times of normality', when 'the *narcotraficante* saw himself as a kind of bandit, but also a gentleman, a *padron*. He would distribute generously, even if it was from prison, make sure the village had electric light, gifts for Mother's Day, presents for children. But this was no different from the manager of the *maquiladora* who allowed his workers a cigarette break or free coffee machine. It meant nothing sincere, it just kept everyone making the product.' Then he reaches for what I have been calling the post-modern or late capitalist, value-free and globalised phase of both society and the narco war: 'But what happens when this system reaches state of crisis?' asks Dr Muñoz. 'Look around you: recession, crisis, factories closing. The narco is in the same position as everyone else, and everyone else is in the same position as the narco. You must keep supremacy, you must keep control. The *narco-traficante* is the most global of all global businessmen, and now he must make you loyal or afraid. And he must do these public executions involving mutilation as a demonstration of power, as all these cultures do, in their final phases.'

I suggest that despite the heinous work he does, Dr Muñoz strikes one as a swarthy man who appreciates the sight of a pretty girl, a good wine, a good meal. 'I spend all day with the dead,' he replies, 'so I have a duty to love life, and live it to the full. When I am with my colleagues, we are always joking about death, and joking *with* death. I live like a man who sits eating a delicious taco on the street there, aware that every moment could be his last. One bullet, and he is dead.'

Notes

Prologue: Amexica

1. Molly Molloy, New Mexico State University, Las Cruces. 'Fronterizo List' bulletin, 31 December 2009. The only reliable count of the dead is that assiduously compiled for Molloy's invaluable 'Fronterizo List'. Molloy's collection of documents is the definitive historical record of the carnage in Juárez. • 2. Annual Report, Chamber of Commerce of Laredo, Texas, 2009 • 3. A good guide to border Spanglish can be found in *Cabo Bob's Mexican Slang*, published on slang101.com. • 4. Tomás Ybarra-Frausto: 'Rasquachismo', published in *Puro Border*, Luis Humberto Crossthwaite, John William Byrd and Bobby Byrd, eds., Cinco Puntos Press, El Paso, 2003, p. 191. • 5. Gloria Anzaldua, *Borderlands – La Frontera*, 1987, third edition, Aunt Lute Books, San Francisco, 2007, p. 25. • 6. As narrated throughout the English translation of Bernadino de Sahagún, *Historia General de las Cosas de Nueva Espana*, aka *A History of Ancient Mexico*, trans. Fanny R. Bandelier Fisk University Press, Nashville, 1932. • 7. Eduardo Matos Moctezuma, *Los Aztecas*, Consejo Nacional para la Cultura y Las Artes, Mexico City/Jaca, Milan, 1989, pp. 31–51. • 8. Interview with Dr Miguel Olmos Aguilera. See his '*Imaginando Fronteras: Representacion y Ficcion en la Frontera del Norte*', paper presented at '*La Frontera: Una Nueva Conception Cultural*', conference Universitad Piloto de Colombia, 2004. • 9. Alejandro Lugo, *Fragmented Lives, Assembled Parts*, University of Texas Press, Austin, 2008, pp. 20–24. • 10. The best history of the frontier itself is Leon C. Metz, *Border: The US-Mexico Line*, TCU Press, Fort Worth/Mangan Books, El Paso, 1989, p. 31. • 11. Ted Conover, *Coyotes*, Vintage, New York, 1987, p. xviii. • 12. Conversation with Roberto Saviano, Rome, 2008. • 13. Daniel Borunda, 'El Pasoans Stay Uneasy as Slayings

Continue', *El Paso Times*, 17 August 2008. • **14**. Chris Kraul, 'Captain Nemo is Grounded', *Los Angeles Times*, 14 December 2008. • **15**. Laurence Iliff, 'Mexico Drug Cartels' Banners Escalate Attacks Against President Calderón's Government', *Dallas Morning News*, 13 December 2008. • **16**. Diana Washington Valdez, 'Firearms in Mexico Have Ties to El Paso', *El Paso Times*, 13 December 2008. • **17**. 'Gunmen Kill Family of Mexican Drug Hero', CBS News/Associated Press, 23 December 2008. • **18**. 'TV Station Targeted in Attack', *Los Angeles Times* wire, 7 January 2009. • **19**. CNN/World Co., 4 February 2009. • **20**. Dan Glaister, 'US Surge Plan to Contain Mexico Drug Violence', *Guardian*, 10 January 2009. • **21**. Molloy, 'Fronterizo List,' 5 December 2009. • **22**. Stewart Powell et al., 'Mexico to Begin Receiving Drug-fighting Aid', *Houston Chronicle*, 4 December 2009. • **23**. Dudley Althaus, 'Zetas Terrorizing Border Outposts', *Houston Chronicle*, 14 December 2009. • **24**. 'Police Arrest Man Linked to Slayings of 2000', *El Paso Times*, 11 December 2009. • **25**. Committee to Protect Journalists, Press Release, 2 November 2009. • **26**. Mark Stephenson, Associated Press bulletin, 18 December 2009. • **27**. Tracy Wilkinson, 'Mexican Drug Raid Hero's Family Slaughtered', *Los Angeles Times*, 23 December 2009. • **28**. Associated Press, 8 January 2010 • **29**. Molloy, 'Fronterizo List'. • **30**. Ibid. • **31**. Associated Press, 31 December 2009.

1 La Plaza

1. Various articles by Alfredo Corchado in the *Dallas Morning News*, especially 30 May 2008, and Elaine Shannon, *Desperados*, Viking, New York, 1988, pp. 31–42. • **2**. Dudley Althaus, 'Cartels Have Mexican Citizens Trembling', *Houston Chronicle*, 19 July 2008. • **3**. For a full account of the American secret services' role in cocaine dealing and the contras, see Gary Webb, *Dark Alliance*, Seven Stories Press, New York, 1998; Shannon, *Desperados*; and Michael Levine, *The Big White Lie*, Thunder's Mouth Press, New York, 1993. • **4**. Don Winslow, *The Power of the Dog*, Arrow, New York, 2005, p. 103. • **5**. See Terrence Popper, *Drug Lord*, Demand Publications, Seattle, 1990, pp. 135–238. • 6. Statement by Anthony Placido, assistant administrator for intelligence, US Drug Enforcement Administration, before the US Senate Judiciary Committee on Crime and Drugs, 17 March 2009. • **7**. Tony Payan: 'The Drug War and the Border,' in *The Last Frontier, South Atlantic Quarterly*, Jane Juffer, ed. Fall 2006.

Duke University Press, 2006, pp. 864–865. • **8**. *Proceso*, no headline – part of summary of killings, 25 February 2009; and *Los Angeles Times*, wire service, 26 February 2009. • **9**. Tracy Wilkinson, 'Women Play Bigger Role in Mexico's Drug War', *Los Angeles Times*, 10 November 2009. • **10**. Marcela Turati, 'Chapos Contra Zetas', *Proceso*, 30 June 2009, and various articles by Alfredo Corchado, *Dallas Morning News*, during 2008. • **11**. Jorge Chabart, op-ed, *El Universal*, op-ed leader article, 20 December 2009. • **12**. Ken Ellingwood, 'Drug Cartel Boss Arturo Beltrán Leyva And The Luxurious RIPs of Mexico's Narcos', *Los Angeles Times*, 21 December 2009. • **13**. Tracy Wilkinson, 'Mexican Family Slaughtered As Drug Lords Take Revenge', *Los Angeles Times*, 23 December 2009. • **14**. See full account in Popper, op. cit., 1990. • **15**. For a full account of Carrillo Fuentes's takeover and running of the Juárez cartel, see Charles Bowden, *Down by the River*, Simon and Schuster, New York, 2002. • **16**. Tracy Wilkinson, 'El Chapo' Has Left the Building', *Los Angeles Times*, 3 December 2008. • **17**. *Los Angeles Times* wire, 18 June 2009. • **18**. *Corriere della Sera*, Milan, 2 October 2008. • **19**. Quoted on Fox News/Associated Press, 3 April 2009. • **20**. Private briefings with Mexican diplomatic sources, London, 2009, UK Interpol sources, London 2009, and US DEA sources, Washington DC, 2008. • **21**. Julia Preston and Samuel Dillon, *Opening Mexico*, Farrar, Straus and Giroux, New York, p. 500. • **22**. Ibid. • **23**. Dane Schiller, 'DEA Bribes Taint Late Mexican Drug Czar', *Houston Chronicle*, 13 May 2009. • **24**. Speaking on MSNBC Television, 9 April 2009. • **25**. Quoted in Leslie Berenstein and Sandra Dibble, 'Border Bloodshed Likely to Worsen', *San Diego Union-Tribune*, 5 October 2008. • **26**. Ken Ellingwood, 'US Shares Blame for Mexico Drug Violence', *Los Angeles Times*, 18 March 2009.

2 *Aqui Empieza la Patria – Here Begins the Homeland*

1. Pablo Vila: '*Identificaciones de Región, Etnia y Nación en la Frontera Entre Mexico-EU*', Universidad Autonóma de Ciudad Juárez, 2004, p.47. • **2**. See Luis Alberto Urrea, *Across the Wire*, Anchor, 1993. • **3**. For a full account of the 'Institute Set' and AFO drug smugglers, see Anne-Marie O'Connor: 'Seduction of a Generation', *Los Angeles Times Magazine*, 28 July 2002. • **4**. For a full account of Alfredo Hodoyán's abduction, and of what the US Embassy in Mexico City did and did not know about it, see

Julia Preston and Craig Pyes, 'Witness to Evil', *New York Times*, 18 August 1997. • **5**. Redaccion, *El Universal*, 25 January 2009; Marc Lacey, 'Mexican Man Admits Using Acid on Bodies', *New York Times*, 26 January 2009. • **6**. Rafael Morales Magaña, '*Edecán Era Informante*', *El Mexicano*, 13 August 2009. • **7**. Dudley Althaus, 'With Mexico's Violence, Nothing is Sacred', *Houston Chronicle*, 2 July 2009. • **8**. See Tim Gaynor, *Midnight on the Line*, Thomas Dunne Books/St Martin's Press, New York, 2009, 'Where Midnight Meets The Road', pp. 77–100. • **9**. See Alfonso Cortez Lara, Megan K. Donovan and Scott Whiteford, 'The All-American Canal Lining Dispute: An American Resolution over Mexican Groundwater Rights', *Frontera Norte* journal, Vol 21, num 41, Enero-Junio, 2009.

3 *El Camino del Diablo – The Devil's Highway*

1. Ruth M. Underhill et al, *Rainhouse and Ocean: Speeches for the Papago Year*, University of Arizona Pres, Tucson, 1997, pp. 89–115. • **2**. Pinau Merlin, *Desert Holes*, Arizona-Sonora Desert Museum Press, Tucson, 1999, pp. 51–53. • **3**. Stephen Trimble, *The People*, School of American Research Press, Santa Fe, 1993 p. 131. • **4**. Luis Alberto Urrea, *The Devil's Highway*, Little Brown, New York, 2004, p.85. • **5**. Richard Felger and Bill Broyles, eds., *Dry Borders*, University of Utah Press, Salt Lake City 2007, p. xiii. • **6**. For full accounts of the Wellton disaster, see Ken Ellingwood, *Hard Line*, Vintage, New York, 2004, and Urrea, op.cit. • **7**. See Metz, *The Border*, op.cit. pp. 385–395. • **8**. Quoted in Urrea, op.cit., p. 12. • **9**. Josh Meyer, 'Sinaloa Cartel May Resort To Deadly Force In US', *Los Angeles Times*, 6 May 2009. • **10**. Interviewed in Salt Lake City, November 2009 – real name withheld. • **11**. Joel Millman, 'Immigrants Become Hostages as Gangs Prey on Mexicans', *Wall Street Journal*, 10 June 2009. • **12**. Ibid. • **13**. For a history of Pitiquito and its mission and church, see Claudio Murrieta, 'Las Paredes Hablan,' Pitiquito, 2004. • **14**. *L'Expreso* (Hermosillo), by La Redaccion, 30 October 2009; and Tracy Wilkinson, 'Mexican Farm-Workers Activist and 14 Others Slain', *Los Angeles Times*, 1 November 2009. • **15**. Winston P. Erickson, *Sharing the Desert: The Tohono O'odham in History*, University of Arizona Press, 1994, p. 25. • **16**. ibid, pp. 69–70. • **17**. Underhill et al, op cit, pp 17–37. • **18**. Ralph Vartabedian, 'US Soldiers, Law Officers Snared in Border Drug Sting', *Los Angeles Times,* 13 May 2005. Also Brenda Norrell, 'US Soldiers Ran Border Cocaine Operation', *Censored News* 23 July 2007, and 'Army Soldiers Sentenced In Drug Sting', *Arizona Daiy Star* • **19**. Carol Ann Alaimo, 'FBI: Military Recruiters Ran Cocaine', *Arizona Daily Star*, 17 December 2006 and Narcosphere.com, 'FBI: Recruiters Caught in Drug Probe' www.unsolvedmysteries.com/usm469076.html?t=conspiracy. • **20**. For a history of the *narcocorrido* genre and Los Tigres' career, see Elijah Wald, *Narcocorrido*, Harper Collins, New York, 2001. • **21**. Randal Archibold, 'Mexican Cartel Violence Spills Over, Alarming US', *New York Times*, 22 March 2009. • **22**. Interviewed by Martin Hodgson, 'Death in the Midday Sun', *Observer*, London, 19 September 2009. • **23**. Tracy Wilkinson, 'Song Banned, Band Pulls Out', *Los Angeles Times*, 29 October 2009. • **24**. Dudley Althaus, 'Singer Shot to Death After Surgery In Matamoros', *Houston Chronicle*, 4 December 2007.

Intermission: The Business End of a .12-Gauge –
Barrett and Morgan's War

1. Miriam Davidson, *Lives on the Line*, University of Arizona Press, Tucson, 2000, p. 13. • **2**. Lee Morgan II, *The Reaper's Line*, Rio Nuevo, Tucson, 2006. • **3**. Interview with former agent Jaime González, Austin, 2009. • **4**. Quoted in Sebastian Rotella in 'Mexican American former Anti-Drug Chief's Reputation On Trial', *Los Angeles Times*, 22 November 2009. • **5**. Stan Tekiela, *Mammals of Arizona*, Adventure Publications, Cambridge, Minnesota, 2008. • **6**. Associated Press, 18 September 2009.

4 Urban Frankenstein

1. Quoted in Steve Fainaru and William Booth, 'An Army Takeover Quells Violence in Mexico', *Washington Post*, 21 April 2009. • **2**. Associated Press, 24 February 2009. No byline. • **3**. CCPSSJ report, quoted in *El Diario de Juárez*, 11 January 2010. • **4**. For an excellent discussion of the city's origins and name, see Lugo, *Fragmented Lives, Assembled Parts*, University of Texas Press, Austin, 2008. • **5**. Quoted in Metz, *Border*, TCU Press, Ft. Worth/Mangan Books, El Paso, 1989, pp. 168–69. The book also contains a detailed account of the development of the twin cities of Juárez and El Paso. • **6**. Charles Bowden, *Murder City: Ciudad Juárez and the Global Economy's New Killing Fields*, Nation Books, New York, 2010. • **7**. Redaccion, *El Diario de Juárez*,

14 November 2008. • **8.** See various entries by Bill Conroy on narcosphere.com. Search 'Ramírez' or click on Conroy byline. • **9.** Redaccion, *El Diario de Juárez*, 11 January 2009. • **10.** Alicia Caldwell, Associated Press, 9 September 2009. • **11.** United States Court of Appeals for the Eighth Circuit, No. 06–1569, 12 January 2007. *See also* Guillermo Eduardo Ramírez-Peyro, Petitioner, v. Alberto Gonzales, Attorney General of the United States of America • **12.** A brief in support of asylum application in the matter of Espi. no Ledezma, Martín. Case no 0 74–816–432 (El Paso, 6 July 2009) • **13.** Tom Russell: 'Since Sinatra Played Juárez,' from the album *Borderland*, Frontera Music/Hightone Records, Oakland, 2001. • **14.** Alejandro Lugo, *Fragmented Lives*, p. 119. • **15.** *El Diario de Juárez*, 17 July 2009. • **16.** For a full account of troops dressing up as criminals and vice versa, see Ignacio Alvarado Alvarez '*Desapariciones y Masacres*', *El Universal*, 8 April 2008. • **17.** Ken Ellingwood, *Los Angeles Times*, 27 February 2009. • **18.** Fainaru and Booth, 21 April 2009, op. cit. • **19.** Ibid. • **20.** *Proceso*, no byline, 15 June 2009. • **21.** Ramon Bracamontes, 'Mexican Cartel Battle Shifts', *El Paso Times*, 23 June 2009; see also Howard Campbell, *Drug War Zone*, University of Texas Press, Austin, 2009, especially chapter on 'Selling Drugs in downtown Juárez', pp. 96–107. • **22.** Molly Molloy, New Mexico State University, Las Cruces. 'Fronterizo List' bulletin, 31 December 2009. • **23.** Redaccion, *El Diario de Juárez*, 9–11 February 2009; and Associated Press, 11 February 2009. • **24.** Algandro Salman and Orlanda Chávez, *Ejentados son in delinquents menos"*, *El Diario de Juárez*, 4 April 2008 • **25.** Jo Tuckman, 'At Least 20 Dead in Mexican Prison Riot', *Guardian*, London, 5 March 2009.

6 *The Wind of Knives*

1. As narrated in the English translation of Bernadino de Sahagun, *Historia General de las Cosas de Nueva Espana*, aka *A History of Ancient Mexico*, Fisk University Press, Nashville, 1932. Also J.M.G. Le Clezio: *The Mexican Dream*, trans. Fagan, University of Chicago Press 1993, chapter two, pp. 41–93. • **2.** *Proceso*, various articles in special edition, 9 December 2009. • **3.** The articles were part of a series over many years by Diana Washington Valdez, narrated in the book *The Killing Fields: Harvest of Women*, Peace at the Border Productions, Burbank, 2006. • **4.** Ken Ellingwood, 'Court Cites Rights Failure by Mexico In Juárez Killings', *Los Angeles Times*, 12 December 2009. • **5.** Ibid.

Intermission: The Road It Gives, and the Road It Takes Away

1. Tom Russell: 'Where The Dream Begins', from the album *Borderland*, Frontera Music/Hightone Records, Oakland, 2001. • **2**. Tom Russell: 'The Road It Gives And The Road It Takes Away', from *Borderland*, ibid. • **3**. Don Henry Ford, *Contrabando*, Cinco Puntos Press, El Paso 2005. • **4**. Alicia Caldwell, Associated Press, various reports during 2009. • **5**. Ryan Bingham: 'Hard Times,' from the album *Mescalito*, UMG music, Nashville, 2007.

7 Eat off the Floor

1. *San Antonio Standard*, 10 March 1996. • **2**. See Enrique Krauze, *Mexico: Biography of Power*, trans. Hank Heifetz, Harper Collins, New York, 1997. Especially the chapter on Miguel Aleman, pp. 526–600. • **3**. Alejandro Lugar, *Assembled Parts, Fragmented Lives*, University of Texas Press, Austin 2008, pp. 148–52. • **4**. Altha J. Cravey, *Women and Work in Mexico's Maquiladoras*, Rowman and Littlefield, Lanham, MD, 1998, p. 49. • **5**. Krauze, op. cit. pp. 697–8. • **6**. Todd Gillman, 'Obama Talks of "Upgrade" to NAFTA With Mexico's Calderón', *Dallas Morning News*, 13 January 2009. • **7**. *Reglamento Interior del Trabajo*, Article 13, 1980. • **8**. Quoted by Diana Washington Valdez, *El Paso Times*, 2 February 2009.

8 Gateway to the Americas/Pax Mafiosa

1. Ginger Thompson, 'Rival Drug Gangs Turn the Streets of Nuevo Laredo Into a War Zone' *New York Times*, 4 December 2005. • **2**. Sara A. Carter, 'Here, We are Prisoners', *San Bernardino Sun*, 28 December 2006. • **3**. Ricardo Ravelo 'Los Zetas: Ejercito de Osiel', *Proceso*, 15 September 2005, and Dudley Althaus and James Pinkerton, 'Violence in Nuevo Laredo', *Houston Chronicle*, 7 August 2005. • **4**. Susana Hayward, 'Drug War Rages in Border Town', *Miami Herald*, 31 July 2005. • **5**. Ricardo Ravelo, Los Zetas, op. cit., and Manuel Roig-Franzia, *Washington Post*, 7 May 2008. • **6**. *Frontera NorteSur*, website, 15 May 2004. • **7**. Alicia Caldwell, Associated Press, 28 January 2010. • **8**. Committee to Protect Journalists, Mexico Annual Country Report for 2008. • **9**. See Cecilia Ballí, *'Ropa Usada'* in *Puro Border*, Crossthwaite, Byrd and Byrd, eds. Cinco Puntos Press, El Paso, 2003, pp. 183–190. • **10**. Ibid,

p. 187. • **11**. Keith Bowden, *The Tecate Journals*, The Mountaineer's Books, Seattle, 2007. See chapter 'Symbols of Power', pp. 219 ff. • **12**. Dudley Althaus and James Pinkerton, 'River to Ruin: Descent of the Rio Grande,' *Houston Chronicle* special supplement, 17 October 1993.

9 *Iron River / Tell Them Who You Are*

1. Tracy Wilkinson, 'Mexico Drug Gangs Turn Weapons on Army', *Los Angeles Times*, 15 March 2009. • **2**. Thomas Koch, *The Militia Battle Manual*, Desert Publications, El Dorado, Arizona, 1996. • **3**. *Full Auto*, Volume One. 'AR-15 Modification Manual', Desert Publications, 1981. • **4**. *Select Fire AK-47 Gigil and Vamlet Conversion Manual*. Desert Publications, 1994. • **5**. Lora Lumpe: 'The US Arms Both Sides in Mexico's Drug War,' *Covert Action Quarterly*, No. 61. Summer 1997. • **6**. Richard Serrano, 'Guns From US Equip Drug Cartels', *Los Angeles Times*, 10 August 2008. • **7**. United States Government Accountability Office, 'Firearms Tracking: US Efforts to Combat Arms Trafficking to Mexico Face Planning and Coordination Challenges,' Report no. GAO-09-709, June 2009. • **8**. FBI press release, 2 May 2009. • **9**. Tracy Wilkinson, 'Ex-General, 2 Others Found Shot To Death Near Cancun', *Los Angeles Times*, 4 February 2009. • **10**. Dudley Althaus, 'Cancun's Top Cop Is Grilled In Retired General's Killing', *Houston Chronicle*, 13 February 2009. • **11**. Ken Ellingwood, 'Killings Uncover Seamier Side of Cancun', *Los Angeles Times*, 2 March 2009. • **12**. Dudley Althaus, 'Beheadings Shake Mexico Town', *Houston Chronicle*, 15 March 2009. • **13**. Tracy Wilkinson, 'Mexico Sees Inside Job in Prison Break', *Los Angeles Times*, 18 May 2009. • **14**. Ken Ellingwood, 'Drug Violence Spilling Into Guatamela', *Los Angeles Times*, 7 June 2009. • **15**. Tracy Wilkinson, 'Mexican Cartel Weapons from Central America', *Los Angeles Times*, 15 March 2009. • **16**. Dudley Althaus, 'Gunfight Near Mexican School Leaves Pupils Traumatized', *Houston Chronicle*, 21 February 2009. • **17**. Lynn Brezosky and Dudley Althaus, 'Blood Flows in Streets of Reynosa', *Houston Chronicle*, 19 February 2009. • **18**. Marc Lacey, 'Drug Tie Seen to Protests in Mexico', *New York Times*, 18 February 2009. • **19**. Tracy Wilkinson, 'Mexican Cartels Buying Public Support', *Los Angeles Times*, 13 March 2009. • **20**. Dane Schiller, TK, *Houston Chronicle*, 1 April 2009. • **21**. Milo Kearney and Anthony Knopp, *Boom and Bust: The Historical Cycles of Matamoros and Brownsville*, Eakin Press, Austin, 1991, pp. 106–

130. • **22**. Antonia Zavaleta and Alberto Salinas, *Curandero Conversations*, University of Texas at Brownsville/Authorhouse, Bloomington, 2009. • **23**. For a discussion of the competing influences of Mexican and Irish Catholicism in the United States, see Manuel Gonzáles, *Mexicanos: A History of Mexicans in the United States*, Indiana University Press, 1999, p. 241. • **24**. See Katherine Boo, 'Letter From South Texas', *New Yorker*, 29 March 2004. • **25**. For an analysis of high school football and Latino identity on the Rio Grande Valley, see Joel Huerta, 'Red, Brown, and Blue: A History and Cultural Poetics of High School Football in Mexican America,' Ph.D. dissertation, University of Texas at Austin, 2005. • **26**. For an analysis of Los Angeles as style capital for Mexican narcos, see Sam Quinones, *True Tales from the Other Mexico*, University of New Mexico Press, Albuquerque 2001. • **27**. Tim Rutten in the *Los Angeles Times*, 28 February 2009, discusses Quinones' theory. • **28**. US District Court/ Southern Texas, *USA v Hernández*, case H-08-317M, filed 24 April 2008. • **29**. Dane Schiller, 'Windshield Repair Man Admits Gun-Smuggling', *Houston Chronicle*, 21 November 2009. • **30**. Dane Schiller, 'Suspected Drug Boss "taunting" Feds', *Houston Chronicle*, 12 July 2009. • **31**. Dane Schiller, 'Mexican Cartels Infiltrate Houston', *Houston Chronicle*, 17 October 2009. • **32**. Dane Schiller and Jacquee Petchel, 'Drug Cartel Chief Sentenced in Secrecy', *Houston Chronicle*, 24 February 2010. • **33**. David Voreacos: 'Wachovia to pay $160 Million to End Money Laundering Probe', Bloomberg.com news, 18 March 2010 and Michael Smith, 'Banks Financing Mexico Gangs Admitted in Well Fargo Deal', Bloomberg.com, 29 June 2010.

Bibliographical Notes

Books and newspaper articles used for reference in this book are anno-
tated and numbered at the appropriate point in the text. But some guide
to sources and further reading may be useful, arranged roughly in accordance
to chapters in this book. Some are referred to in the text and end-notes,
others not, but all the following have been useful to this endeavour in one
way or another.

By far the best general histories of Mexico are *Mexico: Biography of
Power* by Enrique Krauze (English edition Harper Collins, 1997) and *The
Oxford History of Mexico*, a collection of essays edited by Michael C.
Meyer and William H. Beezley (OUP, 2000). The story of the US–Mexican
War, the plunder of Indian lands and raids by the Indians as a Border
narrative, is nowhere better told than in the epic *War of a Thousand
Deserts* by Brian DeLay, Yale University Press, New Haven, 2008. A very
useful recent history is *Opening Mexico* by Julia Preston and Samuel Dillon
(Farrar, Straus & Giroux, 2004).

There are innumerable books on ancient Mexican and Aztec lore, of which
the best (in Spanish) is Eduardo Matos Moctezuma's *Los Aztecas*, published
by the Mexican government's national council for the arts, with Jaca of
Milan, 2000. The definitive original text by Bernadino de Sahagun – his
Historia General de las Cosas de Nueva Espana – is available in a good English
translation as *A History of Ancient Mexico* translated by Fanny Bandelier
(Fisk University Press, Nashville, 1932). For those wanting an English trans-
lation of Bernal Diaz's *The Conquest of New Spain*, that by John Cohen for
Penguin Books has yet to be rivalled. The University of California Press at
Berkeley publishes a reprint of T.T. Waterman's famous book *Bandelier's
Contribution to the Study of Ancient Mexican Social Organisation* (1917).
The Mexican Dream is a famous meditation by J.M.G. Le Clezio on what he

calls 'The Interrupted Thought of Amerindian Civilisations', translated into English by Teresa Lavander Fagan (University of Chicago Press, 2009). The British Museum guide to Aztec and Maya Myths by Karl Taube is an excellent introduction (Trustees of the British Museum, 1993).

There are many books on the US-Mexican border generally. The best history of the frontier itself is *Border: The US–Mexico Line* by Leon C. Metz (Mangan Books/TCU Press, Fort Worth, 1989), who has written many other books about the wars and personalities that make up the border's eventful history. Of the many collections of academic essays on the border, these have proved useful: *US–Mexican Borderlands: Historical and Contemporary Perspectives*, edited by Oscar J. Martinez (Scholarly Resources Inc., Wilmington 1996); *The Last Frontier: The Contemporary Configuration of the US–Mexican Border* edited by Jane Juffer (South Atlantic Quarterly special edition, Duke University Press, 2006); *Crossing Borders, Reinforcing Borders: Social Categories, Metaphors and Narrative Identities on the US–Mexican Frontier*, edited by Pablo Vila (University of Texas Press, Austin, 2000); *Identifaciones de Region, Etnia y Nacion en la Frontera entre Mexico-EU* by Pablo Vila (Universidad Autonoma de Ciudad Juárez 2004). There is also *Life, Death and In-Between On the US–Mexican Border*, edited by Martha Oehmke Loustaunau and Mary Sanchez-Bane (Bergin and Garvey, Westport, 1999), which is specifically about health issues, and the very readable collection of journalism, *Puro Border*, edited by Luis Humberto Crossthwaite, John William Byrd and Bobby Byrd (Cinco Puntos Press, 2003). A good study of Mexicans living in the United States is *Mexicanos* by Manuel G. Gonzáles (Indiana University Press, 2000).

Three main books have been written on the history of the United States' covert involvement in narco trafficking, the most famous of which is *Dark Alliance* by Gary Webb (Seven Stories Press, New York, 1997). Also: the excellent *Desperados* by Elaine Shannon, Viking Penguin, New York, 1988) and *The Big White Lie* by Michael Levine and Laura Kavanau-Levine (Thunder's Mouth Press, New York, 1993).

The best book on Tijuana is Luis Alberto Urrea's *Across the Wire* (Anchor, New York, 1993). Much has been written on migration, the original of which was *Coyotes* by Ted Conover (Vintage, 1987), after which came, notably, *The Devil's Highway* by Luis Alberto Urrea (Little Brown, 2004) about the tragedy in 2001 mentioned in Chapter Two of this book, and *Hard Line* by Ken Ellingwood (Vintage, New York, 2004). There are also: *Lives on the Line* by Miriam Davidson (University of Arizona Press, Tucson, 2000). *No One Is Illegal* by Justin Akers Chacon and Mike Davis (Haymarket Books, Chicago, 2006); *Cutting for Sign* by William Langewiesche (Vintage, New York, 1993) and Tim Gaynor's *Midnight on the Line* (Thomas Dunn Books/St Martin's Press, New York, 2009). *Exodus* is poignantly evocative photographs by Julián Cardona, with a text by Charles Bowden (University of Texas Press, Austin, 2008).

Bowden is *the* writer on the border, whose work centres mainly on Ciudad Juárez. *Juárez: The Laboratory of Our Future* (Aperture, New York 1988) is probably the most terrifyingly insightful book ever written on the city and what it means. Bowden also gave us, as well as many great works of part-fiction, including *Down by the River* (Simon & Schuster 2002) and *Murder City* (Nation Books, 2010) – the only book apart from this one about the current stage of the drug war, as well as the excellent academic study, *Drug War Zone* by Howard Campbell (University of Texas Press, 2009). Campbell's colleague at UTEP, Tony Payan, has written *The Three US–Mexico Border Wars* (Praeger Security, Westport, 2006).

The first book on a cartel chief – and the only time one was ever interviewed for the purpose – was *Drug Lord* by Terrence Popper (Demand Publications 1998). Two great memoirs and one great 'novel' followed Popper's landmark book. *Contrabando* is the autobiography of a drug smuggler, Don Henry Ford (Cinco Puntos Press, 2005) and *The Reaper's Line* is that of customs special agent Lee Morgan, who tried to stop people like Ford (Rio Nuevo, Tucson, 2006), both of which feature in this book, and I'll wager they'd get along just fine. Don Winslow's *Power of the Dog* (Heinemann, London 2005) is fiction – but it all happened for real. Another lovely memoir is of the Rio Grande, navigated by kayak, Keith Bowden's *The Tecate Journals* (Mountaineers Press, Seattle, 2007).

Books on the Tohono O'odham Native American tribe are harder to come by than general histories of those on other tribes. The best is Winston P. Erikson's *Sharing the Desert: The Tohono O'odham in History* (University of Arizona Press, Tucson, 1994), while *Rainhouse and Ocean* by Ruth Underhill et. al. (Museum of Northern Arizona Press, 1979) gives a poetic account of O'odham rituals and speeches. Frank Russell's *The Pima Indians* was recently republished in paperback (Mabu Press, 2006). There are innumerable books on the Arizona desert landscape and natural life – too many to list here – but none is as informative as *Dry Borders*, edited by Richard Stephen Felger and Bill Broyles (University of Utah Press, Salt Lake City 2007). As a literary meditation, Edward Abbey's *Desert Solitaire* stands alone, and there is also Charles Bowden's *Desierto*.

Elijah Wald wrote about *Narcocorrido* (Harper Collins, New York 2001), and the best book on *maquiladoras* is *Fragmented Lives, Assembled Parts* by Alejandro Lugo (University of Texas Press, 2008), focused on Ciudad Juárez. There are also: *Women and Work in Mexico's Maquiladoras* by Altha J. Cravey (Rowman and Littlefield, 1998) and *NAFTA From Below*, edited by Martha Ojeda and Rosemary Hennessy. Ciudad Juárez itself has commanded much attention, and the best sociological study is *La Realdad Social de Ciudad Juárez*, co-ordinated by Clara Jusidman (Universidad Autonoma de Ciudad Juárez, 2007) and a companion statistical volume and DVD, both compiled by Hugo Almada Mireles. On the mass murder of women in Juárez, there is *The Killing Fields* by Diana Washington Valdez (Peace at the Border, 2006) and *Desert Blood: The Juárez Murders* by Alicia Gaspar de Alba (Arte Publico Press, 2005). Others include *Daughters of Juárez* by Teresa Rodríguez, Diana Montané, and Lisa Pulitzer and *If I Die in Juárez* by Stella Pope Duarte (University of Arizona Press, Tucson, 2008).

There are few histories of the Rio Grande Valley as such, but *Boom and Bust: The Historical Cycles of Matamoros and Brownsville* by Milo Kearney and Anthony Kopp (Eakin Press 1991) will do. An excellent academic study in Spanish only is *Estructura Urbana En Ciudades Fronterizas* by Eduardo Alarcon Cantu (Tijuana Colegio de la Frontera del Norte, 2000). A detailed book on patrolling the valley border is *Patrolling Chaos* by Robert Lee Maril (Texas Tech University Press 2004). *Brownsville* by Oscar Casares (Back Bay/Little Brown 2003) is a book of fiction, but speaks volumes about reality. From Laredo come three books: *Nuevo Laredo: A Prelude to War* by Dan Robinson (Shotmakers Inc 1998), *Laredo Stories* by Tony Raunch (Eraserhead Press, Oregon 2008) and *My Border Patrol Diary* by Dale Squint (self-published, 2007). There exist two books in Spanish on the Zetas: *Cronicas de Sangre: Cinco Historias de los Zetas* by Ricardo Ravelo (Random House/Mondadori, Mexico 2007) and *De Los Maras A Los Zetas* by Jorge Fernandez Menendez and Victor Ronquillo (Random House/Mondadori, Mexico, 2007).

So much has been written on Mexican 'Folk Catholicism' as explored in Chapter Nine, but few books in English could improve on D.A. Brading's *Mexican Phoenix: Our Lady of Guadalupe: Image and Tradition across Five Centuries* (Cambridge University Press 2003). The fascinating *Curandero Conversations* by Antonio Zavaleta and Alberto Salinas Jr. is discussed in Chapter Nine.

Index